DYNASTIC IDENTITY IN EARLY MODERN EUROPE

POLITICS AND CULTURE IN EUROPE, 1650–1750

Focusing on the years between the end of the Thirty Years' War and the end of the War of the Austrian Succession, this series seeks to broaden scholarly knowledge of this crucial period that witnessed the solidification of Europe into centralized nation states and created a recognizably modern political map. Bridging the gap between the early modern period of the Reformation and the eighteenth century of colonial expansion and industrial revolution, these years provide a fascinating era of study in which nationalism, political dogma, economic advantage, scientific development, cultural interests and strategic concerns began to compete with religion as the driving force of European relations and national foreign policies. The period under investigation, the second half of the seventeenth century and the first half of the eighteenth, corresponds with the decline of Spanish power and the rise of French hegemony that was only to be finally broken following the defeat of Napoleon in 1815. This shifting political power base presented opportunities and dangers for many countries, resulting in numerous alliances between formerly hostile nations attempting to consolidate or increase their international influence, or restrain that of a rival. These contests of power were closely bound up with political, cultural and economic issues: particularly the strains of state building, trade competition, religious tension and toleration, accommodating flows of migrants and refugees, the birth pangs of rival absolutist and representative systems of government, radical structures of credit, and new ways in which wider publics interacted with authority. Despite this being a formative period in the formation of the European landscape, there has been relatively little research on it compared to the earlier Reformation, and the later revolutionary eras. By providing a forum that encourages scholars to engage with the forces that were shaping the continent – either in a particular country, or taking a trans-national or comparative approach – it is hoped a greater understanding of this pivotal era will be forthcoming.

Dynastic Identity in Early Modern Europe

Rulers, Aristocrats and the Formation of Identities

Edited by

LIESBETH GEEVERS
Universiteit Leiden, The Netherlands

MIRELLA MARINI
University of Antwerp, Belgium and
VU University Amsterdam, The Netherlands

ASHGATE

Published by
Ashgate Publishing Limited
Wey Court East
Union Road
Farnham
Surrey, GU9 7PT
England

Ashgate Publishing Company
110 Cherry Street
Suite 3-1
Burlington, VT 05401-3818
USA

www.ashgate.com

British Library Cataloguing in Publication Data
A catalogue record for this book is available from the British Library

The Library of Congress has cataloged the printed edition as follows:
Dynastic Identity in Early Modern Europe: Rulers, Aristocrats and the Formation of Identities / edited by Liesbeth Geevers and Mirella Marini.
pages cm. – (Politics and Culture in Europe, 1650–1750)
Includes bibliographical references and index.
1. Europe – History – 1517-1648. 2. Europe – History – 1648-1715. 3. Europe – Kings and rulers – History. 4. Royal houses – Europe – History. 5. Aristocracy (Social class) – Europe – History. 6. Group identity – Europe – History. 7. Elite (Social sciences) – Europe – History. 8. Europe – Social conditions.
I. Geevers, Elisabeth Marieke, 1979- II. Marini, Mirella.
D231.D86 2015
929.7094'09032–dc23 2015011129

ISBN: 9781409463269 (hbk)
ISBN: 9781409463276 (ebk – PDF)
ISBN: 9781409463283 (ebk – ePUB)

MIX
Paper from responsible sources
FSC® C013985

Printed in the United Kingdom by Henry Ling Limited, at the Dorset Press, Dorchester, DT1 1HD

Contents

List of Figures

Notes on Contributors

Ronald G. Asch, born in Hamburg in 1953, is a graduate of Tübingen University where he also completed his doctorate after having studied earlier in Kiel and in Cambridge. He has held a research fellowship at the German Historical Institute London (1985–88) and a lectureship at the University of Münster in Germany (1988–1996). From autumn 1996 to spring 2003 he held the chair of Early Modern History at the University of Osnabrück and is now teaching at the Albert-Ludwig University of Freiburg as successor to Wolfgang Reinhard. He is the editor or co-editor of *Politics, Patronage and the Nobility: The Court at the Beginning of the Modern Age* (Oxford: 1991); *Der Adel im Ancien Régime. Von der Krise der ständischen Monarchien bis zur Revolution (ca. 1600–1789)* (Vienna: 2001), and *Frieden und Krieg in der Frühen Neuzeit. Die europäische Staatenordnung und die außereuropäische Welt* (Munich: 2001) and the author of *Der Hof Karls I. Politik, Provinz und Patronage 1625–1640* (Cologne: 1993), a study of the English court before the Civil War. He has also published a short history of the Thirty Years' War in 1997 and a biography of James VI and I: *Jakob I. von England und Schottland: König des Friedens im Zeitalter der Religionskriege* (Stuttgart: 2005). His latest publication is *Sacral Kingship between Disenchantment and Re-enchantment: The French and English Monarchies 1587–1688* (New York/London: 2014)

Sebastiaan Derks (1973) is Head of Digital Data Management and Researcher at the Huygens Institute for the History of the Netherlands. He has published a number of articles on the history and historiography of the Habsburg Netherlands. He is currently working on a dissertation that examines the politics of dynasticism of the Farnese in sixteenth-century Habsburg Europe.

Jeroen Duindam is Professor of Modern History at Leiden University. Duindam studied history at Utrecht University, where he obtained his PhD in 1992 with a critical study of Norbert Elias, translated and published as *Myths of Power. Norbert Elias and the Early Modern European Court* (Amsterdam: 1995). Following this general study, Duindam did research in the archival legacies of dynastic power in France and Austria, leading to his comparative book *Vienna and Versailles. The Courts of Europe's Dynastic Rivals 1550–1780* (Cambridge: 2003). After organising several comparative projects and conferences on dynastic power with Ottomanists and sinologists, Duindam now leads an NWO-Horizon project on 'Eurasian Empires 1300–1800'. His latest publication is a comparative history of dynastic power, *Dynasty. A Global History 1300–1800* (Cambridge: 2015)

Liesbeth Geevers (1979) is a postdoctoral researcher at the Radboud University Nijmegen. From 2008 to 2011 she was a lecturer of Political History at Utrecht University. She obtained her PhD from the University of Amsterdam (2008) on the integration of William of Orange and the counts of Egmont and Horn in the Spanish-Habsburg Monarchy (1559–1567). Recently, she has published on the dynastic identity of William of Orange in the 1560s and the identity of the Nassau dynasty (1541–1616) and is currently studying the position of dynastic juniors in Eurasian empires (1300–1800).

Mirella Marini obtained a Bachelor in Law (1996) and a Master in History (2006) at the Catholic University in Leuven (Belgium). Her Master's thesis was awarded the 'Duke of Arenberg' History Prize in 2006. She then started her doctoral research on the religious patronage of high noble women at the VU University Amsterdam (Netherlands), followed by the University of Antwerp (Belgium). Marini has published a number of articles on Anne of Croy, duchess of Aarschot, for instance on her religious authority or on her funeral arrangements. She has also written about female diplomacy in the sixteenth-century and is currently working on a monography about Anne of Croy's religious patronage in the city of Enghien, as well as on a comprehensive study on the dukes of Arenberg.

Jane Ohlmeyer is Erasmus Smith's Professor of Modern History at Trinity College, Dublin. Professor Ohlmeyer is an expert on the New British and Atlantic Histories. She has published 11 books with major academic presses on a number of themes in early modern Irish and British history, together with articles for major international journals and peer-review anthologies. Her books include *Civil War and Restoration in the Three Stuart Kingdoms* (Cambridge: 1993); *Ireland from Independence to Occupation, 1641–1660* (editor, Cambridge: 1995); and *Political Thought in Seventeenth-Century Ireland* (editor, Cambridge: 2000). Her latest book, *Making Ireland English. The Irish Aristocracy in the Seventeenth Century* on the Irish peerage in the seventeenth century was published in 2012 (New Haven). She is currently working on a study of Colonial Ireland and Colonial India. Professor Ohlmeyer has considerable expertise in overseeing major editorial projects and helped to secure over €5M in funding for the digitisation and online publication of the '1641 Depositions'. On the international and national stages Professor Ohlmeyer is an active proponent of 'Digital Humanities'. She is a Member of the Royal Irish Academy and sits as a member of the Irish Manuscripts Commission and the National Archives Council.

Fabian Persson completed a doctoral thesis *Servants of Fortune: The Swedish Court between 1598 and 1721* at Lund University in 1999. He has contributed to various volumes such as John Adamson (ed.) *The Princely Courts of Europe: ritual, politics and culture under the ancien régime, 1500–1750* (London: 1999) and K. Malettke and C. Grell (eds), *Hofgesellschaft und Höflinge an europäischen Fürstenhöfen in der Frühen Neuzeit (15.-18. Jh.)* (Munich: 2001). He has written about aristocratic marriage, duelling, patronage, women at court and various aspects of aristocratic and court life. Presently he is finishing two different volumes on the Swedish court as well as a monograph on an early modern Swedish nobleman and failed politician. At present Persson is lecturer at the Linnaeus University.

Hamish Scott is Wardlaw Professor Emeritus of International History at the University of St Andrews and an Honorary Senior Research Fellow at the University of Glasgow. A Fellow of the British Academy and of the Royal Society of Edinburgh, he has written extensively on eighteenth-century international relations and government, and is currently completing *The Formation of Europe's Aristocracy c.1300–1750* (Oxford: forthcoming), as well as editing *The Oxford Handbook of Early Modern European History, c.1350–1750* (Oxford: forthcoming).

Violet Soen is Professor of Early Modern History at the University of Leuven. She has been a visiting scholar at Columbia University (Spring 2014) and the École des Hautes Études en Sciences Sociales (Spring 2011). She also held a Max Weber Fellowship of the European University Institute (2008–2009). Her latest book deals with noble, royal and imperial peace attempts during the Dutch Revolt (Amsterdam, 2012). An earlier monograph analysed the peculiarities of sixteenth-century inquisition in the Low Countries (2007). Today, she is working on a book project on transregional noble networks between the Low Countries and France, while coordinating research projects in early modern transregional history (www.transregionalhistory.eu). Additional information on publications and research can be found on her website: http://www.mwpweb.eu/VioletSoen.

Jonathan Spangler is a lecturer in Early Modern European History at Manchester Metropolitan University, England. His doctoral research focused on the foreign princes in seventeenth-century France, notably the Lorraine-Guise, about whom he has published articles in French History and Proceedings of the Western Society for French History, and a monograph, *The Society of Princes: The Lorraine-Guise and the Conservation of Power and Wealth in Seventeenth-Century France* (Farnham: Ashgate, 2009). Recent work has focused on spreading this study more widely, from sixteenth-century Scotland (*The Court Historian*, 2010) to the eighteenth-century "Middle Kingdom" (*Trans-regional and Transnational Families in Europe and Beyond*; 2011). Jonathan took his first degree at William & Mary in Virginia, then worked for several years in Washington and New York as a museum exhibition designer, before completing a DPhil at Oxford University. He has recently taken on the role of co-editor of *The Court Historian*, the journal for the Society for Court Studies.

Avant-propos

Duc d'Arenberg

C'est avec plaisir que j'écris ces quelques lignes à l'occasion de la publication des exposés de la première série des conférences d'Arenberg pour l'Histoire qui a eu lieu à Amsterdam en novembre 2011 sur le thème « Identités dynastiques dans l'Europe moderne – dirigeants, aristocrates et formation d'identités ».

Nous nous réjouissons tout particulièrement du succès de cette conférence organisée de main de maître par madame Mirella Marini (University of Antwerp et Vrije Universiteit Amsterdam) et madame Liesbeth Geevers (Leiden University) à la Vrije Universiteit Amsterdam.

En effet, il s'agit d'une initiative utile qui fait avancer la réflexion historique à un niveau européen et met en contact une nouvelle génération de chercheurs.

La Fondation d'Arenberg, un « think tank historique » sui generis, soutient ce genre d'initiative car elle fait la promotion de l'Histoire et de la Culture dans un esprit européen.

Notre objectif principal est de favoriser la réflexion, la réflexion lente, la réflexion à long terme, la réflexion sur le bon sens collectif et la notion de rapport de force.

De nos jours, le consommateur a bien souvent remplacé le citoyen et la perspective historique fait défaut. En effet, le consommateur paie pour un service et exige une prestation immédiate en négligeant souvent la dimension spatio-temporelle de son action et sa responsabilité personnelle.

Or, tous les parents se basent sur leurs expériences personnelles pour tenter d'éviter de commettre les mêmes erreurs dans l'éducation de leurs enfants qu'ils ont subies eux-mêmes dans leur propre enfance. Pourquoi en irait-il autrement des peuples et de leurs expériences historiques? Ne devons-nous pas tout tenter afin d'éviter les fautes commises par les générations précédentes, même si l'exercice est difficile, voire impossible?

A quoi servirait donc l'Histoire, si ce n'est qu'à tenter de faire progresser la réflexion objective sur l'homo sapiens et les conséquences de son action?

La Fondation d'Arenberg s'engage pour remettre l'Histoire au cœur de nos préoccupations dans un esprit de service public depuis plusieurs décennies et s'intéresse tout particulièrement aux jeunes historiennes et historiens de notre continent qui assurent une réflexion originale sur base d'éléments nouveaux.

Pour ce faire, nous avons mis à disposition d'un large public, en particulier d'un public de doctorants, notre fonds d'archives, le plus grand fonds d'archives familiales des XVII provinces, réparties dans plusieurs pays, dont la Belgique, l'Allemagne, l'Autriche, la France, l'Espagne, la Hollande et la République tchèque.

Nous publions des ouvrages historiques, à ce jour plus d'une vingtaine, en plusieurs langues.

Nous distribuons des prix, à savoir:

- deux prix pour l'Histoire, les prix 'duc d'Arenberg', depuis 1992;
- un prix d'excellence européen, le prix 'Arenberg Coimbra Group' en collaboration avec le groupe Coimbra d'universités européennes depuis 1997;
- un 'College of Europe Arenberg European Prize' depuis 2013 qui récompense un travail consacré à l'étude de systèmes fédéraux dans une optique historique et comparative.

Cette année, nous avons lancé le projet 'biographies européennes' qui s'intéresse à mettre en valeur des personnes peu connues mais remarquables car engagées dans la durée afin de donner idées et exemples aux jeunes générations qui ont soif d'aventure et d'action.

L'an prochain, nous organisons notre premier rallye historique qui reliera des villes et des villages de l'ancien duché d'Arschot. Imaginez une quarantaine d'old timers qui sillonneront les routes du duché; à chaque arrêt, il y aura une brève présentation du passé, du présent et du futur de ces villes et villages par leurs bourgmestres respectifs. De la sorte, nous communiquerons notre passion pour l'Histoire à un large public. Et si tout se passe bien, nous élargirons le parcours du rallye à la France, aux Pays-Bas et à l'Allemagne dès 2016.

Il y a enfin nos conférences et nos séminaires. Cette année, nous mettons sur pied une table ronde sur le thème des petites et moyennes entreprises allemandes à Berlin. En cas de succès, nous tenterons de répéter l'expérience dans d'autres pays.

Nous tenterons d'expliquer à un public averti que ces entreprises ont une raison d'être qui s'enracine dans le passé et nous examinerons les mécanismes qui permettent la création de richesse pour les communautés humaines afin d'assurer leur prospérité.

D'autres projets dorment encore dans les tiroirs et nous demeurons très ouverts pour toutes les bonnes idées qui nous sont communiquées car nous avons fait nôtre la célèbre devise: «l'Union fait la Force».

Pour suivre nos travaux, il suffit de contacter notre site web: www.arenbergfoundation.eu

Meilleures salutations,
Pour la Fondation d'Arenberg
Duc d'Arenberg

Acknowledgements

The majority of the contributions published in this volume were presented at the First Arenberg Conference for History, *Dynastic Identity in Early Modern Europe: Rulers, Aristocrats and the Formation of Identities*, which was organised at the VU University Amsterdam (7–8 October 2011). The stimulating discussions at the conference were led by Prof. dr. Luc Duerloo and Prof. dr. Hans Cools, whom the editors would like to thank for their inspirational input. Their views and comments have greatly benefited the outcome of this volume.

The conference could not have been organised without the generous financial help of the Arenberg Foundation, the Royal Netherlands Academy of Arts and Sciences (KNAW), the Foundation de Moffarts and VU University Amsterdam. We would like to express our particular gratitude to H.S.H. Duke Léopold of Arenberg, who not only awarded the organisation a generous financial stipend, but also allowed us the honour of being the first in a newly created series of historical conferences supported by his Foundation. His collaborator, Michael-W. Serruys, worked tirelessly before and after the conference to make sure everything went as smoothly as possible. And finally we would also like to offer our warmest thanks to the administrative staff of the VU University Amsterdam Department of History for their practical and logistical support.

The editors of this volume have been greatly inspired by all the authors, whom we would like to credit for their enthusiasm and their creativity in translating our ideas into their own research. Last, but not least, we need to express our deepest gratitude for the valuable advice, continuing support and frequent editorial remarks of Prof. dr. Hamish Scott, who also generously agreed to give his closing remarks at the conference, as well as in this volume.

List of Abbreviations

AAE, T	Archives Arenberg Enghien, Testaments
AAE, Bio	Archives Arenberg Enghien, Biographie
AD	Archives départementales
AGS	Archivo General de Simancas
ANF	Archives Nationales de France
ARAB	Algemeen Rijksarchief, Brussels
ASN	Archivio di Stato di Napoli
ASPr	Archivio di Stato di Parma
ASV	Archivio Segreto Vaticano
BL	British Library
BMGN	Bijdragen en Mededelingen voor de Geschiedenis der Nederlanden
BNCF	Biblioteca Nazionale Centrale di Firenze
BNF	Bibliothèque Nationale de France
DBI	*Dizionario biografico degli italiani*
HMC	Reports of the Royal Commission on Historical Manuscripts
KBB	Koninklijke Bibliotheek, Brussels

Figure 0.1 Servaes de Coelx, *The Adoration of the Magi*, oil on canvas 328 × 258 cm, 1617. Altarpiece of the Capuchin Church in Enghien (Hainaut, Belgium). Copyright Studio Berger Enghien.

Introduction
Aristocracy, Dynasty and Identity in Early Modern Europe, 1520–1700

Liesbeth Geevers and Mirella Marini

Introduction

In his pioneering handbook on the European nobility, Jonathan Dewald presented the nobility as an essentially homogeneous social group basically sharing similar privileges, similar beliefs, and similar experiences. He pointed to a 'fundamental similarity in the nobles' experiences' throughout Europe as a result of 'similar economic, political, and cultural problems' to which the nobles responded in 'basically similar ways'.[1] Although this view has been adopted by many historians,[2] European nobilities have also been differentiated according to nationality, locality, or gender, presenting a far more heterogeneous picture of this ubiquitous social group. This volume intends to add another way of looking at the European nobility as a heterogeneous group by focusing on the identities of dynasties and their importance. Therefore the unit of analysis throughout this volume is not the nobility as a whole or individuals within it, but separate dynasties or clusters of families. Our analytical tool for studying such individual dynasties will be the concept of dynastic identity. We contend that each aristocratic dynasty developed its own sense of self, through social, political and religious choices, or through their conception of the family's history and purpose. Even though cultural and political circumstances may have been similar across Europe, every aristocratic dynasty aspired to be seen as 'different'. As the French aristocrat Edmée de La Rochefoucauld (1895–1991) put it: 'chaque foyer, chaque famille a ses habitudes, ses mœurs, sa manière d'être et, en somme, possède cette sorte de civilisation différente de celle des autres familles'.[3]

---

[1] Jonathan Dewald, *The European Nobility 1400–1800* (Cambridge: Cambridge University Press, 1996), xv. See also Jean-Pierre Labatut, *Les noblesses européennes de la fin du XVe siècle à la fin du XVIIIe siècle* (Paris: Presses universitaires de France, 1978).

[2] Later historiography, see Ronald G. Asch, *Europäischer Adel in der frühen Neuzeit* (Cologne: Böhlau, 2008) and the overlapping volume in English which preceded it: *Nobilities in Transition 1550–1700* (London: Arnold, 2003) and Walter Demel, "Die Spezifika des europäischen Adels. Erste Überlegungen zu einem globalhistorischen Thema", *Zeitenblicke* 4 (2005).

[3] Edmée de La Rochefoucauld, *Flashes* (Paris: B. Grasset, 1982), 51. Our thanks to Bertrand Goujon for bringing this quotation to our attention.

Princely courts have been identified as major arenas where the aristocracy was forged, with their own rules of interaction and cultural preferences.[4] These factors were clearly of great importance for forming the identity of the aristocracy as a whole. However, aristocratic identity formation must also be analysed within the context of the aristocratic house. In this volume, it will become clear that dynastic identities were a product of ongoing negotiations between different generations of the family; the rivalries between different branches or with other families; marital strategies and demographic influences; the resulting framing and re-framing of the family's history and the family's honour and loyalty to the ruling house.

The Construction of Identity in a Dynastic Context

Dynasties are essentially groups of people. When people consider themselves a group, they invariably create an identity, based more often than not on a collective memory. Collective memory has been defined as the 'myths, narratives and traditions that constitute who a group is and how it relates to others . . . which are kept alive through the generations by an ongoing process of socialisation and ritual enactment'.[5] Considering the tendency of great lineages to keep alive their genealogical myths and traditions, and their use of education to instil in their youngest generations a sense of dynastic obligation, such a description fits dynasties well.[6] Furthermore, the construction of a dynasty's history (which did not necessarily correspond to historical realities) was often connected to the social position that it held.[7] A collective memory and sense of identity therefore imbued a noble family with shared interests: to uphold the dynasty's position.

[4] See for instance Norbert Elias, *The Court Society* (New York: Pantheon, 1983), English translation of *Die höfische Gesellschaft* (Darmstadt and Neuwied: Luchterhand, 1969).

[5] Alexander Wendt, *Social Theory of International Politics* (Cambridge: Cambridge University Press, 2009), 163.

[6] See for instance Andrew L. Thomas, *A House Divided: Wittelsbach Confessional Court Cultures in the Holy Roman Empire, c. 1550–1650* (Leiden: Brill, 2010) and Karl Vocelka, *Die Lebenswelt der Habsburger: Kultur-und Mentalitätsgeschichte einer Familie* (Graz: Styria, 1997).

[7] As Hamish Scott has previously pointed out, volumes on aristocratic families are still frequently sponsored by descendants of illustrious lineages, aspiring to boost their families' historical significance. Examples of these family histories include: Johan Aalbers et al., *Heren van stand: Van Wassenaer 1200–2000. Achthonderd jaar Nederlandse adelsgeschiedenis* (The Hague: Stichting Hollandse Historische Reeks, 2002); Robert Born, *Les Croy: une grande lignée hennuyère d'hommes de guerre, de diplomates, de conseillers secrets, dans les coulisses du pouvoir, sous les ducs de Bourgogne et la Maison d'Autriche (1390–1612)* (Brussel: Editeurs d'art associés, 1981); George Martin, *Histoire et généalogie des Maisons de Ligne et d'Arenberg*. 2 vols. (Lyon: G. Martin, 2003) and Jan Roegiers et al. (eds), *Arenberg in de Lage Landen: een hoogadellijk huis in Vlaanderen en Nederland* (Louvain: Universitaire Pers Leuven, 2002).

Histories explained how the dynasty had arrived where it was, and implied both an obligation to maintain this position, and guidelines about how to do so. In this sense the constructed dynastic identity created shared interests and at the same served a normative purpose. This volume is mainly concerned with how such identities were shaped.

Apart from a European-wide take on nobilities, nobles are often described in a national context or studied at a local level.[8] Such studies focus on local noble power bases (reinforced by local marital patterns, local economic and political interests and local patronage), or concern, for instance, urban elites or 'the court nobility', and so forth.[9] This crucially allows historians to analyse the development of the

---

[8] For instance: Hamish S. Scott (ed.), *The European Nobilities in the Seventeenth and Eighteenth Centuries* (London and New York: Longman, 1995). Numerous other examples include: Erica Bastress-Dukehart, "Family, Property and Feeling in Early Modern German Noble Culture: The Zimmerns of Swabia", *Sixteenth Century Journal* 32 (2001); Jean-Marie Constant, *La vie quotidienne de la noblesse française aux XVIe et XVIIe siècles* (Paris: Hachette, 1985); Hans Cools, *Mannen met macht: edellieden en de moderne staat in de Bourgondisch-Habsburgse landen (1475–1530)* (Zutphen: Walburg, 2001); Robert Descimon, "Les noblesses à l'époque moderne: chercher de nouvelles voies pour interpréter les phénomènes nobiliaires dans la France moderne: la noblesse, 'essence' ou rapport social?" *Revue d'Histoire Moderne et Contemporaine* 46 (1999); Christophe Duhamelle, "The Making of Stability: Kinship, Church, and Power among the Rhenish Imperial Knighthood, Seventeenth and Eighteenth Centuries", in *Kinship in Europe. Approaches to Long-Term Development (1300–1900)*, (eds) David Warren Sabean, Simon Teuscher and Jon Mathieu (New York and Oxford: Berghahn Books, 2007); William D. Godsey, *Nobles and Nation in Central Europe: Free Imperial Knights in the Age of Revolution, 1750 – 1850* (Cambridge: Cambridge University Press, 2004); Paul Janssens, *De evolutie van de Belgische adel sinds de late Middeleeuwen* (Brussels: Gemeentekrediet, 1998); Gabor Klaniczay, *Holy Rulers and Blessed Princesses. Dynastic Cults in Medieval Central Europe* (Cambridge: Cambridge University Press, 2007); Karen MacHardy, "Cultural Capital, Family Strategies and Noble Identity in Early Modern Habsburg Austria 1579–1620", *Past & Present* 163 (1999); Henk F.K. van Nierop, *Van ridders tot regenten. De Hollandse adel in de zestiende en de eerste helft van de zeventiende eeuw* (Amsterdam: De Bataafsche Leeuw, 1984), there is an English translation which omits the appendices: *The Nobility of Holland: From Knights to Regents 1500–1650* (Cambridge: Cambridge University Press, 1993) and Arie van Steensel, "Kinship, Property and Identity: Noble Family Strategies in Late-Medieval Zeeland", *Journal of Family History* 37 (2012). Violet Soen recently included a list of publications on nobilities and their various contexts in the Oxford Bibliograhies, with a discussion on the merits of these publications in: Violet Soen, 'Nobility', *Oxford Bibliographies in Renaissance and Reformation* (ed. Margaret King), New York: Oxford University Press (online release 15 January 2015).

[9] For instance in: John Adamson (ed.), *The Princely Courts of Europe: Ritual, Politics and Culture under the Ancien Régime 1500–1750* (Londen: Weidenfeld & Nicolson, 2000); Robert G. Asch and Adolf Birke (eds), *Princes, Patronage, and the Nobility: the Court at the Beginning of the Modern Age c. 1450–1650* (Oxford: German Historical Institute, 1991); Frederik Buylaert, "Edelen in de Vlaamse stedelijke samenleving: een kwantitatieve benadering van de elite van het laatmiddeleeuwse en vroegmoderne Brugge", *Tijdschrift*

nobility as a political, social and economic force in a certain area. Most aristocratic dynasties had received titles, territories, honours and offices from their superiors, on which their status as grandees ultimately rested. This was increasingly the case in the course of the seventeenth century, when 'the inflation of honours' meant that titles proliferated and many existing noble families received a higher rank.[10] Also, state service provided an ever increasing portion of noble incomes. In fact, the state plays an increasingly important role through the chapters as we proceed into the seventeenth century. Rapidly expanding armies needed more and more officers, and royal courts needed courtiers, which provided further opportunities for nobles, and also highlights the crucial interdependence of rulers and aristocrats.

Apart from economic interdependence, harmonious nobility–ruler relationships more often than not involved cultural factors as well. After the Reformation had swept across Europe, rulers usually insisted on religious conformity on the part of their nobilities. The weakness of the ruler prevented them from achieving this in all their domains, as the example of Huguenot aristocrats in France and Protestants in the Austrian Archduchies, in Bohemia and later in Hungary demonstrates. However, in the course of the seventeenth century both Louis XIII and Ferdinand II persuaded or coerced their nobilities into accepting their Catholic faith, by making it a *sine qua non* for social and political acceptance, and of advancement within the nobility itself.[11] Excluding dissenting nobles from the bounties of the state was an efficient way to do this.

Such an emphasis on local territorial power bases does not answer all our questions regarding the analysis of the identities or mentalities of great aristocratic houses. This is perhaps mainly due to the fact that the great houses of the early modern period are often hard to capture within a national framework.[12] The Dutch national hero William the Silent fiercely protested his portrayal as a foreigner in

---

voor sociale en economische geschiedenis 4 (2007); Rita Costa Gomes, *The Making of a Court Society: Kings and Nobles in Late Medieval Portugal* (Cambridge: Cambridge University Press, 2003); Wim De Clercq, Jan Dumolyn and Jelle Haemers, "Material Culture and Elite Identity in Late Medieval Flanders", *Journal of Interdisciplinary History* 38 (2007); Frédérique Leferme-Falguières, "La noblesse de cour aux XVIIe et XVIIIe siècles. De la définition à l'autoreprésentation d'une élite", *Hypothèses* 4 (2000); Nathalie Mears, "Courts, Courtiers, and Culture in Tudor England", *The Historical Journal* 46 (2003) and Andreas Pečar, *Die Ökonomie der Ehre: der höfische Adel am Kaiserhof Karls VI. (1711–1740)* (Darmstadt: Wissenschaftliche Buchgesellschaft, 2003).

10 Cools, *Mannen met Macht.*

11 For one dimension of this process, see Karen MacHardy, *War, Religion and Court Patronage in Habsburg Austria: The Social and Cultural Dimensions of Political Interaction, 1521–1622* (Basingstoke: Palgrave, 2003).

12 Robert von Friedeburg, "In Defense of Patria: Resisting Magistrates and the Duties of Patriots in the Empire from the 1530s to the 1640s", *Sixteenth Century Journal* 32 (2001) and Simon Groenveld, "'Natie' en 'patria' bij zestiende-eeuwse Nederlanders", in *Vaderland: een geschiedenis van de vijftiende eeuw tot 1940*, (ed.) N.C.F. van Sas (Amsterdam: Amsterdam University Press, 1999).

the Netherlands because his lineage had held lands there for centuries, but his status as a sovereign prince was derived from a French principality, while the protest song and current Dutch national anthem proclaims his German blood.[13] At the French court the Lorraines held the position of *princes étrangers* – they thus appeared anything but French – yet to this day they are often classified as part of the 'French aristocracy'. Border nobility literally operated on and around 'frontiers', permitting dynastic interests to prevail over narrower political allegiance when family survival depended on it. Upstart Swedish nobles had no interest in presenting themselves as 'Swedish', but instead aspired to a status equal to 'German' princely families. And even a 'proto-Belgian' aristocratic family like the Arenbergs derived its title from a German sovereign principality, while in essence being a younger branch of the Marck family (which amongst other well-known lineages also produced the ducal family of Cleves in the Holy Roman Empire, as well as the dukes of Nevers in France).[14] Even if they were in practice connected to a particular princely court and held office in the service of a particular ruler, the self-fashioning of such aristocrats often occurred in a transnational context.

But some families also identified themselves strongly in opposition to their rulers, casting themselves more as their equals than their vassals. This pertains to many aristocratic families that boasted some kind of sovereign status: the Orange and Arenberg families in the Habsburg Monarchy; the Bourbon-Navarres under the Valois kings; the *princes étrangers* in France. During the seventeenth century such minor sovereigns became increasingly distasteful to centralising rulers, as is shown by the deviating ideas on the ideal Guise heir and the occupations of Lorraine (1634–1661, 1670–1697, 1702–1714) and Orange (in 1672, 1682, 1713). Centralising monarchs demanded greater conformity from their aristocrats, while the interdependence of rulers and aristocrats gave rise to many conflicts.

This interdependence is also visible in matters of culture or identity. Philip II famously failed to come across as a 'Burgundian' on his tour of the Low Countries in 1549, prior to his accession to the throne, while he was also viewed as a stranger at the English court when he travelled there to marry Mary Tudor.[15] Although he valiantly tried to adapt to local custom – heavy beer drinking in the Low Countries, kissing court ladies on the lips in London – he remained conspicuously different. In both cases, his relationship with local aristocracies suffered. His father, Charles

[13] Liesbeth Geevers, "Being Nassau. Nassau Family Histories and Dutch National Discourse from 1541 to 1616", *Dutch Crossing* 35 (2011).

[14] See for a further discussion on the transnational character of these families: Jonathan Spangler, "Those in Between: Princely Families on the Margins of the Great Powers: the Franco-German Frontier, 1477–1830", in *Transnational Families in Europe and Beyond: Experiences since the Middle Ages*, (eds) Christopher H. Johnson et al. (New York: Berghahn Books, 2011), 131–134. This 'reclassification' is for instance visible in: Henk van Nierop, *Van ridders tot regenten.*

[15] Sarah Duncan, *Mary I: Gender, Power, and Ceremony in the Reign of England's First Queen* (New York: Palgrave Macmillan, 2012), 135–64.

V, had experienced the same problems when he made the opposite journey, from his native Low Countries to newly inherited Castile.

In order to analyse identities, it is not only helpful to transcend national borders, but also to shift our focus away from clearly defined political, courtly or military functions. Although such offices and loyalties were often instrumental in forging identities – or were perceived to be one's rightful possession, according to one's self-perception – non-office-holding women were frequently equally important in forging identities. Numerous volumes on the importance and influence of early modern noblewomen – albeit again often belonging to ruling families or occupying a more or less clearly defined political or courtly role – have been published[16] although important gaps remain; as recently as 2008, the Belgian historians Thérèse de Hemptinne and Jan Dumolyn noted the continuing absence of studies concerning noblewomen in the Low Countries.[17] With the recent focus on the study of family history, more and more research is being devoted to the role of women and children and their relationships, as well as the impact these relationships had on the coherence of the wider family.[18] Though heads of noble houses, often advised by councils comprising leading members of the lineage, would usually determine 'family matters', the interaction between individual family members has to be taken into account in the shaping of a dynasty's representational role. In several of the contributions in this volume it becomes apparent that aristocratic men might have had 'a grand design' when it came to the future of their lineages, but they rarely acted alone.

Identity formation in a dynastic context also provides a new framework to interpret the choices, careers and patronage of such families, and the positions assigned to individuals within it. In terms of religious and cultural patronage,

---

16 Nadine Akkermans and Birgit Houben (eds), *The Politics of Female Households. Ladies-in-waiting across Early Modern Europe* (Leiden: Brill, 2013); Jonathan Daybelle (ed.), *Women and Politics in Early Modern England, 1450–1700* (Aldershot: Ashgate, 2004); Katrin Keller, "Frauen in der höfischen Gesellschaft des 17. Jahrhunderts: Amtsinhabe und Netzwerke am Wiener Hof", *Zeitenblicke* 4 (2005), available at: http://www.zeitenblicke.de/2005/3/Keller/index_html; Jan Hirschbiegel and Werner Paravicini (eds), *Das Frauenzimmer: Die Frau bei Hofe in Spätmittelalter und früher Neuzeit* (Stuttgart: Thorbecke, 2000); Isabelle Poutrin and Marie-Karine Schaub, (eds) *Femmes & pouvoir politique. Les princesses d'Europe XVe-XVIIIe siècle* (Rosny-sous-Bois: Bréal, 2007); Pauline Puppel, "Der "Traum" einer jeden Schwiegermutter. Gräfin Elisabeth Charlotte von Nassau-Dillenburg-Schaumburg und Prinz Lebrecht von Anhalt-Bernburg", *Zeitenblicke* 8 (2009), available at: http://www.zeitenblicke.de/2009/2/puppel/Abbildung-2 and Martina Schattkowsky (ed.), *Witwenschaft in der Frühen Neuzeit: Fürstliche und adlige Witwen zwischen Fremd-und Selbstbestimmung* (Leipzig: Leipziger Universitätsverlag, 2003.

17 Thérèse de Hemptinne and Jan Dumolyn, "Historisch adelsonderzoek over de late middeleeuwen en de vroegmoderne periode in België en Nederland: een momentopname", *BMGN – Low Countries Historical Review* 123 (2008).

18 Susan Broomhall and Jacqueline Van Gent, "Corresponding Affections: Emotional Exchange Among Siblings in the Nassau Family", *Journal of Family History* 34 (2009).

families made choices as to which churches and convents to sponsor and in which cities or lordships to build their palaces. Politically and religiously they made their decision as to which side to be on in any conflict, which ruling families to support and into which other aristocratic families to marry. Socially, they decided which persons to accept into their fold and whom to reject, or what standard of conduct to expect from heirs and other members of the family. Culturally, they had a hand in framing the history, heraldry and genealogy of their family, which imperatively needed to be different from other dynasties so as to fit their ambitions and aspirations.[19] Not only the male heads of the family, but a plethora of mothers, siblings, spouses, children and cousins influenced decision-making. These choices – when made with some consistency over time or when presented as being part of a tradition – shaped a family's own identity.

Our focus on individual dynasties is not unprecedented. In fact, in recent decades the study of particularly prominent families has boomed. The primary focus of this scholarship has remained ruling dynasties and their strategic deployment of family members in their bid for European leadership.[20] Our concern with identifying a 'dynastic identity' is partly based on previous analyses of an arguably quintessentially Habsburg dynastic awareness.[21] Anna Coreth's seminal *Pietas Austriaca* has had a lasting influence, inspiring many other related publications.[22] The Austrian historian Karl Vocelka has published a series of studies on the

---

[19] Around 1600 this process was also meant to differentiate between 'new' and 'old' nobilities or even between legitimate nobles and upstart bourgeois who appropriated heraldic devices and acquired noble status. Luc Duerloo, "Het blazoen ontsmet. Adellijke heraldiek als toe-eigening van eer en deugd, 1550–1750", *BMGN – Low Countries Historical Review* 123 (2008) and Paul Janssens, "De la noblesse médiévale à la noblesse moderne. La création dans les anciens Pays-Bas d'une noblesse dynastique (XVe-début XVIIe siècle)", *BMGN – Low Countries Historical Review* 123 (2008).

[20] Ronald G. Asch, *Die Stuarts. Geschichte einer Dynastie* (Munich: Beck, 2011); Michael Brown, "Aristocratic Politics and the Crisis of Scottish Kingship, 1286–1296", *The Scottish Historical Review* 90 (2011); Pablo Fernández Abaladejo (ed.), *Los Borbones: Dinastía y memoria de nación en la España del Siglo XVIII* (Madrid: Marcial Pons/Casa de Velázquez, 2001); Thomas, *A House Divided* and Andrew Wheatcroft, *The Habsburgs. Embodying Empire* (London: Viking, 1996).

[21] See, for instance, Henry Kamen, *The Escorial. Art and Power in the Renaissance* (New Haven and London: Yale University Press, 2010), 64.

[22] Anna Coreth, *Pietas austriaca: Ursprung und Entwicklung barocker Frömmigkeit in Österreich* (Munich: Oldenbourg, 1959). For instance: Luc Duerloo, "*Pietas Albertina.* Dynastieke vroomheid en herbouw van het vorstelijk gezag", *BMGN – Low Countries Historical Review* 112 (1997); Charles Ingrao and Andrew L. Thomas, "Piety and Patronage: The Empresses-Consort of the High Baroque", *German History* 20 (2002); Adam Wandruzka, "Ein Freskenzyklus der 'Pietas Austriaca' in Florenz", *Mitteilungen des Österreichischen Staatsarchivs* 15 (1962) and Gerhard P. Woeckel, *Pietas bavarica: Wallfahrt, Prozession und Ex-voto-Gabe im Hause Wittelsbach in Ettal, Wessobrunn, Altötting und der Landeshauptstadt München von der Gegenreformation bis zur Säkularisation und der 'Renovatio Ecclesiae'* (Weissenhorn: A.H. Konrad, 1992).

mentality and *Lebenswelt* of the Habsburgs.[23] Although the peculiarities of the Habsburg dynasties have attracted special attention, to paraphrase Luc Duerloo, even for the complex realities of the Habsburg dynasty, their family interests have never been fully integrated into the historiography of the composite monarchy.[24] Such discussions are no longer limited to the Habsburgs, as is shown by Kevin Sharpe's recent work on the Tudors and Stuarts,[25] or even to Europe.[26]

This volume will not focus on rulers, but rather on great aristocratic families, such as the Arenberg, the Croÿ and the Guise. Lower ranked noble houses have not been included, although we do not intend to imply that our conclusions about dynastic identity do not apply to them. In more recent years, several valuable monographs have appeared on the persistence of such leading families, their natural preoccupation with survival and continuity, and their significance within the early modern European political constellation. Recent studies have demonstrated that while their aim was broadly similar, dynastic history and traditions could vary significantly from family to family.[27] This means that, even if aristocrats dealt

---

[23] Karl Vocelka and Lynne Heller, *Die Lebenswelt der Habsburger: Kultur- und Mentalitätsgeschichte einer Familie* (Graz: Styria, 1997) and Karl Vocelka and Lynne Heller, *Die private Welt der Habsburger. Leben und Alltag einer Familie* (Graz: Styria, 1998). The conclusions of both works are summarised in Karl Vocelka, *Die Familien Habsburg und Habsburg-Lothringen. Politik – Kultur – Mentalität* (Vienna: Böhlau, 2010). See also Wheatcroft, *The Habsburgs*, xix, who sees the Habsburgs 'as a clan, with its own mythology and covert ideology'.

[24] Luc Duerloo, *Dynasty and Piety: Archduke Albert (1598 – 16 21) and Habsburg Political Culture in an Age of Religious Wars* (Farnham: Ashgate, 2012), 12: 'In order to get the full picture, the dynastic interest needs to be taken into account as well'.

[25] Kevin M. Sharpe, *Selling the Tudor Monarchy: Authority and Image in Sixteenth-Century England* (New Haven: Yale University Press, 2009); idem, *Image Wars: Promoting Kings and Commonwealths in England, 1603–1660* (New Haven: Yale University Press, 2010) and idem, *Rebranding Rule: the Restoration and Revolution Monarchy, 1660–1714* (New Haven: Yale University Press, 2013).

[26] See in particular Lisa Balabanlilar, *Imperial Identity in the Mughal Empire: Memory and Dynastic Politics in Early Modern South and Central Asia* (London: I.B. Tauris, 2012).

[27] Excellent examples include Élie Haddad, *Fondation et ruïne d'une "maison". Histoire sociale des comtes de Belin (1582–1706)* (Limoges: Pulim, 2009); Lawrence E. Klein, "Sociability, Politeness and Aristocratic Self-formation in the Life and Career of the Second Earl of Shelburne", *The Historical Journal* 55 (2012); Peter Marshall and Geoffrey Scott, *Catholic Gentry in English Society. The Throckmortons of Coughton from Reformation to Emancipation* (Farnham: Ashgate, 2009); Gerard Nijsten, *In the Shadow of Burgundy: the Court of Guelders in the Late Middle Ages* (Cambridge: Cambridge University Press, 2004); Jonathan Spangler, *The Society of Princes: The Lorraine-Guise and the Conservation of Power and Wealth in seventeenth-century France* (Farnham: Ashgate, 2009); Ian Verstegen (ed.), *Patronage and Dynasty: the Rise of the della Rovere in Renaissance Italy* (Kirksville: Truman State University Press, 2007) and Hillay Zmora, "The Princely State and the Noble Family: Conflict and Co-operation in the Margraviates Ansbach-Kulmbach in the Early Sixteenth Century", *The Historical Journal* 49 (2006).

with roughly similar processes, such as the Reformation or state formation, they still presented themselves as being quite different from their colleagues – their lineage was thought to be older and more worthy, or their religious affiliations were connected to a specific religious order, or they married in a specific set of other families. Considering these developments in historiography, the concept of dynastic or family identity can serve as a valuable category to contextualise aristocratic choices and actions.

We aim to introduce the concept of dynastic identity as a dynamic notion, constantly challenged and changeable so as to adapt to new contexts. This approach departs from an open view of nobles' experiences, in contrast with the idea of the European-wide noble identity of a 'homogeneous' group, operating within fixed 'national' boundaries. By focussing on these different dynamics, the chapters in this book attempt a better understanding of the worldview and motives of the most powerful individuals and families in early modern societies, who helped shape the European political stage from the Middle Ages until long after the end of the Old Regime.

The Formation of a Dynasty: From 'Kinship' Groups to a Cultural Construction

The first and very obvious question that arises from this new approach is: what is a dynasty? The standard dictionary definitions focus on the generational aspect, for instance: 'a succession of people from the same family who play a prominent role in business, politics, or another field'.[28] Relevant as such definitions are – a dynasty is, after all, a family – this purely biological approach is too narrow for our purposes. Although dynasties are also families, biological kinship alone is hardly sufficient to be able to speak of a dynasty.[29] The composition of dynasties could be and frequently was manipulated. One of the current debates in kinship studies focuses on the shift from broad kin groups to patrilineal families in the period from 1000 to 1300 CE.[30] One of the premises of this discussion is that what

---

28 'dynasty'. Oxford Dictionaries. Oxford University Press. http://www.oxforddictionaries.com/definition/english/dynasty (accessed October 31, 2013).

29 Michel Nassiet, *Parenté, noblesse et états dynastiques, XVe-XVIe siècles* (Paris: Ecole des hautes études en sciences sociales, 2000), 12–13 also distinguishes 'parenté' from its 'substrat biologique'.

30 See, David Warren Sabean and Simon Teuscher, "Kinship in Europe. A new approach to long term development", in *Kinship in Europe. Approaches to Long-Term Development (1300–1900)*, (eds) David Warren Sabean, Simon Teuscher and Jon Mathieu (New York and Oxford: Berghahn Books, 2007), 4–5, for an overview of his debate. See also: Constance Brittain Bouchard, *'Those of my blood'. Constructing Noble Families in Medieval Francia* (Pennsylvania: University of Pennsylvania Press, 2001); David Crouch, *The Birth of Nobility. Constructing Aristocracy in England and France 900–1300* (Harlow: Pearson/Longman, 2005); Amy Livingstone, "Kith and Kin: Kinship and Family Structure

we understand by 'the family' itself has changed. This also means that it is defined, albeit often implicitly. For instance, Constance Brittain Bouchard's definition of family seems to be closely related to the function she ascribes to it: maintaining the family patrimony, continuing the established position of power and possibly improving upon it.[31] Those persons who belong to the dynasty contribute to this process: the fathers or brothers from whom one has inherited, oneself and one's sons who will inherit the patrimony one day.[32] Where there is a secure patrilineal succession, brothers who compete for the patrimony do not belong to the dynasty (but may be considered to have started their own dynastic enterprise), despite obvious biological connections. On the other hand, brothers who *do* support the efforts of their brother might in theory be regarded as members of the dynasty. In an example taken from the fifteenth century, Michaela Hohkamp argued that sisters who, by marrying, cemented a valuable alliance were held in great esteem. But as soon as the alliance fell apart, for instance through death, estrangement or divorce, the sister was no longer useful or valuable to the family, and 'therefore no longer kin'.[33] On another level, this transient inclusion/exclusion of contemporary family members is also visible in the seventeenth century: despite the provocative title *Louis XIV espagnol?* and the introductory remarks that 'kings are also sons of their mothers', it seems farfetched to consider Louis XIV of France as a Habsburg, even though he was Philip III's grandson.[34] Clearly, belonging to a dynasty entailed more than biological kinship.

Wolfgang Weber lamented the lack of sociological theory on dynasties and therefore offered his own definition. According to him, a dynasty is 'an optimal manifestation of the family, that marks itself through a heightened sense of identity and definition to the outside world; a collection of assets that form an expressly collective possession, such as territories, rank, rights and offices; marriages and inheritance practices that are intended to pass on the patrimony undiminished or

of the Nobility of Eleventh- and Twelfth-Century Blois-Chartres", *French Historical Studies* 20 (1997) and idem, *Out of love for my Kin: Aristocratic Family Life in the Lands of the Loire, 1000–1200* (Ithaca: Cornell University Press, 2010).

31 Bouchard, *'Those of my blood'*, 3: 'That is, each individual had to decide which ones, out of all the people to whom he or she was related by blood, were the true family members, those to whom one was allied' and 'the grandsons and great-grandsons of Charlemagne in the ninth century were fully aware that they shared a common ancestry, but they treated their first and second cousins not as family members and allies but as the enemy'.

32 Bouchard, *'Those of my blood'*, 63.

33 Michaela Hohkamp, "Do Sisters have Brothers? The Search for the *'rechte Schwester'*: Brothers and Sisters in Aristocratic Society at the Turn of the Sixteenth Century", in *Sibling relations and the transformation of European kinship, 1300–1900*, (eds) Christopher H. Johson and David Warren Sabean (New York: Berghahn Books, 2011).

34 Gérard Sabatier and Margarita Torrione (eds), *Louis XIV espagnol? Madrid et Versailles, images et modèles* (Versailles: Centre de Recherche du château de Versailles, 2009), 2: 'Les rois sont fils de leurs mères aussi'.

enhanced; and an increased sense of historical continuity. Both the formation and the consolidation should be seen as the result of conscious actions, according to certain elements and patterns'.[35] Weber points out that the formation of a dynasty entailed more than simply mechanisms to safeguard family assets for future generations. Cultural issues were also involved, for instance the 'historicising' of kinship ties by replacing the unclear and recent family roots with the 'discovery' – that is to say in many cases the creation – of a more extended line of descent. Furthermore, the formation of a dynasty was conditional on the premise that not only could physical and psychological characteristics be passed on genealogically, social and legal claims could equally be transferred.[36] The purpose of the dynasty was not only to transmit the family's material and immaterial assets, but also to embody the sense of obligation to keep on doing this. In this way, being part of a dynasty meant a lack of freedom to act in one's own best interest, but rather the obligation to act in the best interest of the wider collective. To impose such discipline, successful dynasties depended on accomplishing the socialisation of the offspring into the dynasty.[37] Weber argues that the improved princely education of the early modern period was directly connected to dynasties' determination to prolong their success. Equally, the improved education or socialising within dynasties meant that excess offspring could be considered useful to connect the family through marriage or patronage with other families or groups, instead of a threat to the main heir.[38]

Wolfgang Weber's definition therefore highlights that a dynasty is to a very large extent a social construction and that a shared identity – based on history, genealogy, patrimony and socialisation – is a central part of it. In addition, living family members are part of the dynasty, but ultimately it consists of a group of people that crucially included both deceased forebears and as-yet unborn offspring.[39] When Philip II built the Escorial, he did not do it for any living family member, but for a dead ancestor: his father. And when his grandson Philip IV

[35] Wolfgang E.J. Weber, "Dynastiesicherung and Staatsbildung. Die Entfaltung des frühmodernen Fürstenstaates, " in *Der Fürst. Ideen und Wirklichkeiten in der europäischen Geschichte*, (ed.) Wolfgang E.J. Weber (Cologne: Böhlau, 1998), p. 95: 'eine optimierte Erscheinungsform der Familie, die sich durch erhöhte Identität (und damit verstärkte Abgrenzung nach Außen), ausdrücklich gemeinsam genutzten (individueller Verfügung durch Familienmitglieder entzogenen) Besitz (Güter, Ränge, Rechte, Ämter), im Interesse ungeschmälerter Besitzweitergabe bzw. maximaler Besitzerweiterung bewußt gesteuerte Heirat und Vererbung sowie daher in der Regel gesteigerte historische Kontinuität auszeichnet. Sowohl die Entstehung einer Dynastie als auch deren Verfestigung sind deshalb wesentlich als Ergebnis bewußter Handelns aufzufassen, welchem entsprechend typische Elemente und Muster zugeschrieben werden können'.

[36] Weber, "Dynastiesicherung", 96–7.

[37] Weber, "Dynastiesicherung", 98–9.

[38] Weber, "Dynastiesicherung", 100–101.

[39] Crouch, *The Birth of Nobility*, 99–100, 131; Nassiet, *Parenté, noblesse et états dynastiques*, 29.

altered the burial arrangements there, he had many future generations in mind.[40] The inclusion of both the deceased and the unborn in dynastic awareness is in fact evident in one of its core elements: heredity, which looks both to the past and the future. Taking our cue from historiography on national identities, we can therefore argue that a dynasty is 'an imagined community', because an important part of its members are no longer alive or have not yet been born and the community as a whole could therefore only be imagined.[41] A dynasty is a timeless entity – at least leaders of dynasties generally aspired to timelessness and projected an image of timelessness – and can be seen as an iceberg: a minority of living family members are visible, while a host of deceased and unborn ones remain hidden.

In contrast with icebergs, the invisible part of the dynasty could be shaped and adapted to suit the needs of the living – in the same way that the history of a certain nation can be manipulated and changed. Thomas DaCosta Kaufmann argues, for instance, that 'dynasties, in expressing their cosmopolitan or supranational character (one thinks here particularly of the Habsburgs), deliberately sought to eliminate elements of topographical and historical contingency that might have weakened their claims to rule'.[42] Dynasties adapted their family history to suit their present needs or support their claims. Families could also connect to certain individuals in the past to reinforce their position. Names were instrumental in this regard. For instance, Henry IV of France gave his eldest son the name Louis at his baptism – although Louis had wanted to be called Henry, after the father whom he worshipped – in memory of St Louis from whom the Bourbons claimed to be descended.[43] And when Philip IV of Spain's third son Fernando Tomás was

---

[40] Juan Rafael de la Cuadra Blanco, "La idea original de los enterramientos reales en El Escorial", *Boletín de la Real Academia de Bellas Artes de San Fernando* 85 (1997).

[41] This concept is taken from Benedict R. O'G. Anderson, *Imagined Communities: Reflections on the Origin and Spread of Nationalism* (London: Verso, 2006, first edition London: Verso, 1983), 6. Anderson explains the term 'imagined' as follows: 'It is imagined because the members of even the smallest nation will never know most of their fellow-members, meet them or even hear of them, yet in the minds of each lives the image of their community'.

[42] Thomas DaCosta Kaufmann, *Towards a Geography of Art* (Chicago: University of Chicago Press, 2004), 137.

[43] E. Soulié and E. de Barthélemy (eds), *Journal de Jean Héroard sur l'enfance et la jeunesse de Louis XIII (1601–1628)* (Paris: F. Didot, 1868), 1:158. On the importance of naming: Barbara Bodenhorn and Gabriele vom Bruck. "'Entangled in Histories': An Introduction to the Anthropology of Names and Naming", in *The Anthropology of Names and Naming*, (eds) Barbara Bodenhorn and Gabriele vom Bruck (Cambridge: Cambridge University Press, 2006); Freya Verstraten, "Naming Practices among the Irish Secular Nobility in the High Middle Ages", *Journal of Medieval History* 32 (2006) and Michael Wolffson and Thomas Brechenmacher, "Nomen est Omen: The Selection of First Names as an Indicator for Public Opinion in the Past", *International Journal of Public Opinion Research* 13 (2001).

born, a court chronicler reminded the child – and his readers – of all the illustrious Ferdinands his parents' families had produced.[44]

Although the existence of biological kinship is not in itself sufficient to be able to speak of a dynasty, the kin group did provide the 'biological hardware' onto which a dynasty could be projected. The development of the concept of kinship is therefore a crucial part of our story. After all, the idea of a dynasty is projected onto a group of people that are united by their kinship ties and the perception of kinship is therefore an important dimension of dynastic awareness. Which persons were considered to be part of the family in the fifteenth through seventeenth centuries? Whereas previously kinship relationships were considered to have developed from a broad group to smaller patrilineal groups with an enhanced awareness of their shared genealogy between 1000 and 1300 CE, more recent historiography situates this development in a much longer period stretching from the post-Carolingian era into the seventeenth century – and really taking off between 1400 and 1700.[45] To give merely one example of the belated development of primogeniture, in Castile all siblings had a right to a share in the inheritance until the *mayorazgo* system was introduced. This system privileged the eldest male heir, who inherited the patrimony, over his younger brothers and all his sisters. This shift began during the Later Middle Ages, but did not reach its climax until the early sixteenth century when the Laws of Toro (1505) systematised what had long been social practice.[46]

The introduction of primogeniture did not mean that the collective nature of late medieval and early modern dynasties disappeared; in some ways it may actually have strengthened it. It is true that through certain marriage and inheritance practices, and through socialisation, the family's material assets and social capital were distributed unequally between siblings. However, it is crucial to stress the distinction between succession and inheritance. Even though the adoption of primogeniture was an extended process which began during the eleventh century, it was mainly the titles and offices together with the principal landed estates to which the eldest male heir succeeded, while the other children received a share of the inheritance through dowries (for daughters), appanages or help launching a career in the army or the Catholic church for younger sons. Sisters continued to play an important role in the dynastic enterprise. If in the fifteenth century sisters were discarded once the alliance they had forged through marriage fell through, from the seventeenth century onwards sisters were deemed important whether they were married or not, simply to advance the possibilities of the main line. However, the long process towards primogeniture did mean that the focus of the kin group on its main branch, and the focus of the members of the main

---

44 Rodrigo Méndez Silva, *Nacimiento y bautismo del Serenissimo Infante de España, D. Fernando Tomas de Austria* (1659), fols. 13–14.

45 Sabean and Teuscher, "Kinship in Europe", 11.

46 The standard authority is Bartholomé Clavero, *Mayorazgo: Propriedad feudal en Castilla 1369–1836* (Madrid: Siglo Veintiuno, 1974; 2nd ed., Madrid: Siglo XXI de España, 1989).

branch on the title-holder both increased. The eldest son was supposed to treat his siblings with 'the generous and wise authority of the father', and in many cases this actually happened.[47]

To illustrate this, it is useful to look again at a case in late sixteenth-century and early seventeenth-century Castile. The *mayorazgo* system led to hierarchisation of the lineage and caused some tensions. Rigorously excluding the younger sons from the inheritance led to many attempts by younger siblings to acquire a larger share of the inheritance through the courts. In spite of such tensions, family solidarity remained intact in the faction struggles at court, where litigating brothers continued to support each other.[48] The onset of primogeniture therefore did not mean that dynasties became smaller family groups; they mostly became more coherent units.

The relationship between the increased coherence of early modern lineages and dynastic identity remains to be analysed, but it seems reasonable to assume that strengthened dynastic identity both fostered coherence and was in turn fostered by it. Wolfgang Weber's emphasis on socialisation gives us a clue as to how families may have granted a more prominent position to the *primogenitus*, while keeping the other siblings on board. This process may have been influenced by the fact that younger siblings were not 'abandoned' to fend for themselves, but neither were they able to maintain status and wealth without their connection to the family unless they could fashion a successful career of their own. The patriarchal nature of both families and society at large meant that the *pater familias* defined the identity of the family members. On the other hand, the siblings of the early modern period were motivated to stress their connection to the head of the family – to uphold their status, which was derived from his, but also to remind their elder brother of his duty toward them.[49] As the examples from sixteenth-century Castile show, the new patriarchal lineages did not all consist of fatherly patriarchs and pliant juniors. Such family structures still allowed for conflict among siblings. But these conflicts were often quite instrumental for the formation of their collective, dynastic identity, as the chapters by Marini, Soen and Geevers all demonstrate. Such conflicts might have reconfigured relationships within the family. In any case, they show that patriarchy is a two-way street. In covering the period ca. 1500–1700, the chapters in this volume explore the formation of dynastic identities

---

47 Christopher H. Johnson and David Warren Sabean, "Introduction. From siblingship to siblinghood: kinship and the shaping of European society (1300–1900)", in *Sibling Relations and the Transformation of European Kinship, 1300–1900*, (eds) Christopher H. Johnson and David Warren Sabean (New York 2011), 3.

48 Antonio Terrasa-Lozano, "Legal Enemies, Beloved Brothers. High nobility, Family Conflict and the Aristocrats' two Bodies in Early-Modern Castile", *European Review of History* 17, no. 5 (2010), 720. See for both sibling support and sibling rivalry Nassiet, *Parenté, noblesse et états dynastiques*, 56–66.

49 Terrasa-Lozano, "Legal Enemies, Beloved Brothers", 723 stresses how the younger siblings were dependent on their eldest brother, who had inherited everything.

against the backdrop of the growing coherence of aristocratic families around the family head.

Most historians who use the term dynastic identity do not take the trouble to define what they mean by it. Thomas DaCosta Kauffman is an exception; he explains what he means by dynastic identity in his work on *The Geography of Art* (2004). In analysing the influence of environmental factors on the production and shape of art, he concludes that the dynastic identity of ruling families had a greater impact than their ethnic or national identity.[50] Dynastic identity is thus defined as 'the continuity of the ruling family over the ages, the sense of self-definition of members of this family as something lasting over a longer period than the life of any one individual. This sort of identity might be seen to be similar to that of ethnic or national identity in that it possesses a superindividual quality'.[51]

Recently, a number of historians have implicitly used the concept of dynastic identity. Jonathan Spangler, who also contributes a chapter to this volume, gave one chapter of his work *The Society of Princes. The Lorraine-Guise and the Conservation of Power and Wealth in Seventeenth-Century France* the title 'The Lorraine-Guise Dynastic identity'. In this work, Spangler focuses on 'the collective resonance of the name [Lorraine-Guise]', which overcame any weaknesses exhibited by the individual family members and was one of the foundation stones of the continuing power and wealth of the House of Lorraine-Guise.[52] Under the heading of 'dynastic identity' he discusses the 'house ideologies' and 'dynastic image' through dynastic history, iconography and display of wealth and patronage.[53]

In 2010, Andrew L. Thomas published *A House Divided. Wittelsbach Confessional Court Cultures in the Holy Roman Empire, c. 1550–1650* (Leiden 2010) in which he analyses the effect of confessionalisation on the dynastic ambitions and patronage of the two Wittelsbach branches of the Palatinate and Bavaria. He employs terms such as confessional identity, dynastic self-perception and, in fact, dynastic identity. Although he is mainly concerned with the influence of confessionalisation on the court cultures of the two Wittelsbach branches, he also analyses the redefinition, or renewal, of their late medieval dynastic ambitions in the sixteenth and seventeenth centuries. Taking his cue from Wolfgang Weber's work, he reconstructs these ambitions by focusing on the education of the dynasty's children, the writing of its histories and its perception by outsiders, among other things. Even more recently, Luc Duerloo devoted a monograph to Archduke Albert of Austria (2012).[54] In this work, Duerloo discusses at considerable length the dynastic rationales for Habsburg policy, and especially that pursued by Albert himself. The 'distinctive styles and set ways of operating on the political stage' shared by all Habsburgs, were complemented by a particular sense of legitimacy

50 Kaufmann, *Towards a Geography of Art*, 143–4.

51 Kaufmann, *Towards a Geography of Art*, 137.

52 Spangler, *Society of Princes*, 4–5.

53 Spangler, *Society of Princes*, 6.

54 Duerloo, *Dynasty and Piety*, 534–6.

through marriages and a proverbial piety.[55] These characteristics were shared by archdukes and *infantes* active all over Europe, and possessed a distinct historical dimension.

When reviewing the use of the term dynastic identity until this point, it is clear that it consists of a construction of a dynasty's history, which serves to educate new members about the family's (perceived) rightful position in society and the achievements in the past which supported and legitimated this status. We might speak of the collective memory of the dynasty, through improved and sometimes frankly incredible genealogies and family histories. Elements such as the aristocratic name, patronage traditions, the representation of identity through works of art and galleries of ancestors, the defining influence of piety or the wish to create a unified group of descendants through a specific set of 'dynastic imperatives', are all instrumental in shaping such a dynastic narrative. We can also think of a particular political activity (for instance diplomacy), connections with certain other dynasties (through marriages, alliances, or rivalries) or distinctive burial practices. All these elements may be used by families to enhance an existing idea of unity or to create a desired community, and in doing so, distinguish the dynasty from other families. The non-static nature of dynastic identity means that there were 'shapers': dominant characters within the dynasty, whether male or female, who mapped new courses and updated strategies to correspond to changing social and political circumstances.

Dynastic Identity as a 'Kaleidoscope': Patria, Caste and Confession Intertwined

What previous studies have in common is that dynastic identity – whether defined or not – is usually portrayed as a category *alongside* other possible categories of identities. Researchers thus make a choice as to what category they prefer, exactly as Thomas prefers confessional identity or Kauffman sees dynastic identity as something *similar* to national identity. However, as becomes clear in the contributions in this volume, dynastic identity is a multi-faceted concept, in which elements such as 'proto-patriotism', loyalty, piety, property or political pre-eminence play an important role. This complex set of elements interacts on various levels and is often held together by a dynamic interpretation of family history. But how should one describe this vague concept, which is able to shift over time and certainly does not offer the benefit of a clearly defined and exclusive category?

One of the most difficult issues to address is that of the widely accepted view of identity as a multi-layered concept.[56] Individuals rarely fit into 'just' one clearly defined category. In our case, while we aim to see dynastic identity as a defining

[55] Duerloo, *Dynasty and Piety*, 534.

[56] Peter Burke, *Cultural Hybridity* (Cambridge: Cambridge University Press, 2010); Jean-François Bayart, *L'illusion identitaire* (Paris: Fayard, 1996).

feature of the European nobility, we cannot overlook research on emerging 'national' sentiments.[57] Nor can we deny the overwhelming power of confessional identities after the Reformation.[58] Gender historians will claim that a person's gender is often at the forefront of his or her decisions and can no longer be set aside when assessing, for instance, noblewomen's political agency.[59] But was there tension between these categories? Was an aristocrat in early modern Europe primarily a nobleman, a patriot, a Protestant or a man? How exactly does dynastic identity embrace all these extensively researched categories? Is it possible to see gender, social group, confession or nation as all facets of the same kaleidoscope, falling to the background or centring in the middle of the view, each time the kaleidoscope turns?

The image of the kaleidoscope is a powerful metaphor in 'identity studies', as psychological and sociological research, for instance, has shown convincingly.[60] It permits a flexible and dynamic approach to individual or collective identities, whereby several facets of personal identity – like gender, ethnicity or social background – work alongside each other.[61] When the kaleidoscope turns, that is to say when social contexts shift, a different facet shifts to the foreground which still interacts with all the other personality traits that only temporarily cede their position. Facets in a kaleidoscope can never be seen separately, they interact continuously with each other. Gender and ethnicity, ethnicity and social background, gender and social background: they are difficult to separate, and attempting to do so would probably create a sterile view on reality. We feel that in the historiography on the

[57] Anne-Marie Thiesse, *La création des identités nationales: Europe XVIIIe-XXe siècle* (Paris: Éditions du Seuil, 2001).

[58] Heinz Schilling, "Die Konfessionalisierung von Kirche, Staat und Gesellschaft – Profil, Leistung, Defizite und Perspektiven eines Geschichtswissenschaftlichen Paradigmas", in *Die katholische Konfessionalisierung*, (eds) Wolfgang Reinhard and Heinz Schilling (Gütersloh: Mohn, 1995).

[59] Susan Broomhall and Colette H. Winn, *Les femmes et l'histoire familiale (xvie-xviie siècle)* (Paris: Champion, 2008); Magdelena S. Sánchez, *The Empress, the Queen, and the Nun: Women and Power at the Court of Philip III of Spain* (Baltimore: Johns Hopkins University Press, 1998); Natalie R. Tomas, *The Medici Women: Gender and Power in Renaissance Florence* (Aldershot: Ashgate, 2003) and Joyce de Vries, *Caterina Sforza and the Art of Appearance: Gender, Art and Culture in Early Modern Italy* (Farnham: Ashgate, 2010).

[60] B. Bradford Brown, Reed W. Larson and T. S. Saraswathi (eds), *The World's Youth: Adolescence in Eight Regions of the Globe* (Cambridge: Cambridge University Press, 2002); Lawrence H. Fuchs, *The American Kaleidoscope: Race, Ethnicity, and the Civic Culture* (Middletown: Wesleyan University Press, 1990) and Joan Z. Spade and Catherine G. Valentine (eds), *The Kaleidoscope of Gender: Prisms, Patterns, and Possibilities* (Los Angeles: Sage, 2011).

[61] Michelle Lamarche Marrese, "'The Poetics of Everyday Behaviour' Revisited: Lotman, Gender and the Evolution of Russian Noble Identity", *Kritika: Explorations in Russian and Eurasian History* 4 (2010).

European nobility too many attempts have been undertaken to strictly categorise the aristocracy into either 'national' nobility, or 'lower' and 'higher' nobility, or even into too strict gender categories.[62]

So in an attempt to open up the discussion, we introduce dynastic identity as a kaleidoscope. As the contributions in this volume will show, aristocratic houses more often than not developed a notion of family history that interacted with the political, the religious or, more generally speaking, the social position the family actually occupied, wished to occupy, or thought it already occupied. Since these politico-religious (not to mention economic and cultural) circumstances in Early Modern Europe shifted constantly, so the various facets of the dynastic kaleidoscope could be manipulated to show a different view, depending on the necessity those circumstances created. What made the kaleidoscope turn is 'family history'; or rather the historicity of shared 'real or imagined' collected and collective memories which produced an amalgam of interiorised historical facts.

Analysing Identity Formation: Actors, Motives and Strategies

The chapters in this volume have been organised under three headings, which aim to identify some of the major social contexts of the formation of dynastic identity: 1) Identity, Ethnicity and Monarchy; 2) Identity Formation and Family Relations; and 3) Manufacturing Identity. In a word, these three categories focus respectively on the influential dynamic between rulers and aristocrats that had a major impact on the identity formation of both rulers and aristocrats; the dynamic within the family, that is between different branches or between generations of the same families, or even between individuals who were each trying to put their stamp on the family's identity; and the dynamic treatment of deceased ancestors, whose legacy could be manipulated by their successors through the construction and manipulation of family histories and genealogies. We do not claim that these three contexts are exhaustive. For instance, we do not consider here the education and socialisation of young family members, although this is clearly an important element of identity formation. Neither do we focus on heraldry, even though this remained an important concern for aristocrats during the period from 1600 to 1750 and an important medium to assert family identity.[63] Instead, we have chosen to focus here on dynastic identity 'in action'.

The three chapters under the first heading all concern the relationship between aristocrats and rulers. Rulers were of enormous importance in the development of

[62] Michaela Hohkamp sometimes refers to 'gender' as a kaleidoscope: sometimes a person's gender will matter, at other times other elements will be more dominant (for instance social class). We prefer to see gender as an element within dynastic identity – a sense of femininity or masculinity that at times becomes dominant within a larger process of identity formation.

[63] Duerloo, "Het blazoen ontsmet", 634.

the identities of aristocratic dynasties. From the viewpoint of leading nobles, their relationship with their liege lord was an important element of definition, in terms of honours, titles, employment and religion. British monarchs were confronted with religious variety in their domains. Jane Ohlmeyer (Chapter 1) highlights the problems aristocrats experienced when their status depended on service to their king and honour demanded that they served their monarch, while their different religious affiliation prevented this. But the building blocks of aristocratic prestige were increasingly at odds with the centralising tendencies of states and rulers. For instance, marriages between aristocrats and members of royal families became less frequent as royals increasingly wed among themselves, depriving aristocrats of their immediate royal connections.[64]

Early modern Europe saw many changes of ruling dynasty, and such changes necessarily involved adaptation on the part of the newly arrived monarch. Ronald Asch focuses on exactly this problem in his chapter on the arrival of Henry IV in France and James VI and I in England (Chapter 2). How could they connect to their new elites, while at the same time maintaining their social distance from them? European interdependence and conflict in both economic and cultural matters is highlighted when we look at the situation in China. Jeroen Duindam (Chapter 3) argues that European elites were exceptional because of the role genealogy played in the legitimisation of their position. Such legitimisation only served the imperial lineage in China – but then this lineage became extremely numerous, encompassing groups comparable to European magnates but also more modest landed nobility.

The second group of chapters focuses on the relationship within aristocratic families. These families were not monolithic blocks, but comprised individuals who might have very different interests. Many of the conflicts regarding dynastic identity took place within the family and originated in problematic successions. The three chapters highlight different aspects of such intra-familial conflicts. Violet Soen (Chapter 4) highlights the problematic division of assets between two brothers – in fact, two nephews of the powerful Burgundian nobleman and preceptor of Charles V, William of Croÿ-Chièvres, who had acquired many new territories during his lifetime and wished to divide his inheritance between his nephews. Enforcing the idea that in the sixteenth century families could easily break up into separate units connected through a shared name and ancestry, she shows how the younger nephew managed to carve out a distinct patrimony for himself, ultimately founding a separate branch with quite different notions of loyalty than its senior branch. Such conflicts did not in the end weaken the dynasty as a whole, but neither does it appear that the division of loyalties between two rival monarchs was the result of deliberate family strategy. Nobles seldom saw their patrimonies solely in terms of nation-states.

Mirella Marini (Chapter 5) reveals the conflict resulting from a reverse development: the merger of two aristocratic houses by means of the marriage of

64 Lucien Bely, *La Société des princes, XVIe-XVIIIe siècle* (Paris: Fayard, 1999).

an heir and an heiress. Such mergers often led to frictions regarding the heiress's patrimony, because two sets of titles and names had to be transmitted to the next generation. Solutions might be found in giving one name to the eldest child and the other to a younger child, a situation still witnessed today in the offspring of the present Duchess of Alba: her eldest son carries his mother's name (Fitz-James Stuart), while the younger children carry their father's name (Matínez de Irujo). Such situations bring to light the position of aristocratic mothers. This role was always important, but gained in visibility if an aristocratic mother was empowered by her independent status as heiress – and was therefore the last guardian of the memory of her own line. However, her children might not share her view of the joint patrimony. In fact, Marini shows how a younger son who turned monk-cum-family historian managed to undo a lot of the identity formation by his own mother. Different generations presented different versions of the family history.

Jonathan Spangler (Chapter 6) discusses yet another problematic succession. Marie de Lorraine, last Duchess of Guise, attempted to choose her successor from among her many kinsmen. Since she was mainly interested in maintaining the family renown, she aimed to bypass her natural heirs – members of the Montpensier and Condé branches of the Bourbon dynasty – in favour of true 'Lorraines'. But her attempts to pass her inheritance to someone who would continue the independence of the *princes étrangers* failed due to the opposition of the head of the Bourbon dynasty, Louis XIV. Ironically, considering the visceral hatred between Bourbons and Guisards during the final decades of the sixteenth century, 'duc de Guise' became a subsidiary title of the Bourbon monarchs in the nineteenth century. Spangler shows in his contribution how the Guisards formed a sizeable clan, consisting of many different branches that were ultimately concerned with the welfare of the whole. In fact, the great numbers of the family were seen as one of its key strengths. In this way, the articles of Soen and Spangler illuminate a development from dynastic fissure to dynastic coherence between the early sixteenth and seventeenth centuries.[65]

The last group of chapters concerns the construction of family histories and the framing of the actions of some family members. As we have mentioned before, the construction of the past is an extremely important part of any kind of identity formation. As memory specialists argue, a family (or any other group) can serve as a social frame for a 'collective memory'. Membership of such a group requires one to 'participate in the group's history', and this is only possible once one has learned about the group's history.[66] Dynastic histories are a codification of the

---

[65] See also the studies by Stuart Carroll, *Martyrs and Murderers: The Guise family and the Making of Europe* (Oxford: Oxford University Press, 2009) and Jean-Marie Constant, *Les Guise* (Paris: Hachette, 1984).

[66] Aleida Assmann, "Re-framing Memory. Between Individual and Collective Forms of Constructing the Past", in *Performing the Past: Memory, History, and Identity in Modern Europe*, (eds) Karin Tilmans, Frank van Vree and Jay M. Winter (Amsterdam: Amsterdam University Press, 2010), 38.

family's memory – however distorted. Although it is an acquired memory, it is nevertheless a memory that concerns a person's identity, since it says something about 'who we are'. Sceptics dismiss the fact that this is a memory at all, and simply call it an ideology or the story, values and anxieties agreed upon by a group. To paraphrase Jan Assmann: a dynasty can only be a dynasty when it considers itself to be so and when it represents itself as such.[67] In both cases, the past is an important shaper of individual identity. Therefore, those who can shape the past also potentially shape the identity of their readership. The three chapters in this section show various sides of this process: the shaping of dynastic history (Geevers and Derks) and the reception of such histories and the role they played in identity formation (Persson).

The shaping of the dynastic past certainly seems to have been internalised by its recipients. For modern historians it seems obvious that this involved some distortion of the truth but, as Fabian Persson argues, the aristocrats involved may have sincerely believed in their version of dynastic history. These constructed histories were therefore 'real in their consequences' whatever their actual veracity. As the past was generally held up to contemporaries to serve as moral lessons and guidelines for behaviour, dynastic histories framed the way future generations would look back on those ancestors they were expected to emulate. Also, dynastic histories reminded family members of the honours, offices, titles and territories once held by their ancestors, and which were therefore to be retained or – if lost – restored. In this way, dynastic histories were carried into the future by the actions and ambitions of the successors.

The chapters in this section highlight different aspects of this process. Sebastiaan Derks (Chapter 7) focuses on the Farnese hero Alessandro and his sons' efforts to shape his memory. Alessandro only escaped a public fall from grace by dying, so his stature was rather besmirched. This posed a challenge for his two sons, who strove to maintain the position of the Farnese dynasty in Italy by recasting their father's memory. As Fabian Persson shows in his contribution (Chapter 8), in Sweden a relatively new aristocracy worked hard to provide itself with a venerable ancestry. However upstart they were – sixteenth-century Sweden was, as Persson notes, an 'impostor's paradise' – Sweden's new aristocracy broadly advertised their ancient and preferably royal descent, married into the royal family and built churches and monuments to match their new-found social status and ambitions, indignantly rejecting any suggestions that their ancestry might not have been as lofty as they or others imagined. Liesbeth Geevers (Chapter 9) focuses on the different perspectives taken by Nassau historians from both the Dutch Republic and Orange to show how different perspectives led to very different views on the overall mission of the Nassau dynasty, the merit of its individual members and even the meaning of the concept of 'the Prince of Orange' – reminding us that titles, too, can have a culturally constructed meaning other than the territorial position

[67] Jan Assman, *Das kulturelle Gedächtnis: Schrift, Erinnerung und politische Identität in frühen Hochkulturen* (Munich: Beck, 2000), 130.

they refer to. All three contributions highlight the fact that dynastic histories were indeed constructions which were at first intended to bolster the position of the contemporary dynasts, but later took on a life of their own. The final contribution, by Hamish Scott, will reflect on all the previous chapters and offer concluding remarks.

PART I
Identity, Ethnicity and Monarchy

Chapter 1
Aristocratic Identity Formation in Seventeenth-Century Ireland[1]

Jane Ohlmeyer

In early modern Ireland the peers were a class of nobility who enjoyed a title (as duke, marquis, earl, viscount and baron), awarded to them by the English monarch, and had the privilege of sitting as temporal lords in the House of Lords, alongside the protestant archbishops and bishops. The greater peers also formed the ruling aristocracy and quickly established themselves as the dominant social group in Irish society. During the early decades of the seventeenth-century the Stuart crown trebled the number of Irish peers. With this inflation of honours, itself an exercise in social engineering, the monarch created a peerage that comprised, in roughly equal numbers, catholic and protestant lords who were charged with making Ireland English. When analysed from an ethnic perspective, the aristocracy was now a mongrel body, combining several distinct groups: the native or Gaelic-speaking Irish; the Old English, as the descendants of the English-speaking Anglo-Norman invaders were known; the New English, as those who had migrated to Ireland from England since the 1530s were labelled; the Scots and the Welsh.

Clearly the ranks of the aristocracy were neither fixed nor impermeable. Some dynasties fell from royal favour and were attainted and their lands forfeited. Upward social mobility also occurred as 'new' lineages joined the established ones, especially with the creations of the 1610s and 1620s. The social background of the peers was varied. By 1641 52 (out of 91) houses were of ancient lineage or noble blood, including the Bourkes of Clanricarde, Butlers of Ormond, FitzGeralds of Kildare, MacDonnells of Antrim and O'Briens of Thomond. The remaining 39 families, like the Annesley, Boyles and Hamiltons, were soldiers or from the gentry or mercantile classes and thus regarded as arrivistes or upstarts. Whatever their background, these titled families, especially the ancient houses, held a disproportionally large amount of Irish land, at least 18 per cent in 1641 rising to 26 per cent by c.1670. They controlled a significant element of the country's wealth and the richest aristocrats in Ireland were on a par with the most prosperous

---

[1] Many of the ideas presented in this chapter derive from Jane Ohlmeyer, *Making Ireland English. The Irish Aristocracy in the Seventeenth Century* (New Haven: Yale University Press 2012) and "The Baronial Context of the Civil War in Ireland", in *The English Civil War. Conflicts and Contexts, 1640–49*, (ed.) John Adamson (Basingstoke: Palgrave Macmillan, 2009).

English or Scottish lords.[2] Men of money, power, prestige and privilege, the peers lived nobly, conspicuously and according to shared notions of honour. They acted as cultural brokers, dressing in the latest London fashions, speaking English (though a significant number would have been native Irish speakers or bi-lingual), and living in 'great houses'. As landlords, developers, entrepreneurs, politicians, and military commanders, they served as the regional and national powerbrokers, exercising influence in Ireland and beyond.

The seventeenth century was a transformational period in Irish history. Years of intense colonisation and Anglicisation characterised the early decades, followed, during the 1640s, by bloody civil warfare. A revolution in landholding and English conquest defined the 1650s, before ushering in the relative peace and prosperity of the Restoration era. By 1688 a bitter sectarian conflict once again engulfed the country and out of this emerged the Protestant Ascendancy of the eighteenth century. This chapter examines the factors that shaped aristocratic identity during this particularly tumultuous period. The fundamental importance of honour, itself closely linked to loyalty to the person of the monarch, cannot be overstated and is a recurring and dominant theme explored here. Irish aristocrats, like their counterparts across early modern Europe, used a variety of devices – genealogy, heraldry, funeral monuments and sermons, along with biographies and family histories – to create illustrious pedigrees and strong dynastic identities for their lineages, to demonstrate their loyal service and to flaunt their Englishness. Yet, given the nature of the times, these developments were often contested and shaped by religious belief, notions of national identity, the choice of a bride and education, as well as senses of loyalty and ideas about honour.

Honour was 'the social glue' for Stuart society.[3] In a number of seminal publications Brendan Kane explores the interface between honour, culture and politics and analyses how honour principles operated in an Irish context, how a distinctive Irish community of honour gelled and how these discussions had a very direct impact on court politics.[4] Using surrender and re-grant agreements, dating

---

[2] David Edwards, *The Ormond Lordship in County Kilkenny, 1515–1642. The Rise and Fall of Butler Feudal Power* (Dublin: Four Courts Press, 2003), 100–102.

[3] Brendan Kane, *The Politics and Culture of Honour in Britain and Ireland, 1541–1641* (Cambridge: Cambridge University Press, 2010), 10. Bernadette Cunningham, "Colonized Catholics: Perceptions of Honour and History in Michael Kearney's Reading of *Foras feasa ar Éirinn*", in *Taking Sides. Colonial and Confessional Mentalités in Early Modern Ireland*, (eds) Vincent P. Carey and Ute Lotz-Heumann (Dublin: Four Courts Press, 2003), 150–64; William Palmer, "That "Insolent Liberty": Honor, Rites of Power, and Persuasion in Sixteenth-Century Ireland", *Renaissance Quarterly* 46 (1993); James Kelly, *That Damn'd Thing called honour: Duelling in Ireland, 1570–1860* (Cork: Cork University Press, 1995); Clodagh Tait, *Death, Burial and Commemoration in Ireland, 1550–1650* (London: Palgrave Macmillan, 2002). Also see Deana Rankin, *Between Spenser and Swift. English Writing in Seventeenth-Century Ireland* (Cambridge: Cambridge University Press, 2005).

[4] Kane, *The Politics and Culture of Honour*; idem, "From Irish Eineach to British Honor? Noble Honor and High Politics in Early Modern Ireland, 1500–1650", *History*

from the 1540s, the crown sought to incorporate the peers into a ruling class and to 'create an aristocratic honour culture' centred on the king. He suggests that despite the very real 'social, cultural and political differences separating English from Irish' the Tudor crown and administration in Dublin 'saw Ireland's Gaelic and 'English-Irish' elites as simply variations on a recognized model of European nobilities'.[5] Kane examines noble honour in three broadly chronological contexts. The first looks at honour in the 'fighting and feasting' culture of medieval Ireland. The second, covering the years between the passage of the Kingship Act in 1541 and the outbreak of rebellion in 1641, explores how being a kingdom influenced notions of honour. There was the 'shift away from culturally (Gaelic) specific honor notions to more broadly negotiated ones' in which 'the honor bond between king and subject was now made explicit'.[6] He argues that 'Irish intellectuals reworked traditional notions of Gaelic honour to fit rapidly and radically changing social, cultural, political and religious circumstances'.[7] He also takes cognisance of the wider European context and demonstrates how 'the influence of Tridentine Catholicism' and continental ideas of honour refashioned Gaelic 'notions of honour'.[8] The third element in Kane's argument 'considers anglicized "British" honor' which, by the mid-seventeenth century, predominated.[9] In seventeenth-century Ireland honour became increasingly linked to service even if lineage remained particularly important for those catholic families denied office because of their faith. Of course, as Cynthia Herrup notes, 'honour was less a single value than a selection from a medley of values. It was … inborn and achieved, self-generated and bestowed, activist and stoical … Honour was both inherited and earned … dependent upon royal favour and community approval'.[10] Honour was its own reward.

Those peers of ancient lineage, like the Kildares, Ormonds, Clanricardes or Thomonds, viewed themselves, thanks to the good fortune of their birth and their chivalric origins, as enjoying a predisposition to honour. They created dynastic lineages by commissioning family trees that traced their ancestry back in time, some to Adam or in the case of the earls of Thomond to Brian Boru, high king of Ireland, and Milo, the first Gaelic invader of Ireland and a descendent of the ancient

Compass 7 (2009); idem, "Making the Irish European: Gaelic Honor Politics and its Continental Contexts", *Renaissance Quarterly* 61 (2008); and idem, "Scandal, Wentworth's Deputyship and the Breakdown of Stuart Honour Politics", in *Reshaping Ireland 1550–1700. Colonization and its consequences*, (ed.) Brian MacCuarta (Dublin 2011: Four Courts Press,).

5 Kane, *The Politics and Culture of Honour*, 21.

6 Kane, "From Irish Eineach to British Honor?" 415, 419.

7 Kane, *The Politics and Culture of Honour*, 46.

8 Ibid., 123.

9 Kane, "From Irish Eineach to British Honor?" 415.

10 Quoted in Cynthia Herrup, "'To Pluck Bright Honour from the Pale-Faced Moon': Gender and Honour in the Castlehaven Story", *Transactions of the Royal Historical Society*, sixth series, 6 (1996), 139.

Greeks. Genealogies and pedigrees focused on the nobleness and legitimacy of particular lineages and helped to differentiate them from the arrivistes.[11] Towards the end of the sixteenth century the Ulster king of arms began to compile coats of arms for peers with Irish titles. By the turn of the seventeenth century the use of heraldic devices was widely established and helped to confirm the exclusive position the aristocracy held in society. Bernadette Cunningham has suggested that 'This interest in heraldry within the context of a settler social hierarchy, and more particularly the associated verification of pedigrees, closely paralleled the work of the hereditary historians in Gaelic society in affirming contemporary social status by reference to ancestry'.[12] The anonymous author of the *Aphorismiscal Discovery of Treasonable Faction* ridiculed the Old English obsession with origin. He took delight in trawling the annals with the intention of exposing the humble beginnings of many of the established lords: 'I haue perused both those chronicles and founde nothinge remarkable, any noble extraction, either in bloude or action, or other thinge, wherof these present gentlmen might bragg off theire proper beinge from thence descended'.[13]

Those lacking an illustrious pedigree simply created one. Richard Boyle, first earl of Cork, stands as an excellent example of someone who used royal service, marriage and death to portray himself as virtuous and his lineage as honourable even if it was clear to contemporaries that he was a grasping, greedy, social climbing commoner who lacked noble virtues and qualities.[14] He purchased armorials and the latest books on the English peerage and ostentatiously adorned his homes with heraldic shields.[15] Clodagh Tait's meticulous analysis of the funeral monuments associated with the first earl of Cork vividly recaptures how the 'upstart earl' (as contemporaries dubbed him) used five funerary monuments 'to bolster, and often create, an official view of the past, the present, and the future'.[16] Cork combined the visual and the verbal in these monuments to portray his new and composite dynasty as an 'ancient' and honourable lineage and to appropriate the reputations

[11] Kane, *The Politics and Culture of Honour*, 158–80; Toby Barnard, *A New Anatomy of Ireland: Protestants in Ireland, 1649–1770* (New Haven: Yale University Press, 2003), 46.

[12] Cunningham, "Colonized Catholics", 150–56.

[13] J.T. Gilbert (ed.), *A Contemporary History of Affairs in Ireland, from AD 1641 to 1653 …* (3 vols, Irish Archaeological Society, Dublin 1879), 1:244–5.

[14] Nicholas Canny, *The Upstart Earl. A Study of the Social and Mental World of Richard Boyle First Earl of Cork, 1566–1643* (Cambridge: Cambridge University Press, 1982), 10–11, 14–15, 19, 23, 43; Clodagh Tait, "Colonising Memory: Manipulations of Death, Burial and Commemoration in the Career of Richard Boyle, First Earl Of Cork (1566–1643)", *Proceedings of the Royal Irish Academy*, 101 Section C (2001); Patrick Little, "The Earl of Cork and the Fall of the Earl of Strafford", *Historical Journal* 39 (1996).

[15] Alexander B. Grosart (ed.), *The Lismore Papers. First [and the second] series … Edited with Introd. and Notes by Alexander B. Grosart from the Original MSS. belonging to the Duke of Devonshire preserved in Lismore Castle* (10 vols., London 1886–88), first series, 5: 84.

[16] Tait, "Colonising Memory", 108.

of the dead for the benefit of the living. These tombs also stood as a testament to the worthiness of Cork's birth, his wealth and the exercise of his influence and power. In short, they celebrated the achievements of the Boyle dynasty, its founder and his family. They also told the life story of a family and provided a snapshot of its changing relationships. For example, Lady Cork's tomb in Dublin (see Figure 1.1) provides 'an abridged pictorial genealogy of the countess of Cork, with each figure described according to their relationship with her'. Her grandfather and parents are represented at the top of the monument. The middle section depicts the countess and her sons and in the bottom tier her daughters kneel in prayer.[17] The coats of arms of the families into whom the Boyles married frame the elaborate tomb and add further colour and splendour. This, like the other Boyle tombs, was a subtle work of propaganda that stressed the virtues of the family and its alliances, its continuities with the past and its potential for the future.

Funerary monuments such as these made powerful statements about the individual and his place in the social hierarchy and the future vibrancy of his lineage. They provided for posterity a powerful visual record of an individual and his lineage. Those that represented a husband and wife and members of their family commemorated a successful marriage and a lord's fecundity. Heraldic shields and devices adorned many monuments and helped onlookers to identify a family and, through the quartering of the arms, to determine the membership of the wider lineage. Heraldic images also helped to convey an ancientness of title and lineage, which was particularly useful for new peers who were eager to establish their social credibility. The nature of the monument and its positioning within the church attested to the status and wealth of the dead peer and, more importantly, to the social connections and political influences of the lineage and to its nobleness and honour. Monuments also celebrated public service, military achievement and private virtue.[18] The elaborate tomb that commemorates Thomas Jones, archbishop of Dublin, and his son, Viscount Ranelagh, illustrates this. It shows the archbishop with churchman's cap and gown (see Figure 1.2). The recumbent figure of Viscount Ranelagh lies below, clad in armour, highlighting the importance of military service. He is surrounded by four female figures, presumably his three daughters and wife, while his son, who is in civilian dress, kneels in prayer.[19]

---

[17] Ibid., 129.

[18] Tait, *Death*, chapter 7; Raymond Gillespie, "The Image of Death, 1500–1700", *Archaeology Ireland* 6 (1992), 8–10; Amy Louise Harris, "Tombs of the New English in Late Sixteenth and Early Seventeenth-Century County Dublin", *Church Monuments* 11 (1996); Rolf Loeber, "Sculptured Memorials to the Dead in Early Seventeenth-Century Ireland", *Proceedings of the Royal Irish Academy* 81, Section C (1981); Paul Cockerham, "'To mak a Tombe for the Earell of Ormon and to set it up in Iarland': Renaissance Ideals in Irish Funeral Monuments", in *Ireland in the Renaissance, c.1540–1660*, (eds) Thomas Herron and Michael Potterton (Dublin: Four Courts Press, 2007).

[19] Tait, *Death*, 125.

Figure 1.1 The Cork tomb. The first earl of Cork combined the visual and the verbal in his family's funerary monuments to portray his new and composite dynasty as an 'ancient' and honourable lineage. This is a photograph of Lady Cork's tomb in St. Patrick's cathedral in Dublin, which shows her grandfather and parents at the top of the monument. Photograph taken by the author.

Figure 1.2 Ranelagh tomb. This elaborate funeral monument in St. Patrick's cathedral in Dublin commemorates Thomas Jones, archbishop of Dublin (c.1550–1619), and his son, Roger, Viscount Ranelagh (d. 1644). Monuments such as this celebrated public service, military achievement and private virtue and provided for posterity a powerful visual record of an individual and his lineage. Photograph taken by the author.

Of course the living used a variety of ways to commemorate the 'breeding' of a deceased lord, his political and marriage alliances, his service and loyalty to the crown. The funeral sermons of protestant lords extolled their public virtues: their 'noble' birth and ancestry, their role as loyal public servants, as brave soldiers, as devoted supporters of the crown and of the established church; together with their personal qualities – their learning, wisdom, tenderness, compassion, hospitality, charity, faithfulness – and, above all, their sense of honour. In 1663 Dr Rust preached the earl of Mount Alexander's funeral sermon and spoke of his virtue, nobleness, wisdom, good nature, loyalty, military ability and his 'zeal and cordial affection for the Church of England'.[20] In short, Mount Alexander exemplified all of the qualities of a true noble:

> a loyal subject to his prince: a dutiful son to the church, a worthy patriot to his country; a tender and affectionate husband to his excellent ladies, real and faithful to his friend; merciful and compassionate towards his tenants, free and charitable to the poor, courteous and obliging to all, in a word, just and righteous, noble and honourable in all his actions.[21]

Other lineages, especially new upwardly mobile ones, recognised the importance of using history to immortalise dynasties and many families oversaw the writing up of their family biographies or else had committed to paper orally preserved stories and testimonies. The earl of Orrery, a younger son of Cork's, perhaps fearful that aspects of his own at times unsavoury past would be exposed, collected materials for his life story with the specific intention of preserving his actions and reputation 'to posterity'.[22] Others did likewise. Prior to his death in 1658 the marquis of Clanricarde had compiled letter books, presumably with a view to writing his own version of events.[23] The MacDonnells of Antrim were anxious to preserve family lore and during the early eighteenth century secured the compilation of detailed genealogies and oral histories of the family.[24] Contemporary writers also chronicled the achievements of the Hamiltons of Clanbrassil and Montgomerys of Mount Alexander and emphasised their noble lineages, their loyalty to the established

20 George Rust, *A Sermon Preached at New-town the 29 of Octob. 1663. At the Funeral of the Right Honourable Hugh Earl of Mount-Alexander, Lord Viscount Mountgomery of Ards, Late Master of the Ordnance, and one of His Majesties Most Honourable Privy Council in Ireland* (Dublin 1664), 37–8, also 32–4.

21 Ibid., 38.

22 Ibid., 27; Thomas Morrice (ed.), *A Collection of the State Letters of ... Roger Boyle, First Earl of Orrery* ... (London 1742), ii.

23 John Lowe (ed.), *Letter-Book of the Earl of Clanricarde 1643–1647* (IMC, Dublin 1983).

24 Hector McDonnell, "A Fragment of an Irish Manuscript History of the MacDonalds of Antrim", *Ulster Journal of Archaeology* 64 (2005) and Hector McDonnell and Jane Ohlmeyer (eds), "New Light on the Marquis of Antrim and the 'Wars of the Three Kingdoms'", *Analecta Hibernica* 41 (2009).

church and the crown and the prominent roles they had played in helping to civilise Ulster.[25] In an article on the Montgomery manuscripts Raymond Gillespie noted that these 'represent a new departure in the writing of Irish history since they are a conscious attempt by a settler family to portray its history since coming to Ireland in a way that demonstrates the success of the settlement. It is not a justification of colonization but rather a description of the founding of a dynasty'.[26]

This was an age when reputation and honour were of paramount importance and peers, conscious of how posterity would judge their actions and those of their lineage, did everything possible to secure reputations and 'to lie well in the chronicle'.[27] This was of paramount importance to the house of Ormond, Ireland's premier aristocratic dynasty during these years. In 1677 Sir Robert Southwell, Ormond's secretary, urged the duke to commission his own history of the 1640s.[28] As Southwell put it:

> And I conceive your long life and many years of employment, and variety of fortunes, will deserve a little care, even from yourself, to see that justice be done; since every man is a debtor to his family, and 'tis not enough to leave great heaps of materials behind, if they must be left to the mercy of those who shall not employ them aright; therefore I am so far in the other extreme that I would even press and importune your Grace to have somebody capable of the work employed in nothing else (while you are in the Government there, and have all papers about you), to write the memories of your whole life, and if not to the world, yet to bequeath them to your family.[29]

Southwell and a scholar called Mr Hill, who later became a professor at the university of Leiden, enjoyed full access to Ormond's 'great heaps of materials' and secured copies of other contemporary histories and began work on compiling a suitable narrative.[30] The monumental task, however, was never completed and

25 T.K. Lowry (ed.), *Hamilton Manuscripts: Containing some Account of Territories of Upper Clandeboye, Great Ardes, Dufferin in the County of Down, by Sir William Hamilton, afterward Viscount Clandeboye* (Belfast 1867) and George Hill (ed.), *The Montgomery Manuscripts (1603–1706). Compiled from the Family Papers by William Montgomery of Rosemount* ... (Belfast 1869). Also see Bernadette Cunningham and Raymond Gillespie, "Brian Maguire of Knockninny and his manuscripts", *Clogher Record* 13 (1988), 41.

26 R. Gillespie, "The Making of the Montgomery Manuscripts", *Familia* 2, no. 2 (1980), 26.

27 Nicholas French, *The Unkinde Desertor of Loyall Men and True Frinds* ([Paris] 1676), 194.

28 *Calendar of the Manuscripts of the Marquess of Ormonde, preserved at Kilkenny Castle* (Old and New Series, 11 vols., London 1895–1920), NS, 3:372.

29 Ibid., 4:374; also 378.

30 Ibid., 4:374, 529.

it was the eighteenth century before Ormond found his historian in the person of Thomas Carte.[31]

During these years Ormond was acknowledged as the greatest royal servant of all.[32] Contemporary historians, like Edward Hyde, earl of Clarendon, represented Ormond as a courageous, selfless, loyal servant who put the interests of the crown before his own.[33] The poet laureate, John Dryden's portrait of Ormond as Barzillai in *Absalom and Achitophel* exemplified Ormond's loyalty in terms of service and sacrifice in civil-war Ireland ('regions waste beyond the flood') and extols his honour ('Barzillai crown'd with Honour').[34] Two years later, Dryden published his translation of *Plutarch's Lives* and dedicated it to the duke. In the preface he emphasised the duke and his family's sense of virtue and honour, his ancient and distinguished lineage, his long and loyal service to the Stuarts, and his remarkable and effective rule in Ireland.[35] Ormond also enjoyed close relationships with some of the other leading literary figures in Stuart England and Ireland, including Aphra Behn, Katherine Philips, Nahum Tate and John Wilson. Writing in 1685 to celebrate the coronation of James II Aphra Behn represented Ormond as 'Stedfast in *Loyalty*, in *Honour* nice'.[36] Like John Dryden these writers were concerned with depicting the family's sense of honour or, in the case of the Butler women, their virtue. They portrayed the duke as a loyal servant to the Stuarts, as the leading courtier and as an extraordinary statesman, and his son, Ossory, as a faithful commander and military hero (comparable to Caesar or 'a Carthaginian prince').[37]

Honour was a collective status and the example of the Ormonds illustrates this vividly. In particular, elegies, written in the wake of the deaths of Ossory and the first duke and his duchess, celebrated their lives and lineage, their military achievements, their public service and their private virtue together with their loyalty to his sovereign, family and friends. Richard Lawrence dedicated *The*

---

[31] Thomas Carte, *The Life of James Duke of Ormond* (6 vols, Oxford: Oxford University Press, 1851); M. Perceval-Maxwell, "Sir Robert Southwell and the Duke of Ormond's reflections on the 1640s", in *Kingdoms in Crisis. Ireland in the 1640s*, (ed.) Micheál O Siochru (Dublin: Four Courts, 2001).

[32] Jane Ohlmeyer and Steven Zwicker, "Patronage and Restoration Politics: John Dryden and the House of Ormond", *Historical Journal* (2006).

[33] Edward Hyde, Earl of Clarendon, *The History of the Rebellion and Civil Wars in England*, (ed.) W.D. Macray (6 vols, Oxford: Oxford University Press, 1888), 2: 492–3 and 'A short view of the state and condition of the kingdom of Ireland from the yeare 1640 to this tyme' (Bodleian Library, Oxford, Clarendon Ms 121C),

[34] E.N. Hooker and H.T. Swedenberg, Jr., (eds), *The Works of John Dryden* (20 vols, Berkeley and Los Angeles: University of California Press, 1953–2000), 2: 817–28.

[35] Ibid., 17: 235–6.

[36] Aphra Behn, *Poems A Pindarick Poem on The Happy Coronation Of His Most Sacred Majesty James II And His Illustrious Consort Queen Mary* (London 1685), [17].

[37] Anonymous, *A Brief Compendium of the Birth, Education, Heroick Exploits and Victories of the Truly Valorous and Renowned Gentleman, Thomas Earl of Ossory* (London? 1680), 3.

Interest of Ireland to Ossory's young heir, later the second duke, and in the preface reprinted many other poems that appeared in the wake of his father's death in 1680. These focussed on his lustrous and ancient lineage, his commitment to protestantism, his loyalty to the Stuarts ('Charles was his Polar Star'), his naval and military victories, his 'publick spirit' and his personal qualities of diligence, affability, humility, charity, and honour.[38] One-page broadsheets also circulated ensuring that the widest possible readership learned of Ossory's bravery, marital acts, fidelity and honour.[39] John Dryden in his opening dedication of *Fables* (1700) deftly linked the three generations and celebrated the Ormonds as a model for the unbroken descent of virtue, honour and charity and suggested that they were 'descended from one of the most Ancient, most Conspicuous, and most Deserving Families in Europe'.[40] Given their position as the premier lineage in Stuart Britain these representations of the Ormonds as the ultimate embodiment of aristocratic honour is understandable, as is the extent to which they became a model for others to emulate.

As this discussion of honour highlights, the centrality of loyalty to the crown in defining noble identity cannot be overstated and often overrode senses of national or ethnic identity. In short, the peers wanted to serve their monarch and to be identified as 'English'. Aidan Clarke's seminal work on the political connections and cultural makeup of the 'Old English' community clearly demonstrates that throughout the first half of the seventeenth century they perceived themselves as the crown's loyal and devoted servants and argued that their Catholicism in no way jeopardised their fealty to a protestant prince nor their ability to serve him as their ancestors had done.[41] Those of Anglo-Norman ancestry, such as the earls of Clanricarde or the Butlers of Ormond, consistently stressed their 'Englishness' often at the expense of their 'Irishness'.[42] Studies largely by Gaelic literary scholars suggest that after the defeat in the Nine Years' War (1594–1603) and the

---

38 Richard Lawrence, *The Interest of Ireland in its Trade and Wealth stated in Two Parts: First Part Observes and Discovers the Causes of Irelands not more Increasing in Trade and Wealth from the First Conquest till Now: Second Part Proposeth Expedients to Remedy all its Mercanture Maladies ... by which it is kept Poor and Low; both mix'd with some Observations on the Politicks of Government relating to the Incouragement of Trade and Increase of Wealth: with some Reflections on Principles of Religion as it Relates to the Premisses* (Dublin 1682), 1:preface.

39 Anonymous, *An Elegy to the Memory of the Right Houorable [sic] Thomas, Earl of Ossory who Depated [sic] this Life July the 30th, 1680* (London 1680).

40 Hooker and Swedenberg (eds), *The Works of John Dryden*, 7:17.

41 Aidan Clarke, "The Policies of the "Old English" in Parliament, 1640–1", in *Historical Studies V*, (ed.) J. L. McCracken (London: Books for Libraries Press, 1965) and idem, "Colonial Identity in Early Seventeenth Century Ireland", in *Historical Studies XI. Nationality and the Pursuit of National Independence*, (ed.) T.W. Moody (Belfast: Appletree Press, 1978).

42 Joep Leerssen, *Mere Irish and Fíor-Ghael. Studies in the Idea of Irish Nationality, its Development and Literary Expression prior to the Nineteenth Century* (Cork: Cork

'Flight of the Earls' in 1607 the native Irish, while acknowledging the centrality of Catholicism to their identity, increasingly adopted the same conciliatory, politique attitude towards the crown which had traditionally characterised the Old English.[43]

Of course the Catholicism of some of Ireland's leading peers did complicate matters. The fact that peers were required to take the oath of supremacy before holding office ensured that the 'service nobility' that James VI and I created in Ireland during the early decades of the seventeenth century was predominately protestant, with only a handful of catholic aristocrats holding senior legal or administrative positions or enjoying military commands in the Stuart army. Hardly surprisingly, the fact that Catholics, especially those who had previously formed part of the ruling elite, were excluded from serving the king became a major grievance. The Old English poet and historian, Richard Bellings, justified the reluctant involvement of the catholic lords in the 1641 rebellion on the grounds that they were denied adequate opportunity to serve:

> We have considered the condition of all the other kingdomes of Europe, and we are the sole subjects, who, being much the more numerous and powerfull, are made incapable of raysing our fortunes by serving our King in any place of honour, profitt, or trust, in that country wherin we were borne, and which God, of his providence, appointed us as a part of the earth which our ancestors for soe many hundred yeares did inhabit.[44]

Ironically it was during the Wars of the Three Kingdoms, that the 1641 rebellion helped to trigger, or in exile during the 1650s that many of these lords finally secured an opportunity to serve the Stuarts. With his restoration after 1660 Charles II endeavoured (not always successfully) to reward those who had stood by him in his darkest hour, but back in late Stuart Ireland opportunities for service were

---

University Press, 1996) offers the best overview of identity formation among the catholic population in early modern Ireland.

43 Breandan Ó Buachalla, "James our True King. The Ideology of Irish Royalism in the Seventeenth Century", in *Political Thought in Ireland since the Seventeenth Century*, (eds) D. George Boyce, Robert Eccleshall and Vincent Geoghegan (London: Routledge,1993). Unfortunately Ó Buachalla's *tome* on the Stuarts and the intelligentsia, 1603–1788, *Ailing ghéar* (Dublin 1997), is not available in English. Also see Mícheál Mac Craith, "The Gaelic Reaction to the Reformation", in *Conquest and Union. Fashioning a British State, 1485–1725*, (eds) Steven Ellis and Sarah Barber (Harlow, Longman, 1995); Bernadette Cunningham, "Irish Language Sources for Early Modern Ireland", *History Ireland* 4 (1996); Marc Caball, "Bardic Poetry and the Analysis of Gaelic Mentalities", *History Ireland* 2 (1994); and Michelle O. Riordan, "'Political' Poems in the Mid-Seventeenth-Century Crisis", in *Ireland from Independence to Occupation*, (ed.) Jane Ohlmeyer (Cambridge: Cambridge University Press, 1995) and eadem, *The Gaelic Mind and the Collapse of the Gaelic World* (Cork: Cork University Press, 1990).

44 J.T. Gilbert (ed.), *History of the Irish Confederation and the War in Ireland, 1641–3* ... (7 vols, Dublin, 1882–91), 1: 36.

once again restricted and limited to the protestant peers. Deprived of opportunities to wield patronage, generate income and secure their noble honour, the continued exclusion of Catholics from holding office and bearing arms undoubtedly contributed to the long-term political and economic demise of catholic lords, especially the lesser lineages.

The association between Englishness, loyalty and 'civility' helps to explain why so many peers, irrespective of their ethnic and religious background, wanted to be perceived as being English. Some touted their 'Englishness' when it was politically expedient to do so. Consider the example of the Butlers of Mountgarret, who took English spouses from well-connected and well-heeled English catholic families over the course of three generations. These connections facilitated Mountgarret opposition to attempts by the government in the late-1630s to confiscate lands in Counties Kilkenny and Tipperary. Then, in the wake of the upheavals of the civil wars, these associations enabled the Mountgarrets to parade their 'Englishness' despite the family's close involvement in the confederation of Kilkenny. The conversion to Protestantism of leading native Irish and Old English lords complicated further matters around identity. Some, such as the O'Briens of Thomond who converted to Protestantism in the late sixteenth century, downplayed their Irish origins and represented themselves as 'English'. By the 1670s, Henry, the eldest son of the seventh earl of Thomond, urged his own heir 'to cherish the English uppon his estate and driue out the Irish, and specially those of them whoe are under the name of gentlemen'.[45]

Particularly intriguing is the extent to which the 'Scottish peers', who settled in Ulster during the first decade of the seventeenth century, became increasingly anglicised. The Scots comprised seven per cent of the resident peerage and represented the smallest ethnic group (the native Irish accounted for 10 per cent, the New English 32 per cent and the Old English 49 per cent).[46] How Scottish were the 'Scottish peers'? Some, especially first generation settlers, retained a strong sense of Scottish identity. Many of the early Scottish planters preferred to deal with Scottish merchants and to surround themselves with Scottish servants and friends.[47] Scottish builders and craftsmen gave a Scottish flavour to the architectural landscape of Ulster as they constructed square baronial tower houses or castles with an L- or T-shaped plan. Many had distinctive Scottish features –

45 John Ainsworth (ed.), *Inchiquin Manuscripts* (Dublin: IMC, 1961), 512.

46 Jane Ohlmeyer, "Scottish peers' in seventeenth-century Ireland' in *Scots in early Stuart Ireland,* (ed.) David Edwards (Manchester: Manchester University Press, 2015), 62-94; Raymond Gillespie, *Colonial Ulster. The Settlement of East Ulster 1600–1641* (Cork: Cork University Press, 1985); Philip Robinson, *The Plantation of Ulster. British Settlement in an Irish Landscape, 1600–1670* (Dublin: Gill and Macmillan, 1984) and M. Perceval-Maxwell, *The Scottish Migration to Ulster in the Reign of James I* (London: Routledge, 1973).

47 Nicholas Canny, *Making Ireland British, 1580–1650* (Oxford: Oxford University Press, 2001), 235.

projecting turrets, crow stepped gables, elaborate corbelling and canonical roofed turrets.[48] The fact that most of the 'Scottish peers' held lands in Ulster facilitated easy and regular exchange between the two kingdoms. Friendship networks within Ireland bound together the 'Scottish peers', especially in the early years.

Table 1.1 Geographic origin of wives of resident peers (based on wives' fathers)[49]

Total sample = 421

Religion of the peer	**Ireland**	**England**	**Scotland**	**Continent**
Catholic (pre-1649)	95 (22.56%)	18 (4%)	3 (0.7%)	2 (0.47%)
Protestant (pre-1649)	46 (10.9%)	56 (13%)	14 (3.3%)	1 (0.2%)
Catholic (post-1649)	58 (13.77%)	22 (5%)	0	1 (0.2%)
Protestant (post-1649)	55 (13%)	48 (11%)	1 (0.2%)	1 (0.2%)
Total pre-1649	*141*	*74*	*17*	*3*
Total post-1649	*113*	*70*	*1*	*2*
Total	254 (60%)	144 (33%)	18 (4%)	5 (1%)

Marriages with fellow Scots reinforced these alliances but only for the first generation of 'Scottish peers'. As the figures in Table 1.1 illustrate, later lords preferred to match with the daughters of the New English elite in Ireland or the nobility in England. The heirs of the Scottish lords invariably travelled to England, especially Oxford, to be educated and confirmed in their commitment to Anglicanism, rather than Presbyterianism. This suggests that the 'Scottish peers' who settled in Ireland did so with the intention of making a permanent commitment and from the outset wanted to become integrated with leading figures in their new communities and used marriage as a means of consolidating powerbases and enhancing political influence. Instead of identifying with their place of birth or with Scottish religious, political and legal institutions and with Scottish culture these lords increasingly looked to their host nation, Ireland, where they enjoyed wealth and status, and to their monarch in England, as the source of honour and continued reward. The passage of time resulted in the bleaching out

[48] E.M. Jope, "Scottish Influences in the North of Ireland: Castles with Scottish Features, 1580–1640", *Ulster Journal of Archaeology*, third series 14 (1951).

[49] Ohlmeyer, *Making Ireland English*, 184.

of the 'Scottishness' of Ireland's 'Scottish peers', much as it did for the Stuarts themselves who became ever more English.[50]

As the examples of the Scottish peers highlight, the choices aristocrats made around key events in their life cycle, especially whom an heir should marry, profoundly shaped senses of dynastic identity. Over a third of resident peers in Ireland married English women, especially as their first wives, aiming to increase their social status by intermarrying with members of the English nobility, landed gentry, or prosperous merchant families (see Table 1.1). As one might expect, protestant peers preferred women from England. More interesting is the number of Irish catholic lords, especially those from the higher ranks (viscounts and above) who took English brides, a trend that continued after 1649. These women perpetuated the family line, infused it with new blood, helped to define a dynasty's identity and, for many catholic houses, secured the political survival of the lineage.

The primary responsibility for any peer was to provide his dynasty with a legitimate heir, ideally an adult son, capable of serving as a head of a house and a royal servant. Though often constrained by the availability of finances, the choice of where to educate a son was a very conscious one, as was the decision to send him on a grand tour, in search of military experience or to spend time at court. The early education, especially of catholic heirs, was contested. The crown did everything possible to educate them in the protestant faith while their fathers and close kin, supported by the clergy, resisted this knowing that a continental education reinforced the family's devotion to Catholicism.

A detailed examination of the fragmentary evidence relating to university education suggests that the heirs of at least 65 resident lords, or 21 per cent of 311 peers who lived in Ireland over the course of the seventeenth century, received some sort of university education, often along with their younger brothers. Of the 65 whose education was documented, 28 (43 per cent) attended Oxford, especially Christ Church and Magdalen colleges; 11 (17 per cent) spent time at Trinity College Dublin; and 10 (16 per cent) at one of the Inns of Court. Of the remaining 16 students, four attended university at Cambridge, two at Glasgow and the remainder at continental colleges (Douai, Louvain and Paris for Catholics and Caen, Saumur and Utrecht for Protestants).[51] Undoubtedly these prolonged

---

50 In this the experiences of the 'Scottish peers' in Ireland differed from those of the Scots who had followed the king south in the years following the Union of the Crowns. A small number of these titled Scots did become highly anglicised, many did marry English women but the majority retained a strong sense of national consciousness and returned home to live in Scotland, see Keith M. Brown, "The Scottish Aristocracy, Anglicization and the Court, 1603–38", *The Historical Journal* 36 (1993) and Neil Cuddy, "Anglo-Scottish Union and the Court of James I, 1603–1625", *Transactions of the Royal Historical Society*, Fifth Series 39 (1989).

51 Estimating how many nobles went to university anywhere in the early modern period is notoriously difficult but the trend was certainly upwards, as was the case of England itself. The share of English nobles attending university never exceeded 40 per

stays at the catholic seminaries influenced the attitudes and mindsets of the Irish catholic peerage and at the very least these helped to create an identity for catholic Ireland that effectively excluded protestant England.[52]

A number of the first generation 'Scottish peers' had attended university in Scotland, usually St Andrews or Glasgow, but increasingly they preferred to send their sons to English institutions, especially Oxford. The predilection for sending boys to Oxford was common. Three generations of the O'Briens of Thomond attended Oxford.[53] In 1629 the earl of Cork dispatched his ward, the 18-year-old earl of Kildare, to Christ Church in the hope he would become 'a great ornament in this kingdom, and an able servant for his Majesty and the Commonwealth'.[54] The second and third earls of Cork spent time at Christ Church, where John Locke tutored the third earl in geography, astronomy and logic.[55] The Butler connections with Oxford were particularly strong and the duke of Ormond served as chancellor between 1669 and 1688. Christ Church was the obvious destination for Ormond's grandson, James, later second duke. The duke instructed his Oxford tutor to ensure that the youth 'may be confirmed and perfectly instructed in the religion professed, practised and best taught in that University' and through this James would acquire 'the principles of honour, virtue and loyalty'.[56] Despite James's academic inadequacies and his reputation as a dullard his years at Oxford prepared him well for his life as a public servant and he went on to succeed his grandfather as chancellor of the university. For others the Inns of Court in London, rather than Oxford, served as an exclusive finishing school where young men 'may learn qualities fit for a gentleman'.[57] A significant minority of catholic lords, especially the higher ranking ones, sent a son to the Inns of Court. This demonstrated the family's commitment to 'civility' and to 'Englishness', something that the state and crown warmly welcomed and actively encouraged.

The wealthier lords also sent their sons on a grand tour. The purpose of foreign travel was primarily educational: to acquire specialised academic and life skills; learn languages (especially French and Italian); appreciate European architecture, fashions, history and culture; observe warfare and understand military techniques

---

cent. Lawrence Stone, *The Crisis of the Aristocracy, 1558–1641* (Oxford: Clarendon Press, 1965), 687–92.

[52] Thomas O'Connor (ed.), *The Irish in Europe, 1580–1815* (Dublin: Four Courts Press, 2001), 16–17.

[53] J.P. Prendergast and C.W. Russell (eds), *Calendar of State Papers relating to Ireland, 1606–1608,* 2: 234, 256.

[54] Public Records Office of Northern Ireland, D.3078/3, 1/5, 4–5, 6–7.

[55] T.C. Barnard, "Land and Limits of Loyalty: The Second Earl of Cork and First Earl of Burlington (1612–98)", in *Lord Burlington. Architecture, Art and Life*, (eds) Toby Barnard and Jane Clark (London: Hambledon Press, 1995), 195–6.

[56] HMC, *Ormonde*, NS, 4: 305 and 355. Also see (for Courcy) ibid., 166–7 and ibid., 5: 337.

[57] Reginald J. Fletcher (ed.), *The Pension Book of Gray's Inn 1569–1669* (London 1901), 295.

and fortifications; and connect with men of comparable rank. The experiences of Hugh Montgomery, first earl of Mount Alexander, the son of a Scottish planter with large estates in East Ulster, were typical. He received a 'liberal education' at home and then travelled 'for his further improvement into foreign countries'. 'The civility he received in his travels in France', noted the family chronicler, 'had bred in him an inclination towards French servants' and he returned to Ireland in 1623 with a French valet 'to confirm his skill in that tongue'.[58] These shared experiences of travel and education undoubtedly shaped the mentalities of Europe's young aristocrats, together with individual identities and tastes, and created pan-European noble networks that were occasionally reinforced by marriage and, more typically, bonds of friendship.

A grand tour, which often included exposure to the exercise of arms, prepared these young nobles for a career in royal service and was typically followed by a sojourn at the Stuart court in London. In the summer of 1639 the heir of Lord Claneboy, of Scottish provenance with estates in Ulster, returned from 'his Travels having taken a generall Survey of Italie and France and seen the severall States and Courts there'. The youth immediately presented himself at court to avoid 'being found a Stranger in England' and then married the daughter of a prominent English earl.[59] The court provided these young men with an opportunity to parade their loyalty, participate in masques, attend plays, dance at royal balls, hunt with the king, imbibe the 'honour culture', and test the marriage market. Above all, it gave them direct access to the person of the king, his family and trusted courtiers and allowed them to experience first-hand royal life and court culture, which so many went on to emulate, and to interact with their peers from across the Stuart kingdoms. In short, these experiences allowed young lords to acquire life skills, secure patrons and forge friendships that would sustain them in later life. Above all education and foreign travel immersed young lords in noble culture and to the ideas that underpinned it, especially those of honour and virtue, and the fundamental importance of royal service. These helped both to forge a common sense of nobleness across the Irish aristocracy that emphasised the exclusivity of their rank and to create links with their counterparts throughout the Stuart dominions and western Europe.

---

58 Hill, *Montgomery Manuscripts*, 257.

59 Grosart, *The Lismore Papers*, second series, 4: 80.

Chapter 2
The Newcomer's Dilemma: Henry IV of France and James I of England

Ronald G. Asch

I

James VI of Scotland (James I of England) and Henry IV of France were not just contemporaries; for all their differences in personality, the *rex pacificus* on the one side and the military hero on the other, they had something important in common. As a newcomer to the French crown in 1589, Henry of Navarre had to find ways to create a secure foundation for his own rule and that of his family. Similarly, James was also confronted with the problem of how to make rule by a Scottish dynasty acceptable to the political nation in England. Of course their situations were different: whereas by the time the last Valois died, France had been torn apart by civil wars for more than 30 years, England had seen no major armed rebellion since 1569 and was a largely peaceful country. Nor was James required to abandon his Protestant faith to claim the English crown. Nevertheless, the problems Henry IV faced in France and James I in England show certain clear parallels.

When James VI ascended to the English throne in 1603, the Stuarts had finally realised a dream that had for decades been uppermost in both James's own mind and in that of his mother. Ever since the death of Mary Tudor in 1558, the Stuarts had tried to obtain the English crown to which they thought they had the best claims, better than those of any rivals and, in Mary Stuart's case, certainly better than the claims of her Tudor cousin Elizabeth.[1] In that sense, James VI was far less of a newcomer in England than Henry of Navarre in France. Although he was King of Navarre prior to 1584, when the last Valois heir the Duke of Anjou died prematurely, Henry was essentially just a high-ranking French nobleman, although he did hold a royal title outside of France. But it is also true that the Guise, his sworn enemies for so many years, were closely related to the Dukes of Lorraine, and as such almost sovereign princes. Not to mention the fact that there were a number of other *princes étrangers*, such as the Dukes of Nevers, related to the rulers of Mantua or the French branch of the house of Savoy, so that the

---

[1] Howard Nenner, *The Right to be King: The Succession to the Crown of England, 1603–1714* (Basingstoke: Macmillan, 1995), 13–25; Susan Doran, "James VI and the English Succession", in *James VI and I: Authority, Ideas and Government, 1566–1625*, (ed.) Ralph Houlbrooke (Aldershot: Ashgate, 2006), 25–42.

position of the Bourbons among the French aristocracy was by no means entirely exceptional before 1584. On the contrary, there were a number of aristocratic families among the *ducs et pairs* who, like the Bourbons, claimed to be related to the royal dynasty, or more specifically to the Valois, although Salic Law did not give them any direct claim to the Crown. Moreover, there were junior branches of the House of Bourbon, like the Condé, who could all too easily become rivals for the main line, in particular if the head of the main line failed to produce a legitimate heir, something which both Henry IV and his son Louis XIII only achieved rather late in life.[2]

The Stuarts, on the other hand, had been Kings of Scotland since the late fourteenth century and had, at least in the fifteenth and sixteenth centuries, chosen their wives – or, in Mary Queen of Scots' case, her first husband – mostly from among the royal families of Europe, in particular the Valois in France, the house of Oldenburg in Denmark, and, last but not least, of course, the Tudors. Mary's own mother had been a Guise.[3] Thus, although James VI and I was a stranger in England, coming from a country which had together with France always been England's most inveterate traditional enemy, he was no upstart, in fact much less so than Henry Tudor, founder of the Tudor dynasty, had been in the late fifteenth century. Moreover, James was careful to base his claim to the English crown exclusively on his hereditary right. He was proclaimed King immediately after Elizabeth I died; Parliament, which was not sitting at the time, played no part in this.[4] This method of settling the succession was by no means a self-evident choice. In the 1580s, there had been attempts to exclude Mary Stuart from the succession because she was a Catholic and Elizabeth's enemy. Either Parliament or a great council of peers and officeholders would have been given the power to bestow the succession on a different candidate, should Elizabeth die, particularly if she were the victim of an assassination.[5] The idea that Parliament and the political nation as represented by the peers and great officeholders could at least examine and perhaps even reject a claim to the succession was certainly not alien to English political

[2] Robert J. Knecht, *The French Civil Wars, 1562–1598* (Harlow: Longman, 2000), 34–40; Klaus Malettke, *Die Bourbonen*, vol. I: *Von Heinrich IV. bis zu Ludwig XIV, 1589–1715* (Stuttgart: Kohlhammer, 2008), 27–40. For the Nevers see Ariane Boltanski, *Les Ducs des Nevers et l'État royal. Genèse d'un compromis (ca. 1550-ca. 1600)* (Geneva: Droz, 2006); for the Guise: Stuart Carroll, *Martyrs and Murderers: The Guise Family and the Making of Europe* (Oxford: Oxford University Press, 2009); Jean Marie Constant, *Les Guise* (Paris: Hachette, 1984).

[3] Ronald G. Asch, *Die Stuarts. Geschichte einer Dynastie* (Munich: Beck, 2011).

[4] Nenner, *Right*, 33, 65.

[5] David Loades, "The English State and the Death of Mary, Queen of Scots", in *Murder and Monarchy: Regicide in European History, 1300–1800*, (ed.) Robert von Friedeburg (Basingstoke: Macmillan, 2004); David Cressy, "Binding the Nation. The Bonds of Association, 1584 and 1696", in *Tudor Rule and Revolution*, (eds) D.J.Guth and J.W. McKenna (Cambridge: Cambridge University Press, 1982).

thought, and, of course, there had been precedents for changing the succession in the fifteenth century.

There were no such precedents in France, and for Henry IV it was even more important than for James Stuart that his right to succeed the last Valois was based merely on the law of succession, in this case on Salic law, which in the eyes of the royalists allowed no discussion at all. In fact, this had been true ever since the King of Navarre had become the heir apparent to the French crown, i.e. since 1584, when his supporters had pointed out that to discard his claims to the crown would be to upset the entire social order and in particular to call into question the privileges and the internal hierarchy of the second order of nobility. In 1576, Henry III had published an edict which confirmed the special place of the *princes du sang* among the *ducs et pairs*. This had given the various branches of the House of Bourbon a special status. The claims of the *princes étrangers*, in particular those of the Guise-Lorraine, that they ranked above the Bourbons had been visibly rebuffed. That the Bourbons would gain such a victory over their rivals had been by no means self-evident in the past; in the first half of the sixteenth century they had lost much of their power and credit because the head of the senior branch, Charles de Bourbon Constable of France, had revolted against Francis I in the 1520s, and fought for the Emperor. Only slowly had the Bourbons been rehabilitated, certainly to some extent in order to create a counterweight against the overambitious Guise.[6] However, with the new order of precedence, the Princes of the blood were henceforth the natural leaders of the entire French nobility,[7] and those who – like the Guise – attacked the highest ranking Prince of the blood royal were trying to subvert the foundations on which the status of all noblemen rested, as argued by Duplessis Mornay, one of the closest advisors of the king of Navarre in the 1580s and early 1590s.[8]

However, despite the fact that after the death of the last Valois, Henry IV was in practice the head of the *Maison de France*, the continuation of which was a necessary precondition for the survival of France as an independent kingdom in the eyes of royalists of all persuasions, he had, unlike James VI, to negotiate his way to power. As Michel de Waele has shown, Henry signed a long series of formal contracts both with cities which were prepared to accept him as King after

6 On the debate about the right of succession between 1584 and 1594, see Myriam Yardeni, *La Conscience Nationale en France pendant les guerres de Religion (1559–1598)* (Louvain: Éditions Nauwelaerts, 1971), 201–93, and for the place of the house of Bourbon among the French nobility, Arlette Jouanna, "Les Guise et le sang de France", in *Le mécenat et l'influence des Guises*, (ed.) Yvonne Bellenger (Paris: Champion, 1997). See also Ralph E. Giesey, "The Juristic Basis of the Dynastic Right to the French Throne", *Transactions of the American Philosophical Society*, New Series, LI, 5 (1961), 29–40.

7 Hugues Daussy, *Les Huguenots et le roi. Le combat politique de Philippe Duplessis-Mornay (1572–1600)* (Geneva: Droz, 2002), 314–15.

8 For the edict of Henry III of 1576, see Jouanna, "Les Guise et le sang de France", 23, 35.

1589 and with his former noble opponents, the leaders of the League. He not only freely granted pardons, money and privileges to those who were prepared to submit to him, he also frequently promised to protect the Catholic religion and, after 1593, to remain a steadfast supporter of the Roman Church.[9] Furthermore, although Henry managed to replace some provincial governors whom he considered unreliable with his own allies and followers, he only did so by buying out the present incumbents at a considerable cost.[10]

Henry's relations both with important cities and with high-ranking nobles were therefore to some extent based on contractual arrangements. At least implicitly, Henry had to accept the revolt of the League as legitimate; otherwise such negotiations would not have been possible. Of course, it was always possible to pretend that the League had only fought against the Calvinists and perhaps against Henry III, and not against the new King, but indirectly Henry gave legitimacy to the rebellion. This may have been one reason that even after the end of the Wars of Religion, and to some extent up to the *Fronde*, it was widely considered permissible for a nobleman to raise troops and fight royal armies to make a political point, or simply to defend his honour and freedom. There was certainly no lack of such revolts in France in the early seventeenth century. The fact that before they came to power the Bourbons themselves had had a long history of getting involved in, and leading major and minor revolts may also have made it more difficult for Henry IV to completely suppress this culture of civil unrest and violence. It certainly survived in many parts of France for decades after 1589, as shown by Arlette Jouanna and more recently by Brian Sandberg.[11]

II

In contrast to the first Bourbon King of France, James VI had governed as a hereditary ruler (in Scotland, of course, not in England), and had been crowned a short time after his birth, although the nobles responsible for this premature coronation had themselves rebelled against James's mother, whom they had deposed. Moreover, Mary Queen of Scots became involved in a series of plots

---

9 Michel de Waele, "Henri IV, politicien monarchomaque? Les contrats de fidelité entre le roi et les Français", in *Le traité de Vervins*, (eds) Jean-François Labourdette et al. (Paris: Presses de l'Université de Paris-Sorbonne, 2000), 120–31 and idem, "Clemence royale et fidelités françaises à la fin des Guerres de Religion", *Historical Reflections* 24 (1998).

10 Robert R. Harding, *Anatomy of a Power Elite: The Provincial Governors of Early Modern France* (New Haven, CT: Yale University Press, 1978), 125.

11 Arlette Jouanna, *Le devoir de révolte. La noblesse française et la gestation de l'État moderne,* 1559–1661 (Paris: Fayard 1989), see also Brian Sandberg, *Warrior Pursuits: Noble Culture and Civil Conflict in Early Modern France* (Baltimore: Johns Hopkins University Press, 2010). For the history of the Bourbons as rebels, see also Denis Crouzet, *Charles de Bourbon, Connétable de France* (Paris: Fayard, 2003).

against Elizabeth I and was eventually sentenced to death for treason and executed, with – or at least so it seemed to some contemporary observers – her son's connivance. One might say that James spent his entire life in an effort to live down this rather questionable start of his royal career. Nevertheless, at least in his younger years, he was frequently forced to seek a compromise with unruly noble subjects and had to bide his time in punishing and destroying those powerful subjects who tried to oppose him or even threatened him in person, as the Earl of Bothwell did more than once in the early 1590s. Bothwell not only gained entry by force into Falkland Palace in 1592, besieging the King in a tower; he also confronted the King in Holyrood House in Edinburgh the following year, having entered the palace fully armed.[12] Thus, even in the early 1590s, James's position in Scotland was still deeply insecure. Born in 1566, he was in the late 1580s the first adult male King to rule Scotland since 1542 (when James V died), i.e. in more than 40 years. His mother had been overthrown by a rebellion in 1567 and was forced to take refuge in England where she was later executed for conspiring against Elizabeth I. Thus, James VI, although the undisputed successor to his mother and his grandfather in Scotland, had in many ways to rebuild almost from scratch a royal authority which had never been particularly stable, even in the fifteenth century. Scotland had not, before 1590, been torn apart by civil wars on a comparable scale to France. Nevertheless, the tendency of nobles to settle disputes through armed conflicts was relatively widespread and most of the regents who had governed Scotland after 1567 had met a violent death, as had most Scottish Kings between 1400 and the early sixteenth century. James's mother had, of course, also met a similar fate, although she was executed in England not in Scotland.[13]

In this respect James's position in Scotland was not all that different from Henry IV's position in France in the 1590s. He, too, had to try to pacify a country that had not seen a reasonably stable political order for a long time. Whatever one may say about James's reign in England, in Scotland he was to all intents and purposes a successful ruler, at least before approximately 1610, when his links with his native country became weaker and the councillors who had followed him to England either died without being replaced by men of comparable standing and capacities, or became uprooted in their own country.

Some recent accounts have credited James with having established a sort of royal absolutism in the 1590s.[14] He certainly managed to raise taxes on a permanent basis, and although the scale of revenues these taxes yielded was very modest, no Scottish King before him had done so. Moreover, he subdued

---

[12] Alan Stewart, *The Cradle King: A Life of James VI and I* (London: Chatto & Windus, 2003), 132–5.

[13] For James's reign in general, see Julian Goodare and Michael Lynch (eds), *The Reign of James VI* (East Linton: Tuckwell Press, 2000), and Julian Goodare, *The Government of Scotland 1560–1625* (Oxford: Oxford University Press, 2004).

[14] Goodare, *Government*, 74–5 and 307–09, cf. Idem, *State and Society in Early Modern Scotland* (Oxford: Oxford University Press, 1999), 325–30 and 66–101.

or destroyed recalcitrant Highland clans and forced unruly nobles to accept the jurisdiction of the royal courts instead of settling their disputes on the field of battle in a blood feud or out of court by arbitration and negotiation. However, James VI could never afford to maintain anything remotely resembling a major army for longer than one or two campaigns, and in extensive parts of the country, in particular the Highlands, he had to rely on the local power of seemingly loyal clan chiefs to control the localities, much as his predecessors had done. Coming from a country where even in 1600 – three years before the death of Elizabeth I of England – it was still conceivable to kidnap the King and take him prisoner to extort concessions from him, as the Ruthvens Earls of Gowrie allegedly did in the infamous Gowrie conspiracy in 1600, James VI must have seen England as a kind of haven of stability and order.[15]

The last major noble revolt had taken place in England in 1569 and it had been a total failure. The second Earl of Essex had attempted a form of putsch against Elizabeth I in 1601. However, he did not get very far and ended up on the block, where he was executed. English nobles and the leading members of the gentry may have resented the fact that the English court was now filled with so many 'beggarly blue caps' as they called James I's Scottish entourage, and some historians think the gun powder plot of 1605 was as much an anti-Scottish as an anti-Protestant conspiracy.[16] Nevertheless, during the reign of James in England, and in contrast to the situation under the rule of his son, civil war or large-scale revolt in the provinces or the capital were never an option, even for those that remained less than fully convinced that it was beneficial for Englishmen to be ruled by a Scottish King. James was, of course, aware of the tensions between his own countrymen and his new subjects. In particular during the first years of his reign in England, one of his most important objectives was to bring about a genuine union of the crowns that was more than a mere dynastic union between Scotland and England.[17] On a constitutional level he failed: the English parliament refused to abandon any of its traditional privileges and was at best prepared to treat Scotland in the same way in which Henry VIII had treated Wales in the 1530s – as a somewhat barbarous province which had to undergo a process of cultural assimilation to English values to become fully civilised.[18] Such a model of a closer union was however not only unacceptable to James himself but also to most if not all Scotsmen.

[15] Maurice Lee, "The Gowrie Conspiracy Revisited", in *The Inevitable Union and Other Essays on Early Modern Scotland*, (ed.) idem (East Linton: Tuckwell Press, 2003).

[16] Jenny Wormald, "Gunpowder, Treason and Scots", *Journal of British Studies* 24 (1985).

[17] Ronald G. Asch, *Jakob I. (1566–1625). König von England und Schottland* (Stuttgart: Kohlhammer, 2005), 62–71.

[18] Asch, *Jakob I.*, 68–9; Bruce Galloway, *The Union of England and Scotland, 1603–1608* (Edinburgh: John Donald, 1986), 93–136.

In England, James was the successor of a Queen, who although much praised as a Princess, impressing her subjects both by her beauty and her wisdom, and who had heroically defended her kingdom against her popish enemies, had nevertheless become increasingly unpopular during the last 10 or 12 years of her reign. Elizabeth expected her nobles to pay for many of the costlier aspects of courtly display and ceremonies, certainly outside Whitehall and the traditional royal palaces, during her royal progresses, for example.[19] Those who pursued a military career were also expected to pay for part of their troops out of their own pockets, at least in times of crisis. This was, of course, by no means unusual at the time, the difference being only that the Queen offered comparatively little as a reward for such services. If one was lucky, one received a stake in a customs farm or in a controversial and unpopular monopoly, or one might be able to buy land in Ireland cheaply, but not everybody was keen to become a landowner governing the bogs of Ireland.[20] To obtain a peerage – if one did not already belong to the peerage – was almost impossible. When Elizabeth died, there were only 55 peers entitled to a seat in the House of Lords, which was no more than in 1487 shortly after the accession of the Tudors. Given the fact that the English population had more than doubled since the late fifteenth century and the landed elite, including the upper strata of the gentry, had probably grown at an even faster pace, this meant that compared to the overall size of the elite, the peerage had become considerably smaller. James decided to remedy this as quickly as he could by distributing honours freely and granting approximately 25 new noble titles in the first three years of his English reign alone; in 1609 there were already 80 peers, and when he died in the mid-1620s there were some 120, so that the peerage had more than doubled in size.[21] Initially, those who had benefited from James's grants were happy enough to have attained the status which they had hoped for for such a long time, but in later years, James simply sold titles to the highest bidder, a policy which was not made more acceptable by his tendency to sell even more titles in Ireland than in England, and at much cheaper rates, too. Older families began to fear for the stability of the social hierarchy, even more so since James's foremost patronage manager from the 1616s onwards was a newly created peer, the Marquess and later Duke of Buckingham. He soon became one of the most hated men at Court, partly because of his monopoly of power, but also because he managed to place his kinsmen and

[19] Mary Hill Cole, *The Portable Queen. Elizabeth I and the Politics of Ceremony* (Amherst, Mass.: University of Massachusetts Press, 1999).

[20] Simon Adams, "The Patronage of the Crown in Elizabethan Politics: the 1590s in Perspective", in *The Reign of Elizabeth I: Court and Culture in the Last Decade*, (ed.) John Guy (Cambridge: Cambridge University Press, 1995).

[21] Charles R. Mayes, "The Sale of Peerages in Early Stuart England", *The Journal of Modern History* 29 (1957); Stone, *Crisis of The Aristocracy*, 755–8.

kinswomen and clients in all the important positions in the central administration, in the provinces and at Court.[22]

By and large, James's generous grant of new titles, his liberal distribution of favours, and his decision to cede so much power to personal favourites can be seen as an attempt to modify existing social hierarchies, if not at times to reverse them. Older families were not, however, entirely marginalised: the crypto Catholic Howards with their different branches, the Earls of Suffolk, Northampton and Arundel, who had in the sixteenth century lost their pre-eminence because their name had been tainted by treason, all clearly enjoyed the King's support. Nevertheless, the influence that first Carr and later Buckingham had on patronage policy forced everyone to seek the favourite's favour. This was seen, at least by some, as demeaning, and the atmosphere of crisis during James' final years was partly due to such factors. In fact, one cannot escape the conclusion that James never quite managed to overcome the deep mistrust which confronted him when he first came to England.

A further difference with France was that neither in Scotland nor in England was James's vision of kingship, which was so closely wedded to ideas of divine right, very popular.[23] James's insistence that all rights and claims to property were subject to his control and could be called into question was from the beginning perceived in England as a danger to the existing legal order, although this insistence may have been no more than a bargaining ploy to gain concessions from Parliament and other corporate bodies.[24] Most English peers were probably prepared to forgive James his sometimes excessive divine right rhetoric; after all, many lords hoped to benefit from the royal bounty in one way or another and a weak or, even worse, a poor King without sufficient revenues was unable to reward the services of his courtiers and officeholders. What was more problematic and irritating about James's idea of kingship was that he clearly rejected most of the values of chivalry which had been so important to Elizabethan court culture. While Henry IV of France was a true *Roi Connétable*, James VI and I was anything

[22] Thomas Cogswell, "The People's Love: The Duke of Buckingham and Popularity", in *Politics Religion and Popularity in Early Stuart Britain*, (eds) Thomas Cogswell et al. (Cambridge: Cambridge University Press, 2002); Alastair Bellany, "'The Enigma of the World'. Memorializing and Remembering George Villiers, First Duke of Buckingham in the Aftermath of Assassination, c. 1628–1642", in *Zwischen Schande und Ehre. Erinnerungsbrüche und die Kontinuitität des Hauses. Legitimationsmuster und Traditionsverständnis des frühneuzeitlichen Adels in Umbruch und Krise*, (eds) Martin Wrede and Horst Carl (Mainz: Zabern, 2007).

[23] Jenny Wormald, "James VI and I – two Kings or One", *History* 68 (1983); Maurice Lee, *Government by Pen: Scotland under James VI and I* (Urbana Ill.: University of Illinois Press, 1981). But cf. Julian Goodare and Michael Lynch (eds), *The Reign of James VI*, in particular idem, "Introduction".

[24] See Johann P. Sommerville, "James I and the Divine Right of Kings: English Politics and Continental Theory", in *The Mental World of the Jacobean Court*, (ed.) Linda Levy Peck (Cambridge: Cambridge University Press, 1991).

but a warlike military hero; he was a rather donnish figure, who tried to excel as a writer and as an orator, or even at times as a theologian and bible interpreter, achievements which were hardly aristocratic and for some aristocrats, definitely below the salt. Moreover, James's effort to present himself as a champion of peace, as a *rex pacificus*, was deeply controversial because it ran counter to the understanding most nobles had of their role and place in society.[25] In Scotland, this sort of self-fashioning may have served its purpose: by presenting himself as a *rex doctus* and a decidedly un-heroic figure, James VI somehow undercut and devalued the prevailing ethos of the Scottish nobility which was all too prone to violence. The fact that the King did not try to compete with the warlike achievements of his nobles was the very reason that he stood apart from – and ultimately above – them. This did not mean that James hesitated to use military power and brute force to subdue unruly highland clans or lowland lords who opposed him, but he was not the ideal boon companion of noble ruffians, quite the opposite. This is not to deny that James, like many nobles, loved to hunt on horseback and was not averse to excessive celebrations involving large quantities of intoxicating drinks.

In England, however, his rejection of the traditional ideals of chivalry even in their more refined and subtler forms was perceived as deeply irritating. Many English noblemen continued to see themselves as called upon to play a leading role in warfare and they now looked for inspiration elsewhere, often abroad.[26] As a military hero, Henry IV certainly continued to be admired by English nobles even after the end of the Wars of Religion.[27] In fact, the contrast between James's image as a monarch and the image Henry IV conveyed and the role he played as first gentleman of his realm could not be more pronounced.

---

[25] Malcolm Smuts, "The Making of Rex Pacificus. James VI and I in an Age of Religious War", in *Royal Subjects. Essays on the Writings of James VI and I*, (eds) Daniel Fischlin and Mark Fortier (Detroit: Wayne State University Press, 2002); cf. Kevin Sharpe, *Image Wars, Promoting Kings and Commonwealths in England, 1603–1660* (New Haven, Ct: Yale University Press, 2010), 74–90, 109–21.

[26] Roger B. Manning, *Swordsmen: the Martial Ethos in the Three Kingdoms* (Oxford: Oxford University Press, 2003); cf. for the situation before 1603 Roy Rapple, *Martial Power and Elizabethan Political Culture. Military Men in England and Ireland, 1558–1594* (Cambridge: Cambridge University Press, 2009) chapter 3.

[27] Kerstin Weiand, "De 'Roi de Guerre' à 'Warrior King'. Réflexions sur un transfert politique et culturel considéré comme enjeu mémoriel", in *Les funérailles princières en Europe, XVIe – XVIIIe siècle*. Vol. 3: *Mémoire monarchique et la construction de l'Europe. Les stratégies funérailles des dynasties princières, 16e et 17e siècle*, (eds) Juliusz Chrosciscki, Mark Hengerer and Gérard Sabatier (Paris: Presses Universitaires de Rennes, 2015). Cf. Paul E.J. Hammer, *The Polarisation of Elizabethan Politics. The Political Career of Robert Devereux, 2nd Earl of Essex* (Cambridge: Cambridge University Press, 1999), 93–4.

III

In many ways, Henry IV's style of kingship was unique. He was a true *Roi Connétable* who had led his noble followers into battle in many campaigns; he was the last French ruler before Napoleon to play this role in a way which was more than merely theatrical.[28] Ostentatiously masculine, as opposed to his half-effeminate, childless and allegedly homosexual predecessor, Henry in many ways embodied the prevailing values of noble culture. Nobles had to prove their heroism and manliness in combat, in duels, and even in feuds and revolts. Nothing worse could happen to a nobleman than to die in his bed. Jean Marie Constant has spoken of the 'mort spectacle' as a cultural model which greatly influenced the behaviour of nobles.[29] Henry, although he was to die not in action but by the knife of an assassin, certainly respected this model and, significantly, he offered to end the Civil War in 1585 by challenging his principal opponent, the Duke of Guise, to a duel. As a true Christian knight, he was prepared to sacrifice his life to save his country.[30] Henry must have known that Guise would not accept this challenge but he nevertheless repeated it often enough until 1589, when Henry III died. As long as he was a mere nobleman, even though first prince of the blood, he was prepared to fight a duel with another nobleman as a personal enemy on an equal footing; one can hardly imagine a Crown Prince in any other European country doing so. Even after 1589, he remained very much a soldier King, rather too much so for some observers who had appreciated the splendour and the refined manners of the Valois court before Henry III's authority gradually collapsed in the later 1580s.[31] Nor were his amorous adventures universally appreciated. To have mistresses and illegitimate children was one thing, but to actually want to marry one of them, as Henry did in 1598 in the case of Gabrielle d'Estrées, was quite a different matter. This might possibly have given a claim to the Crown to Gabrielle's bastard sons. Nor were aristocrats very happy when the King tried to seduce their own wives, as Henry did near the end of his life with Charlotte de Montmorency, who had married the Prince of Condé. Condé had to flee with his wife to Brussels to protect his marriage.[32]

---

28 For Henry IV as *roi connétable*, see Vincent J. Pitts. *Henry IV of France: His Reign and Age* (Baltimore: Johns Hopkins University Press, 2009), 83–175 and for the heroic image of the King see Edmund H. Dickerman and Anita M. Walker, "The Choice of Hercules: Henry IV as Hero", *Historical Journal* 39 (1996); see further Katherine Crawford, "The Politics of Promiscuity: Masculinity and Heroic Representation at the Court of Henry IV", *French Historical Studies* 26 (2003).

29 Jean-Marie Constant, *La folle liberté des baroques (1600–1661)* (Paris: Perrin, 2007), 40–65.

30 Daussy, *Les Huguenots*, 343–4.

31 Constant, *Folle Liberté*, 99–100.

32 Pitts, *Henry IV*, 215–19, Mark Greengrass, *France in the Age of Henri IV* (2nd edn. London: Longman, 1995), 229.

Partly because Henry himself had grown up as a nobleman involved in feuds and civil wars, and partly because he had in some sense himself been a rebel before 1589 and was familiar enough with the culture of honour and of violence which engendered such conflicts, a serious and relentless campaign against duels of the sort which Richelieu orchestrated under the rule of his son, would hardly have been conceivable under Henry. On the other hand, he pursued the efforts of his ill-fated predecessor in emphasising more strongly the distance between the King and the great body of the nobility. Henry III had introduced new ceremonial rules at court which were intended to force his courtiers and other nobles to treat the King with the necessary deference. Henry IV was certainly more relaxed in his manners than his predecessor but he was convinced that, as King, he held a position which was sacred in nature, because of the special, almost priestly or saint-like powers the King enjoyed, and which manifested themselves for example in his ability to heal scrofula. At the same time, Henry saw himself as God's chosen instrument, elected by providence to restore peace and order in France. When confronted by opposition to the Edict of Nantes in the Parisian *Parlement*, Henry had insisted that he was more Catholic than the councillors of the Parliament, for he was truly 'the oldest son of the Church' ('le fils aîné de l'Église'); and because he had – implementing God's will – brought peace to the Kingdom, not only was obedience due to him, but also 'devotion' ('dévotion').[33] The idea of a divine right kingship which, after the end of the Wars of Religion, was based on a fairly broad consensus among the political elite in France, even broader perhaps after 1610 when Henry was murdered by a Catholic fanatic, certainly gave the King a special status which was much more elevated than that of supreme liege lord, martial leader and highest judge. One might say that Henry, precisely because he had been no more than one among a great number of powerful noble magnates before 1589, and even more so before 1584, was more in need of stressing the sacral dimension of kingship than many of his predecessors whose claim to the crown had not been disputed.

What Henry IV achieved after 1589, and in a more pronounced way of course after 1593, when he converted to Catholicism, and after his coronation in 1594, was a real change of identity. He had been a noble among other nobles of almost equal status, an aristocratic rebel and a protestant; now he was a Catholic and a ruler who enjoyed a sacral status, which was enhanced by the traditional rituals of the French monarchy. James VI of Scotland may to some extent have tried to accomplish a similar change of identity, not by abandoning his religion, of course, but by becoming a monarch in the English style, not in the Scottish tradition, and by becoming a major player on the European stage. However, these attempts all too frequently failed or backfired. James's manners, his entire style of kingship, continued to be seen as somehow alien to the English Tudor tradition, and James's

[33] Eric Nelson, "Royal Authority and the Pursuit of a Lasting Religious Settlement", in *Politics and Religion in Early Bourbon France*, (eds) Alison Forestal and Eric Nelson (Basingstoke: Palgrave Macmillan 2009), 124–27 (quotation 125) cf. Joel Cornette, *Henri IV à Saint-Denis. De l'abjuration à la profanation* (Paris: Belin, 2010), 111.

European ambitions, his wish to marry off his son to a princess belonging to a leading Catholic dynasty, ideally to a Spanish *infanta*, clearly did not help dispel this distrust. James tried to create a greater distance between himself and his family by finding a bride for his son who belonged to one of the leading ruling houses of Europe – this almost by definition excluded Protestant dynasties and only left the Habsburgs or the Bourbons – but such a dynastic ambition rendered the Stuarts suspect in the eyes of their Protestant subjects.[34]

On the other hand, the success Henry IV had in winning acceptance for his own rule and that of his family after 1594, and in creating a greater distance between himself and his former companions in arms, should not be overestimated. In many ways, Bourbon rule in France remained unstable until the 1650s, until the *Fronde*, and during Henry's own reign it was all too easy for nobles who were dissatisfied with official policy to find support abroad, in the Spanish Netherlands if they were Catholics, or among the Protestant Princes of Germany and in the Dutch Republic, if they were Huguenots. After all, Spain had until 1598 supported the Catholic League with money and troops, whereas Protestant powers had supported the Calvinists in the Wars of Religion. How unstable the situation in France remained after 1598 became apparent during the conspiracy of the Duc de Biron in 1601–1602. Biron had since 1589 been one of Henry's most loyal followers and military commanders. Raised to the rank of *duc et pair* in 1598 (one of the very few nobles so honoured by the King) he hoped to marry the sister of the King's mistress Gabrielle d'Estrées, who at that time seemed to stand a good chance of becoming the new Queen of France once the King had managed to dissolve his old marriage. In close contact with the Duke of Savoy and Spain, Biron felt increasingly dissatisfied with the way the King treated him, in particular when the latter refused to appoint him Governor of the fortress town of Bourg-en-Bresse, to which Biron himself had laid siege and which he had conquered in the war with Savoy. Accused of treason in 1602, Biron was executed in the Bastille, while many nobles who had been involved in his conspiracy were not punished at all, or only very lightly.[35]

Biron had been a Catholic, although perhaps not a very fervent one, but Henry's former co-religionists resented his style of leadership after 1594, and even more so after 1598, probably even more deeply than Catholic royalists; many of them never quite forgave the King his conversion. These Huguenot nobles were all the more dangerous since they were internationally very well connected. Many had

---

[34] For the politics of the proposed Spanish marriage, see Glyn Redworth, *The Prince and the Infanta: the Cultural Politics of the Spanish Match* (New Haven, Conn., London: Yale University Press, 2003); Alexander Samson (ed.), *The Spanish Match: Prince Charles's Journey to Madrid, 1623* (Aldershot: Ashgate, 2006).

[35] Anne Marie Cocula, "Les trois dimensions de la conspiration de Biron", in *Les lettres au temps de Henri IV = L'Avènement d'Henri IV, quatrième centenaire*, (ed.) Association pour la Commémoration de l'Avènement d'Henri IV au Trône de France (Pau: Association Henry IV 1989, 1991), 4: 341–58.

contacts in England and among German Protestants and the most illustrious among them, the Dukes of La Trémoille and Bouillon, had even married into the House of Orange, the leaders of the Dutch revolt. Henri de la Tour d'Auvergne, who had inherited the Duchy of Sedan from his first wife, a de La Marck, subsequently married a daughter of William the Silent. Extremely well connected both in the Netherlands and in Germany, his sovereign duchy of Bouillon, with the fortress of Sedan, was of great strategic importance. The Maréchal de Biron had in the last resort owed his status to Henry's favour,[36] but Bouillon was different. His family was extremely powerful in the Limousin, and Bouillon itself was an independent principality which gave its lord the status of a Prince of the Holy Roman Empire. Moreover, through his second marriage, Bouillon had become the brother-in-law of the Dutch Stadtholder Maurice of Nassau and of the Elector Palatine Frederick IV. Together with the Duc de La Trémoille, he acted as leader of the Calvinists in France when the King converted to Catholicism in 1593. Involved to some extent in Biron's conspiracy against the King, Bouillon continued to be regarded by Henry with suspicion for creating unrest among the Huguenots. Finally, in 1606, the King, with an army of 16,000 men, prepared to lay siege to Sedan. Bouillon surrendered and was granted a pardon, being allowed to retain his dominions.[37] He had been publicly humiliated, but the power of his family had not been destroyed and in fact, the de La Tour d'Auvergne who saw themselves as the heirs of the medieval Dukes of Guyenne, never quite accepted that they were inferior to the new *maison de France*; it was left to Louis XIV to undermine their power for good.[38]

IV

In his own treatment of the Duke of Bouillon, Henry demonstrated once more that he was capable of combining strength with clemency; but then, of course, he was well advised to do so. In the last resort he could not afford to antagonise families such as the de la Tour d'Auvergne too openly. Their power and international connections were too strong for that. James I was in some respects in the fortunate position that hardly any of his subjects even in Scotland or Ireland were as powerful

---

36 Pitts, *Henri IV*, 281–82.

37 Pitts, *Henri IV*, 281–9; Henri Zuber, "La noblesse protestante (1584–1598). Histoire politique des rapports entre Henri IV et les grands réformés", in *Avènement d'Henri IV. Quatrième Centenaire*, vol. III. *Henri IV. Le roi et la reconstruction du royaume* (Pau: Association Henry IV 1989, 1990), 73–93, 82–88, and Edmund H. Dickerman and Anita M. Walker, "The Politics of Honour. Henri IV and the Duke of Bouillon, 1602–1606", *French History* 14 (2000).

38 Martin Wrede, "Zwischen Mythen, Genealogen und der Krone. Rivalisierende Familiengedächtnisse im französischen Hochadel des 17. Jahrhunderts: die Häuser Bouillon, Noailles und Bourbon", *Zeitschrift für Historische Forschung* 32 (2005).

and as independent as the Duke of Bouillon or some of the other French *ducs et pairs*, such as the Gonzague ducs de Nevers. Neither did he have to cope with junior branches of the royal dynasty. The Hamiltons and the Dukes of Lennox, both great Scottish houses, were distantly related to the Stuarts, but their status was far below that of the French *princes du sang*, and in England there was no equivalent to the French princes of the blood at all. The Tudors were extinct and James was fortunate in having no brothers who could create trouble personally or through their descendants.

Nevertheless, there were nobles in England who had international connections and could thereby accumulate a political and social capital which they could use in domestic conflicts. James I studiously avoided any direct involvement in foreign military conflicts after 1604. Such a policy was at odds with the ideal of many English nobles. In fact, after the end of the Anglo-Spanish war in 1604, those who sought to gain military expertise went abroad, and as Roger Manning has argued, the English aristocracy was by no means so unwarlike as has sometimes been assumed in the past; many aristocrats served in fact in foreign armies. In 1620, more than half of all English peers had fought as soldiers or commanders on land or at sea, and in 1640 this held good for almost 70 per cent of all peers, and many among these soldier-peers had in fact fought in their youth in foreign armies, in particular in the Dutch army.[39] Fighting for the Dutch Republic, men such as Henry Wriothesley, third Earl of Southampton or Robert Devereux, third Earl of Essex clearly felt that they were serving a greater Protestant cause.[40] The tendency to identify with such a cause must have been particularly strong for those peers or aristocrats who felt that the King did not recognise their claims to a sufficient degree, or even that he had slighted them. The third Earl of Essex was certainly an example of this kind of attitude. In his youth, he had married one of the most attractive young aristocratic women of his time, Frances Howard, but the matrimonial alliance with the Howards was a failure, and in 1613 the King persuaded his bishops to dissolve the marriage so that Frances could marry the King's favourite, Robert Carr the Earl of Somerset.[41] A few years later, Frances Howard, who was a true femme fatale, became involved in a sordid affair in which she was charged with murder and poisoning. To some extent, the divorce that

39 Manning, *Swordsmen*, 17–19.

40 For the idea of a Protestant Cause see Simon Adams, "Spain or the Netherlands? The Dilemmas of Early Stuart Foreign Policy", in *Before the Civil War*, (ed.) Howard Tomlinson (Basingstoke: Palgrave Macmillan, 1983) and idem, "England und die Protestantischen Reichsfürsten 1599–1621", in *Dimensionen der europäischen Außenpolitik zur Zeit der Wende vom 16. zum 17. Jahrhundert*, (eds) Friedrich Beiderbeck et al. (Berlin: Berliner Wissenschafts-Verlag, 2003).

41 Vernon F. Snow, *Essex the Rebel: The Life of Robert Devereux, the Third Earl of Essex, 1591–1648* (Lincoln, Nebr.: University of Nebraska Press, 1970); cf. David Lindley, *The Trials of Frances Howard: Fact and Fiction at the Court of James I* (London: Routledge,1993).

the Earl of Essex had to submit to resembles the treatment the Prince of Condé suffered when he tried to protect his wife against the amorous French king, the only difference being that Henry wanted Charlotte de Montmorency for himself, whereas James I, who preferred men to women in his later years, wanted Frances Howard for his favourite. However, in both cases aristocratic pride was wounded, with considerable political consequences.

Although the Earl of Essex remained politically on the side-lines after this humiliation, the outbreak of the Thirty Years War offered him an opportunity to restore his honour as a nobleman. Essex was among those English aristocrats who saw James I's daughter Elizabeth, who had married the Elector Palatine in 1613, as the only member of the ruling dynasty who upheld the tradition of a truly Protestant foreign policy. It was, therefore, for Elizabeth and the Elector Palatine that he chose to fight when he left England in 1620 to join a regiment of English and Scottish volunteers, under the command of Sir Horace Vere, which was to defend the Palatinate.[42] In defending the Palatine Cause, Essex combined a residual loyalty to the Stuart dynasty – as he understood it – with a commitment to a wider religious and political community which included virtually all Calvinist noblemen in Europe who saw it as their duty to fight against popery and the overweening ambitions of the Spanish monarchy. It was to this wider community of honour that he could appeal when his own King refused to grant him the status and pre-eminence at court and in politics to which he believed he had a just claim.[43]

Both Henry IV and James VI of Scotland had as it were to re-invent themselves in middle age. Henry IV had to transform himself from a mere nobleman and leader of a revolt against the ruling monarch into a King who managed to distance himself from his former comrades in arms as well as from his former enemies; he had to prove that they were no longer his equals. He was by no means always successful in doing so, but the international situation which made external intervention in France less likely after 1598 undoubtedly helped him. Moreover most nobles, although still prepared to indulge in small-scale local feuds and the occasional armed uprising, looked for stability and wanted to avoid a return to the full-scale Civil War of past decades. If Henry IV had to re-invent himself as King, James VI of Scotland had to re-invent himself as an English monarch. Many of the problems that had bedevilled him in Scotland played no role in England: there was no large scale noble violence, there were no hectoring Protestant ministers given to theocratic ideals – and despite the serious financial problems he soon faced in England, his revenues were far greater than in the much poorer Scotland.

---

[42] Roger B. Manning, *An Apprenticeship in Arms: the Origins of the British Army; 1585 – 1702* (Oxford: Oxford University Press, 2006), 98–9.

[43] For the importance of allegiance to the Palatine cause among the aristocratic opposition in the 1620s and 1630s, see Thomas Cogswell, *The Blessed Revolution: English Politics and the Coming of War, 1621–1624* (Cambridge: Cambridge University Press, 1989), 102–3; cf. John Adamson, *The Noble Revolt, the Overthrow of Charles I* (London: Weidenfeld & Nicolson, 2007), 361–5.

On the other hand, his rather unrestrained and seemingly undignified personal style and his tendency to speak his mind at great length jarred with traditional conventions in England, the more so since the English had not been governed by an adult male King for over 50 years by the time James ascended the English throne. James rather overemphasised the sacred nature of royal power and was clearly too generous in granting titles, pensions and privileges to his courtiers. Nevertheless, one should not underestimate his success. As opposed to Henry IV, he died in his bed, in the early seventeenth century, when religious fanatics were omnipresent – an achievement in itself. He was a great survivor and thereby demonstrated a talent which he bequeathed to his grandson, Charles II, but which his son, Charles I, clearly lacked.

Chapter 3

Dynasty and Elites: From Early Modern Europe to Late Imperial China[1]

Jeroen Duindam

Introduction

This volume examines dynastic identity in Europe. Around the ruling houses of Europe many families aspired to a semi-autonomous sovereign status. French *princes du sang* or *princes étrangers*, German electors or even newly-appointed 'princes of the empire' in the Austrian Habsburg territories did not comfortably fit into the emerging twofold division between rulers and subjects. The blurry pyramid of multiple forms of dynastic sovereignty only very slowly conformed to the notion of sovereignty as quintessentially single, undivided and, finally, popular. The assertively dynastic stance of high nobles in Europe in this process appears to contrast with the attitudes of elites in other regions of the globe. In this comparative chapter I examine the outlines of hereditary power, dynasty and nobility in imperial China from the downfall of the Yuan dynasty (1271–1368) to the decades preceding the increasing involvement of European powers in China in the early nineteenth century, providing a wider perspective to fellow-Europeanists while suggesting some comparative questions to sinologists.[2] Following this

---

1 For a comparative discussion of dynasty see Jeroen Duindam, *Dynasties. A Global History of Power 1300–1800* (Forthcoming, Cambridge University Press 2015).

2 This periodisation fits with the centuries commonly labelled as 'early modern' in European history. A separate chapter could be written on the problem of 'intercultural' periodisation. The Tang-Song transformation has been presented as the onset of an 'early modern' age in China, complicated by the intervention of the Yuan dynasty, a somewhat understudied phase. The volume edited by Paul J. Smith and Richard von Glahn, *The Song-Yuan-Ming Transition in Chinese History* (Cambridge MA: Harvard University Press, 2003) aims to bridge this gap. Yuan and Ming have likewise been grouped together in the recent overview by Timothy Brook, *The Troubled Empire. China in the Yuan and Ming Dynasties* (Cambridge MA: Harvard University Press, 2010). Alternatively, there is a tendency to stress the continuity between late Ming (1550s onwards) and Qing, although several Qing specialists, Evelyn S. Rawski and R. Kent Guy among them, tend to underline the changes from Ming to Qing, stressing the innovations of the Qing dynasty while others stress continuity. The equation of 'late imperial' and 'early modern' hence is not without its problems; and the impact of the protracted as well as bloody dynastic changeover between Ming and Qing must be kept in mind. On these issues see the various plausible but partly

introduction I will first examine Late Imperial Chinese elites and social mobility in general before concentrating more specifically on the position of the numerous offspring of Ming and Qing rulers.[3]

More often than not, power in the pre-modern world was based on kinship. Relatives formed the most readily available allies and usually served as key figures in power networks. Dynasties and households stand at the core of most forms of political organisation in world history. The dominance of the dynastic principle is confirmed conspicuously by the fact that even rebels usually followed the banner of real or fake scions of a 'legitimate' dynasty. Power arrangements around rulers also mimicked familial relationships; when no actual blood ties were available, fictive forms of kinship were designed to create ties of loyalty and subservience.[4] The metaphor of the family, with the ruler as a benevolent but stern father ruling over his peoples, recurs throughout history. The matriarch may less often be seen to wield power single-handedly, but she was usually very present – idealised as the kind-hearted intermediary for her subjects or decried as the archetypical meddling mother.

All pre-modern empires and states had to confront problems created by geography. Travel and communication presented formidable obstacles to any regime seeking to extend its power beyond the horizon. Rulers were 'involved in a perpetual battle with distance' which in the end they could never conclusively win.[5] Hence, the cooperation of local power wielders was a precondition for the consolidation of central rule. Old chronicles as well as modern textbooks dwell on the altercations between power centres and regions under their control. Historical narratives from all continents depict an alternation between two processes: in the first place the rise of central powers subduing regional warlords and, conversely, in the second place, the gradual erosion of these central powers and their replacement by regional power centres or by rivalling dynasties.

Examples of both processes can be cited *ad libitum*. Several unifying dynasties in China were followed by 'times of troubles' and breakup into separate regimes. Also, within the scope of a single Chinese dynasty an activist, centralising first

---

contesting views in Lynn A. Struve (ed.), *The Qing Formation in World-Historical Time* (Cambridge MA: Harvard University Press, 2004).

3 I have profited from conversations with many sinologists, in addition to reading their works. Clearly, however, this chapter remains the work of an outsider aiming to contribute to academic discussion by connecting two fields rather than by any substantial original research. My thanks go in particular to Harriet Zurndorfer for suggesting important titles, for sharing many of her publications (some before publication) as well as for correcting at least part of my misconceptions. Mistakes and misunderstandings in this chapter are, of course, my own responsibility.

4 See e.g. Peter Parkes, "Fostering Fealty: A Comparative Analysis of Tributary Allegiances of Adoptive Kinship", *Comparative Studies in Society and History* 45, no.4 (2003).

5 P. Brown, *Power and Persuasion in Late Antiquity, Towards a Christian Empire* (Wisconsin: University of Wisconsin Press, 1992), 10.

phase was frequently followed by a second phase in which the localities regained the initiative. The first great Islamic dynasties in West Asia, combining the caliphate with regional hegemony, ended in contestation among rival claimants. Attempts to establish hegemony by a single overarching power among the inheritors of the Roman Empire in the West were never entirely successful and were always followed by contestation and disintegration. It is no coincidence, therefore, that philosophers in Europe and Asia viewed history largely as a cyclical process. Polybius' sequence of state forms, perennially arising from and returning to disorder, is very different from Ibn Khaldun's generational scheme of rise and fall of nomadic tribal dynasties, yet both subscribe to a necessarily cyclical logic. The Chinese understanding of a dynastic cycle matched neither of these views completely. Nevertheless, it also entails an inevitable cycle of waxing and waning. Each of these views, moreover, underlines the subversive power of luxury.[6]

Only in post-revolutionary nineteenth-century Europe did a straightforward model of progress become dominant. It understood the post-1500 economic breakthrough, the rise of 'rationality', and state formation as the intertwining core processes of progress. In this view regional noble power, seen negatively as an archaic force impeding the formation of central government, was first side-lined by activist kings and emperors in the early modern period and subsequently removed by the French Revolution – at least in Western Europe. The strengthening of state powers necessarily entailed the decline of nobility. This axiom of modernisation history has been under scrutiny from the 1980s onwards. Revisionists have stressed the flexible adaptation of nobles to the rise of stronger government, pointing to the active role of nobles in the emerging states. Nobility in its conventional early modern form, with legally sanctioned privileges, has plausibly been presented as an outcome rather than as a casualty of the process of state formation.[7] The European *ancien régime* is no longer seen in terms of the decline of nobilities. Lesser nobles tended towards decline in the age of religious warfare, but at the

---

[6] Peter Bol, "The 'Localist Turn' and 'Local Identity' in Later Imperial China", *Late Imperial China* 24. no. 2 (2003); Frederic Wakeman Jr., *The Fall of Imperial China* (New York: Free Press, 1977), 55–70 stressing chiliastic Buddhism and the expectation of the third 'kalpa'; Brook, *The Troubled Empire* focusing on the sloughs, signs, and cycles in Yuan-Ming history. A religious dimension of cyclical thinking becomes evident in the general wave of Messianic sects and movements, see chapter 5 "Sixteenth Century Millenarianism from the Tagus to the Ganges", in Sanjay Subrahmanyam, *From the Tagus to the Ganges: Explorations in Connected History* (Oxford 2007), 2: 102–37; Polybius, *The Histories*, Vol. III: books 5–8, (eds) F.W. Walbank, Chr. Habicht and W.R. Paton (Cambridge MA: Harvard University Press, 2011); see G.W. Trompf, *The Idea of Historical Recurrence in Western Thought, From Antiquity to the Reformation* (Berkeley, Los Angeles, London: University of California Press, 1979); Ibn Khaldun, (ed.) Franz Rosenthal, *The Muqaddima. An Introduction to History* (Princeton, Oxford: Princeton University Press, 1967); also Robert Irwin, "Toynbee and Ibn Khaldun", *Middle Eastern Studies* 33, no. 3 (1997).

[7] Hillay Zmora, *Monarchy, Aristocracy, and the State in Europe* (London: Routledge, 2001).

same time an upper layer of powerful nobles merged into a new court-related aristocracy, absorbing a group of *homines novi* rising through service in the armies and in the key bodies of the state. This group depended on the state but at the same time held a key position in its apparatus – at court, in the councils, in the army, and in provincial high office.

This revisionist view now represents a near-consensus.[8] It is closely connected to the parallel re-examination of 'absolute' monarchy in Europe. Revisionism reflects two important overlapping shifts in research priorities: the first shifting focus from central institutions and their measures to regional elites; the second moving from studying monarchical rhetoric to the practical implementation of power. The highhanded language of kingship or the submissive tone of local corporations cannot be read as a description of actual relations between centre and periphery. While monarchical power after the 1650s was rarely challenged openly, regional corporations clothed their bargaining for corporate rights and privileges in the language of subservience. The persistent penury of monarchy consistently left openings for lucrative deals.[9] Gradually these changing views, initiated in regional research, have implicated the key centres of power around the ruler: army, court, council.[10] The revisionist perspective never aimed to refute the strengthening of state institutions; it underlined the indispensable role of elites in the consolidation of governance. Even activist rulers such as Louis XIV accepted a *juste mesure* of elite power in general and noble power in particular as inevitable and desirable for the social fabric; even elites with a history of rebellion in the

[8] See Ronald G. Asch, *Nobilities in Transition, 1550–1700: Courtiers and Rebels in Britain and Europe* (London: Hodder Arnold, 2003) and the authoritative collection edited by Hamish Scott, *The European Nobilities in the Seventeenth and Eighteenth Centuries. Northern, Central and Eastern Europe* (London: Longman 1995; second revised edition Basingstoke: Palgrave Macmillan, 2007); the same author has now prepared an important study, Hamish Scott, *Forming Aristocracy: the Reconfiguration of Europe's Nobilities, c. 1300–1750* (Forthcoming).

[9] See e.g. R.J.W. Evans, *The Making of the Habsburg Monarchy 1550–1700. An Interpretation* (Oxford: Clarendon Press, 1979); William Beik, *Absolutism and Society in Seventeenth-Century France. State Power and Provincial Aristocracy in Languedoc* (Cambridge: Cambridge University Press, 1985); Roger C. Mettam, *Power and Faction in Louis XIV's France* (Oxford, New York: Blackwell, 1988); Julian Swann, *Provincial Power and Absolute Monarchy: The Estates General of Burgundy, 1661–1790* (Cambridge: Cambridge University Press, 2003).

[10] David Parrott, *Richelieu's Army: War, Government and Society in France, 1624–1642* (Cambridge: Cambridge University Press, 2001); Guy Rowlands, *The Dynastic State and the Army under Louis XIV: Royal Service and Private Interest, 1661–1701* (Cambridge: Cambridge University Press, 2002); Guy Rowlands, "Louis XIV, Aristocratic Power and the Elite Units of the French Army", *French History* 13 (1999); Jeroen Duindam, *Vienna and Versailles. The Courts of Europe's Dynastic Rivals* (Cambridge: Cambridge University Press, 2003) and other literature cited there.

preceding phase of religious strife looked upon strong kingship as desirable, as long as it respected key interests.

Do these changing views of rulers and nobles in the European context have any relevance for our understanding of Asian dynastic constellations? Clearly, we cannot extrapolate conclusions about Asia from the European revision of 'absolute' rulers and their noble elites. However, the shift from central to regional perspectives and sources appears to be equally relevant in current Asian dynastic history.[11] The European example also suggests that the language of deference can comfortably go together with a keen defence of regional, corporate and dynastic interests. Two general aspects conducive to the rise of regional hereditary power groups, huge distances and strong ties of kinship, were conspicuously present in Late Imperial China, the focus of this chapter. The Qing dynasty not only unified China under its authority, it also 'marched west',[12] conquering extensive territories beyond the traditional borders of China proper. Most computations of the ratio between state magistrates, population, and territory, moreover, suggest that Qing China was relatively sparsely governed. Modest numbers of officials dealt with huge territories, governing a rapidly expanding population.[13] Also, there seems to be universal agreement on the role of the family as the 'strategic core of the social order' in imperial China, not only in terms of respect for parents and the immediate social setting of the family but also through 'ancestor worship' and the construction of genealogies.[14] Yet, although in Late Imperial China the combined forces of distance and kinship were very strong, it still seems to have eluded to some extent the patrimonial pattern so general in the pre-modern world.[15]

---

[11] Harriet Zurndorfer, "Meta-narratives of Song Dynasty Regional Society: an Historiographical Analysis of Western-language Scholarship since 1950", in *Chugoku suka no chiiki-zo: Hikaku-shi kara mita sensei kokka to chiiki*, (ed.) Ihara Hiroshi (Tokyo: Iwata-shoin, 2013).

[12] See Peter C. Perdue, *China Marches West: the Qing Conquest of Central Eurasia* (Cambridge MA: Harvard University Press, 2005).

[13] Around 1800 an estimated 35,000 officials watched over a population of ca. 300,000,000, see e.g. Benjamin A. Elman, "The Social Roles of Literati in Early to Mid-Ch'ing", in *The Cambridge History of China*, vol. 9, *The Ch'ing Empire to 1800* (Cambridge: Cambridge University Press, 2002), 1: 384. Elman cites 20,400 positions for licentiates in 1500, and 24,680 in 1625, assuming a somewhat stronger growth in the eighteenth century. Susan Naquin and Evelyn Rawski, *Chinese Society in the Eighteenth Century* (New Haven: Yale University Press, 1987), 224–5 underline growth, whereas William Skinner, "Introduction: Urban development in Imperial China", in *The City in Late Imperial China*, (ed.) idem (Stanford: Stanford University Press, 1977), 21 points to a long-term decline of the proportion of magistrates in the population from Han to Qing times.

[14] Naquin and Rawski, *Chinese society in the eighteenth century*, 89, on the term Ancestor worship as a misnomer.

[15] See discussion in Gary G. Hamilton, "Patriarchalism in Imperial China and Western Europe: A Revision of Weber's Sociology of Domination", *Theory and Society* 13, no. 3 (1984); Andrew Eisenberg, "Weberian Patrimonialism and Imperial Chinese history",

Post-Tang China: Rags to Riches and Back Again?[16]

'China's was an open society, with no caste system and essentially no ascriptive social statuses apart from the members of the current imperial lineage', F.W. Mote states in a 1998 article. Similar statements can be found throughout the literature on China, outlining the gradual erosion of the power of nobles from the earliest emperors onwards, and the absence of a truly hereditary power elite outside the ruling dynasty in the Late Imperial period (Ming 1368–1644; Qing 1644–1912).[17]

We encounter the decline of hereditary nobilities in the pre-imperial warring states period (475–221 BCE)[18] and again as a result of imperial unification under the Qin emperor (221–210 BCE). Under the Han dynasty (206 BCE–220 CE) hereditary nobles, surviving in the form of regional 'kings' under the emperor's aegis, became increasingly dependent on the evolving state apparatus. However, in the late Han and particularly in the turbulent phase following the fall of the dynasty, 'Chinese society developed in distinctly aristocratic directions', with a relatively small number of families dominating social and political life, relying on pedigree as well as on wealth – a sequence comfortably fitting within simultaneous European experiences.[19] The Tang dynasty (618–907 CE), while not formally recognising the existence of an aristocracy, effectively granted this group supreme offices and

Theory and Society 27, no.1 (1998) and more recently Liping Wang and Julia Adams, "Interlocking Patrimonialisms and State Formation in Qing China and Early Modern Europe", *Annals of the American Academy of Political and Social Science* 636 (2011) on Qing China, stressing the role of bondservants and Aisin Gioro princes as a counterweight to the classic inner–outer power of eunuchs and literati. It connects this balancing act somewhat loosely and not quite plausibly to contemporary monarchical strategies in France (p. 177) but includes interesting statements on the patrimonial lesser and informal extensions of the literature magistrature in the regions (p. 173) or more generally on succession issues as well as on the 'principal-agent' problem.

16 See Rubie S. Watson, "Corporate Property and Local Leadership in the Pearl River Delta, 1898–1941", in *Chinese Local Elites and Patterns of Dominance, (eds)* Joseph W. Esherick and Mary Backus Rankin (Berkeley: University of California Press, 1990), 240 on questioning the cliché of rags-to-riches; Lloyd E. Eastman, *Family, Fields, and Ancestors. Constancy and Change in China's Social and Economic History* (Oxford, New York: Oxford University Press, 1988), 18 on rags-to-riches as topos.

17 F.W. Mote, "Becoming an Emperor", *Proceedings of the Denver Museum of Natural History* 3, no. 15 (1998), 12. In this chapter, I give simplified dates for dynasties, omitting the various shifts within one dynasty or transition periods between dynasties.

18 Mark Lewis, *The Early Chinese Empires: Qin and Han* (Cambridge MA: Harvard University Press, 2010), 31, 44, 70.

19 Patricia Ebrey, "Shifts in Marriage Finance from the Sixth to the Thirteenth Century", in *Marriage and Inequality in Chinese Society*, (eds) Patricia Buckley Ebrey and Rubie S. Watson (Berkeley: University of California Press, 1991), 98; Mark Lewis, *China's Cosmopolitan Empire. The Tang Dynasty* (Cambridge MA: Harvard University Press, 2009), 48.

special legal privileges.[20] The position of these families, gradually developing into a service aristocracy tied to state offices and court-related prestige, in some ways resembles the early modern European court-related aristocracy. However, it would not outlive the dynasty.[21] The single example of a formally ruling woman in Chinese imperial history, Empress Wu (690–705 CE), coincided with a changing relationship between ruler and bureaucracy.[22] Gradually the recruitment of officials through a civil service examination became the accepted route rather than the exception. This made the surfacing of a full-blown hereditary nobility after the demise of the Tang less likely. The rapid expansion of literacy and commerce under the Song dynasty (960–1279 CE) consolidated this change. Typically, this 'Tang-Song transition' has been compared to the European transition from the medieval to the early modern period, showing an analogous pattern of interrelated shifts in the social, economic, cultural and political domains.[23]

Jennifer Holmgren, in the context of her study on imperial marriages, connects the changing nature of elites to the position of the emperor, who developed from a *primus inter pares*, to an autocrat under the Song, to end up as a tyrant with the rise of the Ming (1368–1644) – a terminology that brings to mind the European vocabulary around the rise of 'absolute' power.[24] After the consolidation of the civil service examinations under the Song, we find great aristocratic families only in the context of non-Han conquest dynasties and their allies. The notion of nobility itself did not disappear but remained limited to the merit nobility rewarded for outstanding services and to the relatives of ruling dynasties – the subject of the second part of this chapter. Many sinologists, notably Benjamin Elman, have made clear, however, that the examinations represented a real possibility of social ascent only to a small minority.[25] The lengthy preparation necessary for even the lowest level exam would demand a comfortable financial

20 Lewis, *China's Cosmopolitan Empire*, 49–50.

21 Lewis, *China's Cosmopolitan Empire*, 178, 195–206. See also Bol, "The 'localist turn'", 6.

22 Lewis, *China's Cosmopolitan Empire*, 35–40; 103–4 stresses the 'black legend' around Empress Wu, but is more hesitant than Richard Guisso, *Wu Tse-t'ien and the Politics of Legitimation in T'ang China* (Bellingham: Western, 1978) about her role in the consolidation of the civil service examinations.

23 Lewis, *China's Cosmopolitan Empire*, 178; see a somewhat different assessment of Empress Wu in Denis Twitchett, "Chen gui and Other Works Attributed to Empress Wu Zetian", *Asia Major* 16, no. 1 (2003).

24 Jennifer Holmgren, "Imperial Marriage in the Native Chinese and Non-Han State, Han to Ming", in *Marriage and Inequality*, (eds) Watson and Ebrey, 73.

25 Benjamin Elman, "Political, Social, and Cultural Reproduction via Civil Service Examinations in Late Imperial China", *The Journal of Asian Studies* 50, no. 1 (1991); see also the discussion in Harriet Zurndorfer, "From Local History to Cultural History Reflections on Some Recent Publications", *T'oung Pao*, Second Series, 83, no 4–5 (1997); Joseph W. Esherick and Mary Backus Rankin, "Concluding remarks", in *Chinese Local Elites and Patterns of Dominance, (eds) Esherick and Rankin,* 310–311, 317.

position, limiting actual access to an upper layer of society combining wealth with a tradition of education and learning. This social group is usually labelled as 'gentry', a term with strong European associations, suggesting the untitled and relatively open group of English landed proprietors standing in between the highly exclusive group of titled nobles and broad groups based on commercial or agricultural wealth. In the Chinese context, however, the upper echelon would not be defined by pedigree and hereditary titles but by success in the competition for high office in the imperial bureaucracy. A small minority of candidates passed the thresholds of the three-tiered examinations, and only a handful would reach supreme office at the centre – but a success every now and then would help to maintain the local prestige and wealth of gentry lineages. The promise of office based on merit and the nominal chance of mobility at the individual level made the civil service examinations exceptional in the pre-modern context, even if in practice the system secured social reproduction at the group level.

This daunting gateway into the imperial bureaucracy helped to turn learning and state service into the defining elements of elite status. The civil service examinations created a group of gentlemen-literati aspiring to office or holding office, which connected the localities to the centre and created a powerful shared culture. The Chinese imperial bureaucracy, more elaborate than any European counterpart before the late eighteenth century, developed under the first imperial dynasties. It soon obtained a more or less stable form around six ministries, a separate 'censorate' controlling and reviewing regional magistrates, and a varying group of supreme officials connecting the 'outer court' administrative services to the emperor in his 'inner court' service establishment.[26] A table of nine ranks subdivided into more grades each with their fixed state stipends arranged hierarchy and payment; promotion, demotion, and rotation were based on a system of evaluation and recommendation. In addition, from early Han onwards a series of measures was introduced to keep in check patrimonial tendencies. These 'laws of avoidance' or 'avoidances', expanded and refined under later dynasties, stipulated that officers could not serve in their native areas or under their paternal and maternal relatives.[27] It is unclear whether such rulings could indeed prevent patronage and collusion on the basis of kinship and alliance. More generally, the elaborateness of the Chinese administrative setup and its nomenclature, translated into nineteenth-century European terminology, can create an unduly modern impression: this remarkably sophisticated institution was neither a modern bureaucracy nor necessarily an 'obstacle' to modernisation.[28]

---

[26] Charles O. Hucker, "Introduction: Governmental Organization Era by Era", in *Dictionary of Official Titles in Imperial China* (Stanford: Stanford University Press, 1985), 2–96; see also 318–19 on the six ministries; 593–4 on the censorate.

[27] Hucker, *Dictionary of Official Titles*, 5–6, 263; 397–8; Ebrey, "Shifts in Marriage Finance", 119–20.

[28] See the lucid discussion in Elman, "Political, Social, and Cultural Reproduction via Civil Service Examinations".

It remains important to note that even prestigious and wealthy gentry families in the country could not guarantee high office for any particular individual, although at several points venality crept in for lower degrees or positions, particularly during the later eighteenth and nineteenth centuries.[29] The gentry could effectively marshal wealth and social status to organise access to study and to the examinations. In the absence of examination success, could it use wealth and connections to secure its elite status in the longer term? Or did gentry lineages rise and fall, conforming to the 'rags-to-riches-to-rags' scenario?[30] The relationship between reproduction, production and inequality – or in other words the heredity of wealth and status – has been studied in structural terms by Jack Goody.[31] His initiative was taken up systematically in an important volume edited by Rubie Watson and Patricia Ebrey.[32] Patrilineal descent dominated in both China and Europe, the patriline forming the basis of ancestral piety as well as genealogies. However, the patterns of succession and inheritance differed. Amidst all variations in Europe there is a tendency towards primogeniture after the eleventh century, particularly strong among social elites. European elites developing in tandem with monarchy from the later Middle Ages onwards mimicked the monarchs in adopting primogeniture, adding a variety of instruments protecting their inherited wealth and titles against rash actions by individual family members.[33] The dominance of partible inheritance in China made it more difficult to sustain family wealth over time.[34] The combination of partible inheritance with the practice of concubinage, particularly relevant for wealthy families, may have exacerbated this process.

---

[29] Elisabeth Kaske, "Fund-Raising Wars: Office Selling and Interprovincial Finance in Nineteenth-Century China", *Harvard Journal of Asiatic Studies* 71, no. 1 (2011); Nancy E. Park, "Corruption in Eighteenth-Century China", *The Journal of Asian Studies* 56, no. 4 (1997).

[30] Rubie Watson, "Corporate Property", 240.

[31] Jack Goody and S.J. Tambiah, *Bridewealth and Dowry* (Cambridge: Cambridge University Press, 1973); Jack Goody, *Production and Reproduction: a Comparative Study of the Domestic Domain* (Cambridge: Cambridge University Press, 1976); Jack Goody, Joan Thirsk and E.P. Thompson (eds), *Family and Inheritance: Rural Society in Western Europe, 1200–1800* (Cambridge: Cambridge University Press, 1976); Jack Goody, *The Development of the Family and Marriage in Europe* (Cambridge: Cambridge University Press, 1983).

[32] Rubie S. Watson and Ebrey, *Marriage and Inequality in Chinese Society*; see also James L. Watson and Patricia B. Ebrey (eds), *Kinship Organization in Late Imperial China 1000–1940* (Berkeley, Los Angeles, London: University of California Press, 1986) and Martina Eglauer, "Family and Household in Late-Imperial China", in *Agriculture, Population and Economic Development in China and Europe*, (eds) Rolf Peter Sieferle and Helga Breuninger (Stuttgart: Breuninger-Stiftung, 2003).

[33] On European aristocracy and entail, *mayorazgo*, *fideicommissum* see Hamish Scott, *The European Nobilities in the Seventeenth and Eighteenth Centuries*; and Hamish Scott, *Forming Aristocracy: The Reconfiguration of Europe's Nobilities, c. 1300–1750* (forthcoming).

[34] Esherick and Rankin, *Chinese Local Elites and Patterns of Dominance, 306.*

Concubines' sons were entitled to their share of the inheritance. Daughters, on the other hand, did not as a rule have a right to inherit, although they could obtain some wealth in the form of a dowry.[35] Numerous offspring combined with partible inheritance, without a formalised hereditary status, would make elite downward mobility more likely than in a context where male primogeniture and endorsed hereditary status protected family wealth and invited lucrative marital alliances.

Studies of kinship, by anthropologists as well as by historians, mostly focus on smaller-scale entities: villages or regions. The local varieties they unearth in their work tend to undermine overall generalisations, and take distance from a state-centred top-down perspective. Esherick and Rankin note a shift in emphasis from '… the question of how government controlled local leaders and unified society to issues of how local elites … dominated local arenas and interacted with elites in other arenas.'[36]

Likewise, Michael Szonyi in his study on 'practicing kinship' presents local elites as active agents, using the vocabulary of orthodoxy and the machinery of the state for their own purposes:

> Strategizing in the language of orthodoxy is precisely what ties together all of the different approaches to kinship discussed in this work, tying as well the cultures of elites and common people alike into a single system … . Local elites were important actors in this domain, neither simply representing state interests nor opposing them but rather manipulating the system to serve their own interest … . Organized kinship played an important and complex role in the structuring of both the relationship between the state and local society and local life itself, as a venue for strategic negotiation and competition over local power.[37]

Szonyi's stress on the flexible 'practicing' of kinship shifts attention from the centre to the regions and from normative rules to *ad hoc* routines. This shift neatly matches the basic reorientation mentioned earlier in the context of recent work on European nobles and 'absolutism'.

Not only can we see a convergence in perspectives; there is substantial overlap in the strategies of elites. European noble families could opt for the highest ambition of a court-centred career or choose to stay in the country, developing their landed wealth and local affiliations. Many families, whether planned or *ad hoc*, had these spheres covered by different members of the family or alternated between court and region in a generational pattern. The alternation between local and central strategies, with a 'local' or 'inward turn' usually arising in phases

35 See extensive discussion in Watson and Ebrey, *Marriage and Social Inequality in China*; in Ebrey's introduction and throughout the book; see Eastman, *Family, Fields, and Ancestors*, 17.

36 Esherick and Rankin, *Chinese Local Elites and Patterns of Dominance, 305.*

37 Michael Szonyi, *Practicing Kinship. Lineage and Descent in Late Imperial China* (Stanford: Stanford University Press, 2002), 205–206.

of dynastic weakness, has been suggested for China by Peter Bol as well as by Esherick and Rankin.[38]

The flexibility of elites seems to be a keyword in both domains. Rubie Watson suggests how patrilineal elites could avoid extinction or impoverishment by departing from strict kinship preferences: they relied on matrilineal connections, on uxorilocal marriage by inviting in a son from another patriline to marry their daughter, or on adoption. Could they use filial piety and respect for a common paternal ancestor to strengthen their position? Interestingly, even the solution of protecting the patrimony against infringements by creating a trust (entail or *fideicommissum*), a practice spreading across Europe in the early modern age, had close parallels in China. Several authors point to '... corporate organizations for the primary lineage purpose of defending against the progressive fission of family wealth through the custom of partible inheritance. These lineages thus functioned much as entail did in Europe, producing an undivided and inalienable patrimony'.[39]

Such ancestral estates or lineage trusts helped to maintain the wealth of patrilineal local descent groups over time. They could be organised around ancestral shrines or charitable institutions but sometimes functioned rather like joint-stock companies, bringing together lineage wealth for long-term investments.[40] Kinship rules, usually organised around a revered paternal ancestor, were important in all these initiatives and legitimated them in the eyes of the state.

In their conclusion Esherick and Rankin provide several lucid insights that help to bring in line Chinese and European practices. They differentiate between the social continuity of certain *elites* (nobles, gentry) and the continuity of *personnel* or specific families. Typically, high levels of elite continuity in China were expected to go together with discontinuity at the level of families. Recent research tends to stress the potential of lineages to persist longer, thanks mostly to local *ad hoc* strategies such as those indicated here.[41] In Europe, the level of 'personnel' continuity in the noble elite, usually expected to have been high, was reduced by demography. Between a quarter and a third of noble families we can trace became extinct in the male line within one century. The martial career predominating

---

[38] Bol, "Localist Turn"; Esherick and Rankin, *Chinese Local Elites and Patterns of Dominance,* 307, 340–42.

[39] Esherick and Rankin, *Chinese Local Elites and Patterns of Dominance,* 318; see in the same volume relevant contributions by Brook, Rowe, and Watson.

[40] William T. Rowe, "Social Stability And Social Change", in *Cambridge History of China*, vol. 9, *The Ch'ing Empire to 1800*, (ed.) Willard J. Peterson (Cambridge: Cambridge University Press, 2003), 1: 532–7; these trusts bring to mind the Islamic-Ottoman *waqf* or *vakif*, pious foundations protecting the interests of elite families against the encroachments of the state and other threats.

[41] See the remarkable story of the Ye family, holding on to a comfortable elite position from Ming times into the PRC, Joseph Esherick, *Ancestral Leaves: A Family Journey Through Chinese History* (London, Berkeley, Los Angeles: University of California Press, 2011).

among nobles exacerbated the problem of survival.[42] Bending the rules of succession and inheritance, using maternal relatives to secure continuity, was practised in Europe as well. Families replenished their wealth through marriages with social climbers, rich *roturier* families willing to spend heavily to provide upward mobility (hypergamy) for their daughters, a practice that left patrilineal noble status untarnished in France – although German rules were more rigid in this respect. The presence of mobility at the personnel level, never comfortably fitting noble orthodoxy, was actively concealed by manipulating genealogies and family histories.

The overview of elite strategies in Esherick and Rankin's conclusion provides some parallels between Europe and China. Lineage organisations, however, do not neatly match any noble dynastic organisation in Europe because they went beyond the family or dynasty in numbers and included a socially more diverse membership with its own managerial elite as well as a lower echelon profiting from lineage charity. As we have seen, lineage expedients to maintain wealth and status through the ages did match European elite solutions to some extent. The keywords underlined in various contexts by Esherick and Rankin, networks, patronage and brokerage, appear to have been equally relevant for European and Chinese elites. Patronage and brokerage, at the local level, connecting various localities, and cutting through the social layers, arguably are among the most frequently used terms in European literature on elites.

These similarities of vocabulary and practice should not blind us to remaining fundamental differences. The legitimation of elite power was fundamentally different, with hereditary status serving as the standard in the European hierarchical view, usually connected to a martial ethos rather than to learning.[43] Chinese 'metropolitan' elites based on success in the examinations were far more fluid than court-related aristocracies in Europe, where periodic surges of crisis and mobility contrast with long periods of continuity – some Viennese court families emerging in the later sixteenth century were still very present on the eve of the First World War; most courtier-families sharing Louis XIV's years at Versailles were still in office on the eve of the French Revolution.[44] There is another contrast that can be mentioned only in passing here, although it opens a huge field of discussion.

---

[42] Hamish Scott, *Forming Aristocracy* (forthcoming), introduction and a major chapter on 'succession'.

[43] Though see the reassessment on Chinese Wu and Wen in Nicola di Cosmo (ed.), *Military Culture in Imperial China* (Cambridge, MA: Harvard University Press, 2009) and Harriet Zurndorfer, "What is the Meaning of 'War' in an Age of Cultural Efflorescence? Another Look at the Role of War in Song Dynasty China (960–1279)", in *War in Words: Transformations of War from Antiquity to Clausewitz*, (eds) Marco Formisano and Hartmut Böhme (Berlin, New York: De Gruyter, 2011).

[44] See the definitive statement on this point in Leonhard Horowski's recent *Die Belagerung des Thrones. Machtstrukturen und Karrieremechanismen am Hof von Frankreich 1661–1789* (Ostfildern: Thorbecke, 2012).

Apparently, the Chinese state on the whole preferred a situation where no *corps intermédiaires* complicated the connections between centre and periphery, whereas European monarchs adopted a similar approach only in moments of crisis and on the whole worked together with regional and local corporations.[45] On the other hand, Chinese administrators were so thinly scattered across the population that they could do little to counteract local initiatives as long as these were shrouded in the language of filial piety and deference.

The Imperial Lineage in China: A Nobility?

In China proper, notwithstanding its stress on the male ancestor, no formal hereditary right to high social status and office existed outside of the ruling dynasty. The dynastic principle was conspicuously present in China, but it remained limited to the ruler and his kin. A combination of marriage and concubinage in the Chinese case led to the proliferation of dynastic princes and princesses – a comfortable assurance against extinction of the male line but a challenge in many other respects. Rulers' relationships with their agnates appear to have been thorny in almost all patrilineal dynastic settings. Fierce competition could arise among male claimants to the throne, a tendency particularly strong among dynasties with Central Asian roots.[46] Rulers consistently faced difficult choices in dealing with their sons and brothers. Should they be educated as power wielders, to be entrusted with executive power, acting as their ruling relative's *alter ego* in frontier regions

---

[45] Rowe, "Social Stability and Social Change", 536; Esherick and Rankin, *Chinese Local Elites and Patterns of Dominance*, 337.

[46] I intentionally leave out the common reference to 'bloody tanistry' here, because sibling rivalry and father–son tensions seem to reflect a general pattern in dynastic history; moreover, the Gaelic practices of the term tanistry seem to fit awkwardly with the 'Steppe' traditions highlighted by Joseph Fletcher in his "Turco-Mongolian Monarchic Tradition in the Ottoman Empire", *Harvard Ukrainian Studies* 3–4 (1979–1980); the patterns described by J.H. Stevenson, "The Law of the Throne – Tanistry and the Introduction of the Law of Primogeniture", *Scottish Historical Review* 25 (1927/8) can more easily be connected to patterns of acclamation and variants of succession in the European context. See more general approaches of the succession problem in Jack Goody (ed.), *Succession to High Office* (Cambridge: Cambridge University Press, 1966); specifically on China, Denis Twitchett, "The T'ang Imperial Family", *Asia Major* 7, no. 2 (1994); Patricia B. Ebrey, "Succession to High Office: The Chinese Case", in *Culture, Technology and History: Implications of the Anthropological Work of Jack Goody*, (eds) David R. Olson and Michael Cole (Lawrence NJ: Psychology Press, 2006). In this chapter, I do not address the changing succession rules – the Qing discarded primogeniture and even the precedence of the formal empress's son, leaving room for contestation – a choice which may have reflected the tradition of collective sovereignty. After the endless complications following Kangxi's succession a system of 'secret succession' was introduced which still left room for various choices, but prevented contestation.

or commanding armies? Or conversely, should they be prevented from assuming any serious responsibilities and relegated to a life of enforced leisure under close imperial surveillance?

Princes and their advisors may have pondered these alternatives, but some explicitly addressed them in writing. A remarkable instance of sibling rivalry inaugurated the career of Li Shimin, the second emperor of the Tang dynasty ruling as Tang Taizong (626–649 CE), who ascended to the throne by killing his elder brother, the crown prince, and by forcing his father to abdicate. Nevertheless, Tang Taizong proved able to secure a position among the most idealised emperors of China – a noteworthy feat, probably to be explained in part through his intense involvement in the writing of history at court. Taizong also wrote two highly interesting tracts on rulership: the first early in his reign to legitimise his usurpation, the second towards the end of his reign advising his crown prince.[47] Particularly in the second tract, Taizong offers numerous interesting observations. The emperor, observing the policies employed by earlier dynasties, considered the enfeoffing of relatives wise and necessary, but he added that the fiefs should be many, and their size small. Rulers need their lineages to serve as a 'fence and protection' for the realm. Many relatives make for a prosperous dynasty: 'when the twigs and leaves are luxuriant, the roots will be difficult to pull out'. On the other hand, no single imperial clansmen or house should obtain a pre-eminence approaching that of the ruler, otherwise the throne could be threatened: 'a branch can get so heavy that it breaks the trunk; a tail can get too big to be wagged'. Taizong concludes that 'the best way is to enfeoff many relatives to even up their power and to have them regulate one another and share one another's ups and downs'. Later he added in more general terms: ' … neutralizing the power of subordinates so that none of them gets to be too strong or too weak is indeed the key to securing one's throne'.[48]

---

[47] Tang Taizong 'Golden Mirror' (628) and 'Plan for an emperor' or Ti-Fan (648), translated and printed in Denis Twitchett, "How to be an Emperor: T'ang T'ai-tsung's Vision of His Role", *Asia Major* 3rd ser. 9 (1996). Twitchett (38–49) charts the transmission of the Ti-Fan in China, Korea and Japan; in Japan it seems to have been used for educating crown princes more often than in China, where the historical record of the reign as preserved in court historiography was probably more important. On Tang Taizong literary works, see recently Jack W. Chen. *The Poetics of Sovereignty: On Emperor Taizong of the Tang Dynasty* (Cambridge MA: Harvard University Press, 2010); on court historiography see Isenbike Togan, "Court Historiography in Early Tang China: Assigning a Place to History and Historians at the Palace", in *Royal Courts in Dynastic States and Empires: a Global Perspective*, (eds) Jeroen Duindam, Metin Kunt and Tulay Artan (Leiden, Boston: Brill 2011).

[48] 'Establishing one's kinsmen,' Ti-fan in Twitchett, "How to be an Emperor", 58–63; note important differences in translation between Twitchett and Chiu-yueh Lai in Patricia Buckley Ebrey (ed.), *Chinese Civilization: A Sourcebook* (New York: Free Press, 1993), 112–115, for instance Twitchett 62: 'If the feudatories are allowed to become too powerful, then it will bring about distress over a situation that is impossible [to remedy]. If, however, they are rendered too weak then there will be no foundation for a strong trunk. Speaking on the basis of this, there is nothing as good as establishing large numbers of the

Louis XIV, whose memoirs famously stated that 'La jalousie de l'un sert souvent de frein à l'ambition de l'autre', would have understood.[49]

In the European context royal families remained small and frequently faced extinction. Princes of the blood were few, but they figure prominently in dynastic history, with brothers and uncles in particular serving either as important captains or as leaders of rebellions. Rulers blessed with many sons needed to place them in positions with sufficient prestige without running the risk of undermining their own authority – a balance easily disturbed. Members of the royal family could expect to be paid by the state, with their households and palaces figuring in the same budgets as the court of their ruling relative. In Europe dynastic intermarrying further complicated the issue, with princely houses across the continent accumulating rights of succession to each other's realms. Succession frequently served as a *casus belli* in early modern Europe, although in practice it was always mixed with other sources of conflict. The upper echelon of the imperial lineage in China – uncles, brothers, and sons of ruling emperors, as well as their maternal kin and princesses from the patriline – fits into the pattern of princes of the blood in Europe.[50] The numerous lower echelons of the imperial clan, however, in some respects seem to approximate the European nobility rather than the princes of the blood. Numbers are an important factor here. The imperial clansmen formed a stunningly dense

ruler's kin [in fiefs], but keeping their [individual] power small. *This will cause the great and small to defend one another; and people will share their sorrows and happiness in common* [my italics]. Then, above there will be no suspicious and jealous hearts, below no apprehension of becoming victims of trespass and injustice. This is the lesson to be learnt from enfiefment'. Compared to Chiu-yueh Lai translation in Ebrey, 113: 'Subordinates granted too much power can develop into insurmountable problems for the throne. On the other hand, subordinates granted too little power will not be strong enough to protect the throne. Thus, the best way is to enfeoff many relatives *to even up their power and to have them regulate one another and share one another's ups and downs*. By doing so, the throne need not suspect its subordinates and the subordinates need not worry about being wronged or injured. These are the precautions one should take in granting fiefs. *Neutralizing the power of subordinates so that none of them gets to be too strong or too weak is indeed the key to securing one's throne*'. The two italicised sentences convey a different meaning, made explicit in the final sentence, not to be found in Twitchett: the second translation stresses a *divide et impera* approach explicitly whereas Twitchett's version leaves more room for solidarity among the princes and the ruler – a vital distinction, reflecting two recurring situations.

49 *Mémoires de Louis XIV pour l'instruction du Dauphin*, (ed.) Charles Dreyss (Paris: Didier, 1860), 2:267, where the ministers are discussed, a quote mostly read as relating to the high noblemen at court.

50 For reasons of space and concentration, I leave out here the important domain of marital alliances through paternal sisters and princesses, elaborated lucidly and in great detail, in Jennifer Holmgren, "Imperial Marriage in the Native Chinese and Non-Han State, Han to Ming", as well as John Chaffee, "The Marriage of Sung Imperial Clanswomen" and Evelyn S. Rawski, "Ch'ing Imperial Marriage and Problems of Rulership" all in Watson and Ebrey, *Marriage and Inequality*.

foliage supporting the dynastic trunk, particularly in Ming China. Towards the end of the Ming dynasty apparently some 200,000 persons could claim membership of the imperial clan – admittedly fewer than the French nobility at the same time and certainly a much smaller proportion of the population.[51] While tax exemptions had become typical for European nobilities, imperial clansmen in China were provided for by the state. Stipends and other forms of support were a real burden in financial terms: during the Wanli reign (1573–1620 CE) support for the kinsmen consumed 15 per cent of the overall budget, the largest single category of state expenditure.[52] Finally, imperial clansmen could not aspire to a dignity separate from the ruling dynasty or to long-standing regional ties and networks – two important sources of European noble power.

The Ming princes and princesses, all arising from the 24 sons and 14 daughters fathered by the first Ming emperor Zhu Yuanzhang, ruling as the Hongwu emperor or Ming Taizu (1368–1398 CE), were divided into eight ranks, the lesser ranks of which were far more numerous than the more exclusive upper two ranks of full princes and commandery princes (*qin wang* and *jun wang*). The most important princes lived in 'miniature replicas of the imperial court', and performed all ritual responsibilities of the emperors in the region.[53] Some of the major princes resided in previous capitals, on the site of previous imperial palace compounds. European travellers noticed the Ming princes but usually did not pay them much attention – Europeans mostly visited the eastern coastal fringe of China, a region largely without princely fiefs. Álvaro de Semedo, a Jesuit father who spent some time in Xi'an (ancient Chang'an) in Shaanxi province, did briefly describe the kings or princes in his *History of China*; the more extensive eighteenth-century overview by Jean-Baptiste du Halde, who never visited China, mentions the early Qing princes in passing, stressing their already substantial numbers and their relative poverty.[54]

The founding Ming emperor, Zhu Yuanzhang, in 1370 decreed a policy of enfeoffment of imperial sons:

> As we peruse the ancient ages, ever since the august rulers possessed the land under Heaven, the eldest son born to the primary consort was appointed to the

[51] Richard G. Wang, *The Ming Prince and Daoism: Institutional Patronage of an Elite* (Oxford: Oxford University Press, 2012), 15.

[52] Wang, *The Ming Prince and Daoism*, 15–16

[53] Jérôme Kerlouégan, "Printing for Prestige? Publishing and Publications by Ming Princes", *East Asian Publishing and Society* 1 (2011), 57; see a description in Wang, *The Ming Prince and Daoism*, 11–14; David Robinson, "Princely Courts of the Ming Dynasty", *Ming Studies* 65 (2012), 1 on the Qin prince in Xi'an and the Zhou prince in Kaifeng.

[54] Álvaro de Semedo, *The History of That Great and Renowned Monarchy of China* (London 1655), 121–122; on late Ming princes, J.B. Du Halde, *Description géographique, historique, chronologique, politique, et physique de l'empire de la Chine et de la Tartarie chinoise* (The Hague 1736–1737), 2: 69–71.

> legal position as the heir-apparent. For the other sons, they were to divide and share the land of the country to establish princely investitures. This is the way to mark the distinction between the elder and the young, and the means to stabilize the land from within and without … [55]

At this early stage, Zhu Yuanzhang or Ming Taizu instituted the princes in important fiefdoms, granting them near-autonomous power as well as serious military roles. Apparently they too were to serve, using Tang Taizong's words, as 'fence and protection'. The emperor favoured marriages between princesses and the military elites, seeking to create a strong group of supporters around the throne.[56] This group was exempt from ordinary justice: officials filing complaints against princes through regular administrative channels risked severe punishment.[57] Imperial clansmen were to be judged only by the emperor and a court of fellow-clansmen in the Imperial Clan Court. On the other hand, Taizu's ancestral instructions (1381) for the princes state that it was 'definitely not permissible to recruit eager and clever advisors [or] to receive petitioners' – clearly practices highly important for local power wielders.[58] This ambivalent attitude towards the princes, present in muted form in Ming Taizu's early proclamations appears to have been exacerbated by the conspicuous abuses committed by some of the enfeoffed princes. In 1395, upon the death of the Qin prince, Ming Taizu wrote a 'Funeral Ode' publishing the transgressions of his son:

> Having commanded the land under Heaven I started enfeoffing my sons in order that they would serve as a shield of the imperial house. You Shuang were only junior to the heir-apparent and you were the first to be invested a fief at Qin. But ever since you arrived at your state, no meritorious deeds were reported. Partying with lowlifes, you indulged in profligacy, wine and women, wreaking havoc on the land, and provoked Heaven's wrath. I often admonished and reprimanded you but you were never enlightened and thus lost your life. Even death would not expiate all your sins. Now I adumbrate and publicize the crimes and disgusting misdeeds you had committed in your life time, to which you shall attend.[59]

---

55 Hok-Lam Chan, "Ming Taizu's Problem with His Sons: Prince Qin's Criminality and Early-Ming Politics", *Asia Major* 20, no. 1 (2007), 48.

56 See Wang, *The Ming Prince and Daoism*, 9–10.

57 See Edward Farmer, *Zhu Yuanzhang and Early Ming Legislation: The Reordering of Chinese Society Following the End of Mongol Rule* (Leiden: Brill, 1995), notably the 'August Ming Ancestral Instructions' printed on 114–49 at 132–3; see also *The Great Ming Code. Da Ming Lü*, (ed.) Jiang Yonglin. (Seattle, London: University of Washington Press, 2005).

58 Farmer, *Zhu Yuanzhang and Early Ming Legislation*, 134.

59 Hok-Lam Chan, "Ming Taizu's Problem with His Sons", 77.

Shortly after the accession to the throne of Taizu's grandson, one of Taizu's sons captured the throne by force. Ruling as the Yongle emperor (1402–1424 CE), he was understandably wary about princely power. At the start of the Xuande emperor's reign (1425–1435 CE), the prince of Han challenged the new ruler. This second son-against-grandson rebellion ended in failure, but it must have raised further doubts about the loyalty of the imperial princes. Several other incidents in the fifteenth and sixteenth centuries confirmed the potential for restiveness among the princes. The emperors and their advisors replied with a series of rulings (*fanjin*) radically limiting the freedom of movement of the princes, reducing their political and military roles. They were to stay within the walls of the capital of their regional fiefs and could not engage in martial activities such as hunting.[60] Princes were not allowed to visit each other or to come to Beijing without formal invitation. Discussing the imperial princes, Charles Hucker in his classic study on the Ming states that from the fifteenth century onwards 'the nobility in general was an *ornament* on the *Ming* social scene, not a factor in government'.[61] The ornamental role of the clansmen and the confinement in their urban settings bring to mind the notion of domestication as introduced by Norbert Elias to describe French nobles at Versailles. In this remarkable case of multifocal domestication, the 'empty' ritual role and the confinement ascribed by Elias to the French nobility were scattered over many centres rather than concentrated in one central palace.[62]

Elias based his view of the French nobility at Versailles largely on the *mémoires* of the Duc de Saint-Simon – an immensely rich but notoriously biased source. The duke, an army dropout spending his life around court without holding office, reconfigured the Sun King's policies to turn him into the nemesis of French nobility, a view no longer accepted.[63] The position of Ming imperial princes surely

---

60 See David Robinson, *Martial Spectacles at the Ming Court of China, 1368–1568* (Cambridge, MA: Harvard University Press, 2013) especially chapter 2 on princely hunting showing at least some continuity in this practice. Many thanks to the author for allowing me to read his manuscript before publication as well as for advice.

61 *Hucker, Dictionary of Official Titles*, 71.

62 See Jeroen Duindam, *Myths of Power. Norbert Elias and the Early Modern European Court* (Amsterdam: Amsterdam University Press, 1995) on Elias and domestication, or Duindam, "Versailles, Vienna, and Beyond: Changing Views of Household and Government in Early Modern Europe", in *Royal Courts in Dynastic States and Empires: A Global Perspective*, (eds) Jeroen Duindam, Metin Kunt and Tulay Artan (Leiden, Boston: Brill, 2001) 401–31. Jérome Kerlouégan uses the term 'infantilized' instead of domesticated, Kerlouégan, "Printing for Prestige?" 55. Elias's depiction of Versailles has been compared to the Tokugawa practice of alternate attendance or Sankin-kōtai of the Daimyo; on the separation between Bakufu and the emperor's cultural or ritual power in Japan, relevant to some extent for the discussion of the 'ornamental' Ming princes, see Lee Butler, *Emperor and Aristocracy in Japan, 1467–1680: Resilience and Renewal* (Cambridge MA: Harvard University Press, 2002).

63 See Duindam, *Vienna and Versailles* for a comparative assessment stressing the relatively vested hereditary positions of French court nobles.

was very different, but the notion that they lived in a ritual-ceremonial splendour without any actual influence or connections is now being questioned by several Ming scholars. David Robinson, Richard Wang, Jérôme Kerlouégan, and Craig Clunas have recently stressed the role of Ming princes as cultural and political brokers.[64] They point out that the *literati* administrative elite, adopting a highly critical stance towards the princes, almost entirely monopolised the collective written memory. The official sources generated by the literati elite around court represent a carefully redacted image.[65] Rich archaeological findings in princely tombs and a variety of local gazetteers leave room for a different assessment. Ritual and cultural connections with the urban environments of princely palaces must have been important – even high state officials needed to formally pay their respects to the imperial princely residences by stepping out of their sedan chairs and bowing. Semedo, fully accepting that the princes held no 'Authority and Jurisdiction' underlined that:

> … all the Officers of the Province were obliged to pay him [the prince of Qin in Xi'an] respect suitable to his Title; whence every first and fifteenth day of the Moone they went to do him reverence in like manner, as is done at Court to the King … [66]

Any student of pre-modern culture will find it difficult to offhandedly discard such ceremonial obeisance as simply 'empty show' – the classic nineteenth and early twentieth-century prejudice. Urban populations witnessed this ritual deference towards princes: were they expected to understand it as mere theatre? Moreover, princes were active as patrons of Buddhism and Daoism as well as of literary culture. Their courts must have had an impact on local purveyors and artisans. Finally, what was left of the connections between the princes and hereditary military colonies, so important in the early decades of the princes? It now seems clear that hereditary military households retained their position in the frontier zones, and probably even became stronger in the upsurge of military activity in the late Ming. The presence of long-lasting clans of military leaders, whether or not they maintained connections to the marginalised Ming princes, demands further scrutiny.[67]

---

64 See Wang, *The Ming Prince and Daoism*; Kerlouégan, "Printing for Prestige?", and a special issue 65 of *Ming Studies* (2012) including contributions by David Robinson, Richard Wang and *Xiaoneng Yang.*

65 A view expressed powerfully in *Craig Clunas, Screen of Kings: Royal Art and Power in Ming China* (London: Reaktion, 2013).

66 See Semedo, *History of That Great and Renowned Monarchy of China*, 122; this rule was already included in the 'Ancestral Instruction', see Farmer, *Zhu Yuanzhang and Early Ming Legislation*, 128, nr 34.

67 See Kenneth M. Swope, "A Few Good Men: the Li family and China's Northern Frontier in the Late Ming", *Ming Studies* 49 (2005), 64, 69 underlines that other frontiers

The history of some of the failed rebellions shows not only that the princes were unable to effectively challenge imperial power but also reveals numerous connections at the local level.[68] It seems likely that such connections were the rule, even if princes happily respected the limitations decreed by their august relative. The position of princes under the tutelage of magistrates brings to mind the discussion on noble governors and robe intendants in France, now seen as complementary rather than as antagonistic.[69] The revision of the role of the princes de Condé, princes of the blood, courtiers and governors, long seen as the embodiment of 'domestication', is particularly interesting as a parallel.[70] Whatever results from this ongoing revision, it is clear that the extended group based on the ruler's lineage has some characteristics that can be compared to European nobilities. Louis XIV addressed nobles as 'mon cousin' and cherished the 'honnête familiarité' he enjoyed with his noble courtiers; the fictive kinship reflected in these formulas was real though very distant in Ming China.

Can the Ming imperial lineage be seen as an exception? Contemporaries complained that lesser princes under Ming rule were in a more difficult position than their predecessors under the Song, because they could not enter the key machinery of elite recruitment, the civil service examinations.[71] Hence they were quite limited in entering any career other than passively consuming state stipends and so were likely to lose prestige. The state, moreover, had to spend incredible sums on the maintenance of the imperial clan. While nobles in Europe enjoyed tax exemptions and other privileges, only the small ruling family would be supported

knew similar families; he criticises the standard view that such families had been 'domesticated' (p. 68: note the familiar terminology) under and after the Yongle emperor, stressing their persistence and post-1550 strengthening. See also Frederic Wakeman Jr., *The Great Enterprise. The Manchu Reconstruction of Imperial Order in Seventeenth-Century China* (Berkeley, Los Angeles, London: University of California Press, 1986), 23–86, Swope's 'Northern Frontier', e.g. on 39 citing the fear of a civil official who perceived the military clans as warlords in the making. My thanks go to Barend Noordam for these references as well as for other important comments.

68 David Robinson, "Princes in the Polity: The Anhua Prince's Uprising of 1510", *Ming Studies* 65 (2012).

69 On the French governors Robert R. Harding, *Anatomy of a Power Elite. The Provincial Governors of Early Modern France* (New Haven, London: Yale University Press, 1978) and Horowski, *Die Belagerung des Thrones*.

70 More particularly on the Condé, see Katia Béguin, "Louis XIV et l'aristocratie: coup de majesté ou retour à la tradition, " *Histoire, économie et société* 19, no. 4 (2000); Katia Béguin, *Les princes de Condé. Rebelles, courtisans et mécènes dans la France du grand siècle* (Paris: Champ Vallon, 1999); Christophe Blanquie, "Dans la main du Grand maître. Les offices de la maison du roi, 1643–1720, " *Histoire & Mesure* XIII 3–4 (1998); Swann, *Provincial Power and Absolute Monarchy*.

71 See Wang, *The Ming Prince and Daoism*, 10, mentioning changing attitudes at the Ming court in 1590, and the permission for the lower six ranks to enter the examinations in 1595.

structurally by the state. The lower echelons of nobility, moreover, clearly could not pretend to have any connection with the ruling dynasty. The lowest echelons of the imperial clan can be compared to French country nobles or *hobereaux* on the verge of poverty, yet forbidden by the laws on *dérogation* from engaging in trade or other non-noble pursuits. The association of the lowest princely echelons with the ruling emperor can hardly have increased dynastic prestige. Could this type of foliage, dense but decomposing, still embellish the dynastic trunk? The Qing dynasty rising to power in 1644 learned this lesson and tried to limit the inflation of numbers of the imperial lineage, which still seems to have expanded to more than 70,000 persons by 1915.[72] Qing rulers in many ways reversed Ming policies vis-à-vis the princes. Members of the *Aisin Gioro*, or the imperial lineage, were expected to reside in or around Beijing and were part and parcel of the Qing system of minority rule over Han China. Concentrated in the capital, supported as well as monitored by the dynastic leadership, they could rise to high rank in government and army, escaping the enforced leisure of the Ming princes. An element of merit was introduced into the ranking of Qing princes, and promotions as well as demotions were possible on the basis of their service record. In her impressive study of the Qing court, Evelyn S. Rawski concludes that 'Qing princes were transformed into pillars of the imperium, not its inevitable rivals'.[73]

Behind this reversal of policies, we can see a continuity of tensions and choices entirely relevant also for Ottoman and European settings. This most prestigious layer in the realm deserved honour but needed to be restricted in its potential for political manoeuvring. Numbers were relevant in terms of the budgetary pressure of stipends but also because of their implications for prestige and succession. A small number of potential successors can be expected to be highly prestigious as well as dangerously competitive, whereas huge numbers would no longer be able to maintain a plausible link with succession. As a consequence they tended to lose prestige and mix with the wider population. Finally, the concentration of princes either in the periphery or in the centre strikes the eye. Interestingly, in the Ottoman case residence in the provinces went together with active military and political roles, whereas in the Ming case, it came with enforced passivity. When around 1600 males from the House of Osman were relocated from the provinces to the Topkapı palace, they lost their active roles. Conversely, Qing imperial princes resident in Beijing took up active duties. The fact that the *Aisin Gioro* were the top echelon of a conquest clan, representing only a very small minority of the population, arguably made them more interdependent and coherent, and rebellion a less likely option.

Hereditary rank and nobility did not stop with the Qing imperial lineage itself. While the Qing carefully examined Ming failures in order to adapt their policies, they introduced a far stronger element of nobility into the Han Chinese setting.

---

[72] Evelyn S. Rawski, *The Last Emperors: A Social History of Qing Imperial Institutions* (Berkeley: University of California Press, 1998), 94.

[73] Rawski, *Last Emperors*, 96–126 (chapter on 'sibling policies'), quote on 126.

Military conquest was based upon a careful reinvention of tribal organisation, including Manchu, Mongol, and Chinese allies.[74] This 'eight banner system' formed the core of Qing power until the end of the dynasty. Around the imperial lineage or *Aisin Gioro* stood many important Manchu families. Emperors themselves sought their concubines, as well as the empress, from the ranks of the conquest elite. In addition, strategic alliances of princesses were concluded largely with Mongol grandees.[75] Together, these groups formed an endogamous hereditary semi-tribal layer ruling over Han China – a web of dynasties based on conquest. The nomadic Steppe background of many Asian dynasties, with its stress on collective sovereignty and rule by council, was evident at the beginning of Qing rule and returned in the later eighteenth century.

The Kangxi emperor (1654–1722 CE) not only ruled roughly in the age of Louis XIV (1643–1715 CE), but has often been pictured in the same terms, as the great consolidator and omnipotent ruler.[76] A somewhat closer look at this truly imposing figure shows that some of the problems experienced by Louis were familiar to those of Kangxi. He started his rule under the tutelage of a regency council dominated by Manchu grandees; in 1669 the ouster of these regents, orchestrated by his Mongol grandmother and other nobles at court, started his personal reign. Initially, Kangxi had to carefully manoeuvre around his key minister Songgotu,

[74] Mark C. Elliott, *The Manchu Way: The Eight Banners and Ethnic Identity in Manchu China* (Stanford: Stanford University Press, 2001); there is some resonance here with reinventions of tribal forms around the globe, for example the Safavid case, see e.g. S. Babaie, K. Babayan et al., *Slaves of the Shah. New Elites of Safavid Iran* (London, New York: I.B. Tauris, 2004).

[75] Evelyn Rawski, "Ch'ing Imperial Marriage and Problems of Rulership", in *Marriage and Inequality*, (eds) Watson and Ebrey; see also Shuo Wang, "Qing Imperial Women: Empresses, Concubines, and Aisin Gioro Daughters", in *Servants of the Dynasty. Palace Women in World History*, (ed.) Anne Walthall (Berkeley, Los Angeles: University of California Press, 2008); see also in a comparative perspective the study by Leslie Peirce on the Ottoman Harem, palace women, and intermarriage with the governing elite, *The Imperial Harem. Women and Sovereignty in the Ottoman Empire* (New York, Oxford: Oxford University Press, 1993). On palace women in China more generally see also Bao Hua Hsieh, "From Charwoman to Empress Dowager: Serving-Women in the Ming Palace", *Ming Studies* 42 (2000); various publications by Ellen F. Soullière on Ming Palace Women (including an unpublished 1987 Princeton dissertation, "Palace Women in the Ming Dynasty, 1368–1644"); Priscilla Ching Chung, *Palace Women in the Northern Sung 960–1126 (*Leiden: Brill, 1981).

[76] See the explicit comparison of 'two great rulers' in Joachim Bouvet, *Histoire de l'empereur de la Chine* (Paris 1697), 5, with Kangxi as 'Un prince, qui, comme vous, SIRE, joint à une genie aussi sublime que solide, un coeur encore plus digne de l'empire ; qui est maître de luy même comme de ses sujets, également adoré de ses peuples & respecté de ses voysins […] Un prince, en un mot, qui réunissant dans sa personne la pluspart des grandes qualitez, qui forment les heros, seroit le plus accompli Monarque, qui depuis longtemps ait regné sur la terre, si son regne ne concouroit point avec celui de votreMajesté.'

a Manchu grandee who had supported the coup against the regents.[77] In his later years, the perplexities of dynastic succession and the incompetence of some of his sons put Kangxi under severe pressure. Kangxi's bitter account of his reign, meant to be published to a wider public, was fundamentally changed by his officials, who upon his death turned this remarkably open and poignant testimony into a bland statement of power.[78] In the later eighteenth century towards the end of the reign of Kangxi's favourite grandson, the Qianlong emperor, a Manchu bannerman became the unchallenged favourite at court. While he assembled an immense fortune from the state coffers, there were increasing signs that central power was losing its grip over the provinces.[79]

Manchu and Mongol grandees were an important factor at court, in addition to – and possibly as a counterweight to – the traditional powers of Han Chinese administrators in the outer court ministries. The element of noble and hereditary power at court extended into the frontier provinces under the authority of a separate ministry for 'colonial affairs', the Lifanyuan. The Manchu, Mongol, Uyghur and Tibetan regions were never fitted entirely into the pattern of governance of China proper.[80] Frequent hunting expeditions north of the Great Wall brought together the emperor with Manchu and Mongol elites cultivating their prowess in riding and archery. Hereditary elites in the frontier areas retained their accepted roles. In these respects, Qing China left far more room for noble power than did Ming China, both at the core of the empire and in the periphery. It may be farfetched to compare this large-scale variant of composite monarchy with its European parallels, or the differently governed Chinese provinces with the diversified roles of the *pays d'états* and *pays d'élection* in early modern France. The parallel suggests, however, that it makes no sense to concentrate only on the conspicuous differences between dynastic power in Europe and Asia.

---

[77] I rely here on a presentation given by Michael Chang (George Mason University, Washington DC) "The Recruitment of Lower Yangzi (Jiangnan) Literati to the Kangxi Court, 1670s-1690s" during a conference at Leiden: Servants and administrators: From the court to the provinces, 31 August – 2 September 2011.

[78] Jonathan Spence, *Emperor of China. Self-portrait of Kang-Hsi* (New York: Knopf, 1974) prints both versions.

[79] See Yingcong Dai, "Broken Passage to the Summit: Nayancheng's Botched Mission in the White Lotus War", in *Agents and Interactions. The Dynastic Centre and the Provinces*, (eds) Jeroen Duindam and Sabine Dabringhaus (Leiden, Boston: Brill, 2014) who stresses the role of favourites at the Qing court even before the later Qianlong era, and the changes in the early Jiaqing period.

[80] See e.g. Nicola di Cosmo, "Qing Colonial Administration in Inner Asia", *International History Review* 20, no. 2 (1998).

Epilogue

My tentative remarks confirm that the limitations in communication and the strength of kinship ties provide a general background for the role of elites throughout pre-modern history. China is exceptional because from the Song onwards, a state-controlled mechanism, the civil service examinations, became the foremost factor in the formation of elites. After the Yuan interlude, the examinations regained this position, to lose it only in the final years of Qing rule. Europe appears to be an exception in the increasing role of genealogy in elite legitimation from the later Middle Ages onwards. These processes, stressing merit on one side, birth on the other, need to be put into perspective.

Patrilineal descent was a powerful focus of identity and cohesion both in Europe and in China. Genealogy was important for imperial clans and local lineages as well as for ruling houses and 'noble' dynasties throughout Europe. Heredity in status as well as in office was stronger in Europe than in China – although the difference may have been more outspoken in legitimation than it was in practice. Arguably, both in China and in Europe, wealth obtained through commerce became an increasingly important vehicle of entry into the lower echelons of the elite. There is a clear convergence in another respect. From the Song onwards and from the European later Middle Ages onwards, the central state gradually increased its control over promotion to high elite status, whether defined as high office in the imperial bureaucracy or as high noble rank. Wealth assisted individuals to ascend the ladder of success, but outside of the institutions of the dynastic state, the highest rewards were unavailable. Kinship structures and patrilineal identity, both in China and Europe, formed one element only in an active discourse between local elites and the state: kinship served as a repertoire of arguments and tactics rather than as a rigid rulebook. Elite continuity was strong both in Europe and in China; continuity at the 'personnel' level was stronger in China than used to be taken for granted; conversely, in Europe the dictate of genealogy and heredity left more room for social mobility than was long accepted. Social mobility must have been stronger in turbulent phases than in longs periods of relative order – but this will be a general rule.

The Chinese imperial clan, a conspicuously dynastic and hereditary structure in a social setting stressing fluidity, matches at the top European royal families – showing all the expected tensions between rulers, sons, brothers and uncles, and between the main line and lateral agnatic lines. The more distant members of the Ming imperial clan, starting out as a markedly military elite, were gradually reduced to a prestigious caste living on state coffers without formally fulfilling any active roles other than the ritual representation of their imperial clan status. The role of these princes in their fiefs is currently a focus of research, related to strengthening study of regions and regional sources. The reconfiguration of princely power under the Qing, creating an intricate setup of checks and balances including inner–outer court rivalry, Han-Manchu tensions, the inner court position of empresses, consorts and eunuchs, has been impressively analysed by Evelyn

S. Rawski. The almost too perfect machinery of calculated checks and balances she uncovers raises another question. The succession of the three formidable 'High Qing' emperors, each uncommonly talented and hardworking, tends to confirm an impression of supreme power that in practice may have been more susceptible to a variety of tensions, threats and anxieties. The most effective contemporaneous European rulers had to chart their way through territories they could not easily oversee, depending on the advice and support of numerous figures around them, seen and unseen, formal and informal. Louis XIV warned his son that advice rarely was disinterested, stressing that the closest proximates of the ruler as well as his most trusted advisers were often quick to profit from any weaknesses.[81] Rulers with exceedingly long reigns, such as Leopold I (1658–1705) and Louis XIV (1651–1715), both contemporaries of the Kangxi emperor, were effectively in control only during a part of their long lives, a pattern that seems to match the predicament of the Kangxi emperor and his grandson the Qianlong emperor. Regional sources have helped to reassess views of local elites in China and in Europe; numerous court records in Europe have indicated the vulnerability even of strong rulers and the fragility of order at court. Can similar materials be located in the records of the Chinese court? If so, will they help to our push our understanding of imperial power in China beyond the idealised images of the veritable records, and beyond the easy labelling of rulers as good or bad, strong or weak? Alternatively do we need to accept that such revisions, pertinent for Europe, have little relevance for the Chinese case? I would suspect that on the basis of different sources, a less exalted and more human view even of the most conspicuously successful Chinese emperors would become possible.

---

[81] *Mémoires de Louis XIV*, (ed.) Dreyss, 2: 404; see many parallel passages on the lack of disinterested advice among courtiers and ministers. A new edition of the memoirs is available, Joël Cornette ed., *Mémoires, suivis de Manière de montrer les jardins de Versailles* (Paris: Tallandier, 2007); compare the wary attitude of Charles V as reflected in his advice to his son and heir Philip in Armin Kohnle (ed.), *Das Vermächtnis Kaiser Karls V. Die Politische Testamente* (Darmstadt: Wissenschaftliche Buchgesellschaft, 2005).

PART II
Identity Formation and Family Relations

Chapter 4
The Chièvres Legacy, the Croÿ Family and Litigation in Paris. Dynastic Identities between the Low Countries and France (1519–1559)

Violet Soen

Guillaume de Croÿ, Lord of Chièvres, passed away at the renowned Diet of Worms in 1521. The marriage of this chief councillor to Emperor Charles V had remained childless. In early modern noble families, this generally proved to be a good guarantee for endless legal proceedings on inheritance.[1] In the case of Chièvres, the dispute on his legacy would end up even more hazardous than usual. About two years before his death, the Habsburg advisor had purchased and received a significant series of lands in the enemy Kingdom of France. These lordships were scattered over regions as varied as Champagne, Normandy, Gascony and Languedoc. The other contractor in this noteworthy deal was none other than Germaine de Foix, then widow of the King of Aragon. Sixty years later, this particular heritage of French lordships by the Croÿ family still caused legal proceedings before the Parliament of Paris. In one of the many state-of-affairs made at that occasion, a councillor remarked that Chièvres himself probably thought to have acquired '*deux belles et notables acquisitions … de fait toutes ces terres sont de grande et immense valeur, mais le malheur a voulu qu'en lieu de terres, il acquist des procès a lui et a sa posterité*' [two beautiful and noteworthy acquisitions … In fact, all of this land is of great and immense value, but unfortunately, instead of land, he acquired troubles for himself and for his posterity].[2] The observer might not have foreseen that legal actions in Paris would continue for almost another 80 years, as the lawsuits constantly followed the tide of the wars between the rulers of France and the Low Countries. Meanwhile, members of the Croÿ family and their noble opponents used their loyalties to the respective rulers in order to force the heritage claims to their benefit. As such, not only war, but litigation as well, provided a locus for identity formation of noble families.

---

1 Michel Nassiet, *Parenté, noblesse et états dynastiques XVe-XVIe siècles* (Paris: Ecole des hautes études en sciences sociales, 2000), 24.

2 *Mémoire sur tout l'ensemble du procès, concluant aux revendications précédentes*, 1581: Archives Nationales Série J (henceforth ANF J) 768 52/13.

Hence, through the lens of litigation, this chapter seeks to unravel the impact of geographical anchorage and territorial war on identity formation among noble dynasties in Early Modern Europe. In the Ancien Régime, 'the nobility' was continuously shaped and reshaped around lordships (and accordingly, a *savoir-vivre noblement*[3]), but what happened when these lordships were located in areas where the rulers were at war? For too long, the early modern nobility has been studied within one state and within the borders of that state.[4] Yet early modern grandees often owned possessions spread across political borders, as was apparently the case of Chièvres's legacy. So members of the House of Croÿ have been linked too exclusively to the Burgundian-Habsburg state formation, through which they indeed received many outstanding offices, titles and honours.[5] Still,

---

3 Violet Soen, "Nobility", in *Oxford Bibliographies in Renaissance and Reformation,* (ed) Margaret King, (New York: Oxford University Press), online since January 2015, DOI: 10.1093/OBO/9780195399301-028; Robert Descimon, "*Nobles de lignage* et *Noblesse de service*. Sociogenèses comparées de l'épée et de la robe (XVe-XVIIIe siècle)", in *Épreuves de noblesse. Les expériences nobiliaires de la haute robe parisienne (XVIe-XVIIIe siècle)*, (eds) Robert Descimon and Élie Haddad (Paris: Les Belles lettres, 2010), 279–287; Élie Haddad, "La 'maison' noble: pistes de recherches concernant les contraintes de la transmission dans la noblesse française des XVIe et XVIe siècles", in *Mobilité et transmission dans les sociétés de l'Europe moderne,* (eds) Anna Bellavitis, Laurence Croq and Monica Martinat (Rennes: Presses Universitaires de Rennes, 2009); Paul Janssens was guest editor for a thematic issue on 'Vivre Noblement. The Changing Lifestyle of the Belgian Nobility' of the *Revue belge d'Histoire et de Philologie* 88, no.2 (2010); Jelle Haemers, Wim De Clercq and Jan Dumolyn, "Sumptuary Legislation, Material Culture and the Semiotics of 'Vivre Noblement' in the County of Flanders (14th – 16th centuries)", *Social History* 36 (2011).

4 Rees Davis, "The Medieval State: The Tyranny of a Concept?" *Journal of Historical Sociology* 16 (2003); for the historiography of the nobility in the late medieval and early modern Low Countries: Frederik Buylaert and Jan Dumolyn, "L'importance sociale, politique et culturelle de la haute noblesse dans les Pays-Bas Bourguignons et Habsbourgeois (1475–1525): un état de la question", in *Entre la ville, la noblesse et l'état: Philippe de Clèves (1456–1528), homme politique et bibliophile*, (eds) Jelle Haemers, Céline Van Hoorebeeck and Hanno Wijsman (Turnhout: Brepols, 2008); Thérèse de Hemptinne and Jan Dumolyn, "Historisch adelsonderzoek over de late middeleeuwen en de vroegmoderne periode in België en Nederland: een momentopname", *Bijdragen en Mededelingen betreffende de Geschiedenis der Nederlanden* 103 (2008).

5 Marie-Rose Thielemans, "Les Croy, conseillers des ducs de Bourgogne. Documents extraits de leurs archives familiales, 1357–1487", *Bulletin de la Commission Royale d'Histoire* 124 (1959); Robert Born, *Les Croÿ, une grande lignée hennuyère d'hommes de guerre, de diplomates, de conseillers secrets, dans les coulisses du pouvoir, sous les ducs de Bourgogne et la Maison d'Autriche (1390–1612)* (Brussels: Editeurs d'art associés, 1981) and George Martin, *Histoire et généalogie de la maison de Croÿ* (Lyon 2001: s.n.,1981[1]), both to be consulted with caution; Jan Roegiers et al. (eds), *Arenberg in de Lage Landen. Een hoogadellijk huis in Vlaanderen & Nederland* (Louvain: Universitaire Pers, 2002) situates the history of the Croÿ within the larger history of the House of Arenberg; see now

throughout the sixteenth century, the family tried to manage estates in the Low Countries and France alike, despite the enduring conflicts between Habsburg and Valois. This could expose them to accusations of treason and lese-majesty on both sides of the border, so that confiscation and litigation were always to be expected. Whereas the larger dynastic transregional identity of the family inspired the line of action of the individuals concerned, claims of loyalty and service towards each prince had to be pursued with great care at every occasion, and especially in lawsuits.[6]

As Jonathan Spangler has remarked on an earlier occasion, some early modern transregional families simply defied state formation by their functioning across states and borders alike, while they also contributed to sustaining state power by accumulating offices in border provinces. At that same time, Spangler cited the House of Croÿ as being one of those pan-European 'families in between', demonstrating how in politics, religion and war, family members could choose opposite sides, while simultaneously reiterating the dynastic identity of being a transregional family that was 'hedging the bets'.[7] This chapter observes this apparent conundrum within the juridical sphere. More specifically, it examines the legal proceedings concerning the abovementioned French properties within the Chièvres legacy. As such, it focuses on the area of tension between France and the Low Countries (omitting undeservedly the Holy Roman Empire). The story will be unravelled in three sections. The first will outline how in 1519 the Habsburg councillor Chièvres embodied the dynastic identity of his family by purchasing

---

Violet Soen and Hans Cools, "L'aristocratie transrégionale et les frontières: les processus d'identification politique dans les maison de Luxembourg-Saint-Pol et de Croÿ (1470-1530)" in *L'identité au pluriel. Jeux et enjeux des appartenances autour des anciens Pays-Bas, XIV*[e]*-XVIII*[e] *siècles. Identity and Identities. Belonging at Stake in the Low Countries 14th-18th Centuries,* (eds.) Violet Soen, Yves Junot and Florian Mariage (Villeneuve d'Ascq: Revue du Nord, Hors série, collection Histoire 30), 2014, 209-28.

6 David Potter, "A Treason Trial in Sixteenth-Century France: the Fall of Marshal du Biez, 1549–1551", *English Historical Review* 105 (1990); Simon Hodson, "Politics of the Frontier: Henri IV, the Maréchal-Duc de Bouillon and the Sovereignty of Sedan", *French History* 19 (2005); Kathryn Edwards, *Families and Frontiers. Recreating Communities and Boundaries in the Early Modern Burgundies* (Leiden: Brill, 2002); cf. our project's website www.transregionalhistory.eu.

7 Jonathan Spangler, "Those in Between: Princely Families on the Margins of the Great Powers – The Franco-German Frontier, 1477–1830", in *Transregional and Transnational Families in Europe and Beyond: Experiences since the Middle Ages*, (eds) Christopher H. Johnson, David Warren Sabean, Simon Teuscher and Francesca Trivellato (New York/ Oxford: Berghahn Books, 2011); see also the introduction by the editors and Charles Lipp, "Being Noble in the Borderlands: The Family de Mahuet of Lorraine, 1599–1737", *Proceedings of the Western Society for French History* 29 (2001), 75. A methodological plea to use the term 'transnational history' for the early modern period is provided by Bartolomé Yun Casalilla, "Localism, Global History and Transnational History. A Reflection from the Historian of Early Modern Europe", *Historisk Tidskrift* 127 (2007).

lands in France, and particularly in the province of Champagne. In the second section, it will become clear how the Foix family intentionally challenged the dynastic transregional identity of the Croÿs until the Peace of Cambrai in 1529. The third section will finally reveal how members of the Croÿ clan eventually used litigation in Paris to reconfigure their transregional identity within the House itself. Even so, as mentioned, these episodes running up to the Peace of Le Cateau-Cambrésis in 1559 present only a distinct part of a much larger story, as the lawsuits over the Chièvres legacy continued well into the seventeenth century.[8]

Chièvres in Champagne

Chièvres has gained fame as close councillor to Charles V, which makes it somehow redundant to point out that he was foremost a wealthy aristocrat.[9] At his birth in 1458, though, he was not particularly favoured, being born only as the second son of Philippe de Croÿ and Jacqueline de Luxembourg. Nevertheless, Chièvres did rather well due to the rather common practice of organising and reorganising patrimony among children and siblings, which will be the connecting thread in this story as well.[10] By 1485, the nobleman managed to buy from his father the important lordships of Beaumont and Chièvres in Hainaut, a region where the Croÿ clan had thrived as a very active land purchaser. About a decade later, he received the lordships of Heverlee and Aarschot in Brabant as an advance on his

[8] In fact, indirect information about the sixteenth century can be found in later documents: *Mémoire pour prouver que le roi Henri IV et la maison de Navarre n'ont aucun droit sur les biens provenant de Germaine de Foix, reine d'Aragon, et vendus en 1519 à Guillaume de Croy, seigneur de Chièvres*: Bibliothèque Nationale de France (henceforth BNF) Ms. Fr. 2910 fol. 113; *Pour montrer que le roi ne peut, sous correction, prétendre aucun droit de propriété à Beaufort, Colommiers ... et autres terres qui furent acquises par le sieur de Chièvres de la reine Germaine de Foix. (Pour Pierre Courtillier, demandeur, cousin germain maternel des derniers acquéreurs)*, Paris, 1662, sine nome: BNF FOL-FM-4275; *Eclaircissement du bon droit de messire Philippe Croy-Chimay d'Aremberg, prince ... dudit Chimay, et réfutation des poursuites injustes et imaginaires que font contre lui le sieur de Bercy-Màlon, ... et le sieur René d'Espinoy-Louny,* Paris, 1669, sine nome: BNF FOL-FM-4275 (1). When not cited otherwise, information was deducted from a critical evaluation of these sources.

[9] Guillaume de Croÿ, lord of Chièvres (1458–27/28 May 1521): Georges Dansaert and Thierry de Limburg-Stirum, *Guillaume de Croÿ-Chièvres* (Kortrijk: J. Vermaut, 1942), to be supplemented with the more recent biographical entry in Hans Cools, *Mannen met Macht. Edellieden en de Moderne Staat in de Bourgondisch-Habsburgse landen (1475–1530)* (Zutphen: Walburg, 2001), 200–201.

[10] See the already mentioned study by Michel Nassiet, more recently described for the late medieval County of Flanders by Frederik Buylaert, *Eeuwen van ambitie. De adel in laatmiddeleeuws Vlaanderen* (Brussels: Paleis der Academiën, 2010), 61–4.

share of the legacy among the siblings.[11] So Chièvres obtained, with the lands of Aarschot, one of the *banyeryen* of the duchy of Brabant, which were prestigious lordships that included the rights of high justice and coinage, and foremost enough income to finance private militias and a luxurious lifestyle.[12] As such, Chièvres could easily prosper in Hainaut and Brabant alike. Through his marriage with Marie de Hamal, he then also enjoyed the usufruct of the patrimony in the prince-bishopric of Liège held by her first husband. Finally, for his tutoring of the young prince Charles, he received the duchies of Soria and Archi and the barony of Roccacitta, all in Naples, in 1516. So within one life and career, Chièvres not only managed to adopt a supra-provincial 'Burgundian outlook', as coined by Hans Cools, but also a more imperial one, as conceived by Bartolomé Yun-Casalilla and others.[13] At first glance, his noble identity seemed in tune with the emergence of more delineated composite monarchies at the beginning of the sixteenth century.

What has gone largely unnoticed in traditional historiography, then, is that these wealthy aristocrats easily purchased lands outside the sphere of influence of their rulers. At the age of 61, Chièvres obtained an impressive series of lands in France. First, on 27 July 1519, he bought the county of Beaufort (with the properties of Soulaines and Larzicourt, the viscounty of Saint-Florentin, and the *châtellenies* of Dannemoine and Villers and so forth) in Champagne and the barony of Saint-Pierre de Rudepont in Normandy. He obtained these lands through a *contrat de vendition* [vendition contract] with the already mentioned Germaine de Foix.[14] Moreover, one day later, he received from her the baronies of Coulommiers in Brie-Champagne, Haulterive in Languedoc and Aspet in Gascony, amid many other lands and dependencies. In this instance, Chièvres was the beneficiary of a *contrat de donation* [gift contract] from Germaine de Foix. For many reasons, the double transaction was remarkable, not only because it consisted of a considerable gift, but also because 50,000 ducats of the purchase price of 125,000 ducats were discharged as another donation. Rumours that the rogue Chièvres had forced the widow-queen to these transactions never disappeared. It is more likely that Charles V had a hand in this deal with his step-grandmother, in return for his interventions to wed her to Marquis Johann of Brandenburg. So, comparable to what Frederik Buylaert recently concluded after looking into the marriage patterns of the late

---

11 Cools, *Mannen met macht,* 200.

12 Mario Damen, "Heren met banieren. De baanrotsen van Brabant in de vijftiende eeuw", in *Bourgondië voorbij. De Nederlanden 1250–1650,* (eds) Mario Damen and Louis Sicking (Hilversum: Verloren, 2010).

13 Bartolomé Yun Casalilla, "Introducción. Entre el imperio colonial y la monarquía compuesta. Élites y territorios en la Monarquía Hispánica (ss. XVI y XVII)", in *Las redes del Imperio. Élites sociales en la articulación de la Monarquía Hispánica, 1492–1714,* (ed.) idem (Madrid: Marcial Pons, 2009).

14 *Contrat de vente par Germaine de Foix, veuve du roi Ferdinand le Catholique, et Jean, marquis de Brandebourg, actuellement son époux (seconde noce), à Guillaume de Croÿ, marquis d'Aerschot, seigneur de Chièvres*, 27 July 1519, Copie coll. en Parlement le 5 août 1550: ANF J 768 52/12.

medieval Flemish nobility, grand aristocrats in the Low Countries easily looked outside the Habsburg-Burgundian territories.[15] Moreover, at this juncture, the Habsburg connection even seemed to have facilitated this purchase in the adjacent territory. This was less of a puzzle in the sixteenth century than historiography often seems to hint at.

Actually, Chièvres was acting in line with the dynastic identity of his family, originating from Picardy, a rather loose term for the region around the city of Amiens and considered as *terre de frontière* [borderland]. The noble house of Croÿ took its name after Crouy-Saint-Pierre there, a lordship on the left bank of the Somme, northwest of Picquigny. As such, every genealogy of the family would claim an ancient ancestry from the King of Hungary, as well as a more immediate one from Picardy.[16] Primogenitor Jean de Croÿ had been governor there, before dying heroically at the Battle of Agincourt in 1415. Ever since then, the family had an *hôtel* in Amiens, which served its repeated governmental shares in the region. Gradually, the Croÿ family adhered to the category of Picardian nobles that Werner Paravicini identified as the aristocratic pillars of the Burgundian dynasty in the second half of the fifteenth century.[17] Hans Cools and Mario Damen also unravelled how these kind of Picardian nobles held a relatively greater share of functions and titles at the Burgundian-Habsburg court.[18] The Burgundian-Habsburg dynasty needed noblemen from the frontier, in order to defend, control and extend it. But it is precisely this that ended up being the complicating factor: the King of France obviously thought exactly the same. In this perspective, David Potter showed how Picardian noblemen were attracted by inducements from both the French King and the Burgundian-Habsburg rulers, and how families could be suddenly split in their loyalties as a consequence, or conversely, combine multiple loyalties without problems.[19] The Croÿ family was no exception to this rule of multiple loyalties within a family. With permission from the Dukes of Burgundy

[15] Frederik Buylaert, "La noblesse et l'unification des Pays-Bas. Naissance d'une noblesse bourguignonne à la fin du Moyen Âge?" *Revue historique* 653 (2010).

[16] For example, Jean Scohier, *La généalogie et descente de la très illustre maison de Croÿ* (Douai, Jean Bogard, 1596; anastatic reprint Brussels, 1996).

[17] Werner Paravicini, "Moers, Croy, Burgund. Eine Studie über den Niedergang des Hauses Moers in den zweiten Hälfte des 15. Jahrhunderts", *Annalen des Historischen Vereins für den Niederrhein* 179 (1978).

[18] Hans Cools, "Noblemen on the Borderline: the Nobility of Picardy, Artois and Walloon Flanders and the Habsburg-Valois Conflict, 1477–1529", in *Secretum Scriptorum. Liber alumnorum Walter Prevenier*, (eds.) Wim Blockmans, Marc Boone and Thérèse de Hemptinne (Louvain and Apeldoorn: Garant, 1999); Mario Damen, "Rivalité nobiliaire et succession princière: La lutte pour le pouvoir à la cour de Bavière et à la cour de Bourgogne", *Revue du Nord* 91 (2009). For the Dutch Revolt, see: *Het verdeelde huis: De Nederlandse adel tussen opstand en reconciliatie,* (eds) Luc Duerloo and Liesbeth De Frenne (Maastricht: Shaker, 2011).

[19] David Potter, *War and Government in the French Provinces, Picardy 1470–1560* (Cambridge: Cambridge University Press, 1993), 47–8.

and the Emperor, Chièvres joined the French King Charles VIII in 1494 in his campaign against Naples and he accompanied Louis XII against Milan in 1499.

Given this Picardian background – both real and imagined within the lineage – it might come as a surprise that Chièvres also purchased properties in the adjacent region of Champagne in 1519: the sale primarily included the county of Beaufort and the gift of the barony of Coulommiers in Brie. Yet by the beginning of the sixteenth century, the Croÿ family had been slightly more present in Champagne than in Picardy, where it had lost some of its lands in the wars between Charles the Bold and Louis XI. In Champagne, the House held lands in Tours-sur-Marne, Gandelu, Beaurain and Bar-sur-Aube. In addition, the impressive lordship of Château-Porcien, situated on the Aisne River at the border of the Rethelois, was by far their most important seigniorial estate in the province of Champagne. In the High Middle Ages, it provided one of the seven *pairs* of the Counts of Champagne. Chièvres's grandfather, Antoine le Grand, bought it in 1437–1438; later on he also acquired the adjacent lordship of Montcornet.[20] Less than 20 years later, the lordship was elevated to county by King Charles VII.[21] The castle served as a refuge when Antoine was expelled from the Burgundian court for his francophilia. Although later accepted back into the Burgundian good graces, Antoine preferred to be buried in the chapel of Château-Porcien (which after all provided his highest title). Chièvres's father had also taken refuge there, later on widely refurbishing the castle; he would be buried there too. Within this family context, it is thus less surprising that Chièvres chose territories close to the family patrimony in which his grandfather and father had taken such pride. Still, where Château-Porcien, and especially Montcornet, were lordships on the unstable border between France and the Burgundian-Habsburg territories, this was no longer the case for Beaufort and Coulommiers. As an ambassador of Spain would remark much later: '*Et fait a penser que les terres dont est question sont assizes au milieu du Royaulme de France et ne sont poinct limitrophes*' [And leads one to think that the lands in question are established in the middle of the Kingdom of France and do not touch borders].[22]

20 Antoine de Croÿ (ca. 1402–1475): Albert Châtelet, "Antoine de Croÿ et Hugo van der Goes", in *Der Fall des Günstlings. Hofparteien in Europa vom 13. Bis zum 17. Jahrhundert*, (eds) Jan Hirschbiegel and Werner Paravicini (Stuttgart: Thorbecke, 2004); Paul de Win, "Antoine de Croy, seigneur de Crouy, comte de Porcien", in *Les chevaliers de l'Ordre de la Toison d'or au XVe siècles. Notice bio-bibliographique*, (ed.) Ralph De Smedt (Frankfurt am Main: Peter Lang, 2000), 34–6 and Violet Soen, "La Causa Croÿ et les limites du mythe bourguignon: la frontière, le lignage et la mémoire (1465-1475)" in *Mémoires conflictuelles et mythes concurrents dans les pays bourguignons (ca. 1380-1580),* (eds) Jean-Marie Cauchies and Petit Peporte (Neuchâtel: Publications du Centre d'études bourguignonnes, 2012), 81-97.

21 Jean-Baptiste Lépine, *Histoire de Château-Portien (Ardennes)* (Vouziers: s.n., 1858), 155–60 (facsimile reprint Paris, 1989).

22 *Protestation de l'ambassadeur d'Espagne auprès du roi contre l'appui que celui-ci donne aux revendications du duc et de la duchesse de Guise, au mépris des traités conclus,*

Even if his new lands were purchased at the end of his life, Chièvres seemed to have been particularly concerned about a good destiny for them. Whereas he had originally bequeathed all his properties to his nephew Philippe II de Croÿ, the new Count of Château-Porcien,[23] he changed his opinion some days before his death in his last testament in Worms, dated 21 May 1521. Chièvres then stipulated that only half of the lands acquired from Germaine de Foix would go to his *heritier universel* [universal heir]. The other half of these lands 'situated in the Kingdom of France' would go to his youngest nephew Charles de Croÿ. This new stipulation was remarkable to say the least. Most probably, Chièvres came to this decision as this nephew was already 'currently residing in France'.[24] Charles de Croÿ had indeed continued living in Montcornet after the death of his father in 1514, while his elder brothers had all taken up functions and titles in the Burgundian Low Countries. The legacy of half of the lands that Chièvres acquired *par don et achat* [by gift and purchase] could thus provide a comfortable position for the young Charles in France, as he was not the privileged first-born out of eight children. At the same time, it was a variation in the dynastic theme of reorganising and maintaining property on both sides of the borders, by spreading the risks and bets among different family members. As such, Chièvres's testament stipulated how the family would continue within its dynastic identity of being a transregional family, with a special relevance for the borderlands between France and the Low Countries in Hainaut, Picardy and Champagne alike.[25]

Croÿ versus Foix

Immediately, Chièvres's transactions and his testament were challenged by the Foix clan, eager to regain territories once belonging to their lineage. More captivating though in this legal dispute, is that the dynastic and transregional identity of the Croÿ was clearly challenged. Thomas de Foix, Lord of Lescun, instantly protested Chièvres's gift and purchase. As a collateral relative of Germaine de Foix's, he insisted on claiming the grounds by *retrait lignager* [the heir's preferential right of purchase], which was the customary civil law procedure enabling family members in the closest lines to claim the lands by paying the due price. The Marshal of France alleged that those important lands across France should remain in the hands of nobles who unquestionably served the French king, not in the hands of those serving other rulers. Lescun must have had an impact on his king (if not, his sister

s.d.: ANF J 768 52/9.

[23] Philippe II de Croÿ, Marquis and first Duke of Aarschot (1496–1549): Michel Baelde, *De collaterale raden onder Karel V en Filips II (1531–1578). Bijdrage tot de geschiedenis van de centrale instellingen in de zestiende eeuw* (Brussels: Paleis der Academiën, 1965), 252; Cools, *Mannen met macht,* 196–97.

[24] '*à présent résident en France*': Dansaert and de Limburg-Stirum, *Chièvres,* 291.

[25] Spangler, "Princely Families", 134.

had one as the royal mistress). He soon received the then confiscated lands that Chièvres had obtained from Germaine de Foix, yet without any definitive property rights. For the Croÿs, this was a novel situation. Previously, their multiple loyalties had exposed them to confiscation in times of war, but this was the first time that standard inheritance turned into sequestration, and its impact on the transregional identity of the Croÿs remained to be seen.[26]

In any case, during the renewed Franco-Habsburg War at the end of 1521 onwards, all the lands of the Croÿ were being confiscated, along the more traditional schemes of forcing the enemy's hand. Indeed, as bailiff of Hainaut, Aarschot tried to keep the French army out of Valenciennes and Tournai. As a consequence, both brothers Croÿ seemed not only to have had problems enjoying the lands that they were bequeathed by their uncle, but also those bequeathed by their parents, such as Château-Porcien and Montcornet.[27] As before, peace treaties eventually offered the opportunity to negotiate the mutual release of these confiscations. For Philippe de Croÿ, the new Count of Château-Porcien and Marquis of Aarschot, the death of Lescun in Pavia in 1525 and the subsequent capture of Francis I in Madrid provided welcome incentives to sort things out. He was successful in getting the Emperor to defend his rights and properties in France. According to the 38th article of the Treaty of Madrid of 14 January 1526, Aarschot would henceforth be 'reintegrated and restituted, including all of its counties, baronies, land and seigniories, to the Kingdom of France', so both those inherited from his parents and those inherited from his uncle. The treaty could have been the end of the affair, formally reiterating that the Croÿ family held properties across borders and that this should be respected by both rulers.[28]

---

[26] *Transaction et achapt faict de la conté de Beaufort. Pour Mrs de Lautrec*, 07/08/1529: BNF Ms. Fr. 4651 fol. 24–28, reveals part of the litigation before in the form of the introduction 'Sur le differend qui s'est mehu et offert en proceddant par nous au traicté de la paix en la ville de Cambray, en ce present moys de juilhet 1529, entre messire Philippes de Croy, duc de Sorre et d'Arcy, marquis d'Arset, d'une part, et messire Jehan de Laval, chevalier, baron de Chasteaubriant, et messire Menault de Martory, evesque de Conserans, tuteurs et curateurs des enffans myneurs d'ans de feu messire Odet de Foix, en son vivant seigneur de Laultret, d'aultre part, touchant les terres acquises par le feu seigneur de Chevres de Mme Germayne de Foix, royne douairiere d'Arragon, situées au royaulme de France ... '.

[27] Is to be deducted from the negotiation for the peace Treaty of Madrid in 1526. See also the ensuing *Requête au roi par le duc d'Aerschot, comte de Porcien, pour obtenir l'abréviation des procédures qui doivent suivre la mainlevée de la saisie faite sur son dit comté, faute d'aveu et dénombrement, foi et hommage*: ANF J 768 45/4 holds a whole series of documents on this procedure, which are not dated but cover a later period 1530–1533.

[28] 'reintegré et restitué en toutes ses contes, baronnies, terres et seigneuries estans au royaulme de France', also the Chièvres' legacy and the Lescun plea is mentioned: Treaty of Madrid, 14 January 1526, in *Corps universel diplomatique ...* , (ed.) Henri Dumont (Amsterdam 1739), vol. 4, t. 1, 408.

However, theory differed from practice. Upon the release of Francis I, Aarschot sent envoys to Paris in order to have the treaty implemented. In the capital, they were to find out that the King did not show any willingness to execute the stipulations of the treaty regarding the Croÿ property. The treaty itself soon became highly precarious when Pope Clement VII gave the King of France permission not to comply with the treaty by March 1526 since it had been signed 'under coercion'. As such, the king felt that he was not bound by the treaty whatsoever, by either its general terms or its particular provisions. Instead, Francis I maintained a *saisie féodale* [feudal seizure] of the Croÿ lands. This time, the confiscation was in favour of the dead Lescun's brother, Odet de Foix, Viscount of Lautrec and replacement for his brother as Marshal of France. Nevertheless, Aarschot remained backed by the emperor in order to pursue his claims against Lautrec now. The emperor sent his viceroy of Naples, Charles de Lannoy, and his secretary, Jean Lallemand, to urge for the implementation of the peace treaty, albeit to no avail.[29] Lautrec maintained the incomes from the lands, but he caught an infection during the French military campaigns in Italy and died on 15 August 1528. As such, the Treaty of Madrid remained a dead letter, and the Croÿ brothers encountered further obstructions to their enjoyment of their land and income in France.

Hence, in 1528, Aarschot decided as head of the House to reorganise the lands of his lineage.[30] As mentioned, this was standard procedure within the lineage, but this time the incentive was most probably provided by the multiplying problems with the Chièvres legacy and other lordships in France. A new *partage* [division] was thus concluded in Beaumont, the main family castle in Hainaut, which served as Aarschot's residence when carrying out his tasks as bailiff of the region. The outcome of this division was surprising to say the least: Aarschot had now obtained all the lands of Chièvres's transactions with Germaine de Foix, although his uncle had left half of it to the younger Charles in his last testament. In return for this loss, Charles received the County of Seninghem in Artois and the barony of Montcornet, part of the County of Porcien, and *limitrophe & sises sur les limites & frontières du Royaume* [on the limits and borders of the kingdom].[31] Once more, this division did not take place without accompanying rumours. Some thought that the younger Charles had been forced into a disadvantageous settlement by his brother, while others believed that he indeed preferred to have Seninghem and

---

[29] Cf. footnote 27.

[30] In fact, also Robert de Croÿ, bishop of Cambrai was included in this division of patrimony. So far, I have not been able to reconstruct his part of the deal.

[31] *Factum. Pour Madame la Duchesse de Guyse ayont les droitcts cedez de defunct monsieur le Prince de Portien son premier mary, demanderesse au principe & defenderesse à l'entherinement d'unes lettres royaux de rescision, d'une part contre Messire Philippes de Croy Duc d'Ascot defendeur au principal & demandeur à l'entherinement desdictes lettres Royaux de rescision, d'autre*, s.d.: BNF 4-FM-14869; other typeprint kept under BNF 4-FM-14870.

Montcornet right away, instead of waiting until the Foix stopped litigating and he could enjoy the income of the lands bequeathed in the testament. In any case, Charles now held the title of Count in Artois, while being able to continue to reside in Montcornet in France.

Additionally, the reorganisation left Aarschot free to decide upon the Chièvres legacy in France, without interference from his younger brother. Again, the ongoing peace negotiations between the Habsburg and Valois dynasty for the Treaty of Cambrai in 1529 provided the context for making more definitive settlements. So the mediating ladies not only decided on matters of bilateral peace, but also on the continuing conflict between Aarschot and the tutors of Lautrec's children. The bottom line of the settlement was that the noblemen could not let 'suffer so many nations and persons', and that a *paix universelle* [universal peace] was also to the benefit of '*deux grandes maisons commes celles de Croy et de Lautrec*' [two great houses such as those of de Croÿ and Lautrec]. So prior to the general peace treaty, Aarschot agreed to sell the lands to the Lautrec family, but at the goodly price of 60,000 gold écus (which could be paid in shares).[32] According to some observers, Aarschot had preferred this settlement, knowing that he had chosen to side with the Emperor anyway. Others alleged that he felt forced by the fact that he had not been able to pay the sums for the *relief* of the lands. Maybe the transaction was facilitated by a probable marriage between his niece and Lautrec?[33] Whatever the case, Aarschot would never go back on his decision to sell the lands that Chièvres purchased two years before his death. Again, everything seemed to be sorted out reasonably with the Treaty of Cambrai. Aarschot had sold the most recent acquisitions in France at a reasonable price, avoiding further conflicts and confiscations. Meanwhile, he maintained the traditional family property in Château-Porcien, while his younger brother had been content with taking the adjacent barony of Montcornet and receiving the title of Count of Seninghem in Artois. This seemed as though the Count of Château-Porcien now moved to a more Habsburg profile, while maintaining the ancient family assets still in France. Soon after, he would be honoured by Emperor Charles V as first Duke of Aarschot, the first ducal title granted in the Low Countries.

---

32 *Transaction et achapt faict de la conté de Beaufort. Pour Mrs de Lautrec*, 07/08/1529: BNF Ms. Fr. 4651 fol. 24–28. A transaction of 3 August before the *Eschevins de Cambrai* is mentioned in the 41st article of the Treaty of Cambrai, 5 August 1529: Dumont, *Corps universel*, vol. 4, t. 2, 14.

33 There is a marriage between Odet de Foix, lord of Lautrec and Jeanne de Croy, of the branch of Chimay mentioned by Scohier, *Généalogie*, 50; this must have taken place between the death of his first wife Charlotte d'Albret in 1527 and his own death in 1528; Jean-Baptiste de Courcelles, *Histoire généalogique et héraldique des pairs de France ... et maisons princières de l'Europe* (Paris: s.n., 1822–1833), 1: 57–8, equally mentions that the marriage is stated in family chronicles without being verified by other documents. I have not found other evidence for this marriage, and I do not take it for granted that it took place.

Croÿ versus Croÿ

Although the Treaty of Cambrai seemed to definitively confirm the sale of the Chièvres's legacy to the Foix, this agreement, too, would soon be disputed. This time, things became more interesting. After all, the fight between the Croÿ and the Foix presented a very classic chapter in the book of noble dynasties trying to have their service rewarded, to the detriment of families serving other rulers. After 1529, however, the dispute transformed into an argument within the House of Croÿ itself, during which the transregional identity and its multiple loyalties would eventually be reconfigured. Within this particular episode of the affair, Charles de Croÿ, the new Count of Seninghem, directly confronted his elder brother Aarschot. By then, he had married Renée de la Marck, Countess-Dowager of La Braine and Roucy, daughter of a correspondingly transregional family from the Ardennes. The Count did not particularly gain anything from the marriage contract, but it did establish him as a nobleman in his own right, no longer one by the grace of his elder brother.[34] Soon, Seninghem appealed to Francis I. Most surprisingly, he would (at least partially) be supported in his endeavours by the French king, who played upon the old francophile positions of the lineage. This was no longer the king of France against the 'foreign Croÿ' as had been the case throughout the previous decade. Instead, Francis I favoured the division in the family and tried to influence loyalties by recognising the service of the Croÿ ancestors to the French Crown.

In 1532, Seninghem started legal proceedings in Paris. His main objective was to undo the family division of Beaumont. First, the Count asked for 'his part and portion of the price' of the sale to the Foix family. By July, he had already received royal permission to pursue half of the price. By December of the same year (1532), he also obtained *lettres de annulation* [letters of annulment], which enabled him to petition for half of the lands, so no longer half the price. To cut a long story short, Seninghem henceforth aimed for his share based on Chièvres's testament, which was the only document he recognised. Later on, he started a procedure of rescission before the Parliament of Paris in order to unmake the sale contract preceding the Cambrai Treaty. The judgement forced Aarschot to show the testaments, codicils and division contracts, while requiring an inventory of all goods concerned before the division. Aarschot failed to do so, probably because he was not interested in another procedure in Paris.[35] It was the first time that members of the Croÿ family tried to enforce the inheritance claims through litigation in Paris and by seeking support from different rulers; the lawsuit could have been introduced to the Grand Council in Malines as well, since it was launched by an Artesian Count (through the Treaty of Cambrai, Artois was no longer subject to Parliament's jurisdiction)

[34] *Contrat de mariage de Charles de Croÿ-Senighien avec Renée de la Marche, comtesse douairière de la Braine,* 13 May 1529: BNF Ms. Fr. 4330 fol. 57–72. She was married to Amadeus III de Saarbrücken before.

[35] See the report on this part of the episode in the *Factum* mentioned in footnote 31.

on a division that took place in Hainaut. Yet the procedure concerned lands in Champagne, and the Count of Seninghem now appealed to his sovereign for these lordships, playing upon the rivalry with the emperor to win his cause against his brother.

As before, a new cycle of the Habsburg-French War would complicate the legal proceedings. The old device of transregional families was now set in practice: two sons, two armies. Aarschot continued in the imperial party, but in the heyday of the wars in 1536, Seninghem led 100 French soldiers (with whom he mainly defended his own Montcornet). The Count then cleverly started a new procedure of rescission, only this time with the King's procurator-general and in absence of Aarschot *a l'occasion des guerres estrangeres* [during the foreign wars]. The verdict reinstated the annulment of the division (although it accorded some rights to the Foix). The Emperor reacted with a confiscation of the Seninghem lands under Habsburg control. The ensuing truce of La Fère of October 1538 between Mary of Hungary and Francis I (which was the implementation of the truce signed in July in Nice) obviously had to deal with the affair. The clause concerning the conflict between Aarschot and Seninghem reflected the status quo in the Habsburg-French conflict. Aarschot was assured that the arrangement in the Treaty of Cambrai would take full effect and that all procedures against this sale should stop immediately. Seninghem was assured that he could still appeal at the Court of the Parliament of Paris, and that his demand for a remuneration of this sale was valid. However, he could only initiate procedures for the money; the option of doing this for the lands was no longer possible. The final verdict on this financial compensation would be issued before the Parliament of Paris. So at least Seninghem had reached the conclusion that Paris remained the centre of litigation.[36]

Meanwhile, Seninghem had proceeded to a second marriage, this time with Françoise d'Amboise, Lady of Reynel. By 1541, that marriage had produced a son and heir, not coincidently named Antoine, after the abovementioned Antoine le Grand, one of the founding fathers of the lineage, the first Croÿ to purchase Château-Porcien and Montcornet. Most likely encouraged by these circumstances of a foreseeable dynastic continuity, Seninghem felt eager to turn the clause of the Treaty of La Fère to his benefit. In his request to the king in 1541, he again solicited the possibility of initiating legal proceedings, notwithstanding the royal letters of 1538. Aarschot vainly protested to Francis I, but the king answered that his brother's request did not intervene with what was concluded in Cambrai and La Fère.[37] Afterwards, Francis I redirected the petition from the *conseil privé* [Privy Council] to the Parliament of Paris.[38] In this new procedure before Parliament,

36 Treaty of La Fère, 23 October 1538: Dumont, *Corps universel,* vol. 4, t. 3, 171.

37 *Lettres de François Ier audit duc d'Aerschot, lui disant que, ledit procès ne touchant pas aux traités conclus entre la France et l'empereur, il ne peut dénier audit Charles de Croÿ, son frère, le droit de le poursuivre*, 7 January 1541: ANF J 768 52/3/11.

38 *Extrait des registres du Conseil privé, portant renvoi au Parlement du procès relatif à l'entérinement de la requête présentée au roi par Charles de Croÿ, à laquelle s'oppose*

Aarschot was not even consulted, but after his protest, his representative was heard in the *conseil privé*. The procedure stuck in the renewed war between Francis I and Charles V from 1542 onwards. Aarschot tried to end the conflict with his younger brother by adding a clause in his favour to the peace Treaty of Crépy in 1544.[39] Apparently Aarschot also obtained *lettres patentes en forme de requeste civile* [letters patent in the form of a civil action], including a cassation of previous settlements, from the Parliament of Paris.[40]

Surprisingly, by 1549 this agreement had been turned upside down. Most probably the death of Aarschot was then taken as new impetus to act quickly in Paris. Once again, Parliament ruled in favour of Seninghem, yet this time he got some exceptional compensation. First of all, the division in Beaumont was annulled yet again, so that the whole division was to be done over again. In the meantime, Seninghem could enjoy the title of Count of Château-Porcien by appointment. Two years later he would also receive the lands of Montcornet as compensation by royal letters patent. Seninghem soon used the title of Count of Château-Porcien with great eagerness, although the donation was contested by Philip III de Croÿ, the new Duke of Aarschot. Through his endless legal proceedings in Paris, Seninghem had not only obtained a share of the Chièvres legacy, but also the main property of the whole family in France. All the procedures had made him both Count of Seninghem and Château-Porcien, holding the main family assets in France. In the end, this reconfiguration eventually facilitated family relations within the House of Croÿ, in which the dynastic transregional identity now held a more Habsburg and a more French branch together. When the new Duke of Aarschot was taken prisoner in August 1553 by the French after the battle in Dourlens, his uncle Seninghem and aunt Françoise regularly visited him in the Château de Vincennes. Three years later, Aarschot escaped from his captors, and remarkably, Françoise d'Amboise, Seninghem's wife was suspected for having a hand in it.[41] She was arrested, sent to a Parisian prison but was released in the end.[42] The legal proceedings had thus not excluded reciprocity within the House itself.

Five months after his escape from the Château de Vincennes, Aarschot conceded to a new division arranged in the city of Cambrai. This division was probably a result of the mutual assistance during Aarschot's imprisonment in

Philippe de Croÿ, duc d'Aerschot, 16 March 1541: ANF J 769 52/12.

39 Treaty of Crépy, 18 September 1544, Dumont, *Corps universel*, 4:280.

40 See for other contemporary pending issues also Jean de Saint-Mauris to Charles V, 12/12/1548: Archivo General de Simancas, Série K 1488, doc. 157.

41 Letter of Simon Renard to Philip II, 21/05/1556: *Papiers d'État du Cardinal de Granvelle d'après les manuscrits de la bibliothèque de Besançon*, (ed.) M. Weiss (9 vols, Paris: Imprimerie Royale/Imprimerie Nationale, 1843), 4: 561–5; Bertand Haan, *Une paix pour l'éternité. La négociation du traité du Cateau-Cambrésis* (Madrid: Casa de Velázquez, 2010), 54.

42 Jules Delaborde, "Antoine de Croy, Prince de Porcien", *Bulletin de la société de l'histoire du protestantisme français* 18 (1896).

Paris, and the new Duke now understood the advantages of having a French branch of the family more than his father ever had. The county of Château-Porcien could now remain in Seninghem's hands, while it was recognised that Seninghem had always rightfully enjoyed the title of Montcornet. Château-Porcien would also go to Seninghem's son, but after his death, it was to return to the Duke of Aarschot. Meanwhile, Aarschot would continue as *seigneur de la titre de Croy en Picardie*, holding the name, title and property as the core of the family identity.[43] As a result, the unilateral appointment, done at the instigation of the French King in 1549, was now being arranged and confirmed by a settlement among family members in 1556, and as such it became more authoritative. So with the Peace of Cateau-Cambrésis, Aarschot only asked that everything within the previous treaties be respected and that everything he claimed in justice would be granted to him properly and promptly so that within reason, he could not complain about it.[44] Just as Cateau-Cambrésis meant a standstill in the Franco-Habsburg War, it was also a temporary end to the family strife. The House of Croÿ was now formally divided into a more Habsburg and a more French branch. Seninghem and particularly his son Antoine would gradually behave and present themselves as French nobles, seeking patronage from the French court. By 1561, the county of Château-Porcien was even elevated to a principality, and Antoine also received the title of *pair de France*, exceptional favours for this young branch of the House of Croÿ. Nevertheless, the two branches still remained in contact and exchanged gifts and favours, while Croÿ and Picardy remained vectors of the dynastic identity of the House. The unexpected death of the young Antoine prematurely aborted the experiment of a French branch in 1567. His marriage to Catherine de Clèves, issue of the House of Nevers, meant that the strife over Beaufort and Coulommiers would evolve first into a conflict between the Croÿ and Nevers family. The subsequent marriage of Catherine de Clèves to Henri de Lorraine, Duke of Guise, transformed it into a battle between the Croÿs and the Guises, but these conflicts are another story.

Conclusion

Throughout the Ancien Régime, lordships and landed property offered nobles clear markers to define their identity, whether on the level of individuals or families. The seigniorial estates provided the social capital for their claim to form a privileged order of society. Still, for many grand aristocrats, these lordships gradually became scattered over regions with different rulers. This evolution triggered a very

[43] *Par partage faict à Cambray, le 26 octobre 1556, entre messire Phelippes de Croy, duc d'Arschot, d'une part, et messire Charles de Croy, comte de Senighem, d'autre, les terres qui s'ensuivent demeurent aud. comte de Senighen*, 26 October 1556: BNF Ms. Fr. 4727 fol. 108.

[44] Edited by Haan, *Une paix pour l'éternité*, 220–21.

composite identification process in which a dynastic transregional identity came into being in some cases, as was the situation of the Croÿ family. In this identity, elements of geographical embedment and its intrinsic princely service were easily reinterpreted according to the circumstances of territorial wars and litigation. In the long term, a transregional dynastic identity was certainly a strategy of risk management within the family, which tried to maintain as much property together across borders and to accumulate power across states. In the short term, though, it could turn into a bitter strife between family members, as it did within the family of Croÿ between the Treaty of Cambrai and Cateau-Cambrésis.

Litigation could pay off within the context of the larger identification process of transregional families. The gentlemen's sport (or on other occasions, ladies' sport) could turn into a means of reshaping the loyalty claims surrounding the family and its lordships. As such, litigation in competing centres of political power such as French Paris and Habsburg Malines created opportunities of which the outcome was never to be foreseen, since it depended on the proceedings themselves, the caprices of the rulers and the circumstances of international war. As such, in less than one generation, a 'French' branch was born within the same House of Croÿ due to legal proceedings in Paris, even if the chances of these procedures seemed very precarious at the outset. Paradoxically, or perhaps not, this process was backed and eventually even precipitated by the French king. So litigation was not only the outcome of a process of identity formation, but it could also turn into a constitutive means of that process. The French branch used the same Picardian background as their ancestors to show that they were loyal servants to the French Crown. Still, they remained part of the House of Croÿ, which remained the chief identity marker for the family. Still, the evolution in the first half of the sixteenth century remained very undecided, as the premature death of Antoine de Croÿ demonstrated. After all, the ensuing reorganisation and re-identification across borders was the connecting thread of these kinds of transregional families in the early modern era.

Chapter 5

From Arenberg to Aarschot and Back Again: Female Inheritance and the Disputed 'Merger' of Two Aristocratic Identities

Mirella Marini

The Mighty Widow's Legacy

'We recommend to all our children and grandchildren three things. The first and most important that they always try to have and live by the fear of God and to imitate the good and virtuous life of their late lord and father, without ever doing wrong to the Catholic faith no more than he did, and rather for the defence of it to give up their goods and life. The second that they will always remain good and loyal vassals to their King and Prince his Catholic Majesty, without ever extracting themselves from his obedience. The third that they are careful to guard amongst themselves a true peace, concord and union and to imprint these three points on their children and their subjects, recommending them all to remember us in their prayers and to have others pray to God for us'.[1]

With these well-chosen words Anne of Croy, duchess of Aarschot (1564–1635) and princely countess of Arenberg concluded her last will and testament. She was adamant in the way she wanted those three points to be imprinted on the minds of all of her descendants. Using religion as her medium she wanted to preserve for all eternity the exemplary and pious lifestyle of her husband, the loyalty and obedience to the Spanish king as well as the absolute unity of the family. Religion,

[1] 'Nous recommandons à tous noz enfans grands et petits trois choses. La première et principale qu'ils tachent toujours d'avoir et de vivre en la crainte de Dieu et d'imiter la bonne et vertueuse vie de feu leur Seigneur et Père sans jamais manquer en aucune chose de la loys Catholique non plus qu'il n'a fait, plustost pour sa déffence de prendre leur biens et exposer leur propre vie. La deuxième qu'ils ayent toujours à demeurer bons et fidelz vassaux de leur Roy et Prince sa Majesté Catholique sans jamais se denoyer de son obéissance. La troisièsme qu'ils soyent soigneux de maintenir entre eux tous une vraye paix concorde et union et d'imprimer ces trois poinct en l'esprits de leurs enfants et subjects, leurs recommandans à tous de se resouvenir de nous en leur priers et de faire prier Dieu pour nous': Archives Arenberg Enghien (AAE), Testaments (T) 1, fol. 319r–320v.

princely loyalty and family loyalty were key issues on the duchess's mind when she died, to be passed on from generation to generation.[2]

The duchess of Aarschot was one of the most important aristocratic women in the early seventeenth-century Habsburg Low Countries. She was of the highest descent, married a popular courtier, supported the Counter Reformation in a truly impressive way, and her inheritance propelled the Arenberg family into the highest echelons of noble society. But in the 'official' Arenberg family history, she plays only a marginal role. In 1660, almost 30 years after she died, the capuchin Charles of Brussels finished his *Marques des grandeurs et splendeurs de la maison souveraine des Ducs d'Arenberg*, detailing the Arenberg descent from Roman times until his own.[3] This capuchin brother had formerly been known as Anthony of Arenberg (1593–1669), fourth son of the duchess. Throughout his religious life, he would meddle in politics and landscaping alike, as well as spend years researching and writing his family's history.[4] So if his mother's accomplishments did not make it into his manuscript, it is because her son consciously decided to omit them.

Although religion and loyalty, foremost on the duchess's mind when she died, are taken for granted in the *Marques des Grandeurs*, they were highly contested at the time. The pious Arenberg image was created by the duchess herself, half her offspring was involved in the Noble Fronde of 1633 – including father Charles of Brussels – and mother and children had been involved in the worst family conflicts imaginable, making the idea of family concord quite a comical one.[5]

Identity formation in the Arenberg family took place around several pivotal moments in its history. But the pivotal moments which took place before 1660 are too often interpreted in the light of the *Marques des Grandeurs*. Of course father Charles of Brussels based quite a few of his ideas on these events, but he made no mention at all of alternative interpretations on what the Arenberg identity constituted. And during his mother's lifetime, these alternatives existed, and were key contributing factors to the birth of a dominant Arenberg identity. It is this pivotal point in Arenberg history which will be analysed in this contribution.

---

[2] For an account of the duchess's funeral and the way the funeral rituals interacted with the wording in her will see: Mirella Marini, "Pendanten in leven en dood: Vroomheid, identiteit en autoriteit in de testamentaire beschikkingen van Anna van Croy, hertogin van Aarschot en prinses-gravin van Arenberg (1564–1635)", in *Graven spreken. Perspectieven op grafcultuur in de middeleeuwse en vroegmoderne Nederlanden*, (ed.) Peter Bitter et al. (Hilversum: Verloren, 2013), 153–70.

[3] AAE, Biographie (Bio) 1.

[4] For a full account on father Charles's life see Fredegand Callaey, *La vie religieuse et familiale en Belgique au XVIIe siècle: étude sur le Père Charles d'Arenberg, frère-mineur capucin (1593–1669)* (Paris: Librairie Saint François, 1919).

[5] For a full account on the possible treason of the Arenberg children and the captivity of the eldest son see: René Vermeir, "Le duc d'Arschot et les conséquences de la conspiration des nobles (1632–1640)", in *Beleid en bestuur in de oude Nederlanden: liber amicorum Prof. dr. M. Baelde*, (ed.) Hugo Soly and René Vermeir (Gent: Gent RUG, 1993), 477–89.

Figure 5.1 Portrait of Anne of Croy. Detail of Antoon Van den Heuvel, *Our-Lady-of-the-Rosary*, oil on canvas, ca. 1633. Altarpiece of the chapel of Our-Lady-of-the-Rosary in the Saint-Nicolas Church Enghien (Belgium). Copyright Studio Berger Enghien (Belgium).

Three important questions will be discussed, all surrounding female inheritance and its influence on the transferral or transmission of dynastic identity. First we will determine how identity was transferred through a contract, in this case the marriage contract between Anne of Croy and the princely count of Arenberg, detailing the conditions for female succession rights and its consequences on the identity of future children. Then we will question the actual transferral of identity and family heritage through women and the way the realities of demographic pressure forcibly intervened with the strict interpretation of contractual clauses. And thirdly it is necessary to see how conflicts surrounding female inheritance could influence the development and transmission of identity, especially when women and their (male) heirs defended conflicting interests. In this case, Anne of Croy and her eldest son were often at odds with each other, although presumably they both acted in accordance with the family's best interests. As we will see, the transferral of Arenberg-Croy family identity would not go as planned, although many of what are seen as determining identity markers within the family were actually the product of Anne of Croy's creative imagination. How these events were translated in the *Marques des Grandeurs* will also be discussed.

The 'Official' Family History

For this contribution I used the early twentieth-century unpublished and handwritten copy of the eighteenth-century transcript of the seventeenth-century original of the *Marques des grandeurs et splendeurs de la maison souveraine des Ducs d'Arenberg écrit en l'an 1660 de la main propre du Père Charles d'Arenberg et copié en 1782 par ordre de S.A.S. Monseigneur Louis Englebert Duc d'Arenberg et d'Arschot par J.F. Grosfils. La copie actuelle a été faite en 1907 par ordres de SAS Monseigneur le Duc Engelbert-Marie d'Arenberg par la Soeur Vincent des Filles de la charité de Saint Vincent de Paul à Héverlé.*[6] As this version of the manuscript shows, the *Marques des Grandeurs* was deemed so important for the transmission of the Arenberg identity that it was copied time and time again. Even more so, the manuscript itself and its many unaltered copies suggest the Arenberg identity is a fixed concept, born in the murkiest beginnings of the empire and forever unchanged until the present day. Undoubtedly, this is exactly what the good capuchin intended when he undertook to 'investigate' his family's history. However, in many ways, the *Marques des Grandeurs* is more an extended political pamphlet than a cultural history, documenting and explaining the political position of the Arenberg family between 1644 and 1660.[7] The year 1660 especially seems

[6] AAE, Bio 1.

[7] See also my argument in: Mirella Marini, "Interlocking dynasties: netwerking en huwelijkspolitiek van de familie Arenberg tijdens de Opstand", in *Het verdeelde huis: de Nederlandse adel tussen opstand en reconciliatie*, (eds) Liesbeth De Frenne and Luc

to be the determining date. It is said that the fact that father Charles of Brussels' work was finished (or at least halted) in 1660 is a coincidence, and that it hasn't got so much to do with the events within the family of that year.[8] I do not agree.

Not only has this manuscript rewritten and reinvented Arenberg family history in favour of the notions of sovereignty and independence as defining identity markers, it did so in order to redefine the family's social and political position after one of the most painful decades in its history, when the Fronde had left deep cuts in family pride.[9] In 1660 Philip-Francis (1625–1674), duke of Arenberg and Aarschot and grandson to Anne of Croy, was presented with the manuscript by his uncle the capuchin.[10] In that year Philip-Francis celebrated the wedding of his younger brother and heir, who would hopefully provide the family with ample offspring.[11] Without a next generation the family would perish. Arenberg family history is one of ruptures, conflicts, demographic crises and loyalty in spite of possible ruin. The house of Arenberg stood at the brink of extinction more than once, never more so than during the long seventeenth century, and only managed to survive through sheer luck and the providence of a few of its shiniest members. One of these was Anne of Croy.

As David Warren Sabean and Simon Teuscher have argued in *Kinship in Europe. Approaches to Long-Term Development (1300–1900)*, aristocratic notions on what defined a family, and hence its family identity formation, underwent a definite change after the Thirty Years' War.[12] Inheritance practices in families more and more stressed a territorial identity and descent, to the detriment of the old idea of widely defined kinship groups. Luc Duerloo has argued that the Low Countries' nobility developed a clearer sense of an aristocratic 'class' identity after their Habsburg princes published a number of edicts on the use of heraldry, titles

---

Duerloo. Publicaties van de Vlaams-Nederlandse Vereniging voor Nieuwe Geschiedenis 10 (Maastricht: Shaker Publishing, 2011), 55–78.

8 For instance in: Martin Wrede, *Ohne Furcht und Tadel – Für König und Vaterland. Frühneuzeitlicher Hochadel zwischen Familienehre, Ritterideal und Fürstendienst*, Beihefte der Francia 75 (Ostfildern: Jan Thorbecke Verlag, 2012), 178, it is suggested this has to do with the military offences of Louis XIV of France.

9 Wrede, *Ohne Furcht und Tadel*, 186–87 for what this author identifies as the 'identity capital' of the Arenberg family.

10 In fact, Philip-Francis is omnipresent in the manuscript. Even in those descriptions that focus on events before his birth, he is still very frequently mentioned and praised. For instance: AAE, Bio 1, fol. 242, 252 and 257 all dealing with the Croy-Aarschot inheritance.

11 Philip-Francis had a younger half-brother Charles-Eugene (1633–1681), who married Marie-Henriette de Cusance et de Vergy in 1660. When Philip-Francis died childless in 1674, Charles-Eugene succeeded him. Family survival remained an issue, and only from the second half of the eighteenth century would a duke again father more than one (male) heir. See also Marini, "Interlocking dynasties", 56.

12 David Warren Sabean and Simon Teuscher, "Kinship in Europe: A New Approach to Long-Term Development", in *Kinship in Europe. Approaches to Long-Term Development (1300–1900)*, (ed.) David Warren Sabean et al. (New York: Berghahn Books, 2007), 9.

etc. from 1595 onwards.[13] This 'class awareness' brought an increasing emphasis on the so-called correct uses of heraldry and an obsessive focus on noble quarters as instruments of distinction, within the peer group and without. In this case, the Arenberg were forced to develop a stronger territorial identity because of the political pressure caused by the Dutch Revolt, and yet again, a fear of extinction.[14] This caused them to develop an actual 'Arenberg' identity, while at the same time very much continuing to act as a younger branch of the Marck dynasty. However, it is that 'temporary' invention of tradition set off around 1570–1580, arguably the first pivotal point in family identity formation, which was then used by the capuchin family historian as proof of his family's identification with the sovereignty and independence of the small princely Arenberg seigniory. In this chapter it will be stated that at the beginning of the seventeenth century this strong territorial identity was by no means a given.

The Sources: Arenberg Family Archives

The *Marques des Grandeurs* cannot merely be used as a source of historical facts or even of historical sentiments. The identity developed within its pages is a created one, of special use in 1660, but not one that can be conveyed to the mind-set of the Arenberg family around 1600. Unfortunately, on many occasions, historians like August Roeykens and recently also Martin Wrede, have used it as a source, turning it into the logical – or even almost eschatological – product of the family history before 1660.[15]

The documents used in this chapter, and indeed in many of the publications regarding the family, are for the most part found within an archival collection called 'Biographies' in the Arenberg family archives.[16] But the very first and most elaborate of these so-called biographies were collections of important contracts,

[13] See his argumentation in Luc Duerloo, "Het blazoen ontsmet. Adellijke heraldiek als toe-eigening van eer en deugd, 1550–1750", *BMGN-The Low Countries Historical Review* 123 (2008), 633–54.

[14] See for this argument: Marini, "Interlocking dynasties" and Mirella Marini, "Dynastic relations on an international stage. Margaret de la Marck (1527–1599) and Arenberg family strategy during the Dutch Revolt", in *Women, Diplomacy and International Politics since 1500*, (eds) Glenda Sluga and Carolyn James (London: Routledge, 2015), 46-67.

[15] Family archivist and capuchin brother Roeykens did attempt to debunk some of Charles of Brussels' argumentations, without however doubting the actual historicity of the identity claims presented in the manuscript. August Roeykens, "Une grande dame de nos provinces au XVIe siècle: Marguerite de la Marck, Princesse-Comtesse d'Arenberg", *Annales du Cercle Archéologique d'Enghien* 15 (1967–1969), 297–424 and Wrede, *Ohne Furcht und Tadel.*

[16] The private archives of the Arenberg family are held in the small Hainault city of Enghien. Enghien was once part of the Arenberg patrimony and is of special importance to

letters, etc., all brought together by Anne of Croy.[17] She assembled portfolios of documents per child, but also of herself, presumably mostly for legal reasons and for the express purpose of memoria.[18] Although they are often treated as an easy source of correspondence, in many ways these portfolios are the heart of the original family archives. They are much more than biographies of individuals and are actually something like 'state papers', dealing with the relationship between Anne of Croy and family members, but also detailing the governance of the house of Arenberg. On the other hand, it has to be taken into account that if a certain letter or contract was preserved, it happened with a reason, and that reason was mostly to defend and support the duchess's position within the Arenberg family. Many of Charles of Brussels' writings were based on documents the duchess had expressly copied, for instance the life story of her mother-in-law.[19] The capuchin father used these individual documents to support his own claims, and to do so, he decontextualised them to fit into his own story. If he was to be in any way successful, he had to 'forget' to mention that his mother's archival diligence was at the source of his 'slightly altered' family story. But where Anne of Croy had collected these documents to support her claim on a mixed Croy-Arenberg identity – for instance by combining Arenberg and Croy family documents within the same portfolio – her son needed to 'downsize' the Croy heritage.[20] The reason

---

the family since the family crypt is located there as well. For the family archives see: www.arenbergfoundation.eu.

[17] Since the seventeenth century numerous archivists have been working for the family, who have at some point created the 'Biographies' collection. Today, it consists of an amalgam of documents all brought together in a 'Biographie', each one more or less relating to an individual member of the Arenberg family. This tradition is continued today. In a sense, it is a pity that this way the original portfolios created by Anne of Croy seem to have almost completely lost their archival context.

[18] For instance the 'Biographie 8' (AAE, Bio 8): *Livre de copies de lettres de Philippe D'Aremberghe filz aisné de Son Excellence autenticquées pour servir à d'originelles toutes selon leurs années. Depuis 1616 jusques 1621*, or the 'Biographie 10' (AAE, Bio 10): *Dedans ce livre sont les promesses que plusieurs de la Maison de madame Anne de Croy luy ont fait de la servir toutte sa vie et ne la point quitter jusques après sa mort et leurs instructions comme madame veut qu'ils se gouvernent en son service et ce que'elle leurs donne chacun a part* or indeed the 'Biographie 3d' (AAE, Bio 3d): *Copies des principaulx pappiers originaulx autenticques et simples touchantz messeigneurs et mesdames parens et parentes de Monseigneur touttes autenticquées pour servir à l'advenir d'originaulx chacuns mis à part et selon leurs années faict en l'an 1624.*

[19] AAE, Bio 3d, fol. 1r–17v, *Brief discours de la vie et conduicte des affaires de Margeruite de la Marck Comtesse de la Marck et d'Aremberghe depuis sa naissance.*

[20] AAE, Bio 2, *Receuil des pappiers originaulx autenticques et simples de tous Messeigneurs et Mesdames parens et parentes de Madame, come aussy ceulx de Monseigneur et de Madicte Dame lesquelz sont autenticquéz pour s'en servir à l'advenir d'originaulx chacuns mis à part selon leurs années*, 1624. Instead of creating a distinct portfolio for the documents pertaining to herself and her husband, she chose to incorporate them into the Croy portfolio.

behind this decision has to be seen against the backdrop of his nephew's wedding in 1660 and the political events leading up to that point, but also, in part, in the context of the emotional rupture this Croy heritage caused within his family.

The Transferral of Identity through a Marriage Contract

In 1587 a marital agreement was drawn up between Charles (1550–1616), princely count of Arenberg and Anne of Croy. The most important articles of this agreement specified Croy's claims to the Aarschot inheritance.[21] Anne of Croy was the eldest daughter of Philip III of Croy (1526–1595), duke of Aarschot.[22] The duke had promised his daughter the duchy of Aarschot in case her older brother were to die childless.[23] That was not a far-fetched idea at all. After almost 10 years of marriage, this young Croy heir still had no children.[24] So when Arenberg and Anne of Croy married, she had a very realistic chance of inheriting one of the most sought-after titles in the Low Countries. Anne of Croy's parents had actually gone to some lengths to ensure their eldest daughter inherited the Croy-Aarschot patrilineal patrimony. They explicitly named her next in line after her brother in their will, they concluded an '*avis de père et mère*' (dated 18 April 1579) and now the marriage contract again confirmed her rights.[25]

21 AAE, Bio 2, fol. 192v–205v, *L'originel traicté de mariage de leurs Exces faict au Chasteau de Beaumont le XVI de septembre 1586.*

22 It was at that time the only ducal title in the Netherlands, apart of course from the ducal titles of Luxemburg, Limburg, Brabant and Guelders, which were all part of the Habsburg patrimony. For more on the house of Croy see: Robert Born, *Les Croy: une grande lignée hennuyère d'hommes de guerre, de diplomates, de conseillers secrets, dans les coulisses du pouvoir, sous les ducs de Bourgogne et la Maison d'Autriche (1390–1612)* (Brussel: Editeurs d'art associés, 1981).

23 The Croy dynasty consisted of several branches in the sixteenth and seventeenth centuries, as the contribution of Violet Soen in this volume also shows. This particular 'branch' of Aarschot was the main Croy-branch and thus the duke of Aarschot had the honour of being 'head' or 'chef' of the entire Croy family. See also: Wilhelm Karl von Isenburg and Frank Freytag von Loringhoven, *Europäischen Stammtafeln. Stammtafeln zur Geschichte der europäischen Staaten* (5 vols, Marburg: Stargardt,1956–1978), vol. 4, table 98–100.

24 For more details on his childless marriage with his first wife Marie de Brimeu see: Marie de Villermont, *Grands Seigneurs d'autrefois: Le duc Charles de Croy et d'Arschot et ses femmes Marie de Brimeu et Dorothée de Croy* (Brussel: Dewit, 1923) or more recently: Anne Mieke Backer, "Tuinkunst tijdens de Nederlandse Opstand. De prinses van Chimay, Marie de Brimeu en de 'humanisering' van de bloem 1550–1605", *Cascade. Bulletin voor Tuinhistorie* 15, 2 (2006): 14–39, available at: http://www.cascade1987.nl/bulletins/TuinkunstOpstand-A.M.Backer-CascadeBulletin-2006-2.pdf [accessed 25 Sept. 2014]

25 AAE, Bio 2, fol. 39v, *Copie du testament de Monsieur le Ducq D'Arschot père à Madame faict à Beaumont le 19e septembre 1595* and fol. 48v, *Copie de l'advis de père et mère faict par Philippe Sire de Croy et Dame Jeanne de Hallewin du 18 avril 1579.*

According to the Croy-Arenberg marriage contract, if Anne of Croy indeed came to inherit, then 'the eldest son of said damsel Anne will have to carry name and coat of arms of Croy' and in that case 'said eldest son will hold the title of duke of Aarschot with the name and the coat of arms of Croy, divided by those of Arenberg'.[26] Only the second son of the couple would 'hold title and arms of the principality of Arenberg, having as his part the goods from the paternal side'.[27] In case only one son were to be born (or survive), he would have to take 'the two names and arms of Croy and Arenberg'.[28] So the contract specifically arranged the transferral of the Croy name and arms to the eldest son of Anne of Croy, making the matrilineal patrimony the most important patrimony to be distributed to potential offspring. This firstborn son would start his own dynastic enterprise, only revealing his Arenberg descent in his coat of arms, not in his name or in his title. A second son would continue the Arenberg dynasty and take its name and title. Arrangements like these were of course quite useful if the survival of a dynasty were in some ways in jeopardy. Nor were these contracts the exception. Other aristocratic houses transferred names, titles and patrimony via the eldest daughter to the (preferably) male heirs of her body.[29] What is important in this contract however is not just the issue of female inheritance, but the continuation of the matrilineal dynastic name, and hence, its identity. The duke of Aarschot clearly saw this arrangement as a good way to save his dynasty and to keep his titles 'in the family'. But even so, it was the other party, the Arenberg family, that would stand to gain, and to lose, the most with this contract.

[26] 'le filz aisné de laditte damoyselle Anne seroit tenu porter le nom et armes de Croy' and 'ledict filz aisné d'elle porte tiltre de ducq d'Arschot avecq nom et armes de Croy parties de celles d'Aremberghe': AAE, Bio 2, fol. 192v–205v, *L'originel traicté de mariage*. The following citations are also from this document.

[27] 'portera nom tiltre et armes d'Jcelle principaulté d'Aremberghe, ayant pour partaige les biens venans du costé paternel'.

[28] 'les deux noms et armes de Croy et d'Aremberghe'.

[29] Female inheritance is of course not an exception among royal houses, as for instance the royal house of Hannover inherited the English throne through the rights of a female ascendant. But in that case a royal title was inherited but the name of the dynasty would continue as Hannover. Female inheritance and the continuation of the matrilineal dynasty (and its name) is for instance better demonstrated by the history of the Grimaldis of Monaco. Not only was the Monegasque title transferred, but the matrilineal dynastic name of Grimaldi was perpetuated: Pierre Delorme, *Les Grimaldi. 700 ans d'une dynastie* (Poitiers: Aubin Imprimeur, 1998).

Female Inheritance in the Arenberg Family

Traditionally it is said that the Arenberg originated from the Eifel region in the Holy Roman Empire.[30] Arenberg was a sovereign principality, only subjected to 'God and the Emperor' as it was stated.[31] As mentioned before, this emphasis on the Arenberg territorial identity and these notions of sovereignty and independence are actually based on the 1660 account of family history by father Charles of Brussels.[32] Although the Arenberg consistently presented themselves as imperial nobility, the Marck-Arenberg had been forging dynastic links with the Liège and Low Countries nobility from the fourteenth century onwards. The core of their patrimony thus consisted of a string of seigniories in Liège, Luxemburg, Brabant, Holland, Drenthe and Friesland.[33] However, in spite of these family connections, it would be false to consider them 'Dutch' nobility. The Arenberg were a younger branch of the Marck family.[34] During most of the sixteenth century they boasted a 'close' family relation to the dukes of Cleves and the other Marck branches.[35] Politically speaking, their interests lay on a European transborder level, underlined by a fierce effort to maintain European-wide marriage connections, as well as friendship ties, following the dynastic example of the other Marck branches.[36] The emphasis on the territorial Arenberg identity was 'a new thing', an invention of

---

[30] See for a detailed history of the family and a definitive 'setting' in the Eifel: Peter Neu, *Die Arenberger und das Arenberger Land*. 6 volumes (Koblenz: Verlag der Landesarchivverwaltung Rheinland-Pfalz, 1989–2001).

[31] As posed by Charles of Brussels in AAE, Bio 1 fol. 4 and 52–3. See for the importance of this status at the Brussels court, especially after obtaining the *Reichsfürstenwürde* in 1576: Luc Duerloo, "Arenberg in de Habsburgse Nederlanden", in *Arenberg in de Lage Landen: een hoogadellijk huis in Vlaanderen en Nederland*, (ed.) Jan Roegiers (Leuven: Leuven University Press, 2002), 58–80.

[32] Or as he stated it: 'La véritable définition de la souveraineté est l'indépendance': AAE, Bio 1, fol. 51.

[33] Jan-Engelbert d'Arenberg, "De heren, graven, prins-graven en hertogen van Arenberg", in *Arenberg in de Lage Landen: een hoogadellijk huis in Vlaanderen en Nederland*, (ed.) Jan Roegiers (Leuven: Leuven University Press, 2002), 13–51 and Jean-Pierre Tytgat, "Van rentmeesters en intendanten: het beheer van de Arenberggoederen", in *Arenberg in de Lage Landen: een hoogadellijk huis in Vlaanderen en Nederland*, (ed.) Jan Roegiers (Leuven: Leuven University Press, 2002), 132–44.

[34] It is also argued that the house of Arenberg in the sixteenth century was actually a younger branch of the Ligne family (also named the Third House of Arenberg). In *Europäischen Stammtafeln*, vol. 6, tables 94–5 this becomes painfully clear. This is probably an incorrect interpretation of the 1660 family history by father Charles of Brussels. Contemporary Arenberg never portrayed themselves as a younger Ligne branch. See: Marini, "Interlocking dynasties" and "Dynastic relations" and Wrede, *Ohne Furcht und Tadel*, 154.

[35] For a detailed overview of all the Marck branches see: *Europäischen Stammtafeln*, vol. 6, tables 16–20.

[36] Marini, "Interlocking dynasties".

tradition, cunningly introduced in the beginning decade of the Dutch Revolt.[37] So now in 1587 at the time of the Croy-Arenberg marriage, as a younger and perhaps less successful Marck branch, accepting the terms of this marriage contract was a way of obtaining the ducal title that they craved so much.

Female inheritance was something the Arenberg were quite comfortable with. The Arenberg family had faced extinction in the male line at least twice in its known history.[38] Only in the early sixteenth century a more or less clearly defined 'Arenberg' patrimony was passed on, but its members would still use the dynastic name 'de la Marck' and refer to Arenberg not as a name, but as a title.[39] The last descendant of this 'Marck-Arenberg' line, Margaret de la Marck, countess of Arenberg, married John of Ligne, baron of Barbançon (1525–1568) in 1547. They were the groom's parents and thus father Charles of Brussels' agnatic grandparents. In the *Marques des Grandeurs* this Ligne-Marck marriage was again described in terms of sovereignty and independence, since Barbançon would be 'promoted' from 'the quality of a younger branch' to 'a grand, independent and distinct house'.[40] So only four decades before the Croy-Arenberg marriage, the Arenberg had been able to survive as an 'independent dynasty' because a similar marital agreement had been made between Margaret de la Marck and John of Ligne. Their marital contract specified that the matrilineal Marck-Arenberg patrimony would go to their eldest child (male or female) who would then use 'the title, name and coat of arms of the counts and countesses de la Marck and Arenberg'.[41] Only a second child would take the Ligne-Barbançon name, coat of arms and title from its father.

If we compare this clause to the Aarschot-clause in the Arenberg-Croy marriage contract, it appeared that only a generation later the Arenberg were prepared to make their name and coat of arms temporarily 'subordinate' to Croy survival. This

---

37 Marini, "Interlocking dynasties".

38 In the fourteenth century the heiress of Arenberg had married the count de la Marck. This is how the title Arenberg was passed on in the Marck family. Their two sons Adolf II and Everhard I would each go on to head their own families. From Adolf II descended the dukes of Cleves (extinct in the male line in 1609), the dukes of Nevers (extinct in the male line in the sixteenth century), and the counts of Ravenstein (extinct in the sixteenth century). From Everhard I descended the counts of Marck-Arenberg (later the dukes of Arenberg), the lords (later princes and dukes of Bouillon) of Sedan (extinct in the male line in the sixteenth century), the barons of Lummen and the lords of Rochefort (extinct). To make things even more complicated, several individuals in the family used the name 'Arenberg', even those that today we would not count as descendants of the Arenberg line sensu strictu. This is of course a result of German succession laws, where all the children could use the title (and name) of their father.

39 For more details on this 'de la Marck' identity see: Marini, "Interlocking dynasties".

40 'la qualité d'une famille puisnée' and 'une grand maison distincte et indépendante': AAE, Bio 1, fol. 303.

41 'de tytele, naem ende wapenen van graven ende gravinnen vander Marckque ende tot Arenberghe': as cited by Roeykens, "Une grande dame", 338.

becomes clear when looking at the conditions of this contract in case the Arenberg-Croy couple only had one son. This sole heir would have to combine both names and titles, but the Croy name is mentioned first in line. During his lifetime, as sole representative of two dynasties, this heir would in all likelihood prefer to use his more attractive Aarschot ducal title, exposing his Arenberg descent only through his coat of arms. Only a generation later a 'resurrected' and separate Arenberg dynasty would again be formed, if there were enough sons. This is speculation of course, but it does raise questions about the nature of the Arenberg dynasty, or rather the strength of its identity at the time of contracting the Croy marriage. One of the possible explanations for a weaker Arenberg identity at this time might be the fact that this branch of the Marck dynasty actually had a history of troubled successions. Margaret de la Marck (1527–1599) had only inherited when her older brother had died young and childless. And he had only inherited the county of Arenberg from his grandfather three years previously.[42] Succession in the Arenberg family was never a given.

Margaret de la Marck's and Anne of Croy's contracts thus do not differ that much. The most striking difference is probably the succession in terms of equal primogeniture in the older contract and the specification of male primogeniture in the newest contract. This difference can be easily explained by the difference in German and Low Countries inheritance and name-giving practices. But otherwise, both contracts laid out the consequences of female inheritance in some detail. The only other difference was in their personal circumstances. Margaret de la Marck had married as a confirmed heiress, she was a countess in her own right. Anne of Croy only had a prospect of inheriting when she married. In order to fully make her claim, her brother had to die childless. Her position was much less secure.

In the event, both the Arenberg and the Aarschot inheritances would pass on to the eldest son, who was expected to take name and coat of arms from the matrilineal inheritance. Both contracts specified an important dynastic change, where the eldest child would be the 'arch founder' of a new dynasty, whereas a younger child would continue the patrilineal dynasty and its identity. Yet the outcome of these two contracts would be very different.

---

42 In fact Margaret de la Marck's father had died at the age of 30, before he could inherit the county. To make matters more complicated, Margaret de la Marck's grandfather had also inherited by chance, as his older brother had died childless. When Margaret de la Marck thus inherited at the age of 17, the young Arenberg-Marck branch had not known a stable succession in three generations: *Europäischen Stammtafeln*, vol. 6, table 18.

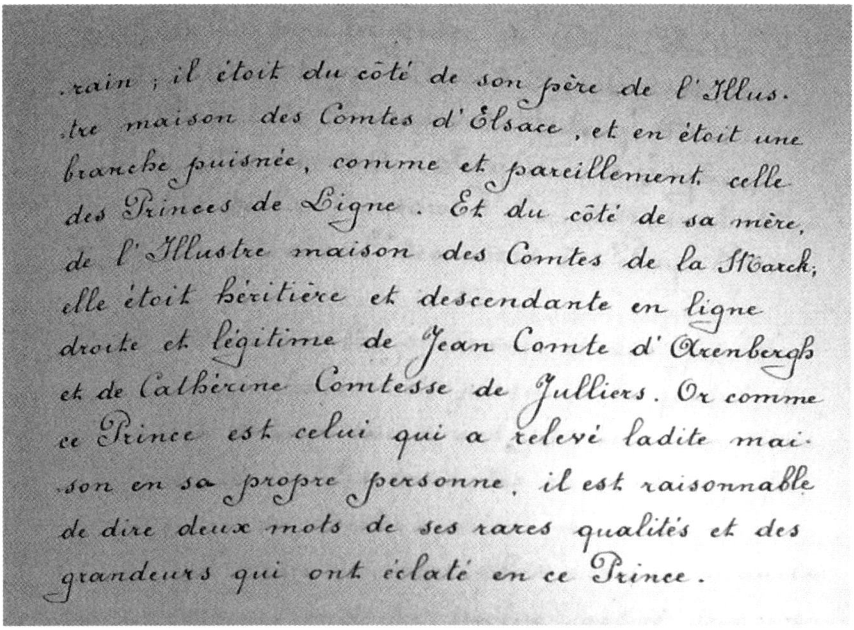
.rain ; il étoit du côté de son père de l'Illus-
.tre maison des Comtes d'Elsace, et en étoit une
branche puisnée, comme et pareillement celle
des Princes de Ligne. Et du côté de sa mère,
de l'Illustre maison des Comtes de la Marck;
elle étoit héritière et descendante en ligne
droite et légitime de Jean Comte d'Arenbergh
et de Catherine Comtesse de Julliers. Or comme
ce Prince est celui qui a relevé ladite mai-
son en sa propre personne, il est raisonnable
de dire deux mots de ses rares qualités et des
grandeurs qui ont éclaté en ce Prince.

Figure 5.2 *Marques des grandeurs et splendeurs de la maison souveraine des Ducs d'Arenberg*. AAE, Bio 1, fol. 189, in which Charles of Arenberg is named arch founder of the 'new' Arenberg dynasty. Copyright: Arenberg Archives in Enghien (Belgium).

In the event, the first child born out of the Ligne-Marck marriage had been a boy, our groom Charles of Arenberg (1550–1616). To our knowledge however he never called himself a 'de la Marck'.[43] He seemed to limit himself to the (territorial) denomination 'of Arenberg', which was in all likelihood the product of the 1570–1580 identity formation process.[44] In his coat of arms his mixed Arenberg,

43 Martin Wrede explains that this was part of the marital agreement between Margaret de la Marck and John of Ligne: Wrede, *Ohne Furcht und Tadel*, 153. However, in the contract itself, it is clearly stated that the de la Marck name of his mother was very much part of the deal: Roeykens, "Une grande dame", 338 and 341.

44 In historiography Charles of Arenberg is often named Charles of Ligne, princely count of Arenberg. Where this name comes from is not clear. Neither is it clear if the count actually used this name in correspondence. In the Arenberg archives I have never encountered this specific way of naming the count, not in his correspondence and neither in signed contracts. In any case, that name would actually be quite illogical. On the other hand, in Jean-Baptiste Maurice, *Le Blason des Armoiries de tous les Chevaliers de l'Ordre de la Toison d'Or depuis la première institution iusques à present. Avec leurs noms, surnoms, titres et cartiers. Ensemble leurs Eloges déscrites en bref* (The Hague: Jean Rammazeyn

Marck and Ligne-Barbançon descent were of course visible.[45] The capuchin family historian saw Charles of Arenberg as the one who 'has restored said house in his own person'.[46] It is clear that when the capuchin monk wrote his story in 1660, his father was considered to be the arch founder of the 'new' Arenberg dynasty. The transferral of this matrilineal Arenberg identity to the eldest son does not seem to have imposed any problems or conflicts. Charles of Arenberg's younger brother Robert did indeed inherit from his father and called himself 'of Barbançon'.

Demographic Pressure because of 'Too Many' Heirs as a Disrupting Factor in Identity Formation

The Arenberg-Croy marriage turned out to be quite successful in many ways. Arenberg earned prestige in the military, as a diplomat and as a statesman, especially during the reign of the 'Archdukes' Albert (1559–1621) and Isabella (1566–1633), sovereigns of the Netherlands since 1598.[47] While he frequently travelled in Habsburg service, his wife administered the Arenberg patrimony. She was particularly successful in settling her husband's many debts.[48]

The couple had 12 children, 10 of whom survived into adulthood, five sons and five daughters. Although it may seem that they were lucky with such ample offspring, a lot of the conflicts between parents and children were actually the result of this demographic pressure. The Arenberg patrimony, which was already heavily compromised by the Dutch Revolt, would increasingly suffer under

Imprimeur, 1667), 306 he is indeed called 'Charles de Ligne'. For the 1570–1580 point in history see: Marini, "Interlocking dynasties".

45 See for his entrance in the Livre du Toison d'Or as 'Charles Prince et Conte d'Arenberge Seigneur de Barbanson et de Zevenberge': Die Bayerische Staatsbibliothek CodIcon Online, Cod.icon. 285, *Livre du Toison d'Or institué et fundé par le bon Duc Philippe de Bourgogne*, end of sixteenth century, Netherlands, fol. 72r, available at: http://codicon.digitale-sammlungen.de [accessed 11 Sept. 2014]

46 'a relevé ladite maison en sa propre personne': AAE, Bio 1, fol. 189. The French verb 'relever' has a lot of different meanings. In this sentence it points to restoring the ancient house of Arenberg, but it also points to lifting something up, ennobling it. Using this word places Charles of Arenberg in family history as some sort of saviour.

47 See for the Netherlands under the Archdukes and their court: Werner Thomas and Luc Duerloo (eds), *Albert & Isabella 1598–1621: Essays* (s.l.: Brepols, 1998) and Dries Raeymaekers, *One Foot in the Palace: The Habsburg Court of Brussels and the Politics of Access in the Reign of Albert and Isabella, 1598–1621* (Leuven: Leuven University Press, 2013).

48 AAE, Bio 2, fol. 225r–226v and fol. 227r–230r: two powers of attorney from Charles of Arenberg to Anne of Croy, 26 November 1587 and 23 August 1600, conceding the financial administration of the family patrimony to his wife. See also: Mirella Marini, "Female Authority in the *Pietas Nobilita*: Habsburg Allegiance during the Dutch Revolt", *Dutch Crossing: Journal of Low Countries studies* 34, no. 1 (2010), 5–24.

financial stress. All of these 10 children depended on it, maybe not all in equal measure, but considering the social status of the couple it was imperative that they received patrimonial shares according to their 'quality'. Although the capuchin family historian made a show of emphasising how blessed the couple were with so many children, this was mostly rhetoric of the church.[49] When it came to safeguarding a family patrimony, fewer children were a better ticket to financial health. In a way, a generation earlier, Margaret de la Marck had it a lot easier. Besides providing her daughters with honourable dowries, she had only two sons. And both these sons had two clearly defined patrimonies, thanks to Margaret de la Marck's marriage contract. But with 10 children things were different. After all, the Arenberg-Croy contract had only made clear arrangements for two possible sons. With the birth of every new child, the parents made a new will. What has been difficult to explain, is why these wills did not seem to name the eldest son of the couple the principal heir of the patrilineal patrimony.[50] In the early testaments of the couple their third son seemed to be favoured, resulting in discussions on the morality of this 'disinheritance' of the 'rightful' heir. The explanation however is at once simple and very complex.[51] Philip of Arenberg, the eldest son, was never destined to become an Arenberg at all. In view of the Croy-Arenberg marriage contract, Philip – not coincidentally named after Anne of Croy's father – was to become a Croy.[52]

Anne of Croy bore five sons: Philip (1587–1640), Charles (1588–1613), Alexander (1590–1629), Anthony (1593–1669) and Eugene (1600–1635).[53] Second son Charles, who is not to be confused with our capuchin historian father Charles of Brussels, was immediately destined for the church.[54] He was given

[49] AAE, Bio 1, fol. 192–5. He expressly referred to previous marriage negotiations for the young princely count, with two noble women who turned out to be 'sterile' as he put it: Louise de Vaudémont (future wife of Henry III of France) and Sybilla of Cleves (who would marry Charles of Habsburg, marquis of Burgau). Father Charles saw it as divine providence that these marriages fell through, which is actually, considering these marriage candidates, absolute nonsense of course.

[50] See AAE, T 1, T 3 and T 20 for the various wills and codicils of the couple.

[51] And of course we now know there was no such thing as a strict male primogeniture among the imperial nobility in the first place.

[52] Of course the name Philip also referred to king Philip II, but most noble families in the Low Countries boasted children with names like Charles and Philip, all named for Charles V and his son. The important issue however is that this first name also directly connected their firstborn to the Croy family, where successive Philips had been governing the house since 1475, thus honouring their connection to the Burgundian dukes.

[53] In this contribution nothing further will be said on her daughters: Ernestine (1589–1653), Clara (1594–1670), Albertine (1596–1652), Dorothea (1601–1655) and Caroline (1606–1630). All of her daughters would marry and so all of them would be provided with a considerable dowry.

[54] In this contribution the majority of noble men under discussion were called Charles, after the great emperor Charles V, which can be confusing at times. That is why in most

a prebendaryship and was entrusted to a tutor. Before even reaching adulthood he signed a family contract in which he explicitly renounced his rights on the Arenberg inheritance 'for the good and benefit and conservation of the grandeur of our house'.[55] When Charles junior died unexpectedly in Rome in 1613, youngest son Eugene was to take over his older brother's ecclesiastical career.[56] Eugene was thus only briefly treated as one of the Arenberg heirs. This left three sons to provide for: Philip, Alexander and Anthony. Third son Alexander also received a prebendaryship at a young age, which explains why fourth son Anthony would perhaps feature prominently in some of his parents' wills.[57] But these plans were abandoned before Alexander's teenage years. Fourth son Anthony would have a brief, but intense, career at court, before entering the capuchin order after his father's death. Anthony took the religious name Charles in honour of his father, and Brussels was his place of birth. Hence father Charles of Brussels, who would go on to create his family's history.

In the first decade of their marriage, Charles of Arenberg and Anne of Croy had quite limited financial resources, partly because their northernmost seigniories were either sequestered or sacked during the Dutch Revolt.[58] They could hardly even meet their most pressing financial obligations.[59] This meant that the bulk of their financial means was invested in the education of eldest son Philip. However, help came from an unexpected source. In 1595, Anne of Croy's father had died. Her elder brother Charles of Croy (1560-1612) had thus inherited the ducal title of Aarschot. Only a few years after that, the new duke of Aarschot received a second ducal title from the French king Henry IV, and would now style himself Charles, duke of Aarschot and duke of Croy. In 1600, Alexander and Anthony were 'claimed' by this childless uncle of Aarschot, who felt these boys were best educated by him.[60] This might explain why plans to entrust Alexander to the church were halted. In any case, the Arenberg-Croy couple decided to agree with

---

cases preference has been given to use a person's title, instead of his name.

55 'pour le bien et utilité et conservation de la grandeur de notre maison': AAE, Bio 5, fol. 23v–24v, *Minute du consentiment et aggréation de feu Monsieur Charles d'Aremberghe*.

56 AAE, Bio 105 and Callaey, *La vie religieuse*, 57–61. It actually had become clear much sooner that Eugene was of such a 'delicate nature' that he would best pursue an ecclesiastical career.

57 AAE, Bio 5, fol. 1r, Age dispensation for Charles and Alexander of Arenberg.

58 Neu, *Die Arenberger*, 1: 242 and Roger Vermeulen, "Vorselaar, Retie en Lichtaart", in *Arenberg in de Lage Landen: een hoogadellijk huis in Vlaanderen en Nederland*, (ed.) Jan Roegiers (Louvain: Leuven University Press, 2002), 156.

59 AAE, Correspondence Charles of Arenberg (CKA), nr 50–nr 58, *Margaret of Ligne, countess of Lalaing to Charles of Arenberg*, from 1602 to 1611: Charles's sister complains year after year about his inabilities to pay her dowry. In 1603 his debts already amounted to 28 years' worth of unpaid rents to his sister.

60 AAE, Bio 5, fol. 1r; Callaey, *La vie religieuse*, 50 and A.-K. Van Laer, "Ceste servirat pour vous baiser humblement les mains: de mentaliteit van de hoge adel gezien

the duke of Aarschot's plans. Both Alexander and Anthony stayed with their uncle from 1600 until 1610. They studied at the university in Leuven, and were only permitted to visit their parents about two weeks a year.[61] In 1610, at 17 years old, Anthony was 'released' from his uncle's care and sent to the Brussels court.[62] He then spent more time with his parents, apparently mostly with his mother, who promptly expected her fourth son to provide for her in old age.[63] Also in 1610, the duke of Aarschot's plans with his other nephew Alexander became more outspoken. Amongst other things, a contract was drawn up in which Alexander was promised the Croy palace at the Brussels Coudenberg.[64] These were probably the first cracks in Anne of Croy's chances to inherit from her brother, although she did not recognise them as such. In fact, both Anne of Croy and her husband had signed and thus ratified this contract 'as heirs apparent of this house and of said lord duke'.[65]

Growing up, eldest son Philip's position was thus quite ambiguous. He was raised as the eldest and 'most important' son in every way possible. He was sent on a Grand Tour to visit the places and the courts his father had been to before him.[66] So everywhere Philip went he must have been welcomed as his father's heir, an Arenberg. [67] He was undeniably brought up to follow in his father's footsteps, while at the same time he knew he was not expected to inherit from him, nor even take his name. The question is what kind of an identity he actually developed. Did he identify with his father's family, or was his upbringing distinct enough to instil in him a sense of dynastic expectancy, the knowledge that he was somehow different vis-à-vis his brothers? In any case, thanks to the support of his uncle, it was mostly Alexander who seemed to have learned what it was like to be a Croy, while distant Philip, away on his tour for several years, mostly met with his father's dynastic allies.

---

door de familiecorrespondentie van Karel van Arenberg en Anne van Croy (1600–1635)" (Master's Thesis in History, Katholieke Universiteit Leuven, 1988), 111–15.

61 Van Laer, "Ceste servirat", 112.

62 Callaey, *La vie religieuse*, 62–3.

63 AAE, Bio 5, fol. 125v, *Anne of Croy to Antonia-Wilhelmina of Arenberg,* 27 March 1616.

64 National Archives in Brussels (Algemeen Rijksarchief Brussel, ARAB), Archival collection Arenberg (FA), MG 1154 nr. 1, *Donation d'entre viff que fait Charles sire et duc de Croy et d'Arschot à Alexandre d'Aremberg,* 22 January 1610.

65 'nostre propre d'héritiers plus apparent d'icelle maison et dudict Seigneur Ducq': ARAB, Arenberg, MG 1154 nr. 1.

66 Neu, *Die Arenberger*, 2:35 and Van Laer, "Ceste servirat", 102–5.

67 For an overview of the European network of Charles of Arenberg and his connections to Bavaria and other members of the imperial nobility see also: Marini, "Dynastic relations".

Changing Fortunes

Philip's position changed drastically around 1605, coincidentally the year he returned from his European tour at the age of 18. The duke of Aarschot and his first wife had lived separately for almost 20 years when she died.[68] The duke quickly remarried in the hopes of still procuring a (legitimate) child. In 1605, he married his young cousin Dorothea of Croy, daughter of the marquis of Havré.[69] This marriage must have shocked the Arenberg-Croy couple. If the young duchess had a child, the Aarschot-clause of Anne of Croy's marriage contract would be void. Moreover, the duke made a show of marrying within the Croy family to make sure the Croy patrimony remained united. This tactic, a 'cousin-marriage', is often seen as the defining mark of nineteenth-century family strategy, aimed at preserving and enlarging family fortunes, and according to Sabean almost completely absent in seventeenth-century Europe.[70] But as this example shows, in the early seventeenth century the prospect of a female succession to a patrilineal inheritance – although still quite common – nevertheless already pushed some families into following this practice.

Anne of Croy, who spent the first 20 years of her marriage believing she would bring the Aarschot inheritance into the Arenberg family, now became a most unlikely heir. The years 1605–1606 are therefore a pivotal point in the life of the Arenberg dynasty. Coincidentally or not, Anne of Croy and her husband decided to buy the seigniory and city of Enghien in 1606.[71] The Arenberg patrimony was heavily mortgaged just to make this purchase possible. Until that time, the couple did not possess a castle or town that could be seen as a worthy 'dynastic seat'; now suddenly they did. Arenberg ostentatiously devoted himself to the renovation of his castle and gardens in Enghien, while deciding to retire from an active political career. Eighteen-year-old Philip had just returned from his Grand Tour and upon arrival started his military career in the Habsburg army and took over his father's prominent place at court. Philip was now firmly installed as the principal heir of the Arenberg patrimony, expected to continue the name and title of Arenberg. In 1608 he was given the barony Zevenbergen in Brabant, which had been of special importance to his grandmother Margaret de la Marck, since her husband John of

68 As mentioned before, this childless marriage had prompted Anne of Croy's father to name her second in line for his inheritance.

69 The marquis of Havré was a younger half-brother of Charles of Croy's father, and thus the duke's uncle.

70 David Warren Sabean, "Kinship and Class Dynamics in Nineteenth-Century Europe", in *Kinship in Europe. Approaches to Long-Term Development (1300–1900)*, (ed.) David Warren Sabean et al. (New York: Berghahn Books, 2007), 301–13.

71 For more on this purchase see Yves Delannoy, *La cession de la seigneurie d'Enghien par Henri IV à Charles d'Arenberg en 1607*. Gemeentekrediet historische uitgaven. Reeks in-8° 76 (Brussels: Gemeentekrediet, 1988).

Ligne was buried there.[72] It was an important dynastic symbol. So in the years to come, his role as likely heir to the Aarschot fortune changed into a role as the confirmed heir of the Arenberg patrimony. The identity he had been prepared to embrace was replaced by one he was never intended to learn. The crucial nature of this episode was not recognised as such in the *Marques des Grandeurs*. The beauties and importance of Enghien were of course evoked, but it was not recognised as an identity marker, or at least not anymore in 1660.[73] But in the crucial decades of 1605–1640 it was the main canvas upon which Anne of Croy painted her version of the family identity.

In 1610, the year the duke of Aarschot made up a new will and seemed to be grooming Alexander of Arenberg to succeed him, Philip of Arenberg married Anne-Hypolite de Melun (+1615), daughter of Pierre de Melun, the prince of Epinoy.[74] His marriage turned out to be a happy one, and his wife gave birth to two daughters in 1611 and 1613. But Philip was unhappy. He was subjected to bouts of melancholy and seemed to be emotionally unstable.[75] He claimed to be at a disadvantage, because he could not possibly hold up his station at court with the allowance he received.[76] Since his mother was the administrator of the family finances, his complaints were directed against her. It is not clear whether there was any truth in his complaints. Later events suggest Philip was not very prudent in the management of his financial affairs, something he was reprimanded for by his mother.[77] More and more, the relationship between Philip and his mother became strained, only kept in check as long as the head of the dynasty, his father, was still alive.

72 Van Laer, "Ceste servirat", 102–5.

73 AAE, Bio 1, fol. 204–23, *Achat de la terre d'Enghien.*

74 On Melun's treason see: Charles Piot, "Melun (Pierre de)", *Biographie Nationale*, 14 (Brussel, 1897), 332–5.

75 ARAB, FA, nr. MG 925 (6), *Philip of Arenberg to the Infanta Isabella*, s.d.: a desperate plea to the Infanta about his over-controlling mother and AAE, Bio 6, *Anne of Croy to Philip of Arenberg,* 22 February 1620: about his ill health and continuing melancholy.

76 AAE, Bio 7, fol. 17r–17v, *Philip of Arenberg accepts that his 10.000 fl. annual allowance is reduced to 5.000 fl. annually in consideration of his siblings*, s.d. and Bio 8, fol. 79v, *Anne of Croy to Philip of Arenberg,* s.d. and fol. 42r, *Philip of Arenberg to Anne of Croy,* 5 February 1620.

77 AAE, Bio. 8, fol. 43r, *Philip of Arenberg to Anne of Croy,* 25 February 1620. Others were quick to profit from his distress, see also: Marini, "Female Authority". Up until 1615 however his mother seemed to be content with his frugal life style see: Callaey, *La vie religieuse*, 85–7.

The Croy-Aarschot Inheritance: The Struggle to Justify Female Inheritance Rights

Although the duchess Dorothea, the duke of Aarschot's wife, was very young, her expected pregnancy held off. Aarschot thus devised a new way of keeping his sister – and her Arenberg descendants – away from his inheritance. Around 1610, he decided to name his father-in-law universal heir to his fortune.[78] His sister still appeared in his new will, as universal heir to the moveable goods he did not dispose of.[79] This was a meagre consolation prize, as everything 'of value' was now lost to her. Aarschot quite adamantly referred to the Arenberg as a 'different' family. So where the old duke, Anne's father, had believed female inheritance would save his dynasty, her brother was convinced it would be the ruin of it: 'that I would be the last of my house, and that by dying without descendants, my house, falling to the distaff, would be lost, and that such beautiful goods and grand titles would go to another house'.[80] From the wording in his will, it is clear he could not see Philip, his sister's eldest son as a Croy. Although apparently he stressed his blood ties to Anne of Croy herself, his vision of what constituted the Croy-Aarschot dynasty was clearly not defined by the closest blood ties, his next of kin, but by a male dominated identity, only passed on by men carrying the Croy patronym.[81] He made it plainly clear that a woman could not possibly inherit these titles. Applying Salic Law to both his ducal titles of Aarschot in the Low Countries and of Croy in France, the duke defended the idea that his double ducal title was one and undividable, and thus, could not be inherited by his sister. When he died in 1612, these dispositions could not be accepted by the Arenberg.

The duke's apparent aversion to female inheritance did not prevent him from naming Alexander of Arenberg heir to the county of Beaumont and the principality of Chimay.[82] Alexander in return was expected to carry the name Croy-Chimay-Arenberg. Aarschot's decision to favour Alexander over Philip must be seen in light of his personal relationship with Alexander. By giving Chimay and Beaumont to his sister's child, Aarschot did in a way recognise the validity of female inheritance, or at least, when it concerned lordships acquired through female inheritance in the first place, like Chimay. On the other hand, ignoring his sister's place and

[78] Baron de Reiffenberg, *Une existence de grand seigneur au seizième siècle: Mémoires autographes du Duc Charles de Croy* (Brussel: Muquardt, 1845) and Piet De Fraine, "1612–1640: le Duché d'Aerschot passe de la Maison de Croy à la Maison d'Arenberg", *Le Folklore Brabançon* 173 (1967): 67–89.

[79] De Fraine, "1612–1640: le Duché d'Aerschot", 77–80.

[80] 'que j'éstois le dernier de ma maison, et qu'en mourant sans délaisser génération, ma maison, tombant en quenoille comme elle faisoit, éstoit perdue, et que tant de beaux biens et grand tiltres fussent venus à un aultre maison': as cited in Karel Slos, "Karel van Croy en de recuperatie van de Zuid-Nederlandse adel onder de aartshertogen" (Master's Thesis History, Katholieke Universiteit Leuven, 1997), 23.

[81] For the emphasis on this blood tie see: Wrede, *Ohne Furcht und Tadel*, 130.

[82] De Fraine, "1612–1640: le Duché d'Aerschot", 67–89.

assigning them directly to one of her sons, also stressed female inheritance was not necessarily about a woman inheriting directly. The bulk of Aarschot's inheritance, with his two ducal titles, went to the Croy-Havré, the younger Croy branch headed by his uncle/father-in-law.[83]

Figure 5.3 Coat of Arms of Anne of Croy, sculpted on the enclosure of the chapel of Our-Lady-of-the-Rosary in the Saint-Nicolas parish church in Enghien (Belgium), the confraternity of which she founded in 1631. Both her husband's and her own complicated dynastic descent is visible. For Charles: Arenberg-Marck – Ligne-Barbançon. For Anne: Croy-Renty. Copyright Studio Berger Enghien (Belgium).

Anne of Croy successfully challenged her brother's will. Through a ruling by the court of Brabant in 1614, the duchy of Aarschot was awarded to her and her descendants.[84] However, Salic Law did apply to the ducal title of Croy, as to the honorary title of 'head of the Croy family', both of which could not possibly be carried by a woman and were appointed to the Croy-Havré.[85] The duchess however

[83] Most likely Alexander of Arenberg had known about these plans, or at least it is said that Alexander actually wrote the will for his uncle, acting as an ad hoc secretary: Callaey, *La vie religieuse*, 51 and Slos, "Karel van Croy", 23 and 48.

[84] AAE, Bio 1, fol. 450r.

[85] See also Wrede, *Ohne Furcht und Tadel*, 133.

never accepted this ruling, and transferred her claim to the Croy ducal title to her heirs.[86] Her victory in the Aarschot case was widely applauded.[87] But from then on, the family would be immersed in the worst disputes imaginable.

The Clash of Identities: Arenberg, Croy or Croy-Arenberg?

As long as the princely count of Arenberg was alive, all was seemingly well. But when he died in 1616, when some of the legal issues surrounding the Aarschot inheritance were not completely settled yet, the problems started. The dynastic identity as developed by Charles of Arenberg and Anne of Croy was almost brand-new. Although the capuchin Charles of Brussels made it seem like an old and fixed identity had long ago been consolidated, the actual truth is that in 1616, no clear identity had been consolidated. The insecurity surrounding the Croy inheritance and then the actual incredibly messy succession had interrupted the consolidation of a dominant identity. Hence, Anne of Croy needed to build on the dynastic vision as expressed in her marriage contract. During her entire two decades as a widow, she tried to fabricate a mixed Croy-Arenberg identity, presenting this identity as the almost logical consequence of her marriage. But in 1616, the realities of succession, and the realities of the development of a different dynastic consciousness by her sons, would constantly interact and clash with her own vision.

Alexander, who through his mother's legal actions saw his chance of forming his own Chimay dynasty thwarted, was bought off with a compromise. He did not inherit Chimay and Beaumont directly from his uncle, but received these two lordships from his parents through a family agreement. In return, he would have to pay his mother 100,000 fl.[88] So actually Alexander did call himself Croy-Chimay-Arenberg and is considered the founder of a new dynasty, a younger branch of the Arenberg.[89] Alexander's marriage contract, signed in 1613, still considered him a possible heir, both of the Arenberg and of the Aarschot inheritances. For the Arenberg titles he was fourth in line after his older brother Philip and his younger brothers Anthony and Eugene. But for the Aarschot title he was next in line after Philip.[90] This shows again the pre-eminence of the Croy-Aarschot inheritance,

[86] AAE, T 1, fol. 294v and 297v.

[87] The Archdukes seemed to be siding with the Arenberg in this conflict: AAE, Bio 2, fol. 207v, *Archduke Albert to Charles of Arenberg*, 21 October 1614.

[88] AAE, Bio 20, *Alexander of Arenberg to Anne of Croy*, 23 May 1615 and 10 May 1617.

[89] See Maurice, *Le Blason des Armoiries*, 383 for how this new identity was translated in his coat of arms.

[90] AAE, Bio 4, fol. 76r–82r, *Marriage agreement between Alexander of Arenberg and Magdalena of Egmont*. Interestingly, if Alexander was to be sole heir to both patrimonies, his eldest son would have to resurrect the Arenberg dynasty, thus implying that the Arenberg

as well as an inability to completely sidestep the dying wishes of the duke of Aarschot. As long as Alexander's father was alive, relations between mother and son remained cordial. But after Charles of Arenberg's death, Alexander seemed to 'ignore' his mother's position in the family more and more. Before any peace could be made between them, Alexander died on the battlefield in 1629.[91]

It is not clear exactly how Philip felt, when all of a sudden he became the Croy-Aarschot heir again, especially since he also lost a decent part of his inheritance in favour of his younger brother Alexander. He does not seem to have had a bad relationship with Alexander.[92] Philip did profit from his other brother Anthony's actions. Upon the death of his father, Anthony had decided to enter a capuchin monastery in 1617.[93] However, his mother had only just provided him with an honourable share of her patrimony.[94] She had given it under some sort of apanage: Anthony could not dispose of his share freely.[95] If he was unable to have heirs, or if he in some way contradicted his mother, his share automatically fell back to his mother's patrimony.[96] When he entered the monastery without permission, he should have been legally held to return his lordships to his mother, but instead he made a will and left everything to his older brothers Philip and Alexander.[97] So now, both sons Alexander and Anthony had committed some sort of 'dynastic treason' by not following the dynastic plan set out by (one of) their parents.[98]

The duchess's relationship with Philip was worse. Recently widowed Philip shockingly considered following his brother Anthony's example in joining the capuchin order.[99] This prompted the duchess to spur the Archdukes into action.[100] Albert and Isabella had been understanding where Anthony, a fourth son, was concerned. They could not however permit a leading man of the Low Countries' nobility and the principal heir to the highest noble title in the Netherlands to forsake his duties. In fact, the panic with which the duchess of Aarschot reacted against

---

and Croy-Aarschot patrimonies were intended to remain separate and that the (re)creation of two different dynasties was the ultimate goal.

91 His new dynasty of Croy-Chimay-Arenberg was short-lived. By the end of the seventeenth century it had died out. The Chimay title was inherited by the Hénin-Liétard family and was hence lost for both the Croy and the Arenberg families.

92 However, their respective heirs would face each other in court over the payment of the 100,000 fl. They would settle it by a 'cousin-marriage' between the young branches.

93 For a full account on his decision and its result see Callaey, *La vie religieuse*.

94 Callaey, *La vie religieuse*, 110–17.

95 See also Callaey, *La vie religieuse*, 143.

96 AAE, Bio 5, fol. 45r, *Papier originelle d'une promesse que Anthoine d'Aremberghe Comte de Seneghem faisoit à feu Monseigneur le Duc son père et Madame sa mère*, 17 November 1613.

97 Callaey, *La vie religieuse*, 110–17.

98 Youngest son Eugene would also enter a capuchin monastery, but he was excused for it.

99 Even his siblings thought this was outrageous: Van Laer, "Ceste servirat", 69.

100 And even the papal nuntius was against these plans: Neu, *Die Arenberger*, 2:37.

her son's pious wishes, was the result of a new emerging demographic crisis. Of her five surviving sons, only two had children, and all of those grandchildren were girls.[101] Despite her own fecundity, her Arenberg-Aarschot dynasty was in peril of dying out. But her decision to include the Archdukes and to expose her son as a nobleman forsaking the divine duty to his dynasty and his princes, cannot have warmed Philip's heart to his mother. Strikingly, she evoked the prospect of the entire Arenberg-Aarschot patrimony falling to another family by the future marriage of his five-year-old daughter and heir. She used the argument of the insecurities of female inheritance to convince her son to marry again.[102] In the event, Philip didn't enter the capuchin order, but he would hold off remarrying for another few years.

In 1617, the duchess accorded Philip the right to use the title 'duke of Aarschot', while at the same keeping control over the Croy-Aarschot patrimony itself.[103] Philip had inherited the Arenberg patrimony when his father died, but his mother held the 'gardenoble' of her (underage) children, thus retaining financial rights to the Arenberg patrimony. She was also entitled to the lordships she had acquired with her late husband.[104] Years of endless public disputes arose over the financial management of the duchy of Aarschot.[105] Philip took his problems to court and surprisingly was confirmed in his claims. In 1619 the sovereign court of the duchy of Brabant, more commonly known as the Council of Brabant, ruled that Anne of Croy had never inherited the duchy herself.[106] It had passed 'through her body' to her husband, and then when he died, directly to the eldest son. Anne of Croy was not a duchess, but a dowager-duchess. This was somewhat contradictory to the council's earlier ruling and it did not end all conflicts, as the duchess was still entitled to manage the duchy's financial affairs.[107]

The way Anne of Croy represented herself in the conflicts with her son are interesting. In a letter to him, she wrote: 'and if you do not do it, I will show you

---

[101] Philip's two daughters were five and three years old respectively. Alexander also had two daughters when his father died: a one year old and one newly born. Anthony had in fact conceived a child before becoming a capuchin. Apparently he had impregnated an unknown woman at the Brussels court. The child was a girl, but of course she had no rights to (part of) the Arenberg patrimony.

[102] ARAB, FA, MG nr. 4001, *Certains poinctz que Madame la Duchesse d'Arschot remonstre à Monsieur le Ducq d'Arschot son filz aisné*, s.d.

[103] De Fraine, "1612–1640: le Duché d'Aerschot", 83.

[104] AAE, Bio 2, *L'originel traicté de mariage de leurs Exces faict au Chasteau de Beaumont le XVI de septembre 1586* and Marini, "Female authority".

[105] See for the public nature of these disputes: ARAB, FA, nr. MG 925 (6), *Philip of Arenberg to the Infanta Isabella* and Birgit Houben, "Wisselende gedaanten. Het hof en de hofhouding van de landvoogden Isabella Clara Eugenia (1621–1633) en de kardinaal-infant don Fernando van Oostenrijk (1634–1641) te Brussel" (PhD diss., Ghent University, 2009), 127.

[106] De Fraine, "1612–1640: le Duché d'Aerschot", 80–87.

[107] Wrede, *Ohne Furcht und Tadel*, 158 and 183.

that I am your mother and to him [a counsellor of Philip] that I am Anne of Croy'.[108] That expression is one of the most striking examples of how her own dynastic identity was placed opposite to that of her children. The same kind of viewpoint is also expressed in her will when she reflected upon her efforts to set the finances of the Arenberg family straight.[109] In her relations with people, she very much remained a Croy. The Croy identity was a very dominant one. But the ruling of the Council of Brabant in 1619 was interesting: if Anne had never inherited the duchy and it had passed directly to her husband, did that mean that the duchy of Aarschot became part of the Arenberg patrimony?[110] They were both transmitted to descendants under fideicommisum, but did the same fideicommisum apply to both these patrimonies? Did the articles in the Croy-Arenberg marriage contract relating to her eldest son's name and coats of arms still stand? Judging by the way successive counts (and later dukes) of Arenberg inherited both these titles and patrimonies, it did seem that they were 'merged' into one undividable Arenberg-Aarschot patrimony, if not de iure than at least de facto. But these descendants always stressed their Arenberg sovereign rights and titles, stemming in other words from a very dominant Arenberg identity.

Philip can be seen as a transitional figure. He used his Aarschot title and was habitually called 'Aarschot' and not 'Arenberg' by his peers. On the other hand, he was also the first Arenberg to use the 'simplified' coat of arms, which was clearly Arenberg.[111] He seems to have juggled between his identities: Aarschot when it supported his political power in the Low Countries, Arenberg when it supported his claim on precedence over his peers and a privileged treatment by the Habsburg. But the events of the Fronde interfered with this double identity. Philip spent the last years of his life in captivity in Madrid. The king stated that in his lands – the Spanish Low Countries – Philip was indeed Aarschot, and thus a vassal of the king, subjected to his authority.[112] His sovereign, Arenberg, identity was of no consequence. Philip's eldest son Philip-Francis was educated at court in Madrid and was manoeuvred into a Spanish marriage.[113] In 1644, nine years after Anne of Croy's death, the imperial county of Arenberg was elevated to a duchy. And from then on, the Aarschot identity, which was implied to make the Arenberg 'dependent' on the person of the king, was made subordinate to the new Arenberg ducal title. They became dukes of Arenberg and Aarschot, independent and sovereign. It is that identity which father Charles of Brussels needed to teach his nephew and his heirs. But although the Croy identity was not fully incorporated

[108] 'et si vous ne le faicte je vous monstreray que je vous suis mere, et à luy que je suis Anne de Croy': AAE, Bio 8, fol. 79v., *Anne of Croy to Philip of Arenberg*, s.d.

[109] AAE, T 1, fol. 319v–320r.

[110] Martin Wrede points to the fact that de iure they would remain separate: Wrede, *Ohne Furcht und Tadel*, 130–33 and 156–8.

[111] See Maurice, *Le Blason des Armoiries*, 372 for his coat of arms.

[112] Neu, *Die Arenberger*, 2: 93.

[113] Neu, *Die Arenberger*, 2: 86–7.

into the sovereign ducal Arenberg identity, Anne of Croy's legacy of religion, loyalty and family union oozed off the pages of the *Marques des Grandeurs*.

Conclusion: Croy-Arenberg for all Eternity

The cover illustration of this volume is the altar piece of the capuchin church in Enghien, painted in 1617 by the rather obscure Servaes de Coelx.[114] The painting faces the entrance to the Arenberg family crypt in the church floor. It demonstrates quite aptly which version of their family's identity Anne of Croy and her husband wished to transmit to their descendants. The painting was finished around early 1617, but it had been ordered almost a year before, so probably right before Charles of Arenberg died. The way the family is represented in this painting and the values it was supposed to transmit, are rather striking. I have argued elsewhere that this painting, the rituals surrounding Anne of Croy's funeral and the wording of her will form a curious trinity. They all point to her desire to be seen as a 'pendant' of her husband, or rather of his authority, his dynastic position and of his exemplary lifestyle, even if she died almost 20 years after it was finished.[115]

About 50 or so members of the Croy and Arenberg families are represented in this painting.[116] Now, we could assume that the couple had a number of options in the representation of their family members, even though the theme in itself – The Adoration of the Magi – asked for certain 'fixed' elements. The division along gender lines of these families does not have to be considered a lucky coincidence or just a reflexion of gender roles in the church or the artist's creative freedom. Considering the whole theme of the painting revolves around the Arenberg-Croy couple as saviours of the dynasty and bringers of prosperity, the Arenberg and Croy family members were most likely 'mixed' on purpose.[117] It is no coincidence that so many people made it into the painting, rather it gives the impression of a strong and long 'historical' dimension in their family identity. By mixing up these families an impression of dynastic continuity is given, and the fluid nature of what constitutes a dynasty becomes clear. It is as if the Arenberg-Croy couple formed the apotheosis of the combined family histories of both the Croy and the Marck-Arenberg families, who passed on this 'merged' identity to their children, all depicted on the first rows behind them. The smaller children on this painting were actual grandchildren of the couple, while the angels might be deceased children and grandchildren. The painting is thus an almost exact translation of the

114 Servaes de Coelx, *The Adoration of the Magi*, oil on canvas 328x258 cm, 1617.

115 Marini, "Pendanten in leven en dood".

116 Landelin Hoffmans, *Les portraits des d'Arenberg dans les tableaux religieux des XVIIe et XVIIIe siècles à Enghien* (Enghien: Imprimerie Delwarde, 1941) gives a detailed overview of the supposed identity of the people portrayed. However, some of his interpretations are disputable.

117 See for more about the theme of this painting: Marini, "Female Authority", 12–18.

generational life of the Croy-Arenberg dynasty: all the ascendants and descendants of the couple, united in their admiration for 'Christ', the 'holy product' of this prosperous couple. In a sense, this painting also represented the 'victorious' couple, winning the legal war around the Aarschot inheritance and claiming the Croy legacy as their own.

Since dynastic loyalty – towards their Habsburg princes, their family (as in forebears and descendants) and the church – is prominently present in this painting, as well as in Anne of Croy's will, this sense of dynastic representation had to be transmitted to the main heir. Eldest son Philip – in the painting represented as King Balthasar – was supposed to interiorise these ideals of a merged identity, supported on the combined family histories of the Croy and the Arenberg. And since Anne of Croy positioned herself as the guardian and creator of this merged identity, Philip was supposed to honour her will to transmit her version of dynastic loyalty to his descendants. It was as tangible a good to be transferred as her jewels or her houses. And by accepting the terms of her will and taking control of his inheritance, he was also held to accept this 'mixed' version of Arenberg-Croy family identity. But as stated in this contribution, the duchess's views on her family identity were heavily compromised by the conflicts surrounding the Aarschot inheritance. Interestingly enough, the image of the pious Charles of Arenberg as saviour of the Arenberg dynasty, as constructed and perpetuated by the duchess, did make it into the Arenberg family history written by their son the capuchin. It was an image she spent decades building, mostly in order to confirm her own authority. But where this image was readily accepted and transferred within the dynasty, her own Croy identity was lost in the process.

One could argue that the familiarity of the Arenberg family with female inheritance prompted their undisputed acceptance of the same terms, when it concerned the prestigious and very promising Croy-Aarschot inheritance. However, when in 1612 Anne's brother, Charles of Croy, duke of Aarschot and duke of Croy, indeed died without producing legitimate offspring, a fierce legal battle ensued. The five sons and possible heirs of the Arenberg-Croy couple had all developed different identities. Some chose ecclesiastical careers, the eldest was educated in an especially ambiguous way, and his younger brother had been clearly groomed to become a Croy.

Succession rights as determined by the couple were continually tinkered with, not in the least by the childless duke of Aarschot. The consolidation of the Arenberg identity had been put on hold, and was forced to develop rapidly against the backdrop of family conflicts and political survival. The Arenberg identity as it was created by Charles of Brussels had to fine-tune a previously weakened identity, still influenced by older notions of the de la Marck heritage. It now excluded any further weakening of this original, dominant, 'old' and fixed identity, by no longer incorporating legacies left through the female inheritance of a title that had ultimately compromised the family, politically, as well as emotionally.

Chapter 6

Points of Transferral: Mademoiselle de Guise's Will and the Transferability of Dynastic Identity

Jonathan Spangler

The lure of the grand heiress has provided rich storylines for countless myths and dramas, from the ancient Greek legend of Atalanta to the tragic opera *Turandot*. Royal fathers steered the fates of their daughters by imposing trials of strength or wit to determine worthiness of potential heirs. In stories such as these we learn little about dynastic identity. What traits of the bride's family are perpetuated once the successful suitor has taken over her father's throne? Is dynastic identity transferable?

History provides very real examples of spectacular heiresses being pursued by ambitious men and can illuminate us further by the outcomes of such matches. Sometimes these were negotiated by parents or other surviving family members, with or without the participation of the heiress, while in other cases the heiress was a widow, and thus operating at a more independent level. Such is the case of the well-known 'Monkey Duchess', Elizabeth Cavendish, heiress of properties from both her father, the duke of Newcastle, and more significantly of her late husband, the duke of Albemarle (Christopher Monck, hence her nickname). Displaying a tinge of madness, she declared she would re-marry none but a crowned head, and was duly wooed by the earl of Montagu in 1690, who posed as the emperor of China.[1] The outcome was that the Albemarle name and identity was lost, as its fortunes served to forge a new dynastic identity by elevating the Montagu family to the rank of duke (1705). In this case, a mentally impaired heiress was no more successful than her fictional counterparts in transferring her dynastic identity intact.

But can we find counter-examples? Could princely or aristocratic heiresses in the early modern world exercise agency in selecting their own heirs or in controlling the passage of dynastic identity from one lineage to another? What factors enabled them to do so, and what factors limited their choices and actions? This chapter will examine one of the greatest heiresses of seventeenth-century France, Marie de Lorraine, Mlle de Guise (1615–1688), who was presented with an opportunity to preserve her family's name and reputation as she came to the end of her life. The last member of her family, she had never married, and as a woman

1 Edward C. Metzger, "Montagu, Ralph, First Duke of Montagu", *Oxford Dictionary of National Biography* (Oxford, 2004), http://www.oxforddnb.com/view/article/19030 [accessed 6 July 2012].

in her seventies, was unlikely to re-start a dynasty through marriage. She was thus faced with the option, like a Roman emperor, to choose her successor based on a set of criteria that was important to her, and which we can identify as a Guisard dynastic identity. I will argue that the twin poles of this identity, foreign princely status and Catholic orthodoxy, both helped and hindered Mlle de Guise's attempts to secure the transferral of her family's 'property' (physical and ideological) to the most suitable heir. In the end, Mlle de Guise was unsuccessful, in large part due to the incompatibility of her dynastic ideals with Louisquatorzian notions of a centralised absolutist state, one that was 'French', or even 'national', with no room for non-royal princes who were by definition 'trans-national'. As we will see, Mlle de Guise's bar was set too high. Yet her case is valuable in demonstrating that female agency was at least a possibility; it is thus useful to begin with a brief survey to identify other women with similar opportunities in this period.

What's in a Name? Heiresses and Dynastic Preservation Strategies

The central issue Marie de Lorraine grappled with was survival of a name and its 'renown', more than merely material concerns such as estates, buildings and movable wealth. Such things came and went, but a name endured. This was neither a new concept in the 1680s, nor would it cease to be an issue for aristocrats for centuries to come. A standard strategy since the middle ages had been to give the name (and arms and properties) of an heiress's defunct family to a second son: for example, the House of Laval endured from the thirteenth century as a cadet branch of the Montmorency.[2] This strategy remained a European standard, even at the highest levels, the most famous example being that of Maria Theresa of Austria and Francis Stephen of Lorraine: in this case the senior princes took the name Habsburg (or 'Austria'), while 'Lorraine' was retained by the cadet line established in Tuscany.[3]

Some noble families in early modern France relied on another strategy: they kept the heiress within the dynasty by marrying her across lines of *cousinage*, often niece to uncle. In the eighteenth century, the grandest court families of

[2] Genealogical data for the following paragraphs is derived primarily from Père Anselme de Sainte-Marie, *Histoire Généalogique et Chronologique de la Maison Royale de France, des Pairs, des Grands Officiers de la Couronne & de la Maison du Roy, des anciens Barons du Royaume, avec les qualitez, l'origine, le progrès et les armes de toutes leurs familles* (9 vols, Paris: La Compagnie des libraires, 1726–33).

[3] Other name preservation strategies existed in early modern Europe, including more 'agglutinative' systems such as those used in Britain or Iberia, where surnames were simply added rather than lost, in increasingly long chains: Temple-Nugent-Grenville-Chandos-Brydges in eighteenth-century England, and today's Duquesa de Alba in Spain, personally representing four leading dynasties: Álvarez de Toledo, Silva, FitzJames-Stuart and Colón de Portugal.

Montmorency, Rohan and La Tour d'Auvergne employed this strategy, almost to exclusion of any other; they had more than estates and a name to preserve – they had ducal and princely rank to guard, with relevant fiscal and honorific privileges. In contrast, nobles of lesser rank sometimes defied their blood relatives and natural heirs, aiming for something bigger: to preserve the name within a *different* lineage, one with ducal or princely status. This can be seen in the actions of the heiresses of the families of Albret-Pons or Montlaur-Maubec with regard to the House of Lorraine. In both cases, the family names were preserved not in surnames, but in titles given to younger sons (and exalted; for example, 'prince de Pons', though no real principality existed).[4] This strategy was not always successful. The last Gouffier duc de Rouannais defied the hopes of his collateral cousins by becoming a monk in 1667, and selling his duchy – as well as his sister – to the comte de la Feuillade d'Aubusson, with the idea that he would take the Rouannais title. But the Count rose quickly in favour at court and as a military commander, and became known as the maréchal-duc de la Feuillade, the Gouffier and Rouannais names being lost.

But were any of these instances demonstrably cases of female agency? Did any of the heiresses have a say in their use as 'points of transferral'? In some cases, it seems certain: Antoinette de Pons (d. 1632), was heiress of her son from her first marriage, and transferred his duchy of La Rocheguyon to a son from her second marriage.[5] An attempt was made by Charlotte de la Marck, sovereign duchesse de Bouillon and princesse de Sedan, who chose her own husband (Henri de La Tour), but died in 1594 in childbirth. Nevertheless, her husband used his significant political credit at the French court and with the Protestant princely hierarchy to transfer her inheritance to his children by a second marriage (significantly, to Elisabeth of Nassau), despite the protests of Charlotte's natural heirs in the La Marck family.[6]

This example brings us closer to the case of Mlle de Guise, by highlighting that a significant impetus for these alliances was in the transfer of princely status. The most notable examples of this in the seventeenth century are the Grimaldis of Monaco, the Rohan-Chabot and the Montmorency-Luxembourg. In each case, the aspiring suitor hoped to gain not just a name and property, but princely rank and the privileges that went with it. In some cases they succeeded: Jacques Goyon de Matignon successfully transformed himself in 1731 into SAS Prince Jacques

---

4 Jonathan Spangler, *The Society of Princes: The Lorraine-Guise and the Conservation of Power and Wealth in Seventeenth-Century France* (Farnham: Ashgate, 2009), 193–5.

5 Perhaps she had greater flexibility in her actions as a former royal mistress (of Henri IV).

6 Charlotte did have a son who lived long enough to make his father at least the co-heir, legally. See Simon Hodson, "Politics of the Frontier: Henri IV, the Maréchal-Duc de Bouillon and the Sovereignty of Sedan", *French History* 19, no. 4 (2005). The La Marcks continued to call themselves dukes of Bouillon until 1652, when they too became extinct, leaving a daughter who took the name (and claims) to the House of Eschallard de la Boulaye.

I of Monaco. In other instances they were only partly successful: François-Henri de Montmorency-Bouteville married the heiress of a *prince étranger* family, Madeleine-Charlotte, duchesse de Luxembourg; her duchy-peerage was re-erected for him in 1661. But her efforts to have their sons recognised as princely – potentially as sovereigns of Luxembourg itself – fell upon deaf ears.[7] Similarly the marriage of Henri Chabot to Marguerite, duchesse de Rohan, enabled him to acquire her duchy in 1648, but the subsequent Rohan-Chabot heirs were not recognised as princes, unlike their 'true' Rohan cousins of Soubise and Guéméné. Again, we must ask, how much say did these heiresses have in these manoeuvres? Saint-Simon claims that Marguerite de Rohan, the greatest heiress of the mid-century, made a love match of her own choosing, despite opposition to Chabot being a Catholic.[8] In contrast, in the case of the Grimaldis, Saint-Simon indicates that while the heiress Louise-Hyppolite was confined in a convent in Aix, matters were arranged by her father, the prince of Monaco, the groom's uncle, the maréchal de Matignon, and the bride's maternal grandfather, Louis de Lorraine, comte d'Armagnac. After 15 years of waiting in an unhappy marriage, the Princess only reigned in Monaco for 306 days before following her father to the grave after a bout of smallpox in 1731. Her husband succeeded her as prince of Monaco, taking her name and arms, and her dynastic identity.[9]

Any survey of the major princely (but non-royal) heiresses in this period in France must include the two heiresses of the House of Savoy-Nemours (who spurned offers from the House of Lorraine to marry the duke of Savoy and the king of Portugal),[10] as well as their aunt by marriage, the duchesse de Nemours. Marie-Anne d'Orléans (1625–1707), duchesse de Nemours, became, as a widow, sole heiress of the House of Longueville. Her attempts to donate her sovereign principality of Neuchâtel in the 1690s to her bastard cousin, the chevalier de Soissons, led her into significant entanglements with the French legal system and the foreign policy aims of Louis XIV.[11] Her case leads us back to similar attempts to manage her own succession by Mlle de Guise.

---

7 Guy Rowlands, *The Dynastic State and the Army under Louis XIV* (Cambridge: Cambridge University Press, 2002), 327–9.

8 Saint-Simon (Louis de Rouvroy, duc de), *Mémoires*, (ed.) Y. Coirault (Paris: Gallimard, 1983), 2: 809.

9 Saint-Simon, *Mémoires*, (ed.) A. de Boislisle (Paris: Hachette, 1879–1928), 2: 34; 4:679–80; 9:37–9.

10 Robert Oresko, "Maria Giovanna Battista of Savoy-Nemours (1644–1724): Daughter, Consort and Regent of Savoy", in *Queenship in Europe, 1660–1815: The Role of the Consort*, (ed.) C. Campbell-Orr (Cambridge: Cambridge University Press, 2004).

11 Sarah Hanley, "The Family, the State, and the Law in Seventeenth- and Eighteenth-Century France: The Political Ideology of Male Right versus an Early Theory of Natural Rights", *The Journal of Modern History* 78, no. 2 (2006). This otherwise excellent article suffers from serious misconceptions about sovereignty, underpinning much of the argument with notions that France somehow had juridical rights over Neuchâtel, an Imperial fief (today in Switzerland).

Seeking an Appropriate Heir 'who will bear the name Guise'

The Très Haute et Très Puissante Princesse, Son Altesse Marie de Lorraine, duchesse de Guise, princesse de Joinville, duchesse de Joyeuse, comtesse de Montrésor, dame de Marchais et Liesse, and so on, died on March 3 1688, in her Hôtel de Guise in Paris. She was the last of her house, guardian of its treasures and its legacies since the death of her great-nephew, François-Joseph, in 1675. Her emblem printed on contemporary portraits aptly demonstrated her status, the last tree standing in a now empty forest.[12] (see Figure 6.1) At 73, she was still a maiden – at least officially – having been variously promised to princes and nobles including the king of Poland and the duc de Beaufort since she was a young girl.[13] But her family's great wealth and dominant political position repeatedly prevented any union, particularly as Marie came of age in the waning years of princely rebellion and political instability. Not flashy and heroically popular like her male Guise forebears – most notably her brother, the last fully adult duc de Guise – she instead seems to have inherited her mother's sense of duty, piety and fiscal responsibility. Like her mother, Henriette-Catherine de Joyeuse (d. 1656), she had common sense and managerial skills so lacking in her infamously foolhardy brother, Duke Henri II.[14] Even before Henri's death in 1664, Marie had taken over the family finances from her mother, as seen in her significant efforts to reduce the Guise debts, and guardianship of the Duke's heirs.[15]

---

[12] The Latin *inscriptio*, 'succisas dat coniectare superstes' can be translated as 'the survivor lets us imagine those who were cut down', but *coniectare* can also imply 'gather together': Mlle de Guise collected the remnants of both the Guise properties and their qualities as princes. It is interesting to note in the context of this chapter that the object of this sentence is feminine, referring no doubt to *arbores*, 'trees', but also, perhaps to Mlle de Guise's female predecessors. My thanks to Professor Alison Adams and Dr Gavin Kelly for help with this translation.

[13] A thorough biography of Mlle de Guise emerges from the writings of Patricia Ranum, notably her "Mademoiselle de Guise, ou les défis de la quenouille", *XVII*^{e} *siècle* 144 (1984); and *Portraits Around Marc-Antoine Charpentier* (Baltimore: Dux Femina Facti, 2004). In both works, Ranum presents evidence for a secret marriage to Mlle de Guise's friend and agent, the comte de Montrésor.

[14] The 1648 Neapolitan adventure of Henri II, duc de Guise (an attempt to replace Spanish rule with his own), is the focus of a new collection of essays, edited by this author, Jessica Munns and Penny Richards, *Aspiration, Representation and Memory: The Guise in Europe, 1506–1688* (Ashgate, 2015), which includes a chapter by this author on Guise's relationship with his mother, Henriette-Catherine de Joyeuse.

[15] Archives Nationales de France (henceforth ANF), R^{4}* 1060, 'Succession de Guise: Recueil des pièces concernant la succession' (Série R, Papiers des princes, Apanage d'Orléans).

Figure 6.1 Marie de Lorraine, duchesse de Guise, princesse de Joinville. Engraving by Antoine Masson (1684), after a painting by Pierre Mignard. Collection of the author.

In February 1686, feeling old age begin to wear her down, Mlle de Guise called together her lawyers and notaries to the Hôtel de Guise, and created two documents, a will and a donation. Through these two documents, she attempted to create a legal web that would enable her succession to pass intact to the heir of her choosing, thus bypassing her natural heirs who were not members of the House of Lorraine. But Marie's quest to cultivate an appropriate heir precedes her actions of 1686 by several decades. Since the early 1660s, she had groomed her under-aged nephew, Louis-Joseph, as Guisard heir. Again following in the footsteps of her pious and sensible mother by firmly associating herself with the *dévot* cause at court, she obtained the support of the Queen Mother and the Queen, undoubtedly crucial in obtaining a bride of the highest rank (if not of the best health) in 1667: Isabel d'Orléans, Mlle d'Alençon, a first cousin of Louis XIV and also half-Lorraine.[16] These royal links further ensured that when Louis-Joseph died in 1671, Marie was named regent of his infant son, François-Joseph – instead of the boy's mother – and was assisted by one of the ablest men in France, Jean-Baptiste Colbert.[17] Marie planned for this child to grow up as *more* than a glorious Guisard prince, a semi-royal prince, as reflected in the name he went by: duc d'Alençon. A duke four times over (Alençon, Guise, Angoulême and Joyeuse), half-Lorraine, half-Bourbon, with a huge fortune, he would enjoy his own private chapel, a personal composer and orchestra to rival the King's, and a legacy of popularity with the people of Paris that still, after nearly a hundred years, slightly un-nerved the Crown. When the child died in March 1675, Mlle de Guise was in despair.[18]

Marie therefore examined her family tree for heirs among her cousins in the House of Lorraine resident in France. As she says in her donation of 1686, the lands of the House of Guise had for centuries been held by younger sons of the House of Lorraine, and should therefore continue to do so, 'both for the justice and the glory of that house'.[19] The next-in-line senior male member of her family was Charles III, duc d'Elbeuf, but Mlle de Guise never seems to have considered him – the reason for which I have yet to uncover. Perhaps she was wary of his reputation

[16] Her parents were Gaston de France, duc d'Orléans, and Marguerite de Lorraine.

[17] Bibliothèque Nationale de France (henceforth BNF), Clairambault 1204, fols 179–222; Joly de Fleury 120, fol. 216.

[18] Strictly speaking, she was not the last member of her branch of the family, as her cousin, Henriette, abbess of Jouarre, outlived her by six years, but as a professed nun, she was legally 'dead' to the world, and thus incapable of claims to the succession. Of the two Guise widows living in 1675, one was an imbecile locked away in her château, the other a royal princess who, although she continued to bear the name 'Mme de Guise', retained her own separate identity as a *Petite-Fille de France*. See Jonathan Spangler, "Benefit or Burden? Elite Widows in Seventeenth-Century France", *Proceedings of the Annual Meeting of the Western Society for French History* 31 (2003).

[19] ANF, R^3 117, "Recueil de pieces concernant la succession de Son Altesse Mlle de Guise", (Série R, Papiers des princes, Maison de Conti), fol. 6, "Escrit fait entre Mademoiselle de Guise et Monsieur de Couvonges", 1 February 1686.

as a former Frondeur; this was 30 years in the past, but Marie would have been aware of Louis XIV's long memory when it came to the Frondes. Perhaps she disliked him personally, for his marital choice of a recently converted 'heretic', Elisabeth de La Tour d'Auvergne. But this too was in the past, as the Duchess had died in 1680, and the Duke had re-married, more appropriately, the daughter of a prominent *dévot* couple, the duc and duchesse de Navailles. Nevertheless, Mlle de Guise may have felt that his heir, Henri d'Elbeuf, retained a taint from his formerly Huguenot mother and was unsuitable to bear the name Guise. Or perhaps she felt that, as Elbeuf already had a duchy-peerage of his own, dynastic strategy would suggest that she pass her properties to a younger son; the Guise had indeed employed this strategy several times in previous generations, with the duchy-peerages of Aumale, Mayenne and Chevreuse.

In the early 1680s therefore, she looked to the duc d'Elbeuf's younger brother's son, the prince d'Harcourt. Alphonse de Lorraine was establishing himself as a soldier, had royal blood (as a great-grandson of Henri IV and Gabrielle d'Estrées), and had large estates adjoining Mlle de Guise's duchy of Joyeuse in Languedoc. His wife was a *dévot*, close to the emerging power at Versailles, the King's secret wife, Mme de Maintenon. Harcourt's sister, Marie-Anne-Françoise, had recently succeeded Mlle de Guise's own sister as abbess of the traditionally Guise-held abbey of Montmartre.[20] This seemed ideal, so in 1684 or '85, Mlle de Guise settled a transaction with the prince and princesse d'Harcourt selling them the duchy of Guise in return for some of the Guise debts being paid (by the Prince's mother's significant treasury).[21] But the transaction was never completed – though at least one property, Roquelaure in the Rhône valley, was exchanged – and the records are unclear why. Some funds were transferred, but the Duchy was not sold, and the name Harcourt disappears from Mlle de Guise's will and donation made the following year. An inventory done after the death of Mlle de Guise tantalisingly lists a memoir of pieces 'hidden away' by Mlle's archivist Gourdon at the end of 1685.[22] Why did the Harcourts suddenly lose favour? It seems likely that Marie became disgusted by the public scandal of a lawsuit involving the Prince in adultery, not with a common serving wench, but with the wife of a prominent

---

[20] Georges Poull, *La maison ducale de Lorraine* (Nancy: Presses universitaires de Nancy, 1991).

[21] Spangler, *Society of Princes*, 227, citing ANF, Minutier Central XCIX, no. 297; and Archives Départementales (henceforth AD), Ardèche, B 115, fol. 154. An entry in Dangeau's journal for 10 July 1684 notes that 'M le Prince d'Harcourt came to Versailles to inform the King that his treaty with Mlle de Guise, for the duchy of Guise, had been concluded and declared; it is claimed that he purchased it for 3,000,000 livres, of which he would only pay 2,200,000, and that, besides the gift of 800,000 livres which Mlle de Guise makes to him, she gives him also 30,000 livres *rente* on the City [of Paris]'. Dangeau (Philippe de Courcillon, marquis de), *Journal*, (eds) E. Soulié et al. (Paris: Firmin Didot frères, 1854–60), 1: 36.

[22] ANF, R^4*1056, "Inventaire après le decès de Mlle de Guise en 1688", item 146.

royal counsellor and finance officer.[23] Harcourt would leave France altogether in 1688 to seek military employment elsewhere.

We can see from the above that Mlle de Guise was developing a list of criteria for the 'appropriate' Guise heir. He was to be a member of the House of Lorraine, preferably with royal blood, whose estates would augment the Guise estates in a coherent block, someone with no taint of scandal or links with families with a Huguenot past, and not offensive politically to Louis XIV. But a further criterion that becomes apparent is the desire for an heir who might revive the Guise legacy of princely glory in the defence of the Holy Mother Catholic Church.

By moving her finger one branch further down the Guisard family tree, to the son of Elbeuf's youngest brother, Mlle de Guise found a good choice. Charles de Lorraine, prince de Commercy, was also already beginning to show great promise as a military commander and a Catholic hero, albeit on the plains of Hungary in Habsburg service not as a servant of the Bourbons. Like his cousin Harcourt, he also shared the blood of Henri IV and possessed large estates in Champagne adjoining Mlle de Guise's principal seat at Joinville.[24] Commercy also represented a link back to the senior sovereign branch of the House of Lorraine, and, as will become clear, this mattered a great deal to Mlle de Guise in her deliberations. His father had been an able general and advisor to Duke Charles IV of Lorraine in the 1660s–70s, and his mother was the Duke's own illegitimate daughter. In 1686 Commercy was serving in Vienna as a Generalfeldwachtmeister under the command of the new duke of Lorraine, Charles V, the hero of the defence of Vienna in 1683; he had left France in frustration in 1684 after being passed over for a regiment by Louis XIV, along with a fellow *prince étranger* and cousin, Prince Eugene of Savoy.[25] But although Mlle de Guise would make a significant donation to Commercy in 1686, she would not name him as her heir.

We can see the growing admiration of Mlle de Guise for her distant cousin, the head of her house, Duke Charles V of Lorraine, in the wording of her testament of February 1686. Here she notes that in a previous act, she had donated a relic of the True Cross to the Abbey of Saint-Mihiel in Lorraine, where many of her kin were buried. Now she enhances that gift with a huge annual *rente* of 1,000 livres, with the intention of 're-thanking God for the victories which He has given to the Christian armies under the conduct of SAS Msgr le Duc de Lorraine in the last war against the Turks, and to obtain for all the princes of our house the perseverance in the Catholic religion, and the grace to augment in them the zeal for maintaining

23 BNF, Collection Morel de Thoisy, vol. 95. Catherine le Breton was the wife of Nicolas de Chanterais, Sieur Dormoy, king's counsellor and comptroller of the regiment of the Royal Guard. Harcourt was at first anonymous in the court documents of 1685, since his identity and rank would force the case to be moved from the civil court of Paris to the Parlement. But by summer 1686, Harcourt was fully named and shamed.

24 For Commercy, see Spangler, *Society of Princes*, 245–8.

25 Alain Petiot, *Au service des Habsbourg. Officiers, ingénieurs, savants et artistes lorrains en Autriche* (Paris: Messene, 2000), 40–41.

it'.[26] It is this attachment that convinces her to make one final leap in her decision: her proper heir will be a son of the Duke himself. Amongst her significant legacies and donations to charities (schools, hospitals, convents) and domestic servants in both Paris and the provinces – totalling 624,000 livres in donations and 51,000 in pensions, or about 1.1 million livres capital – the last pension named in her will specifies the princely sum of 12,000 écus (35,000 livres), per year for a younger son of the Duke of Lorraine, 'who will bear the name Guise'.[27]

But it was in the donation of 1 February 1686 that Mlle de Guise chose to be more explicit. In this document she donates not just a pension, but her entire paternal estates to an un-named son of the Duke of Lorraine – at the time, there were three, all under the age of ten: Leopold, Charles and Joseph – who will not have already been ear-marked for an ecclesiastical career, who will take the name and arms of Guise, and who will come to live in the Hôtel de Guise.[28] This donation includes the crown jewels of the patrimony, the duchy of Guise in Picardy and the principality of Joinville in Champagne, plus her major financial holdings: the *rentes* on the Cinq Grosses Fermes and on the Hôtel de Ville in Paris, valued at over 1.1 million livres.[29] She states that she does this, since, on reflection of all God has willed she accumulate, it is what she *should* do ('que nous avons crû en devoir faire'). It is significant to note that this was a repeat of the donations in 1506 of the same properties, Guise and Joinville, to Marie's ancestor, Claude de Lorraine, the younger son of Duke René II, and for the same expressed reasons.[30] Here another important aspect of the dynastic identity of the House of Lorraine is recalled: defenders of the Catholic faith. Mlle de Guise, in her collections of portraits, precious objects and sacred relics, materially had 'gathered together' (as in the words of her personal emblem) the memories of her Guise forebears, the champions of the Catholic League during the Wars of Religion; martyrs for the Faith in the assassinations of 1563 and 1588.[31] But even more broadly, the House of Lorraine maintained its identity as leaders of the defence of the faith from the earliest days of the Reformation, for example, against the Lutheran peasant armies (the 'Rustauds') in 1525.[32] Other images displayed in the Hôtel de Guise

---

26 Testament of 6 February 1686, British Library (henceforth BL), Sloane, 2885, 80. There are also copies of this testament in Paris, Nancy and Vienna.

27 BL, Sloane 2885, 82.

28 Donation of 1 February 1686, ANF, R^3 117, 1.

29 "Estimations from 1697 inventory", ANF, R^3 117, 77.

30 Testament of René II, Duke of Lorraine and Bar, AD, Meurthe-et-Moselle, 3F 432, fol. 181.

31 Jonathan Spangler, "Material Culture at the Guise 'Court': A Tapestry, a Bed and a Devotional Dollhouse as Expressions of Dynastic Pride and Piety in Seventeenth-Century Paris", *Seventeenth-Century French Studies* 34, no. 2 (2012). For a useful summary and re-appraisal of the Guise in the sixteenth century, see Stuart Carroll, *Martyrs and Murderers. The Guise Family and the Making of Europe* (Oxford: Oxford University Press, 2009).

32 Guy Cabourdin, *Encyclopédie illustrée de la Lorraine: Les temps modernes – 1. De la Renaissance à la guerre de Trente ans* (Nancy: Éd. Serpenoise u.a., 1991), chapter 4;

alluded to the even older associations of the House of Lorraine with the Crusader hero, Godfrey de Bouillon, the chronicler Jean de Joinville and the Kingdom of Jerusalem, both in its physical and spiritual forms.[33]

To solidify this support for the glory of her house, Marie de Lorraine refers obliquely in her testament to two other donations made elsewhere: the duchy of Joyeuse (her maternal inheritance) to the prince de Commercy; and the seigneuries of Lambesc and Orgon in Provence to another cousin, Louis de Lorraine, comte d'Armagnac.[34] Armagnac was by 1686 rapidly becoming the *de facto* head of the House of Lorraine in France, as Master of the Horse and one of Louis XIV's few identifiable favourites.[35] Either Mlle admired him as a prince of her house acquiring glory at the French court, or, more cunningly, as someone who would defend her donation since he had something to gain from it, since Louis XIV was not likely to look favourably on the donation of two of the grandest fiefs in France (in both size and honours) to a prince being raised at the Imperial court by a Habsburg mother (Archduchess Eleonora Maria, half-sister of the Emperor). With this in mind, 'for the greatest security and validity of said donation', Mlle de Guise added one final legal twist to her preparations. The donation names as formal beneficiary not the unnamed prince of Lorraine, but Charles-François de Stainville, comte de Couvonges, who would receive and administer the properties until such time as the prince would be able to come to France to claim them. The Stainvilles were a typical Franco-Lorraine border family with strategies of divided service: while the elder son had served the king of France as a lieutenant-general, governor of Casale and commander of troops in Catalonia, the younger, Couvonges, served the duke of Lorraine as Grand Chamberlain of his court-in-exile in Innsbruck, and as diplomat and secret agent.[36] With attachments on both

William Monter, *A Bewitched Duchy: Lorraine and its Dukes, 1477–1736* (Geneva: Libr. Droz, 2007).

33 As analysed by Robert S. Sturges, "The Guise and the Two Jerusalems: An Early Modern Family's Medievalism", in Munns, Richards and Spangler, *Aspiration, Representation and Memory*, 25-46.

34 I have not located these *donations entrevifs* as they are named in the testament (and referred to even more vaguely in the donation of 1686).

35 For Armagnac, see chapter 3 of Spangler, *Society of Princes*. His brother, the chevalier de Lorraine, was the well-known favourite of the King's brother, Philippe, duc d'Orléans.

36 The Stainvilles had held significant posts in the duchy of Lorraine since the thirteenth century, and would continue to be prominent in the history of both Lorraine and France well into the eighteenth, notably in a nephew and heir, the Minister Choiseul. Jean-Joseph Expilly, *Dictionnaire géographique, historique et politique des Gaules et de la France* (1764), 2: 524; F.-A. Aubert de La Chesnaye-Desbois and J. Badier (eds), *Dictionnaire de la noblesse* (Paris: Schlesinger frères, 1863–77), 18: 681–2. The Archives des Affaires Etrangères in Paris holds cartons specifically dedicated to Couvonges: Correspondence politique, Lorraine, vol. 45 (1681–96), as envoy from the duke of Lorraine to France; and vol. 68 (1695–98), as 'secret agent'.

sides of the fence, Couvonges therefore was the perfect go-between for Mlle de Guise and her potential heir, a 'placeholder' of dynastic identity, the reliable representative of centuries of loyalty. Mlle de Guise underlines this fact, requiring that the heir, once in place, will give a pension to Couvonges, 'in order that he would be more in a state to sustain the glory of the House of Lorraine in France'.[37] Couvonges, along with Commercy and Marie's lawyer, Favieres, was also named as an executor of her testament.

By the new year 1688, Mlle de Guise felt her health was worsening and feared for the security of her donation. The duchy of Lorraine had been occupied since 1670, and despite attempts to negotiate a settlement at Nijmegen in 1679, it remained so.[38] As stated above, Louis XIV was unlikely to favour a donation to a sovereign prince being raised in an enemy camp. He had recently rejected an advantageous marriage proposed for a sister of Commercy (with the duke of Modena), stating that he 'would not involve himself' in the affairs of a family which engaged itself in interests contrary to his own.[39] Nevertheless, Marie renewed the terms of the donation, 8 January, again before lawyers and notaries,[40] then revised the testament at the end of February with her first codicil.[41] This gives the specifics of gifts and pensions for domestics, musicians, lawyers and other servants of her household (about 70 people), adds a few more pious legacies, including a pension for Père La Chaise, to 'demonstrate her great esteem' for him (or, more cynically, was this in reality a bribe for someone very close to the King?), and makes two significant additions. The first is to augment by 200,000 livres the previous donation of 100,000 livres each to the sisters of the prince de Commercy, solidifying her commitment to that particular branch of the family. The second recognises that, as Couvonges and Commercy are no longer in the country (and thus likely to be pursued rather than rewarded by the French judicial system), they should be replaced as executors of her will by the Administrators of the Hôtel-Dieu in Paris. Here too Mlle de Guise was being quite shrewd: she added a large donation of 50,000 livres for the poor of the Hôpital Général, with the condition that this money would not be paid out until *after* the other pious legacies, thus holding the Administrators hostage until they did her bidding.

A few days later, 2 March, Mlle de Guise called her notaries to her bedside once more, added a gift and pension for Couvonges, and named a few more charities. She also changed her mind about gifts she had made of a large tapestry and a ceremonial bed to the Duke of Lorraine and a jewel-encrusted wooden model

---

37 ANF, R³ 117, 6.

38 For the most recent research on this topic, see Phil McCluskey, *Absolute Monarchy on the Frontiers: Louis XIV's Military Occupations of Lorraine and Savoy* (Manchester: Manchester University Press 2013).

39 Sourches (Louis-François du Bouchet, marquis de), Mémoires sur le règne de Louis XIV, (eds) G.-J. de Cosnac and A. Bertrand (Paris: Hachette, 1882), 1:456, November 1686.

40 ANF, R³ 117, 3.

41 BL, Sloane 2885, 85.

of the House of the Virgin at Loreto to his wife the Duchess.[42] These were now to be sold like the rest of her movable goods to pay off the Guise debts. The reasoning for this change is not given. But the very next day, she made a third codicil, in which the tapestry and the bed were to be given to Louis XIV *himself*, as a gesture (in her words) to show all of Europe marks of her recognition of his kindnesses, 'as proof of her zeal and respect'.[43] She also added still more pensions, gifts to the Jesuits of the rue Saint-Antoine in Paris, and another major donation, 100,000 livres to the princesse d'Harcourt (and a discharge for the 40,000 livres the Harcourts still owed her from the partial transaction of 1685). Is this third codicil nothing more than the desperate act of a dying woman, considering that the Jesuits were close to Père La Chaise, and Harcourt was close to Maintenon, the closest intimates of the King himself? It seems too coincidental for these to be anything but calculated gifts to win the favour of Louis XIV. But who else did Mlle de Guise need to worry about challenging her will? Who were the natural heirs she was attempting to bypass?

Why not let the Succession pass to the Natural Heir?

In wishing to keep the Guise patrimony together in 1688, Mlle de Guise was in a similar position as her contemporary, King Charles II of Spain, whose vacillations over appointing an heir demonstrate his concerns – or those of his counsellors – for the preservation of his empire and its identity. The legal battle over the Guise Succession was by no means as epic as the War of Spanish Succession, but it did drag on for decades and involved hundreds of litigants, inside France and out.

Why? The Guise succession did not simply consist of properties (movable and immovable); it also included intangible honours such as the peerage of the duchy of Guise, with quite tangible privileges such as the right to have lawsuits heard before the Parlement of Paris (as a tribunal of peers) or the King's Council itself. But, as seen in the Rohan-Chabot and Grimaldi-Matignon marriages, the Guise succession also involved the potential transferral of princely rank, with a further attendant set of privileges, though these were much less clearly defined. Aside from ceremonial privileges such as the right to wear a hat in the company of foreign ambassadors or to sit in the Queen's presence, the *princes étrangers* enjoyed levels of private access to the monarch and a degree of judicial immunity that were crucial to the maintenance of their dynastic identity.[44] Louis XIV was

42 Spangler, "Material Culture at the Guise 'Court'", 158–75.

43 BL, Sloane 2885, p. 91.

44 Robert Oresko, "Princes étrangers", in *Dictionnaire de l'Ancien Régime*, (ed.) Lucien Bély (Paris: Presses universitaires de France, 1996), 1019–20; Spangler, *Society of Princes*, chapter 1. These privileges were not fully codified until the reign of Louis XV, when, for example, decrees were issued stating that children of *princes étrangers* were to be formally received at court as if they were princes of the blood.

not keen to have this semi-autonomous group of senior aristocrats augmented at his court, as can be seen in his unwillingness to extend princely privileges to the House of Fürstenberg in the 1660s, despite his otherwise favouring them personally.[45] Princely status was not in question in Mlle de Guise's donation to the son of the duke of Lorraine, who was a prince by birth; rather it would have established another branch of foreign princes in France, and with a peerage to anchor their position.[46] We can say clearly then, that Guise dynastic identity was built on the twin pillars of this quasi-independence from the Crown, and a long history of defence of the Catholic Church – an issue currently at the forefront of many minds in France in the 1680s due to Louis XIV's ongoing quarrels with Pope Innocent XI.[47] Like Charles II deciding the fate of the Spanish monarchy, Mlle de Guise had no desire to see the Guisard identity subsumed into the identity of her natural heirs. In both cases this was the House of Bourbon.

The paternal heirs of Mlle de Guise were led by the prince de Condé in the name of his wife and her sister. The maternal heirs also put forward a claim in the person of Mlle de Montpensier. Two branches of the House of Bourbon thus laid claim to the Guise succession. The Condé lawyers arrived to take possession of the Hôtel de Guise within hours of Mlle de Guise's death on 3 March. The deceased's closest paternal heirs, the sisters Anne-Henriette-Julie, princesse de Condé, and Bénédicte-Henriette, duchess of Hanover, were daughters of Anne-Marie de Gonzague, known as the Princesse Palatine, who had died only four years previously. She was in turn the daughter of Catherine de Lorraine-Mayenne, duchesse de Nevers, from the branch closest in descent from the Guise.[48] Why was there no claim put forward by the duc d'Elbeuf, as the next *male* heir of the House of Lorraine? The letters patent for the duchy-peerage of Guise (1528) make it

45 Spanheim (Ezéchiel, baron), *Relation de la Cour de France en 1690*, (ed.) E. Bourgeois (Paris: Mercure de France, 1973), 125; Primi Visconti (Giovanni-Battista, conte di San Maiolo), *Mémoires sur la Cour de Louis XIV, 1673–1681*, (ed.) J.-F. Solnon (Paris: Perrin, 1988), 10.

46 In the perceptive words of Saint-Simon: 'although a great princely lineage is pretty, *cela ne tenoit qu'à une bouton*, and there is nothing in France of more true and solid grandeur than a duchy-peerage. The House of Lorraine, to whom true princely status cannot be disputed, has thought thusly even at the height of its power'. *Mémoires*, (ed.) Y. Coirault, 4: 432.

47 Joseph Bergin, *Crown, Church and Episcopate under Louis XIV* (Yale: Yale University Press 2004), chapter 7, "A Decade of Crisis".

48 The princesse de Condé (1648–1723), and the duchess of Hanover, aka Brunswick-Lüneburg (1652–1730), had they not been Catholic, would have been deemed closer to the Stuart Succession than their aunt, the Electress Sophia. The Duchess was a widow; her late husband, Johann Friedrich (d. 1679), converted to Catholicism in the 1650s and became a devoted francophile, building Herrenhausen in emulation of new buildings at Versailles, to the annoyance of his brothers, including Ernst August, the husband of Sophia. 'Mme de Hanovre' returned to France in 1679 and lived with the Condés, then at the Hôtel de Guise during the succession lawsuits. Saint-Simon, *Mémoires*, (ed.) Coirault, 7: 718–20.

clear that although the duchy was created for 'heirs and claimants, whether sons or daughters at whatever degree, forever perpetually', the peerage created at the same time was for males only.[49] So technically the peerage did pass to Elbeuf, but was redundant as he was himself already a peer, though this is mentioned in none of the vast succession dossiers I have seen. Nor do any of the legal documents generated by this case ask by what right Mlle de Guise had attempted to bypass her natural heirs for her Lorraine cousins in Innsbruck.

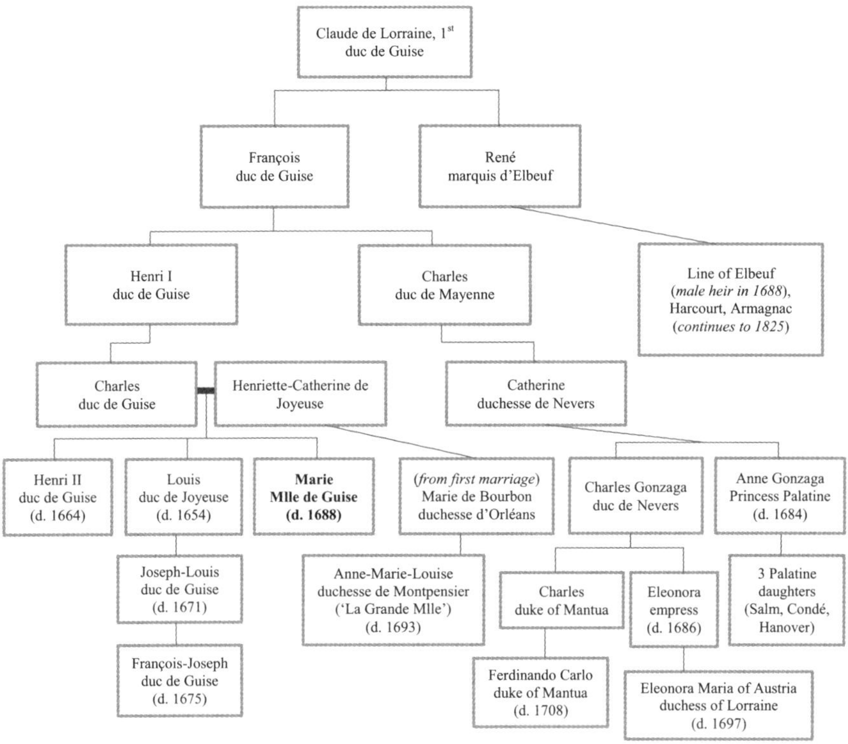

Figure 6.2 Relationship chart between Mlle de Guise and her close kin: Gonzaga, Palatine, Lorraine (simplified)

A closer analysis of the genealogical records, however, reveals another significant factor in the breaking of the donations of Mlle de Guise: the French law

49 BNF, Ms. Fr. 2758, fol. 195. Mlle de Guise was either not aware of this distinction between the estates and the peerage of the duchy of Guise, or else she considered that she held a *new* peerage, since the death of her great-nephew in 1675. She was, rather incredibly for a woman, referred to as a 'pair de France' in formal homage documents from July 1675 (ANF, P 20[1], no. 7). Nor did Elbeuf ever claim precedence based on the date of creation of the earlier peerage: 1528, compared to his own of 1581.

known as Droit d'Aubaine. The two Palatine sisters had a senior agnatic kinsman, higher up in the ranks of natural succession: the duke of Mantua, Carlo Ferdinando Gonzaga. Moreover, the thus far childless Duke would have been followed in strict lineal succession by another cousin: none other than the duchess of Lorraine herself, Archduchess Eleonora Maria, daughter of the Empress Eleonora Gonzaga. The young Lorraine princes, to whom Mlle de Guise was hoping to pass both the Guise estates and identity, could thus be counted as her closest natural heirs.[50] Droit d'Aubaine would make the donation necessary, however, because Mlle de Guise's lawyers knew that this law prevented French estates from passing to persons born outside the Kingdom, unless they had been specially naturalised by letters patent. Duke Charles V of Lorraine had been born in Vienna, and although he had been naturalised in the 1650s, his children, born in Innsbruck and Vienna, had not.[51] The reliance on the Droit d'Aubaine becomes clearer when considering that the two Palatine sisters had another sister (now dead), who was in fact older; although this eldest sister, Louise-Marie, had been born in Paris, her son, the prince of Salm, had been born in Aachen and raised alongside the future Emperor Joseph I in Vienna.[52] The duke of Mantua was born in Mantua and Archduchess Eleonora Maria was born in Regensburg. The natural heirs according to French law were therefore the Palatine sisters, French-born, and were recognised as such by the Parlement of Paris in an *arrêt* of 26 April 1689.[53]

But the primary legal challenge to the will had come from Mlle de Guise's maternal heir, Anne-Marie-Louise, duchesse de Montpensier (1627–93), better known to posterity as 'La Grande Mademoiselle'. The two women had been battling in the courts since the 1650s when Montpensier felt she had been cheated of her portion of the Joyeuse succession by yet another complicated will, that of Henriette-Catherine de Joyeuse, Montpensier's grandmother, and Mlle de Guise's mother.[54] Here finally was the opportunity Montpensier had been waiting for, in

---

50 Indeed, this is underlined when in 1708, the succession of the duke of Mantua was contested by the houses of Lorraine and Bourbon-Condé. Guy Cabourdin, *Encyclopédie illustrée de la Lorraine: Les temps modernes – 2. De la paix de Westphalie à la fin de l'Ancien régime* (Nancy: Éd. Serpenoise u.a., 1991), chapter 6. The Empress Eleonora (d. 1686) had supported the exiled Lorraine court financially, as niece of a former duchess of Lorraine herself. It is difficult to see how the Guise and the Gonzagas could not have seen themselves as anything but members of an international 'society of princes'.

51 Stephane Gaber, *Et Charles V arrêta la marche des Turcs ... Un lorrain sauveur de l'occident chrétien* (Nancy: Presses universitaires de Nancy, 1986).

52 No claims were ever put forward by Ludwig Otto, prince of Salm (1674–1738), though he was probably naturalised at some point to enable him to inherit his family's sizeable French properties.

53 *Arrêt* of Parlement printed in ANF, R^3 117, 17. For Droit d'Aubaine, see Peter Sahlins, *Unnaturally French: Foreign Citizens in the Old Regime and After* (Ithaca, NY: Cornell University Press, 2004).

54 BNF, Factum 14859. Mademoiselle discusses her conflicts with Mlle de Guise at length in her memoirs: *Mémoires de Mlle de Montpensier, petite-fille de Henri IV*, (ed.)

the donation made to the prince de Commercy of the duchy of Joyeuse. Joyeuse was located in Languedoc, in the region of 'Droit Romain', a legal code which forbade the transmission of patrimony by donation if there was an obvious heir. The Parlement of Paris agreed, and by the *arrêt* of April 1689, declared the donation of 1686 null and void. The donations for Commercy, Armagnac and Couvonges were struck down, and Couvonges (in absentia) was condemned to damages, interests and all legal expenses.[55]

Droit d'Aubaine and Droit Romain had thus served as double blows to demolish the donations of Mlle de Guise. But a *requête* of May 1689, a month after the Parlement's ruling, brought to light the first of many snags Mlle de Guise's will had placed in the path of her heirs. Here the comte d'Armagnac made it clear that Lambesc and Orgon were not Guise patrimony but 'acquisitions' of Mlle de Guise – through a sleight of hand, in that her mother had redeemed debts on these properties with her own money – so although located in Provence, 'Pays du Droit Romain', they were not subject to it. Armagnac certainly was not a foreigner (though ironically his status at court depended on his rank as a *prince étranger*). His *requête* was followed shortly by those of other members of the House of Lorraine, the princesse d'Harcourt and Commercy's sisters, followed by creditors, domestics, and legatees, led by the Hôtel Dieu, the abbess of Montmartre and the bishops of Autun and Toul, claims eventually numbering in the hundreds. Legally the debts had to be paid before the heirs would receive anything, and the largest debts, with dowager privilege of preferred payment, were the pensions of Mme de Guise (Isabel d'Orléans, 40,000 livres) and Mme de Joyeuse (Françoise-Marie de Valois-Angoulême, 15,000 livres). There was also a claim put forward for a third dowager pension, for the late Honorine de Berghes, jilted bride of Henri II, duc de Guise, which was pursued endlessly (and ultimately fruitlessly) by her nephew the prince de Berghes.[56] These huge debts and legacies would block the heirs for several years in legal wrangling, aided by the fact that the prince de Commercy was condemned as a traitor in 1690. The power of the heirs, maternal and paternal, was strengthened significantly in spring 1693, when La Grande Mademoiselle died and was succeeded by her heir, the King's own brother, Monsieur (Philippe, duc d'Orléans). By 1701, most everything was settled: Joinville passed to Monsieur (a paternal property being used to satisfy maternal debts), Guise to the Condés, and, surprisingly, the duchy of Joyeuse was granted to the heirs of the prince de Commercy: his sisters.

Was the Guise name and identity lost? The son of the princesse de Condé was indeed re-created duc de Guise in 1704,[57] but none of his successors used this title in court parlance (instead they continued to go by traditional Bourbon

A. Chéruel (Paris: Charpentier, 1858), 2: 381–2; 2: 431–43; 3: 243–7.

[55] ANF, R^3 117, 17.

[56] Succession documents collected in ANF, R^3 117, with further detail in R^4 *1060, and the archives of the House of Orléans, 300 AP I, cartons 97 to 107.

[57] Anselme, *Histoire généalogique*, 3: 483.

names: Enghien, Clermont, La Marche), and on the whole the Guise estates were submerged within the fortunes of the House of Bourbon-Condé.[58] The Hôtel de Guise was sold during the litigation to the princes of Rohan, who rebuilt it into what we see today as the Archives Nationales.[59] The jewel in the Guise crown, the château of Joinville in Champagne, fared much worse. It was abandoned, and demolished and sold for scrap by the House of Orléans in the later eighteenth century.[60] But as a postscript, we can add that in the nineteenth century, the now royal House of Orléans did assign the title prince de Joinville to a younger son.[61] The Orléans also inherited the estates of the House of Condé in 1830, and the pretender to the French throne in the 1930s was – rather ironically from the point of view of purported Guisard ambitions during the Wars of Religion – known as the duc de Guise.[62]

Mlle de Guise's vision was picked up by her successors in other ways. From 1698, the newly restored duke of Lorraine, Léopold, indicated his desire to re-establish the prominence of the cadet branches of his dynasty: 'during the thirty years of his rule, Léopold displayed an active sentiment of familial solidarity … whether they were established in France, in Germany or elsewhere, he called to them, invited them to his court, and procured offices, benefices and distinctions for them'.[63] He promoted the careers of his cousins, first the prince de Commercy, whose principality bordered Lorraine (but who was killed in Italy in 1702), then the prince d'Harcourt, to whom the Duke sold several fiefs in Lorraine which he erected into a principality under the name 'Guise'.[64] This new 'prince de Guise' never became a major actor in eighteenth-century France, and his line became extinct in 1747. By then the dukes of Lorraine themselves had left the region, first to Tuscany in 1737, then to Vienna where they transformed themselves into Habsburgs.

---

58 Daniel Roche, "Aperçus sur la fortune et les revenus des princes de Condé à l'aube du XVIIIe siècle", *Revue d'histoire moderne et contemporaine*, XIV (1967); Katia Béguin, *Les Princes de Condé: Rebelles, courtisans et mécènes dans la France du Grand Siècle* (Paris: Champ Vallon, 1999), 278.

59 Charles-Victor Langlois, *Les hôtels de Clisson, de Guise & de Rohan-Soubise au Marais* (Paris: J. Schemit, 1922).

60 Emile Humblot and Roger Luzu, *Les seigneurs de Joinville* (Saint-Dizier: Impr. A. Brulliard, 1964).

61 Prince François d'Orléans (1818–1900).

62 Prince Jean d'Orléans (1874–1940).

63 Zoltan Harsany, *La Cour de Léopold, duc de Lorraine et de Bar* (Nancy: Idoux, 1939), 117.

64 Poull, *Maison ducale de Lorraine*, 457–8. For more on the return of the Guise cadets to Lorraine in the reign of Duke Léopold, see this author's chapter, "Les strategies d'accroisement de la gloire ducale par le rappel des princes du sang lorrains", in (ed.) Anne Motta, *Echanges, passages et transferts à la cour du duc Léopold (1698–1729) (Rennes: Presses universitaires de Rennes, forthcoming).*

Nevertheless, one branch of the House of Lorraine did survive in France beyond the 1740s, and continued to enjoy the privileges of *princes étrangers* (and indeed continued to be referred to as 'Guisards'): the descendants of the comte d'Armagnac. As a way of referring to their kinship to Mlle de Guise and her illustrious forebears, some of them assumed the title 'prince de Lambesc', for the property in Provence willed to them by Mlle de Guise in 1686. Lambesc is a small town, but in terms of dynastic identity it represented a great deal to the Lorraine princes. It was a reminder, however faint, that their ancestors had claimed the vast Angevin empire ruled by 'le bon roi' René I, king of Sicily and Jerusalem (both in name only), duke of Lorraine and sovereign count of Provence. Mlle de Guise's father, Duke Charles, had been governor of Provence in the 1620s, and in a distant echo of this inheritance, the prince de Marsan (Camille-Louis de Lorraine) was named one of the last royal governors of Provence in 1770.[65]

This last transferral brings us to a final point, that dynastic identity consisted of more than simply individual desires, or even those of families or clans. At its broadest conceptualisation, the 'House of Guise' embodied also its domestics – well known to historians of the family – and indeed its lawyers, creditors, suppliers, clients and tenants. There is no clearer illustration of this than a tiny reference to a transaction, lost among the hundreds of pages of the Guise Succession documents, by which Mlle de Guise, in taking over the affairs of her late brother in 1664, made a contract with the inhabitants of Lambesc and Orgon. She promised that if she sold her properties there (as her brother had been planning to do), she would only sell them to a Lorraine prince, 'because they had been ruled by that family for so many centuries'. In return, the townspeople would renounce debts they were owed.[66] She honoured this promise, and the name Lambesc, not Guise, was in fact the very last one held by the last of the Lorraine princes in France, in a place of honour at Versailles as Master of the Horse and kinsman of the queen, Marie-Antoinette.[67]

Mlle de Guise was not a typical heiress. She was of the highest, semi-sovereign rank, and was far too old to be considered for marriage. She was not a widow and she had no immediate kin to place restrictions on her legal actions. The succession strategies of Marie de Lorraine nevertheless usefully demonstrate that, although her attempts ultimately failed, opportunities at least did arise for aristocratic women to express their dynastic identities independently of men. Her failure, as with those of the duchesse de Nemours or the duchesse de Luxembourg, and the successes of the duchesse de Rohan or the princesse de Monaco, illustrate the ongoing struggle of aristocratic women in a patriarchal world; a world increasingly dominated by

---

65 Edouard Baratier, *Histoire de la Provence* (Toulouse: Privat, 1969), 370.

66 ANF, R[4] * 1060.

67 The attempt of Charles-Eugène de Lorraine, prince de Lambesc (1751–1825), as Commander of the Royal Allemand-Dragoons Regiment, to defend the Tuileries, was one of the initial sparks of the French Revolution. Paul Spagnoli, "The Revolution Begins: Lambesc's Charge, 12 July 1789", *French Historical Studies* 17 (1991).

centralising, even 'nationalising' states; a world in which semi-autonomous trans-national princely families, or families whose power derived from confessional divisions, would struggle to maintain their place.

PART III
Manufacturing Identity

Chapter 7
The Fruits of War: The Representation of Alessandro Farnese in Paolo Rinaldi's Liber Relationum[1]

Sebastiaan Derks

From Khair ad-Din Barbarossa, the grand admiral of the Ottoman fleet, to Emanuele Filiberto of Savoy, who won a resounding victory at Saint Quentin, the war-torn sixteenth century produced many remarkable commanders. Perhaps the most famed among them was Alessandro Farnese, Duke of Parma and Piacenza. Success stories about this outstanding warrior abound, from his strategic brilliance and military daring, his attention to detail in the planning of his operations, his icy self-control and perseverance, to an unparalleled series of conquests, which restored Habsburg authority over the greater part of the Low Countries. Yet, his most notable feat was undoubtedly the capture, after a hard-fought and brilliantly executed siege of more than a year, of the metropolis of Antwerp. The siege was one of the marvels of the age, and as a reward Alessandro regained the fortress of Piacenza from the Habsburg King – a prize his family had coveted for decades.[2] Not surprisingly, his campaign of reconquest provided the subject matter for a flurry of chronicles and panegyrics. These battle narratives celebrated Alessandro as the military leader *par excellence*, as evidenced in the many representations of him as a latter-day Alexander the Great. Although most of these contemporary

---

[1] An earlier version of this chapter was published in Italian in *Militari italiani dell'esercito di Alessandro Farnese nelle Fiandre. Atti della giornata di studio, Fontevivo, 24 settembre 2011*, (ed.) G. Bertini (Fidenza: Mattioli, 2013).

[2] L. van der Essen, *Alexandre Farnèse, prince de Parme, gouverneur général des Pays-Bas (1545–1592)* (5 vols. Brussels: Librairie nationale d'art et d'historie, 1933–1937) and P. Fea, *Alessandro Farnese, duca di Parma, narrazione storica e militare, scritta colla scorta di documenti inediti* (Turin: Bocca, 1886). Both biographies are still fundamental due to the loss of archival material in September 1943; see also the overviews offered by G. Bertini, "Alessandro Farnese fra Italia, Spagna e Paesi Bassi", in *Uomini di governo italiani al servizio della Monarchia spagnola (secoli XVI e XVII)*, (eds) C.J. Hernando Sanchez and G. Signorotto (Spec. Issue: *Cheiron*, 27/53–4) (Rome: Bulzoni, 2011) and L. van der Essen, "Alexandre Farnèse 1545–1592: les principaux aspects de sa personnalité", *Revue générale belge*, no. 68 (1951).

accounts proved to be of ephemeral value, some of them undeniably had an important bearing on the shaping of subsequent narratives about him.[3]

One of the most influential and extensive of the early histories of Alessandro Farnese is that written by the courtier Paolo Rinaldi, within a few years after the duke's death. His historical narrative, known as the 'Liber relationum eorum quae gesta fuere in Belgio et alibi per serenissimum D. Ducem Alexandrum Farnesium', holds particular importance because it offers an insider's account of Alessandro's protracted campaign in the Low Countries. Indeed, it is often considered as the nearest we have to an official history of the commander. This Italian vernacular text, although never printed, has had a long but intermittent history of influence from the time of its compilation. In the first half of the seventeenth century, the Roman Jesuit Famiano Strada used it, together with correspondence lent by the Farnese family, for his widely circulated and frequently translated work on the Low Countries wars.[4] His history, and specifically his narration of Alessandro's military exploits, became a central point of reference for many works of history that followed. However important this early recognition may have been, Rinaldi's text has only in modern times acquired a certain renown, through the solid work of the eminent Belgian scholar Léon van der Essen. In his authoritative multivolume biography of Alessandro, for which he extensively mined the text, he branded it as one of the principal sources of information on the personal attitudes and perceptions of the duke. Van der Essen also recognised the manuscript, on the basis of textual comparison with Strada's book, as being closely linked to the ducal inner circle, and identified Rinaldi as its author.[5] Although subsequent studies have

---

3 Cf. M. Stensland, *Habsburg Communication in the Dutch Revolt* (Amsterdam: Amsterdam University Press, 2012), 108–11; R. Sabbadini, "L'uso della memoria. I Farnese e le immagini di Alessandro, duca e capitano", in *Il 'perfetto capitano'. Immagini e realtà (secoli XV-XVII): atti dei seminari di studi Georgetown University a Villa 'Le Balze', Istituto di Studi Rinascimentale di Ferrara 1995–1997*, (ed.) M. Fantoni (Rome: Bulzoni, 2001); B. de Groof, "Alexander Farnese and the origins of modern Belgium", in *La dimensione europea dei Farnese*, (eds) idem and E. Galdieri (Spec. Issue: Bulletin de l'Institut historique belge de Rome 63) (Rome-Brussels: Institut historique belge de Rome, 1993).

4 L. van der Essen, *De auteur en de beteekenis van de Liber relationum eorum quae gesta fuere in Belgio et alibi per serenissimum D. Ducem Alexandrum Farnesium* (Antwerp: Standaard, 1943), 9–11. Also see F. Strada, *Della guerra di Fiandra, deca prima* (Rome: Hermanno Scheus, 1638), 481–2; R. Zapperi, *Eros e Controriforma. Prehistoria della galleria Farnese* (Turin: Bollati Boringhieri, 1994), 77; F. Neumann, *Geschichtsschreibung als Kunst. Famiano Strada S.I. (1572–1649) und die ars historica in Italien* (Berlin-Boston: De Gruyter, 2013), 214–16, 250, 253.

5 Van der Essen, *Alexandre Farnèse*, 1:xxi–xxii; idem, *De auteur*, 5–14. Rinaldi's manuscript had been acquired by the Koninklijke Bibliotheek, Brussels (hereafter KBB) in the 1880s: J. van den Gheyn, *Catalogue des manuscrits de la Bibliothèque royale de Belgique* (Brussels: Lamertin, 1901), 7: 561. Cf. the earlier assessments in "Chronique: L. van der Essen (Louvain), Une source inconnue pour l'histoire du gouvernement

accepted this attribution, surprisingly little attention has been paid to the wider political context of Rinaldi's codex and its underlying purpose.

Military matters have always been the main focus of scholarly interest in Alessandro Farnese. It is therefore not surprising that the 'Liber relationum' was generally placed alongside similar military narratives of the Low Countries war.[6] For the period of Alessandro's command, there are several eyewitness accounts by veteran officers, ranging from brief reports of services rendered, such as the account of Francesco Biumio, to recollections of considerable length, such as those of Carlos Coloma, Alonso Vázquez, and Francisco Verdugo.[7] Much important work has been done in the past three decades on what texts like these actually intended to represent. One of the major problems with these complex sources of information – inevitably tainted with personal bias – is that they raise as many questions as they solve with respect to their historical veracity. While it has become accepted that these first-hand accounts do not always provide an accurate depiction of military events, they undeniably do reflect contemporary perceptions of warrior ethos and military glory. The importance of such texts, thus, rests primarily in the ways the combatants represented their wartime experiences and attempted to transform these into military exempla.[8] However, one area that has not been adequately explored, is the specific princely or noble

d'Alexandre Farnèse aux Pays-Bas espagnols", *Revue belge de philologie et d'histoire* 9 (1930): 685, and E. Gossart, *La Révolution des Pays-Bas au XVIe siècle dans l'ancien théâtre espagnol* (Brussels: Hayez, 1910), 86.

[6] Cf. L. van der Essen, *Kritische inleiding tot de studie van het Spaanse leger en van zijn oorlogvoering in de Nederlanden gedurende de XVIe eeuw* (Brussels: Paleis der Academiën, 1949); and the Spanish edition in idem, *El Ejército Español en Flandes 1567–1584*, (ed.) G. Janssens (Cuacos de Yuste: Fundación Academia Europea de Yuste, 2008); idem, *Alexandre Farnèse*, 1: xxi–xxii.

[7] See, e.g., the "Narrativa di quanto ha fatto Francisco Biumio detto Corradino capitan de lancie per servitio di S.M.tà sotto il carico del Serenissimo Duca di Parma, governatore et capitan generale delli stati di Fiandra", published as appendix III in *Militari italiani dell'esercito di Alessandro Farnese*, (ed.) G. Bertini, 243–61; C. Coloma, *Las guerras de los Estados Bajos, desde el año de 1588 hasta el de 1599* [first published in 1625] (Biblioteca de Autores Españoles 28) (Madrid: Editorial Atlas, 1948); A. Vázquez, *Los Sucesos de Flandes y Francia del Tiempo de Alejandro Farnesio*, (3 vols, Madrid: Miguel Ginesta, 1879–1880); *Commentario del coronel Francisco Verdugo de la guerra de Frisa en XIIII años que fue governador y capitan general de aquel estado y exercito por el rey D. Phelippe II, nuestro senor*, (ed.) H. Lonchay (Brussels: Kiessling, 1899): re-edited in *Francisco Verdugo: Verslag over mijn jaren als legerleider en gouverneur namens Filips II in Stad en Lande van Groningen, Drenthe, Friesland, Overijssel en Lingen (1581–1595)*, (ed.) J. van den Broek (Groningen: RHC Groninger Archieven, 2009).

[8] On Habsburg military autobiographies, see Y. Rodríguez Pérez, *The Dutch Revolt through Spanish Eyes. Self and Other in Historical and Literary Texts of Golden Age Spain (c. 1548–1673)* (Bern: Peter Lang, 2008); R. Puddu, *Il soldato gentiluomo: autoritratto d'una società guerriera, la Spagna del Cinquecento* (Bologna: Il Mulino, 1982); A. Cassol, *Vita e scrittura. Autobiografie di soldati spagnoli del Siglo de Oro* (Milan: LED, 2000);

context in which these texts were written. It is often not clear with what political motives warriors wrote, what they hoped to gain, and how their accounts were employed in the political arena. Moreover, scholars have arguably been too ready to view these first-hand accounts as a distinct strand of history-writing: in practice, however, they were difficult to distinguish from biographies of notable warriors and justifications of military actions (often in imitation of Caesar's *Commentarii*).[9] It should, therefore, be stressed that the 'Liber relationum' was part of a wider culture of historical writing in the sixteenth century, which took an intense interest in the lives of contemporary and near-contemporary military heroes.

Biographies and chronicles of great captains were for the most part produced in response to the needs of ruling families. The prime purpose of these texts was to immortalise the military exploits and the heroism of family members, and to advance the dynastic agenda. There was obviously something highly attractive in the use of history in storms of criticism, when a family's reputation and status was at stake. In particular, biographies written by witnesses, often relatives or gifted secretaries, were considered important instruments for forging dynastic identity and for vindicating family honour.[10] The lucid biography of Ferrante Gonzaga by his secretary Giuliano Gosellini, for instance, was primarily intended to uphold the family's good name and to refute the accusations surrounding Ferrante's removal from office as governor of Milan.[11] In a similar way, the *Vita dell'illustrissimo signor Camillo Orsino* by Giuseppe Orologi, and Lorenzo Capelloni's *Vita del prencipe Andrea Doria*, had to portray the captains as their offspring wished them to be perceived. More than anything else, these biographies had to accentuate the virtue and martial valour of the protagonists and strengthen the dynastic reputation,

---

Y.N. Harari, *Renaissance Military Memoirs: War, History, and Identity, 1450–1600* (Woodbridge: Boydell, 2004).

[9] T.C.P. Zimmerman, *Paolo Giovio: The Historian and the Crisis of Sixteenth-Century Italy* (Princeton, N.J.: Princeton University Press, 1995), 165, 190, 256, 267–9. Cf. also G. Ianziti, "I 'Commentarii': appunti per la storia di un genere storiografico quattrocentesco, " *Archivio storico italiano* 50 (1992).

[10] Cf. M. Fantoni, "Il perfetto capitano: storia e mitografia", in *Il 'perfetto capitano'. Immagini e realtà (secoli XV-XVII)*, (ed.) idem, 29–34; G. Brunelli, "'Sopra tutto fu inclinatissimo alla religione'. La *Vita dell'illustrissimo signor Camillo Orsino* di Giuseppe Orologi", in *Nunc alia tempora, alii mores. Storici e storia in età postridentina. Atti del convegno internazionale, Torino, 24–27 settembre 2003*, (ed.) M. Firpo (Florence: Olschki, 2005), 429–31. Also see V. Caputo, *La 'bella maniera di scrivere vita': biografie di uomini d'arme e di stato nel secondo Cinquecento* (Naples: Edizioni scientifiche italiane, 2009), 15–32, 77–104.

[11] G. Gosellini, *Vita del prencipe don Ferrando Gonzaga* (Milan, 1574). On Gosellini, see the entry by M.C. Giannini, in *Dizionario biografico degli italiani* (hereafter *DBI*) 58 (2002), 110–14 and Caputo, *La 'bella maniera di scrivere vita'*, 192–210. See on Ferrante's removal also M.J. Rodríguez Salgado's excellent essay, "Ferrante Gonzaga: the Champion of Innocence", in *Ferrante Gonzaga. Il Mediterraneo, l'Impero (1507–1557). Atti del convegno di studi, Guastalla, 5–6 ottobre 2007*, (ed.) G. Signorotto (Rome: Bulzoni, 2009).

purposely distracting attention from more contentious aspects of their lives. For this reason, such works of history could be valuable instruments of justification and propaganda, something most princes and captains did not want to do without.[12] As we shall see, the same point can be made for Rinaldi's account of Alessandro Farnese's campaign. To disclose the full meaning of this manuscript, we need thus to add another dimension, namely that of the relevance of the dynastic culture that produced it.

This chapter therefore examines the various dynastic expressions in the codex of Paolo Rinaldi to see to what extent they resonated with the concerns of Alessandro's sons, Ranuccio and Odoardo Farnese. The analysis of the 'Liber relationum' is pursued in two steps. In the first section, I examine the collapse of Alessandro's authority in the Low Countries and his fall from royal grace. This larger framework and the cast of principal characters involved will enable us to further investigate the political aspirations of the Farnese, and how these were represented in the 'Liber relationum'. In the second section, I chart the genesis and structure of the text of Paolo Rinaldi in comparison with other works of representation and glorification of the Farnese dynasty. It is not my aim to present a detailed description of the contents of the codex, but rather to demonstrate its function as essentially a vehicle of ducal representation and justification. In addressing these issues, I will draw upon a significant, but largely unnoticed source of information: a second copy of the 'Liber relationum' which survives in the Biblioteca Nazionale Centrale in Florence.[13] This codex provides critical details about the compilation history of Rinaldi's text, and reveals important clues about its immediate context. However, the most significant sources of information are the letters written by the Farnese to each other, and those they received from their various officials. Although incomplete, this evidence allows us to comprehend more fully the intentions of the author and his patrons. Taken as a whole, the intention of this chapter is to show that the manuscript was designed as a piece of historical propaganda which has much to teach us about the dynasty's policies and ambitions at the end of the sixteenth century.

---

[12] On princely and noble manipulations of the past, see inter alia Ch. Grell, W. Paravicini and J. Voss (eds), *Les princes et l'histoire du XIV*[e] *au XVIII*[e] *siècle*, (Bonn: Bouvier, 1998); H. Carl and M. Wrede (eds), *Zwischen Schande und Ehre. Erinnerungsbrüche und die Kontinuität des Hauses. Legitimationsmuster und Traditionsverständnis des frühneuzeitlichen Adels in Umbruch und Krise* (Mainz: Zabern, 2007); R.L. Kagan, *Clio and the Crown: The Politics of History in Medieval and Early Modern Spain* (Baltimore, MA: Johns Hopkins University Press, 2009); and recently M. Wrede, *Ohne Furcht und Tadel. Für König und Vaterland. Frühneuzeitlicher Hochadel zwischen Familienehre, Ritterideal und Fürstendienst* (Ostfildern: Thorbecke, 2012).

[13] P. Rinaldi, 'Historia di Fiandra del tempo che comandò l'armata il Duca Alessandro Farnese', Biblioteca Nazionale Centrale di Firenze (hereafter BNCF), *Fondo Magliabechiano*, Ms. II-I-235. See the description in G. Mazzatinti, *Inventari dei manoscritti delle biblioteche d'Italia* (Forlì: Bordandini, 1898), 8:75.

Dynastic Politics

Past historiography on Alessandro's campaigns has often downplayed or neglected the significance of dynasticism for his activities as commander of the Habsburg forces. His dynastic interests, however, are of fundamental importance for a proper understanding of his policies and priorities in the Low Countries.[14] Although Alessandro devoted great commitment and energy to his role as commander, the political designs of his family always remained at the heart of his concerns. It is no coincidence, then, that in the early 1590s, when his health collapsed and Alessandro became convinced that he was nearing his end, securing the prosperity of his dynasty became his foremost aim. Unable to leave the war in the north and to make his preferred arrangements for succession, he was acutely aware of the problems he was leaving his son Ranuccio: their reputation had suffered severe blows on account of the unrelenting opposition to his government in the Low Countries, their patrimonial finances were overburdened, and their pre-eminent position within the Habsburg system of power was more and more called into question. Against this canvas of problems and a pervasive sense of political regression, Alessandro realised that it would be a daunting task for the young ducal heir just to consolidate the power of the dynasty. To make matters even worse, Ranuccio would find himself almost alone in this difficult political game, and could only look to his younger brother, Cardinal Odoardo, for support. With the successive deaths of his grandparents Margherita of Austria (1522–1586) and Duke Ottavio (1524–1586), his great-uncle, Cardinal Alessandro (1520–1589), and now the imminent demise of his father, all within a few years of each other, the dynastic situation started to take a dramatic turn. Alessandro, therefore, had many reasons for concern. In these inauspicious conditions, he knew very well that the only ray of hope for his sons was their close kinship with the Spanish Habsburgs.[15]

In the relations between both dynasties, however, unmistakable signs of disagreement and mutual friction surfaced at this stage. Indeed, beneath all the reassurances of appreciation, the Habsburg King Philip II was in serious doubt about the obedience and reliability of Alessandro as governor of the Low Countries, and increasingly distrusted his motives. Philip's support for his nephew was undeniably faltering. The reasons for this deterioration of relations seemed justified: the king was extremely dissatisfied with Alessandro's opposition to the war in France. The commander had shown great reluctance to intervene in

---

[14] See esp. M.J. Rodríguez Salgado, "Almost a Royal Eagle. Alexander Farnese and the Spanish Monarchy", in *Alexander Farnese and the Low Countries* (forthcoming); cf. V. Soen, "Philip II's Quest. The Appointment of Governors-General during the Dutch Revolt", *The Low Countries Historical Review* 126 (2011). Compare also the remarks in A. Cauchie and L. van der Essen, *Inventaire des archives farnésiennes de Naples au point de vue de l'histoire des Pays-Bas catholiques* (Brussels: Kiessling, 1911), lxxix–lxxx.

[15] Cf. G. Drei, *I Farnese: grandezza e decadenza di una dinastia italiana* (Rome: Libreria dello Stato, 1954), 169.

France in support of the Catholic League, as this would open another front and interrupt his offensive against the rebel forces in the Low Countries. Alessandro had repeatedly complained that the transfer of troops and resources could only lead to an erosion of royal power in the north.[16] His misgivings were, however, at odds with the resolute dedication of the king to the French cause. Alessandro's insistence on this matter was based on his strategic beliefs, but also reflected his fear that the interim governor, Count Peter-Ernst von Mansfeld and his son Karl, would use his absence to malign him publicly and obstruct his authority as royal governor. Alessandro had, in fact, like many Habsburg governors before him, become the focal point of a barrage of criticism during these years, in which the corruption and financial mismanagement of his government was being targeted.[17] But there was more: as evidenced by highly critical reports, Alessandro had put his clientele, mostly Italians, in command of garrisons and fortified places, and had thereby alienated the Spanish troops.[18] Hence it was not surprising that the king watched Alessandro's government with increasing alarm, whilst at the same time he knew that the commander would be difficult to replace. Although the two had quarrelled before, Philip gradually became sufficiently irritated by Alessandro's independent and disobedient conduct, that he lost all confidence in his leadership. Thus, in December 1591, despite the great consideration he had always shown him, the king decided to remove him from office. This meant that the duke would be summoned to Madrid, with all the honours and dignity he deserved, in an attempt to keep his reputation intact and to avoid suggesting that he was actually being replaced.[19]

---

[16] See Rodríguez Salgado, "Almost a Royal Eagle"; cf. eadem, "Philip II and the Post-Armada Crisis: Foreign Policy and Rebellion, 1588–1594", in *IX Jornadas de Historia Maritima. Despues de la Gran Armada: la historia desconocida (1588–16..)* (Madrid: Instituto de Historia y Cultura Naval, 1993); Van der Essen, *Alexandre Farnèse*, 5: 276–89.

[17] On the rivalry with the Mansfelds, cf. H. de Schepper, "Le gouverneur général Peter Ernst von Mansfeld et les agents espagnols Fuentes e Ibarra aux Pays Bas en 1593", in *España y los Países bajos, siglos XVI-XVII. Agentes e identidades en movimiento*, (eds) R. Vermeir, M. Ebben and R. Fagel (Madrid: Silex, 2011); H. de Schepper, "De katholieke Nederlanden van 1589 tot 1609", in *Algemene Geschiedenis der Nederlanden* (Haarlem: Fibula-Van Dishoeck, 1979), 6: 280–81; B.J. García García, "Mansfeld contre Farnèse. Dessins satiriques de Charles de Mansfeld contre le gouvernement du duc de Parma, Alexandre Farnèse", in *Un prince de la renaissance. Pierre Ernest de Mansfeld (1517–1604). II. Essais et catalogue*, (eds) J.-L. Mousset and K. De Jonge (Luxemburg: Musée national d'histoire et d'art, 2007), 129–34.

[18] L. van der Essen, "Une critique de l'administration d'Alexandre Farnèse aux Pays-Bas par Don Juan de Idiáquez, secrétaire d'Etat de Philippe II (1592)", *Bulletin de la Commission royale d'histoire* 100 (1936); see also Bertini, "Alessandro Farnese fra Italia, Spagna e Paesi Bassi", 83–7.

[19] See Van der Essen, *Alexandre Farnèse*, 5: 372–5; Rodríguez Salgado, "Almost a Royal Eagle".

Figure 7.1 'The funeral procession for Duke Alessandro Farnese in Brussels', 1592–1594. Engraving, by Frans Hogenberg. 210 × 280 mm. Amsterdam, Rijksmuseum.

According to one of his biographers, Alessandro, although oblivious of the plans for his removal, was well aware of the rumours circulating about him and expected negative repercussions to follow.[20] Therefore, he felt increasingly compelled to take action to strengthen his reputation, and persisted in his kinship and identification with the Spanish Habsburgs.[21] In fact, throughout the early 1590s, Alessandro frequently asked his uncle Philip for favours, suggesting that he always put the king's interests ahead of his own. Still in the glow of his military triumphs, he tried to press the king to give assurances with regard to the future of his son Ranuccio. Philip was particularly careful and reluctant to enforce the status of the Farnese family, as their dynastic aspirations, and

[20] Van der Essen, *Alexandre Farnèse*, 5: 376–80.

[21] See, for example, Alessandro Farnese to Philip II, (copy), [November 1592], in P. Fea, *Il duca Alessandro Farnese e le carte dell'Archivio napoletano* (Parma: 1914), 25–6: request to 'concedere a me et miei discendenti priuilegio di esser cognominati, non d'Austria, ma Farnesi Austriaci, come perpetui servitori et dependenti della Real Casa Sua'. Cf. also Fea, *Alessandro Farnese*, 504.

in particular their claims to the throne of Portugal, might interfere with his own plans. The king therefore objected to a marriage between Ranuccio and a niece of Pope Sixtus V, but in 1591 offered them a safe match with a Habsburg archduchess instead. These negotiations were, however, cancelled when the bridal candidate unexpectedly died, leaving the Farnese still without a prestigious marriage for Ranuccio.[22] Philip was also hesitant in his support to secure a cardinal's hat for Alessandro's second son Odoardo, and when finally elected, he was disinclined to give him lucrative offices and benefices.[23] In so doing, Philip signalled his intention to protect his own dynastic interest at all costs, and to keep the ambitions of his nephew and great-nephews in check as much as possible. Not suprisingly, the king's piecemeal concessions of favour frustrated his Farnese relatives. In the autumn of 1592, Alessandro, seeing no other option, took a more aggressive stance and ordered Ranuccio to go to Madrid. He had decided to send his son, in secret and without royal consent, to offer the king his resignation from the governorship. It was a last attempt to regain the initiative, and to extract himself from the progressively more hostile environment in the Low Countries, before he would be removed.

Alessandro realised that to recover the king's full favour for his family, he had to prove that he could not be blamed for the problems which were under investigation. Ranuccio's instructions, preserved in a lengthy memorandum, were therefore explicit and left little room for misinterpretation. The young prince had to inform the king extensively about the state of affairs in the Low Countries, and to give reasons and justifications for his father's conduct. Alessandro's defence against the charges levelled at him was founded on his claim that he had used every means at his disposal to protect Habsburg interests in the north, but that his policy had been completely obstructed through the mismanagement of the Mansfeld family. The memorandum, then, was a piece of pure self-exculpation. However, the more significant part had to make clear that, as Alessandro was now on the brink of death, he could no longer continue the war as the loyal provinces wanted him to. The governor asked the king to be allowed to retire and to attend, in the little time left to him, to his own affairs. Moreover, by sending Ranuccio to the royal court, Alessandro communicated the clear message to the king that he genuinely desired a rapprochement

---

[22] Zapperi, *Eros e Controriforma*, 28–9; J.A. von Hübner, *Sixte-Quint: d'après des correspondances diplomatiques inédites tirées des archives d'État du Vatican, de Simancas, Venise, Paris, Vienne et Florence* (Paris: Franck 1870), 2: 146 ; Rodríguez Salgado, "Almost a Royal Eagle". On their claim of Portugal, cf. A.E. Denunzio, "Strategie diplomatiche e vicende dinastiche: le pretese dei Farnese nella successione al trono di Portogallo (1578–1580)", in *Maria di Portogallo, sposa di Alessandro Farnese, principessa di Parma e Piacenza dal 1565 al 1577*, (ed.) G. Bertini (Parma: Ducati, 2001).

[23] Rodríguez Salgado, "Almost a Royal Eagle"; see also R. Zapperi, "Odoardo Farnese principe e cardinale", in *Les Carrache et les décors profanes* (Rome: École française de Rome, 1988), 335–40; idem, *Eros e Controriforma*, 76–81.

between their families. Another reason was, predictably, to offer his son the opportunity to meet with his great-uncle Philip, and to follow his father's example by offering his services and personal loyalty. Most literature refers to this apologetic memorandum as Alessandro's 'political testament', but it constituted only the first part of his last message to his heir.[24]

On his deathbed, as one would expect, the duke had also dictated another text for his son, in which he instructed him on the outstanding dynastic matters for the negotiations with the king. Firstly, Ranuccio was to ask for Philip's opinion with regard to his marriage. This issue was the main purpose of his mission, his father insisted, and had to be treated with great circumspection. He was not to make any new proposals, but just had to remind the king of their strong preference for a Medici princess, hoping that Philip would throw his political weight behind it. Only in the unlikely case that the king had changed his mind, could Ranuccio propose a union with the eldest daughter of the Polish king. Most importantly, Ranuccio's marriage had to bring him a large dowry, enabling him to improve the precarious financial position of the dynasty. Secondly, Ranuccio had to secure Habsburg protection in their prolonged dispute with the Landi family over Borgo Val de Taro.[25] This strategically valuable Apennine fief had to remain firmly in their hands. Thirdly, he had to express their hopes of acquiring the territories of Pontremoli and Casalmaggiore, imperial fiefs situated in the Lunigiana and Po valleys, to incorporate them into their duchies of Parma and Piacenza. Lastly, he had to acquaint the king with the needs of his brother Odoardo, who as cardinal of a princely family and member of the Habsburg faction in Rome required a splendid court to represent his lineage and the king in a proper manner. The Farnese prince had to convince Philip that the best way to solve this financial problem was to bestow a number of rich benefices in the kingdom of Naples. Alessandro was aware that it might

[24] See e.g. L. van der Essen, "Le testament politique d'Alexandre Farnèse. Dernières instructions du gouverneur général à son fils, Ranuccio Farnèse, au sujet des affaires des Pays-Bas (novembre 1592)", *Bulletin de la Commission royale d'histoire* 86 (1922) ; idem, *Alexandre Farnèse*, 5: 379–81. Van der Essen published the memorandum, entitled 'Instruttione sopra le cose di Fiandre per voi Ranuccio mio figlio', from the Archivio di Stato di Napoli (hereafter ASN), *Archivio Farnesiano*, b. 1720, which has been destroyed. A surviving copy is in ASN, *Archivio Farnesiano*, b. 1624 (II). See also Cauchie and Van der Essen, *Inventaire des archives farnésiennes*, 362–3.

[25] On the counts of Landi and the dispute over Borgo Val di Taro, see e.g. M. Rizzo, "Gli Austrias e l'Italia centrosettentrionale nella prima età moderna. Una rapsodia geopolitica", in *Feudi di Lunigiana tra Impero, Spagna e Stati italiani (XV-XVIII secolo)*, (eds) E. Fasano Guarini and F. Bonatti (La Spezia: Accademia lunigianese di scienze Giovanni Capellini, 2008); A. Koller, "Reichsitalien als Thema in den Beziehungen zwischen Kaiser und Papst: Der Fall Borgo Val di Taro", in *Das Reich und Italien in der Frühen Neuzeit* (Contributi dell'Istituto storico italo-germanico in Trento 17), (eds) M. Schnettger and M. Verga (Bologna: Il Mulino, 2006); G. Tocci, *Le terre traverse. Poteri e territori nei ducati di Parma e Piacenza tra Sei e Settecento* (Bologna: Il Mulino, 1985), 48–66.

be expedient to offer the king territorial compensations, in order to bring the negotiations to a speedy conclusion. He urged his son that all possible effort had to be made to soon relieve their family from 'the oppression of debts' that they had contracted to continue the war in the Low Countries. In this second memorandum Alessandro spelled out everything he believed necessary to make the king more inclined to compromise and reward the Farnese for his services.[26]

Around the same time political change came to the north in very distinctive forms. In the autumn of 1592, news had begun to circulate that a royal emissary, the experienced warrior Pedro Enríquez de Acevedo, Count of Fuentes, was on his way to the Low Countries. However, the precise scope of his mission remained unclear, leading to fierce speculation about the king's intentions. At the end of November, when Fuentes finally arrived in Brussels, he found the royal government in a state of utter confusion and paralysis, with everyone waiting for him to take over the leadership.[27] Learning that Alessandro had already left for France in mid-November to prepare for his next campaign, Fuentes knew he had no choice but to chase after the commander-in-chief. However, seeing the chaotic situation, he procrastinated, until the long-awaited news came that Alessandro had died in Arras on the night of December 3, 1592. The duke's death, predictably, created more problems than it solved, as Fuentes could never quite stabilise his position as the governor-designate and was inevitably caught up in prolonged conflicts with Peter Ernst von Mansfeld. It was Mansfeld who eventually assumed the governorship in Brussels, but the two continued to quarrel over the government and defence of the Low Countries and took every opportunity to publicly question each other's authority. Nevertheless, despite their personal animosity, they were forced to cooperate to overcome the problems of the Habsburg armed forces and to implement the necessary financial reforms.[28]

The change in government became still more apparent when, the following spring, Spanish officials stepped in to restore order and take over the management of the royal finances in the Low Countries. Foremost among them was Esteban de Ibarra, the new secretary of war, who was to play a central role in the

---

26 'Memoria et instruttione di quello, che voi Ranuccio mio figlio havete da trattare in Spagna per servizio vostro e del Cardinale mio, et della casa', December 1592 (Arras), in ASN, *Archivio Farnesiano*, 1624 (II). With regard to Farnese's finances in 1592, see M.A. Romani, "Finanza pubblica e potere politico: il caso dei Farnese (1545–1593)", in *Le corti farnesiane di Parma e Piacenza (1545–1622)*, (ed.) idem (Rome: Bulzoni, 1978).

27 Papal commissioner Girolamo Matteucci to Cardinal Pietro Aldobrandini, 20 October 1592 (Brussels), 24 October 1592 (Brussels), 28 October 1592 (Brussels), and 30 November 1592 (Brussels), Archivio Segreto Vaticano (hereafter ASV), *Segretaria di Stato, Fiandra*, b. 5, ff. 109–10, 117–18, 120–24, 190.

28 De Schepper, "Peter Ernst von Mansfeld", 91–3, 98–109. Cf. Matteucci to Aldobrandini, 26 December 1592 (Brussels), 31 December 1592 (Brussels), and 2 January 1593 (Brussels), ASV, *Segr. Stato, Fiandra*, b. 5, ff. 280–281, 287–293, 294–295.

rationalisation of the military-financial administration.[29] He was determined to make a clean sweep and end the endemic corruption, the unwarranted intrusions, and the squandering of royal funds. Soon after his arrival, Ibarra had initiated an administrative review of the conduct of Alessandro's confidants, in particular with regard to their handling of military funds. Therefore, throughout the spring and summer of 1593, his chief concern was to bring together a whole series of accounts and papers so as to facilitate an intensive audit. With the help of Fuentes he had seized some of the late governor's records, but the main problem was that Alessandro's principal secretary, Cosimo Masi, had sent the bulk of the evidence to Parma.[30] Masi, for so long seen as the embodiment of Farnesian abuses, now came under venomous attack: he was accused of embezzling money from the military treasury and from important customs revenues. It was thought that Paolo Rinaldi had been involved too.[31] In March, Fuentes and Ibarra informed Masi that he was detained in Brussels, pending the delivery of the requested papers relating to administration of the army under Alessandro's command. It was not until the end of September 1594 that Masi was granted a safe-conduct to return to northern Italy.[32] Earlier, at the beginning of his governorship, Mansfeld had already ordered the Privy Council in Brussels to initiate an investigation into the abuse and mismanagement of financial resources, thus ousting the auditors of the licents and contributions from office and requiring them to submit their accounts and papers to the Habsburg Council of Finances. Furthermore, Ibarra had proposed creating an ad hoc criminal tribunal for the Low Countries. Growing impatient with the pace of change, the king eventually agreed with him and appointed five judges

---

29 See, e.g., J.E. Hortal Muñoz, "La visión de un ministro 'castellanista' sobra la situación de los Países Bajos al final del siglo XVI: los advertimientos de Esteban de Ibarra", *Bulletin de la Commission royale d'histoire* 174 (2008), and De Schepper, "Peter Ernst von Mansfeld", 93–9.

30 Fuentes to Philip II, 24 January 1593 (Brussels), Archivo General de Simancas (hereafter AGS), *Secretaría de Estado,* leg. 604, 18; see also "Relaçion de los despachos y papeles que Cosme Masi secret. que ha sido del Duque de Parma que este en cielo entrega", in ibid., leg. 604, 55. Cf. Cauchie and Van der Essen, *Inventaire des archives farnésiennes*, xix–xxxi.

31 Bertini, "Alessandro Farnese fra Italia, Spagna e Paesi Bassi", 91–3; De Schepper, "Peter Ernst von Mansfeld", 93–6. On Masi, see the entry by G. Bertini in *DBI*, 71 (2008), 586–8, and also L. van der Essen, "Correspondance de Cosimo Masi, secrétaire d'Alexandre Farnèse, concernant le gouvernement de Mansfeld, de Fuentes et de l'Archiduc Ernest aux Pays-Bas, 1593–1594", *Bulletin de l'Institut historique belge de Rome* 27 (1952).

32 Cf. Matteucci to Aldobrandini, 25 March 1593 (Brussels), ASV, *Segr. Stato, Fiandra*, b. 5, f. 382–3; Fuentes to Philip II, 30 March 1593 (Brussels), AGS, *Estado*, leg. 604, 54; Jean Richardot to Ranuccio Farnese, 6 May 1593 (Brussels), 3 October 1594 (Brussels), Archivio di Stato di Parma (hereafter ASPr), *Carteggio Farnesiano Estero*, b. 116, s.f.; Cauchie and Van der Essen, *Inventaire des archives farnésiennes*, xx–xxxi, 219, 222.

to investigate and penalise fraud and abuse of the military treasury.[33] Although these Habsburg interventions for reforming the financial organisation did not attain their goals, they unintentionally fanned national sentiments that could not easily be contained.

Indeed, the early 1590s showed clear signs of ethnic antagonism in the officer corps of the Habsburg forces. Relations between the Spanish and the Italian army officers were severely strained by disputes over appointment practices, and with it, over the hierarchy of the high command. The increasing interference of Alessandro's entourage in military matters had inflamed the animosity of the captains and colonels of the Spanish nation. The Spaniards lamented that the duke had upset the balance between the nations, and, worse, had deprived them of their right of precedence. It was clear that the frustration and alienation of Spanish officers had sparked a volatile, hostile atmosphere in the army, and provoked outbursts of anti-Italian rage. Alessandro's death only deepened the internal divide in the army and opened an 'abyss of confusion', as the intense competition in the top ranks spread to the troops and resulted in military insubordination and mutiny.[34] The first indications of this crisis surfaced at the 'almost royal' obsequies for Alessandro in Brussels, when violent confrontations over precedence erupted between Spanish and Italian soldiers. Because of all these difficulties, the year 1593 proved to be an *annus horribilis* for the members of the Farnese contingent in the Low Countries, in which fear and despair alternated with hope for new dynastic success. In their eyes, everything hinged on Ranuccio's ability to execute the commands of his father and to win the king's favour.[35]

But the situation looked different to the new Duke of Parma and Piacenza. As much as Ranuccio may have desired to follow his father's will, serious problems in the Po valley led him to delay his voyage to Spain. In the year prior to his accession, he had become embroiled in a feud with Vincenzo Gonzaga, Duke of

---

[33] De Schepper, "Peter Ernst von Mansfeld", 97–9; Hortal Muñoz, "Los advertimientos de Esteban de Ibarra", 96–9. Cf. J. Lefèvre, "Le Tribunal de la Visite (1594–1602)", *Archives, bibliothèques et musées de Belgique* 9 (1932) and A. Esteban Estríngana, *Guerra y finanzas en los Países Bajos católicos: De Farnesio a Spínola, 1592–1630* (Madrid: Laberinto, 2002), 30–37.

[34] Cf. F. González de León, *The Road to Rocroi. Class, Culture and Command in the Spanish Army of Flanders, 1567–1659* (Leiden-Boston: Brill, 2009), 98–101; Bertini, "Alessandro Farnese fra Italia, Spagna e Paesi Bassi", 83–7. On national sentiment and identity in premodern Italy, see e.g. G. Signorotto, "Identità e interessi nell'Italia dei potentati", in *Le sentiment national dans l'Europe méridionale aux XVIe et XVIIe siècles (France, Espagne, Italie)*, (ed.) A. Tallon (Madrid: Casa de Velázquez, 2007).

[35] Masi to Ranuccio Farnese, 13 January 1593 (Brussels), ASPr, *Carteggio Farnesiano Estero*, b. 115, s.f. For Alessandro's obsequies, see B. de Groof, "Una questione di priorità: spagnoli, italiani e fiamminghi alla morte di Alessandro Farnese", in *I Farnese. Corti, guerra e nobiltà in antico regime. Atti del convegno di studi, Piacenza, 24–26 nov. 1994*, (eds) A. Billotto, P. Del Negro, C. Mozzarelli (Roma: Bulzoni, 1997).

Mantua, and now worried about the designs of the latter on his dominions. This conflict resulted from a verbal clash with Alfonso Felice d'Avalos, Marquis of Vasto, cousin of Vincenzo, over his alleged involvement in the destruction of a Mantuan armory by fire. Crucially, the conflict came to a head during a particularly tense and hostile period in the relations between the two sovereign houses following the annulment of Vincenzo's marriage with Ranuccio's sister Margherita. As the collective honour of their respective families was again on the line, neither Ranuccio nor Vincenzo could afford to back down. Within a few months, the dispute escalated into a major incident, as both young rulers were building up support from other powers on the Apennine peninsula to ensure the safety of their states. As the threat of war began to loom large in the region, the pope and the Habsburg king felt compelled to intervene and solve the conflict. Finally, by late June 1593, the quarrel between the two dukes was patched up in accordance with the instructions of Philip II.[36] But since relations with Mantua remained fraught with mutual mistrust and hostility, Ranuccio still did not feel completely confident about leaving for the royal court. However, the Farnese officials in the Low Countries, who from the beginning had opposed these Padan distractions, voiced serious concerns about further postponement of his departure. They repeatedly urged Ranuccio to follow the plan set out by his father, since 'the merits of the notable services' of his family were still 'so fresh' in the king's mind. In the view of these officials, the best chance for him to heighten his status and to constrain competitive peninsular rivals, was to gain full Habsburg support and patronage.[37] But Ranuccio refused to take their unsolicited advice. Instead, as we will see in the next section, he initiated the production of representative works of visual art, poetry, and histories about his father's campaign. In his position of vulnerability, Ranuccio knew that he had to communicate the outstanding military achievements in the Low Countries as the hallmark of the Farnese dynasty.

Dynastic Propaganda

In the early phase of his reign Ranuccio modelled his image as ruler primarily on the military exploits of his father. The works that he and his brother Odoardo planned and commissioned were designed to mythologise the accomplishments

[36] R. Canosa, *I segreti dei Farnese* (Rome: Sapere, 2001), 70–85; Drei, *I Farnese*, 86–188. See on the collapse and annulment of the marriage A. Bellù, "Margherita Farnese, sposa mancata di Vincenzo Gonzaga", *Archivi per la storia* 1 (1988), 381–420; V. Finucci, *The Prince's Body: Vincenzo Gonzaga and Renaissance Medicine* (Cambridge, MA: Harvard University Press, 2015) and the novelistic treatment in M. Bellonci, *Segreti dei Gonzaga*, rev. edn (Milan: Mondadori, 1981), 39–80.

[37] Cf. Richardot to Ranuccio Farnese, 12 January 1593 (Brussels), and Masi to idem, 13 January 1593 (Brussels), ASPr, *Carteggio Farnesiano Estero*, b. 115, s.f.

of the dynasty as well as emphasise their familial relationship with the Habsburg monarchy. In these memorial projects – such as Simone Moschino's over-lifesized marble statue representing 'the apotheosis of Alessandro Farnese', the important engraving of this statue by Francesco Villamena, the grand decorative scheme of Alessandro's *Fasti* for the Salone Grande in the Roman family palace, and Cesare Campana's encomium on the siege of Antwerp – Ranuccio, in accordance with his warrior ambitions, encouraged the comparison, or amalgamation of him with his father. In the past three decades, much work has been done on these commissions, and on their importance as acts of ducal legitimation and representation. The project for the Salone Grande in particular has drawn attention from scholars who have read it as part of the pre-history of Annibale Carracci's famous Galleria Farnese.[38] Yet, while modern scholarship has acknowledged the centrality of Alessandro's campaigns to Farnese visual and literary culture in this period, few have tried to account for the ways in which it was framed and represented to fit the ducal claims. It was predominantly through metaphors and narratives about his father's governorship in the north that Ranuccio legitimised and redefined his ducal authority. In this section, I hope to correct this imbalance by offering a first analysis of Paolo Rinaldi's text, and of its role in the dynasty's struggle for rewards and recognition. The 'Liber relationum' is a crucial text for reconstructing the political agendas behind many Farnese projects, as it can be directly linked to the train of thought of Ranuccio and his personal entourage. My argument in what follows will be that this manuscript can be characterised as constituting a first attempt at a comprehensive dynastic history of the Low Countries war.

[38] See e.g. D. Bodart, "Cérémonies et monuments romains à la mémoire d'Alexandre Farnèse duc de Parme et de Plaisance", *Bulletin de l'Institut historique belge de Rome* 37 (1966); E. Leuschner, "Francesco Villamena's 'Apotheosis of Alessandro Farnese' and Engraved Reproductions of Contemporary Sculpture around 1600", *Simiolus* 27 (1999). On the Salone Grande project (and the Galleria Farnese), cf. Ch. Dempsey, "Annibale Carrache au Palais Farnese", in *Le Palais Farnèse*, I.1 (Rome: École française de Rome, 1981); and the seminal studies by R. Zapperi, "Le Cardinal Odoardo et les Fastes Farnese", *Revue de l'art* 11 (1987); idem, "Odoardo Farnese principe e cardinale",; idem, *Eros e Controriforma*; idem, "Per la storia della Galleria Farnese. Nuovi ricerche e precisazioni documentarie", *Bollettino d'arte* 84 (1999); idem, "Annibale Carracci e Odoardo Farnese", *Bollettino d'Arte* 95 (2010); C. Robertson, "Osservazioni sul mecenatismo del Cardinale Odoardo Farnese", in *I Farnese. Arte e collezionismo. Studi*, (ed.) L. Fornari Schianchi (Milan: Electa, 1995), 70–79; eadem, *The Invention of Annibale Carracci* (Milan: Silvana 2008), 101–5.

Figure 7.2 'The Apotheosis of Alessandro Farnese', 1600. Engraving, by Francesco Villamena. 210 x 178 mm. London, British Museum. (View of Simone Moschino's statue honouring Alessandro Farnese as the conqueror of the city of Antwerp. The epigram to the right is dedicated to Alessandro's son Ranuccio and compares him to his father).

Before delving into Rinaldi's version of ducal military history, a brief look at contemporaneous history-writing in Farnese service will help to clarify the genesis of his project. In his early days as ruler of Parma and Piacenza, Ranuccio had already reassured Alessandro's trusted secretary, Cosimo Masi, of his intention to commission histories in order to glorify his father's merits. Masi had convinced him of the need to publish historical works to refute the malicious charges and to reaffirm the indisputable loyalty of the Farnese to the Habsburg monarchy. It seemed imperative to launch a counter-offensive to recover the honour of Alessandro and to defend the ducal territories from external threats.[39] Ranuccio certainly maintained a great interest in historiography, and was a particularly dedicated patron of historical treatises and orations. We can safely assert, therefore, that in this period Parma developed into an important centre of historical activity, attracting the services of Cesare Campana, Gabriello Chiabrera, Giovan Battista Marino, and other scholars as much-needed promoters of Farnesian interests. Among the first results was Campana's remarkable *Assedio e racquisto d'Anversa, fatto dal Sereniss. Alessandro Farnese*, published in 1595, which recounts the events of the long siege of the Scheldt city. This text, which was widely disseminated, substantially embellishes the military enterprises of Alessandro. Evidently, Campana's work had a twofold purpose: to present a favourable image of the main character, the 'gran padre', and to evince Ranuccio's similarity with him.[40] In this manner, historiography was manipulated to forge a dynastic narrative which was deeply relevant to the Farnese court. This promising start to the rewriting of the Farnesian past did not, however, ensure success. Of the many scholars who tried to win ducal patronage, it was Antonio Querenghi who in 1595 managed to secure a commission for a *Belgica Historia*. He was expected to narrate the whole of Alessandro's operations in the north in the form of a voluminous encomium. However, once commissioned, Querenghi proved a complete disappointment. His relationship with the Farnese rapidly soured,

[39] Masi to Ranuccio Farnese, 13 January 1593 (Brussels), ASPr, *Carteggio Farnesiano Estero*, b. 115, s.f.; idem to Ranuccio Farnese, 19 August 1593 (Brussels), in L.P. Gachard, "Les archives farnésiennes à Naples", *Compte rendu des séances de la Commission royale d'histoire* 9 (1869), 335.

[40] See also the reprint of this text: *Imprese nelle Fiandre del Sereniss. Alessandro Farnese* (Cremona: Francesco Pellizzari, 1595). On Campana and the Farnese, see G. Nori, "Una biografia parallela di Alessandro Farnese: Pomponio Torelli e Cesare Campana", *Aurea Parma* 62, fasc. I (1978) and the entry by G. Benzoni in *DBI* 17 (1960). For Ranuccio's patronage of historiography, see Sabbadini, "L'uso della memoria"; Cauchie and Van der Essen, *Inventaire des archives farnésiennes*, ccx–ccxiv; A. Biondi, "L'immagine dei primi Farnese (1545–1622) nella storiografia e nella pubblicistica coeva", in *Le corti farnesiane di Parma e Piacenza, 1545–1622*, I: *Potere e società nello stato farnesiano*, (ed.) M.A. Romani (Rome, Bulzoni 1978); C. Pérez Bustamante, *El cronista Antonio de Herrera y la historia de Alejandro Farnese* (Madrid: Tipografía de Archivos, 1933).

allegedly due to problems over the disclosure of information.[41] As a consequence, Ranuccio remained without an all-encompassing history of his father's rule in the Low Countries.

It seems plausible to assume that the 'Liber relationum' sprang from this new culture of historiography regarding the wars in the Low Countries. Paolo Rinaldi, after all, was himself a high-ranking member of the ducal court. Unfortunately, due to the loss of much of the material pertaining to the early Farnese period, little is known about his personal background and career trajectory.[42] What seems certain, however, is that Rinaldi came from a Florentine family of some standing, and that he gained his first military experience fighting in the war of Siena in 1554/55. He was also involved in the Habsburg invasion of the Papal States in 1556.[43] Further evidence indicates that in the early 1570s Rinaldi obtained a position within Alessandro's household. We should also note that he joined him in the naval expedition against the Ottomans, which ended with the Holy League's victory at Lepanto.[44] Later, Rinaldi's name resurfaces in a list of captains and servants who had followed Alessandro to the Low Countries. More importantly, according to this document, he had been given the office of major-domo, which meant that he served as master of the household and enjoyed continuous and assured access to the Farnese ruler.[45] In practice, Rinaldi also appears to have

41 Cf. C. Volpi, "Odoardo al bivio. L'invenzione del Camerino Farnese tra encomio e filosofia", *Bollettino d'arte* 83 (1998) ; eadem, "Odoardo e il Camerino Farnese. 'Virtù' politica o 'Virtù' privata", in *Studi di Storia dell'Arte in onore di Denis Mahon*, (eds) M.G. Bemardini, S. Danesi Squarzina and C. Strinati (Milan: Electa, 2000); U. Motta, *Antonio Querenghi (1546–1633). Un letterato padovano nella Roma del tardo Rinascimento* (Milan: Vita e pensiero, 1997); Robertson, *The Invention of Annibale Carracci*, 104–5. See also the comments by A. Cadoppi, *Gabriele Bombasi, letterato reggiano (1531–1602): una vita fra l'Ariosto, il Correggio, i Farnese e i Carracci* (Modena: Nuova Futurgraf, 2010), 165–6.

42 The Farnese dynasty's archives in Naples were largely destroyed in September 1943. See M. Dierickx, "Les Carte Farnesiane de Naples par rapport à l'Histoire des anciens Pays-Bas, après l'incendie du 30 septembre 1943", *Bulletin de la Commission royale d'histoire* 112 (1947); R. Filangieri, *L'Archivio di Stato di Napoli durante la seconda guerra mondiale*, ed. S. Palmieri (Naples: Arte Tipografica, 1996). See also G. Ramacciotti, "Le vicende storiche dell'Archivio Farnesiano a Napoli e la sua reale consistenza", *Archivio storico per le province parmensi*, ser. IV, 2 (1949–1950) and 4 (1951).

43 Cf. Rinaldi, "Liber relationum", KBB, Ms. II.1155, ff. 9v, 117v–18. For his Florentine origin, see the notarial act by Cosimo Masi of January 27, 1586, in ASPr, *Carteggio Farnesiano Estero*, b. 113, s.f.; Cadoppi, *Gabriele Bombasi*, 195.

44 Rinaldi, "Liber relationum", KBB, Ms. II.1155, ff. 49v, 117v–18. Cf. the "Rolo delle persone che vano con l'Ecc.a del S.or Principe alla guerra", 18 June 1571, published in A. Cappelli, "Alessandro Farnese ed i Parmigiani alla Battaglia di Lepanto", *Aurea Parma* II, fasc. 1–2 (1913). On his presence in Alessandro's household, see Rinaldi, "Liber relationum", KBB, Ms. II.1155, ff. 246, 247.

45 Algemeen Rijksarchief, Brussels (hereafter ARAB), *Audience*, 33/4, ff. 38–50 (39): "Estat et declaracion de ceulx qui doibvent estre francqz et exemptz de touttes maltottes et

handled important administrative and financial tasks of the Habsburg government, such as the control over customs revenues. This was probably the result of the close links he had established with Cosimo Masi and Jean Richardot, the two ministers who wielded most influence at the court of the duke.[46] In late spring 1592, Rinaldi returned to Parma and Piacenza, with the assignment to reform the ducal finances and to reduce the suffocating burden of debt. It provided Rinaldi with the opportunity to play a significant part in the steering of the Farnese states: he attended council meetings, had frequent interviews with ducal intendants and servants, and he carefully monitored the affairs at Ranuccio's court. In November of that year, Alessandro also appointed him chamberlain of the ducal exchequer.[47] In sum, Rinaldi had a long career in Farnese service, leading him through martial service, financial management, and high court office. Whatever the messages concealed in his 'Liber relationum', we are clearly dealing with an account from an influential participant in Farnesian politics.

While Rinaldi's narrative was for the most part founded on what he had personally witnessed, he nonetheless interspersed it with information from various official documents. As a consequence, his account has the immediacy of a first-hand history, but is also far more detailed than anything produced by his contemporaries. The method adopted by Rinaldi emanates in many ways from Ranuccio's programme for ordering the dynasty's archives. One of the first initiatives of the newly acceded duke had been to create a central repository inside the ducal palace in Parma and to collect all relevant records for future historical use. In particular, his secretaries were instructed to assemble the archival patrimony pertaining to the government of the Low Countries, as it was fragmented and dispersed over different chanceries.[48] The central figure in this process of documentary transfer and storage was Cosimo Masi, who had been closely involved in the production of most of these archives, and had extensive knowledge of the principles along which they were organised. For this reason, as we have seen, Masi had also been locked in a protracted struggle with Habsburg officials over the archives of Alessandro's government in 1594/95. Around the

---

impositions", 8 January 1586.

46 See the memo by Frédéric Perrenot, 21 December 1589, in *Mémoires de Frédéric Perrenot, sieur de Champagney, 1573–1590*, (ed.) A.L.P. de Robaulx de Soumoy (Bruxelles: Société de l'histoire de Belgique, 1860), 253–300; De Schepper, "Peter Ernst von Mansfeld", 94–5. For Perrenot's criticisms, see also Stensland, *Habsburg Communication*, 120–21.

47 Cf. Rinaldi to Masi, 20 August 1592 (Piacenza), 21 August 1592 (Piacenza), idem to Ranuccio Farnese, 9 July 1592 (Piacenza), 15 July 1592 (Piacenza), ASPr, *Carteggio Farnesiano Interno*, 176, s.f.; idem to Ranuccio Farnese, 13 October 1592 (Parma) and 12 November 1592 (Parma), ASPr, *Carteggio Farnesiano Interno*, 177, s.f. For the appointment, see Cappelli, "Alessandro Farnese", 7.

48 G. Drei, "Gli archivi farnesiani", *Archivio storico parmense* 29 (1929), 153–4; N. Barone, *Notizie riguardanti l'archivio farnesiano ora conservato nell'Archivio di Stato di Napoli* (Naples: D'Auria, 1898), 5; Cauchie and Van der Essen, *Inventaire des archives farnésiennes*, ix–xliv.

same time, moreover, Ranuccio instructed him to present Cesare Campana with a set of secret government documents and first-hand reports.[49] More importantly, Masi himself had tried his hand at writing a comprehensive history of Alessandro's campaign in the north, using correspondence from the ducal archives. But his draft manuscript, which intermittently covered the period from his arrival in the Low Countries to the siege of Maastricht in 1579, was left unfinished.[50] We do not know if and to what extent the 'Liber relationum' did rest on Masi's narration. However, it is clear that, throughout the writing process, Rinaldi enjoyed privileged access to the ducal repository to acquaint himself with its secret contents, the *arcana principis*. It can, in fact, be observed that there are many references in the text indicating his substantive reliance on documents from the Farnese archives.[51] The immediate context and composition of Rinaldi's text has long remained shrouded. The introductory letters included in the Florentine copy of the text, however, reveal that the work was completed in the summer of 1599. This means that Rinaldi wrote his history in a period during which, as we will see, Ranuccio's prospects and politics came to a critical juncture. Unfortunately, beyond being commissioned by the duke to produce an elaborate encomium of the great commander, Rinaldi offers in these letters no information on the dynastic leitmotifs of his project.[52] It is therefore to the 'Liber relationum' itself that we shall now turn, to explicate his redefinition of dynastic history.

Rinaldi summarises the contents of his account in the first book of his text and points to the exceptional importance of the narratives contained in it. His work chronicles the decades of Farnese rule in the Low Countries, starting with a general overview of the government of Alessandro's mother, Margherita of Austria, who had been put in charge shortly before the king's departure for Spain in 1559. In this first book Rinaldi emphasises the extent of the threat posed by militant Protestantism and its support among the nobility. Although Margherita's regime followed a policy of persecution, the evils of heresy continued to spread, ending in iconoclastic riots and collective protest by lesser nobles with protestant leanings. But through force of arms and the adoption of a more moderate policy,

[49] Cf. the "Relaçion de los despachos y papeles tocantes al serviçio de S.M.d … ", 1595, edited and contextualised in Cauchie and Van der Essen, *Inventaire des archives farnésiennes*, xiv–xxxiv. See also Pedro de Laudans to Masi, 13 April 1595 (Brussels), ASN, *Archivio Farnesiano*, b. 1722 (II). For Campana and Masi, see A. Barilli, "Nuovi documenti su Alessandro Farnese", *Archivio storico per le province parmensi*, ser. III, 3 (1938), 91–2, and the entry by G. Bertini in *DBI* 71 (2008).

[50] See Cauchie and Van der Essen, *Inventaire des archives farnésiennes*, ccxiii, 261, 300.

[51] Cf. Rinaldi, "Liber relationum", KBB, Ms. II.1155, ff. 1, 10, 21, 241, 252–2v.

[52] Rinaldi to Ranuccio Farnese, 21 September 1599 (Parma); and idem to Odoardo Farnese, 28 September 1599 (Parma), in Rinaldi, "Historia di Fiandra", BNCF, *Fondo Magliabechiano*, Ms. II-I-235, ff. 1–4; the text of this codex is fragmentary and incomplete. Book VI, for instance, has only six folio-sides: Ibid., ff. 165–7v. Cf. also Rinaldi to Ranuccio Farnese, 9 July 1599 (Parma), ASPr, *Carteggio Farnesiano Interno*, b. 211, s.f.

Margherita eventually succeeded in re-establishing obedience to the king. Seen from this perspective, the arrival in Brussels of royal forces under the command of the Duke of Alba could only 'put everything that she had organised and secured with so much difficulty and industry, into disarray and in danger again'.[53] Not surprisingly, Rinaldi does not hesitate to recount that Alba's six-year rule experienced a series of catastrophic reverses. This first book also narrates the inadequate and ineffective military operations of Alba's immediate successors, in their chronological order up to the beginning of Alessandro's government. In contrast to this rather uneven coverage, the remaining nine books of the 'Liber relationum' concentrate entirely on the exploits of Alessandro Farnese, trumpeting his military and political gains in the north. Rinaldi's history of reconquest appears thus as a massive narration of military operations, but barely touches on the complex political events in the Low Countries. Moreover, Rinaldi enhances his description of the awe-inspiring conquests by stressing the recognition Alessandro received from other commanders and rulers. Here, he often lapses into hyperbole and long digressions to express his admiration for Alessandro. Finally, to close his account of the Farnese campaign in the Low Countries, Rinaldi offers a large collection of maxims that were allegedly coined by the duke and were intended to accentuate his moral virtues in politics and warfare.[54]

Like most sixteenth-century writings on notable captains, the 'Liber relationum' glorified the late Duke of Parma and Piacenza as an ancient warrior-hero. Rinaldi's emphasis of the link between Alessandro and his ancient namesake stands out in particular. In his description of the famous pontoon bridge over the river Scheldt – a determining factor in the recapture of the rebellious city of Antwerp – he equated it explicitly to the causeway built by Alexander the Great to the island city of Tyre. Rinaldi also repeatedly refers to the risks the duke took on the front line that were in no way necessary for him. These descriptions indicate that both Alessandro and he had understood the importance of the image of an exemplary hero amidst the perils of war. In his account Rinaldi clearly demonstrates that the Farnese commander excelled far above all others in terms of military ability and bravery. More importantly, his heroic representation of Alessandro – consistent with a strong dynastic tradition of identification with Alexander the Great – also had political overtones. Indeed, it is important to note that the Hellenistic identification allowed for parallels between the service of Alessandro under the Habsburg King Philip II and that of Alexander under his father Philip II of Macedonia. This allusion was an attempt to accentuate the blood ties with the Habsburg dynasty, and presented the captain-general symbolically as an adoptive son of the king.[55] In addition, Rinaldi compared him to Caesar to enhance the duke's reputation as

---

53 Rinaldi, "Liber relationum", KBB, Ms. II.1155, ff. 5–20v; see the quote on f. 18v.

54 Ibid., ff. 257–9.

55 Ibid., ff. 165v, 251–2. See Sabbadini, "L'uso della memoria", 163, 172–3 and idem, *La grazia e l'onore. Principe, nobiltà e ordine sociale nei ducati farnesiani* (Rome: Bulzoni, 2001), 192–3, 199–200.

the greatest commander of his own day. The image of the duke as a superior ruler was inescapable. Nonetheless, the symbolism of pagan heroes also served as a counterpoint to the image of a pious Christian conqueror. The 'Liber relationum' contrasts Alessandro's piety and modesty with the brutality and haughtiness of the ancient rulers. It evinces that Alessandro was an excellent, modest Christian captain, who seemed to be indifferent to the temptations of admiration and honour. Of great interest in this respect is Rinaldi's remark that the duke was deeply averse to glorification of his merits by panegyrical writings.[56]

Another example of this pro-Farnese rewriting occurs in the passages in which Rinaldi reflects on the role of the Spanish officers in the Habsburg army. Although he draws attention to the significant part that they played in military operations, he does not present them in a very positive light. Their *esprit de corps* and attitude towards combat, Rinaldi stresses, were different from that of his fellow-Italians. He seems in no doubt that the Spanish nation suffered from unwarranted authoritarianism and arrogance, and that it unjustifiably considered itself superior to other nations.[57] This demonstrates that the echoes of the intense conflicts between the Iberians and Italians over authority and hierarchy in the high command had not died down. Of course, a multinational army such as the Habsburg forces in the Low Countries was likely to produce extreme competition between nations, fuelled by public justifications of combat effectiveness and qualities of the different ethnic groups. The commander-in-chief had the unenviable duty to control and remedy such rivalries and disputes, and failure to do so would seriously damage his reputation. Therefore, Rinaldi pinned the blame for the ethnic strife within the Habsburg high command on the Spanish officers, who had failed to appreciate Alessandro's leniency toward them and had remained intransigent. It is in this context that he emphasises the duke's efforts to place the Spaniards in command of the major fortresses, ignoring the demands of the native population.[58] Rinaldi's text can thus be seen as a deliberate attempt to give legitimacy to the military leadership of Alessandro and to counter the charges of the Spanish captains.

---

56 Rinaldi, "Liber relationum", KBB, Ms. II.1155, ff. 165v, 250–52, 254v. See also the remark by Pomponio Torelli, count of Montechiarugolo, and Farnese courtier, "che il S.r Duca non haveva mai havuto mira ad altra gloria che quella della S.ta Fede et che fusse vero che non haveva mai voluto sopportare che alcuno scrivesse le sue historie", in Barilli, "Nuovi documenti", 91.

57 Rinaldi, "Liber relationum", KBB, Ms. II.1155, ff. 43v, 217.

58 See Ibid., ff. 244, 252–5v. Cf. the more extensive discussions in A. Spagnoletti, "Le dinastie italiane e la guerra delle Fiandra", *Società e storia*, n. 125 (2009); idem, "Quale patriottismo per i soldati napoletani al servizio della Monarchia Cattolica?" in *Guerra y sociedad en la monarquía hispánica: política, estrategia y cultura en la Europa moderna (1500–1700)*, (eds) E. García Hernán and D. Maffi (Madrid: Laberinto, 2006); idem, "Onore e spirito nazionale nei soldati italiani al servizio della monarchia spagnola", in *Militari e società civile nell'Europa dell'età moderna (secoli XVI-XVIII)*, (eds) C. Donati and B.R. Kroener (Bologna: Il Mulino, 2007).

Throughout his account Rinaldi extols his protagonist's martial abilities and portrays him as the restorer of peace and concord in Habsburg Europe. His text offers an implicit, but consistent narrative that fuses the captain's personal qualities with the mastery of the Farnese lineage in warfare. Rinaldi's narration of the death of Alessandro's father, Ottavio Farnese, illustrates this perfectly. The achievements of Ottavio are here succinctly recalled, from his involvement in the wars in Algiers and in the Holy Roman Empire, in the service of his father-in-law, the Habsburg Emperor Charles V, his successful defence of Parma against the joint forces of the emperor and of the pope, to his leadership in the Habsburg war effort against Ferrara. Clearly, underlying this appraisal is the conviction that the military exploits of Ottavio foretold those of Alessandro.[59] Rinaldi likewise claims that Ranuccio had inherited his father's military acumen, referring to the young commander's battlefield feats in the French campaign of 1591/92. This representation of a dynastic chain of intergenerational military excellence plays into the idea that Duke Ranuccio too was worthy of leading the Habsburg forces and possessed all the qualities of a great warrior. Actually, the young duke did believe that the best path for his dynasty lay in military service. In 1596 Ranuccio came very close to realisation of his warrior pursuits: the Venetian state had offered Ranuccio the post of captain-general for its Illyrian campaign, but withdrew the offer to avoid any sort of involvement in the lingering conflict between Mantua and Parma. Consequently, throughout Ranuccio's reign, securing an appointment to high Habsburg military command – the only option left to him – was a major concern, demanding much diplomatic effort. In line with these ducal designs, the 'Liber relationum' focuses on the merits and successes of the family in the service of the Habsburg crown. In his text Rinaldi repeatedly stresses that Alessandro Farnese had reconquered most of the lost territories in the Low Countries and had solidified Habsburg control over them. What emerges from his description of the military distinction of the dynasty, and Alessandro in particular, is the message that the overall command of the Habsburg forces would be in excellent hands if entrusted to the Farnese.[60]

In another variation of this pro-Habsburg view, the 'Liber relationum' heralded Alessandro's warrior values in keeping with the ideal type of the great captain. The text presents him in the language of service, loyalty and self-sacrifice. By holding up the magnanimous deeds of Alessandro as a model for military leadership, Rinaldi gives the impression that Philip II's honour largely derived from having such a warrior at his disposal. But this discursive path can only be maintained by referring to the close, harmonious relations between the Habsburg king and his commander. Rinaldi therefore presents Alessandro as unconditionally loyal

---

59 Rinaldi, "Liber relationum", KBB, Ms. II.1155, ff. 48, 203v–204.

60 See, for example, Ibid., ff. 40, 239, 241, 256. See B.J. García García, "Ranuccio I Farnesio y la gloria del principe", in *I Farnese. Corti, guerra e nobiltà in antico regime*, (eds) Billotto, Del Negro and Mozzarelli, for Ranuccio's attempts to be appointed to military command.

to the Habsburg cause.[61] This perspective may also explain the marginality of the duchies of Parma and Piacenza and the other possessions of the Farnese family in his description of the captain's life. Evidently, Rinaldi felt that the glorification of Alessandro as a small sovereign prince was irreconcilable with the idea of loyal service to the Habsburg overlord: his narrative of Alessandro's commitment and dedication to Habsburg service simply left no room for conflicts with the king and ducal attempts to increase his status or territories. Insisting on the territorial sovereignty and dynastic logic of the commander could only undercut his discourse about the sacrosanct relationship and reciprocal loyalty between the Farnese and the Habsburgs.

In light of these observations, it is not surprising that several passages in the 'Liber relationum', particularly in the final books, are concerned with the material needs of the Farnese. Rinaldi did not forget to acquaint his readers with the vexed question of rewards. Alessandro's self-effacing demeanour, therefore, features prominently as a mode of interpreting the relationship between the king and the Farnese. Rinaldi represents Alessandro as the epitome of the sacrifice of one's own family interests for service to the Habsburg monarchy. Thus the Duke of Parma and Piacenza, even with the position of his own dynasty at stake, continued to serve in this campaign out of a sense that it was his duty as a loyal ruler. 'Alessandro has always spent large sums in the service of the Catholic King', Rinaldi writes, 'without any recognition or gratitude'. Clearly his purpose here was to portray Alessandro as a modest commander-in-chief, who had served the king 'with his own resources, health, blood, and life' without ever petitioning for rewards.[62] Such a portrait highlights the losses the Farnese had incurred in their great service to the Habsburg king. Rinaldi details the nefarious effects of Alessandro's 14-year-long stay in the Low Countries: the crippling debts that the Farnese had accumulated during the campaign ran to over a million ducats, the dynasty's income had diminished considerably due to the deaths of Margherita of Austria and Cardinal Alessandro Farnese, and most importantly, the two young princes Ranuccio and Odoardo were left in unfavourable circumstances, with all the perils of being without paternal presence and advice. In spite of his father's sacrifices, however, Ranuccio still had not been compensated with significant rewards by the king, monetary or otherwise. It is thus clear that the vast canvas of military achievements in the 'Liber relationum' also served to address the issue of the king's debt of gratitude to the Farnese.

All in all, it can be argued that the dynasticism of Ranuccio's early rule had strong resonances in Rinaldi's work. As we have seen, following the death of his father, the duke was faced with a precarious relationship with the Habsburg King

[61] Cf. Rinaldi, "Liber relationum", KBB, Ms. II.1155, ff. 252–252v.

[62] See Ibid., ff. 203–4, 218, 254–4v, 257v. Thirteen years later, Rinaldi claimed that the king was willing to grant Alessandro the fiefs of Pontremoli and Casalmaggiore, if he had only asked for them. Cf. Rinaldi to Ranuccio Farnese, 8 April 1612 (s.l.), in Barilli, "Nuovi documenti", 81.

Philip II, also ruler of Milan, and intense pressure from the Gonzaga duchy to the north-east. Moreover, the problems described in the will of Alessandro had remained unresolved, which meant that the dynasty was locked in a situation of considerable uncertainty. The central elements in Farnese strategy during these years were therefore the arrangement of a marriage for Duke Ranuccio and the repair of the dynasty's financial power. In 1597 the Farnese brothers hoped to secure a marriage alliance with the Bavarian Wittelsbach dynasty, which could reinforce their position within the Habsburg imperial sphere. This effort rapidly turned into a fiasco, as the Wittelsbach Duke Wilhelm V did not have the adequate financial resources and Philip II refused to provide the dowry. Ranuccio repeatedly asked the king for support and a remuneration of the debts his father had contracted during his governorship, but it seemed to be a futile hope.[63] At the time he wrote his account, Rinaldi was well informed of the duke's arguments about the pressing dynastic needs. We would thus be wrong to assume that Rinaldi had taken on such politically sensitive matters on his own personal initiative. It seems likely that his 'Liber relationum', as a *pièce justificative*, was intended to complement the diplomatic campaign waged by Ranuccio.[64] The distinctly problematic situation of the Farnese changed promptly, when they entered into negotiations for a bride from the papal Aldobrandini family. At the end of 1599, after months of haggling over the dowry, the two parties signed a marriage pact, which gave Ranuccio a large dowry to pay off the debts incurred by his father, and provided Odoardo with major benefices. This papal match also strengthened the hand of the Farnese in international politics and opened up a new phase in ducal relations with the Habsburg dynasty. Indeed, when Ranuccio first visited the royal court in 1601, he was appointed to the highly exclusive Order of the Golden Fleece, and gained generous pensions from King Philip III for himself and his brother Odoardo.[65] With this sudden shift in Farnese–Habsburg relations, the 'Liber relationum' obviously lost much of its relevance as a vehicle for dynastic legitimation and justification.

---

[63] For these marriage negotiations, see Odoardo Farnese to Ranuccio Farnese, 30 August 1596 (Caprarola), 4 September 1596 (Caprarola), 21 September 1596 (Caprarola), 19 February 1597 (Rome), 2 June 1599 (Rome), 7 July 1599 (Rome), ASPr, *Carteggio Farnesiano Interno*, b. 1080/B, Protocollo 1588/1602, ff. 22r, 24r, 32r, and 33v. See also Zapperi, "Per la storia della Galleria Farnese", 87–90; idem, *Eros e Controriforma*, 28–9.

[64] Cf. G. Nori, "Pomponio Torelli: una ignorate missione diplomatica in Spagna (1598–1599)", *Archivio storico per le province parmensi*, ser. IV, 29 (1977), 296–305.

[65] Zapperi, *Eros e Controriforma*, 29–36; M.A. Visceglia, *Roma papale e Spagna. Diplomatici, nobili e religiosi tra due corti* (Rome: Bulzoni, 2010), 124; García García, "Ranuccio I Farnesio", 128–9.

Conclusion

Alessandro's death signified a dramatic transformation in the political prospects of the Farnese. The new generation of the dynasty had to endure a long period of uncertainty largely due to the problematic legacy of the duke's government in the Low Countries. It was no coincidence then that, in such times of crisis, the new Farnese ruler, Duke Ranuccio, resorted to historiography. He was certainly aware of the necessity of forging a favourable history of the dynasty's recent past for the protection of his interests and for rebuilding lost authority. In this chapter I have made an effort to investigate how historiography was put to practice by the Farnese in advancing their political agendas and in constructing a strong warrior identity. The 'Liber relationum' of Paolo Rinaldi, evidently, represents a key text in this context of the reinvented history of Alessandro Farnese. What emerges most clearly is that Rinaldi's text presents itself not only as a campaign narrative, but above all as a work of propaganda which expresses many Farnesian concepts. His text had to set the dynastic record straight and fight off the incessant accusations of misconduct and disloyalty. The 'Liber relationum' is therefore an important text for investigating the way in which the Farnese developed dynastic arguments and precepts. More research is needed on the role of history at the courts of other warrior princes to establish how exceptional the Farnese were in this respect. The evidence presented here seems to indicate that the political value of historical writing for these military elites was much greater than we may have assumed.

As the example of Rinaldi's text also shows, holding a governorship in the service of a more powerful monarch did not always pay off for rulers of small principalities. Moreover, it often left them with a past full of criticism and opposition, as was the case with most Habsburg governorships or viceroyalties. Strengthening their reputation and securing their rewards proved to be major challenges for these rulers and their families. The case of the 'Liber relationum' illustrates the variety of defences and justifications they could use to claim their rewards or to expunge the stains on their honour. It seems natural, in the light of such problematic pasts, that the political significance of histories, chronicles and panegyrics grew. Indeed, as anxiety about dynastic status and honour mounted in the sixteenth century, so did the interest in historical accounts of battlefield feats. This evidently also implies a common perception of what was praiseworthy by the standards of the period. The small-state princes, for instance, knew all too well that it was essential to present themselves as modest rulers, who had no other interest than to serve the Habsburg king. In this text Alessandro Farnese appears as a magnificent commander, but also as a metaphor for the virtue and self-effacing service of his dynasty. According to Rinaldi 'the duke never asked him [the king] for anything, by saying: he who serves well makes claim enough'.[66]

---

66 Rinaldi to Ranuccio Farnese, 8 April 1612 (s.l.), in Barilli, "Nuovi documenti", 81.

Chapter 8

To Give to Airy Nothing a Local Habitation and a Name: Creating Two Great Swedish Noble Families

Fabian Persson

At the very zenith of aristocratic power in Sweden in 1669 senior members of the powerful De la Gardie family submitted a petition to the teenage King Charles XI.[1] The letter fumes with righteous indignation. The De la Gardies demanded an end to evil calumnies besmirching the memory of their grandfather Pontus De la Gardie who died in 1585. He had arrived as a condottiere in Sweden in 1565 and proceeded to a brilliant career. Now, however, it was claimed that he was not a nobleman but a simple shoemaker posing as an aristocrat. This surprising claim originated in a book published in 1605 by the Flemish Jacob Typotius.[2] He had been a secretary to King John III and a contemporary of Pontus De la Gardie.

The outraged De la Gardies stated 'that our late grandfather was of an old and prominent noble family, is painstakingly proven by his family that has lived in the same place in France until thirteen years ago'. Their French relatives had testified about Pontus De la Gardie 'what the whole country well knew, both their own great uncle's Noble birth, as well as the fact that he with honour used the same name he received in baptism until he died. The French relatives had also provided 'a detailed genealogy showing every person since 1382'. The rumour from Typotius was a grievous pain that 'incredibly hurts the honest name our ancestors brought to their graves'.

The only problem was that the French testimonies and genealogies were all lies. Pontus De la Gardie was not born as the accomplished nobleman Pontus De la Gardie but as the ambitious commoner Ponce Scroperier.[3] How had such a man become a distinguished nobleman in the first place? This chapter will address the question of how Swedish noble families conjured up an aristocratic identity.

Early modern aristocratic and princely families built up what could be called a dynastic memory.[4] This dynastic memory would be both a memory of what

---

1 Peter Wieselgren (ed.), *De la Gardiska archivet eller handlingar ur Grefl. Dela Gardiska Bibliotheket på Löberöd* (Lund: Hörberg, 1836), 7: 143–5.

2 Jacob Typotius, *Relatio historica de regno Sveciae* (Frankfurt,1605), 14–15.

3 Lorenz von Numers, *De hemliga rummen* (Stockholm: Norstedt, 1980), 29–63.

4 The author will further expand on this concept in coming publications.

the dynasty had experienced and also a way for a dynasty to develop its own identity. We can also discern how certain dynasties will begin to see themselves as having some inherent values. In such dynastic memories ideas of the dynasty's destiny were linked to various individuals and occasions which were given special importance. To have any form of dynastic memory in the form of a remembered past was in itself a claim to legitimacy. Thus it was paramount for early modern dynasties to either have or create a dynastic memory.

The Formation of a Swedish Nobility

To understand how people such as Ponce Scroperier could craft a new noble identity it is important to review the confused state of the Swedish nobility in the sixteenth century.[5] To an impostor, sixteenth-century Sweden was the promised land. The chief bureaucrat of King Gustav's government between 1538 and 1543, Conrad von Pyhy, was exposed in 1543 as a fraud who had lied about his identity. He was in reality an extremely able German commoner called Peutinger. Other fraudsters included a German who married into the Swedish high aristocracy by posing as noble. As the example of Scroperier shows, von Pyhy was hardly the only one. Their efforts were made easier by the fact that nobility was a highly fluid concept in Swedish society at the time. It didn't even strictly become hereditary until 1569. A number of people can also be seen as 'halvfrälse' – or half noble. Often these were husbands or sons of noblewomen. Successful upstarts marrying into an established family could usually lay claim to nobility even though it was all a haze with no clear boundaries. Noble families did not normally carry different names from peasants. A few had family names such as Sture but most of them used 'patronymikon' such as Persson, Eriksson and Jönsson until about 1600 in the same way peasants did. King Gustaf was known as Gustaf Eriksson before his elevation to the throne and the name Vasa for his dynasty is a later construction based on the family crest. The Swedish aristocracy was also unusually small with a few dominant, rich families and an overwhelming majority of aristocrats who were little better than slightly dressed up and hopefully washed peasants. Scarcity could thus in a Swedish context be turned into an advantage. In a better ordered society with more documentation you cannot create a past as easily. Under such circumstances behaving and looking the part of a nobleman went a long way in early modern Sweden.

Out of this chaos a number of families emerged as influential noble dynasties that would dominate early modern Swedish politics in the sixteenth and seventeenth centuries. The foreign upstarts De la Gardie, already mentioned, and the Swedish Brahes are two examples of families that managed to become great aristocratic houses with their own dynastic memories. How did they manage to do

5 Jan Samuelson, *Aristokrat eller förädlad bonde?* (Lund: Lund University Press, 1993), 260–61.

this? This chapter will review the strategies undertaken by these two families to answer this question.

Several strategies were employed by these families. Ponce Scroperier changed his name to appear more noble. The Brahes did not need to resort to this. However, both families were concerned with their own history and genealogy. A dynastic memory can be created fairly quickly, as will be illustrated.

Another important strategy consisted of marriage alliances which would proclaim and consolidate the family's illustrious position. Both families married into the royal families. It is striking, however, that even though both the De la Gardies and the Brahes were related to the royal family, that was not the main thrust of the dynastic building. Instead of harping on matrilineal royal descent, patrilineal descent was still considered more important. The Vasa heritage was not in the forefront when the Brahes and De la Gardies showcased their families.

The noble families also tried to leave behind a legacy in stone and images. Several methods could be employed. One was naming places after family members. Another was erecting memorial stones such as the ones littering the county of Per Brahe the younger. A further way was to create a family shrine in a particular church. Here tombs, coats of arms, statues and family heirlooms could be collected. Another way to state the dynastic nature of the family was to publish genealogies both in Sweden and abroad.

In the following paragraphs I will consider how the de la Gardies and Brahes employed all these strategies in order to craft their aristocratic and dynastic identities.

Creating a Gilded Past

In sixteenth-century Sweden only a select few families could boast old noble descent going back centuries. The Natt och Dag, Bonde and Bielke families could trace their roots to the thirteenth century and the royal Vasa family as well as the Oxenstiernas, Stenbocks and Tre Rosor to the fourteenth century. This comparative lack of ancient ancestors was something of an embarrassment. Even the newly baked royal house of Vasa could be attacked as non-noble, though such an attack was completely unjustified. When Tsar Ivan the Terrible had accused Gustav Vasa of being a mere peasant, Vasa's son King John III wrote a famous furious 'scolding letter' in response: 'As your letter still claims, which is a big and insolent lie, that our late dear father was a peasant from Småland and not of a noble family – everytime you say that you lie most shamefully'.[6]

Until the reign of Gustav Vasa, none of these families held titles, until Erik XIV created a Swedish titled nobility. He handed out at his coronation in 1561, the titles of Count and Baron to families related to the royal family. These families

---

[6] Harald Hjärne, "Ur brefvexlingen emellan konung Johan III och tsar Ivan Vasilievitj", *Historiskt bibliotek* 7: 8 (1880), 531–4.

consisted of the old nobility, but also of aristocratic families related to the Vasas. King Gustav was married three times and his later two wives came from the Swedish nobility. He also had cousins and a nephew who were given important positions. The first three counts were King Erik's cousin Per Brahe and his father's cousins Svante Sture and Gustav Johansson (Tre Rosor). Nine barons were also created. The following year lands, counties and baronies were handed out to go with the title. At first these lands were small but they would grow considerably over time.

Thus the monarchy was an all important factor in building the dynastic fortunes of the Brahes and, later, the De la Gardies. By latching on to strengthening royal power aristocratic families could receive rewards in lands, offices and from the 1560s in titles as well. Families outside the royal nexus and with no presence at court would find themselves losing ground. The Vasa dynasty had resources surpassing previous rulers when rewarding their kin and loyal servants.

The Brahe family was thus one of the most important noble families in the 1560s. It was, however, also embarrassingly new as a prominent family. The high status of the Brahes was based entirely on Per Brahe's father having married King Gustav's sister Margareta. This sorry state of affairs was about to be rectified.[7] In the 1540s Sweden's foremost archivist Rasmus Ludvigsson had looked into the Brahe family and not found any illustrious background. The earliest known Brahe was Per Brahe's great grandfather Magnus Laurensson. Obviously something better was needed – and something did turn up.

In the 1560s a manuscript was unearthed that suddenly gave the Brahe family a completely new and distinguished background. Vadstena convent was founded by the Bridgettine order and, naturally, they had a special interest in the family of Saint Bridget herself. She had belonged to the highest Swedish nobility in the fourteenth century. Several nuns wrote descriptions of Saint Bridget's family and relations and in one of these the Brahes now made a surprise appearance. The manuscript was tampered with in the 1560s, possibly by the abbess Karin Bengtsdotter wanting to ingratiate herself with the powerful new count. The archivist Rasmus Ludvigsson also appears to have been in on this act. According to this new changed manuscript the Brahe family was a cadet branch descending from a brother of Saint Bridget.

The enchanted count Per Brahe was soon convinced of his family's newly discovered distinction. In a letter from 1573 he takes the relationship with Saint Bridget as a given and asks Rasmus Ludvigsson if he has any more information about 'my paternal family'. Not only was Brahe now descended from Saint Bridget's brother but it was also demonstrated that Saint Bridget's family itself was a cadet branch of the royal family of King Sverker (reigned 1130 to 1156). From being a rather new family the Brahes were now one of the most ancient ones in Sweden – indeed the most ancient and royal to boot! When Per Brahe's son

[7] Jan Liedgren, "Föreställningar om den heliga Birgittas släkt: traditioner och konstruktioner", *Personhistorisk Tidskrift* 79 (1983), 1–16.

Joakim was buried in 1567 the Vadstena convent church was chosen. The newly created dynastic memory in the form of the connection between the Brahes and Saint Bridget would be reinforced over the coming century.

The De la Gardies, as mentioned at the beginning, were also given a genealogical make-over. The French mercenary Pontus De la Gardie had begun life as mere Ponce Scroperier, son of a wealthy merchant in southern France. Leaving France, and life in a Benedictine monastery behind him, Ponce Scroperier invented a new, more aristocratic sounding name – De la Gardie. The name came from a farm owned by his family. He switched from Danish to Swedish service in 1565. He soon rose high in King John's favour and was made baron of Ekholmen in Veckholm parish in 1571. Nine years later he was given the King's illegitimate daughter Sophia Gyllenhielm as a wife. His title and his royal marriage now marked him as one of the foremost aristocrats in Sweden.

In 1605 Ponce Scroperier was exposed, posthumously, by Jakob Typotius as an impostor but his son Jakob De la Gardie acted later to remedy the damage. Securing letters and testimonies from relatives in France a fraudulent genealogy was concocted. Thus Typotius's claims could be refuted and a glittering ancestry of centuries of French lower nobility displayed. This form of dynastic memory had nothing to do with the reality of the past but all to do with the ambitions of the present. Both the De la Gardies and Brahes thus entered the seventeenth century with improved and impressive genealogies stretching far back into the middle ages.

Marriages – On the Up and Up

The ambitions of the Brahes and De la Gardies can also be seen in their marriages. When we review these marriages, it becomes clear it is important to grasp that these families did not merely wish to rise above ordinary Swedish noble families. They wished to be seen as the peers of German princely families. Marrying could make or break a family.

Per Brahe (1520–1590) married Beata Stenbock, younger sister to Queen Catharina, last wife of King Gustav. As noted above, the Stenbocks belonged to the oldest Swedish nobility. His sons continued the trend to fortify the family position by marriage. Erik Brahe, the second count, married Elisabeth, daughter of Duke Otto of Braunschweig-Lüneburg. It proved to be a brilliant but unhappy union. She would write home to her relatives in Germany complaining about his mistreatment and in the 1590s he almost lost Visingsborg county when the Swedish regent considered confiscation because of count Brahe's 'continued whoring, not once, but many times'. He finally had to flee abroad after being too compromised politically. Erik's brother Gustav Brahe was considered to be courting Princess Anna, daughter of King John III. This was considered an unlikely, but not completely impossible union. The Princess's brutal uncle, Duke Charles, lampooned the liaison in his rather badly written rhymed chronicle. The third

Brahe brother, Magnus, married Brita Leijonhufvud, niece of Queen Margareta, second wife of King Gustav. The fourth brother, Abraham Brahe married Elsa Gyllenstierna whose stepmother was a sister of Queen Gunilla, second wife of King John III, and a member of the ancient Bielke family. As can be seen, the marriages were confined to a very small number of families.

Pontus de la Gardie's descendants also connected themselves through marriage with both the oldest and newer nobilities. As mentioned, Pontus De la Gardie married King John's illegitimate daughter while his sons Johan and Jakob married an Oxenstierna and a Brahe respectively. Jakob De la Gardie's wife Ebba Brahe had been courted by King Gustavus Adolphus in the 1610s – his love letters to her still exist.[8] In the seventeenth century the families strove to uphold this exclusivity. Per Brahe the younger married first a Stenbock and then a De la Gardie. Having become part of this exclusive social group, the De la Gardies became very careful to uphold their status in all circumstances. When his sister Christina Brahe wanted to marry the young general Åke Tott he was worried. Åke Tott was, despite being a grandson of King Erik XIV, not a count or even a baron. That Per Brahe's sister would take a rank below others was inconceivable. Before the marriage Brahe wanted assurances that his sister would retain her rank as the daughter of a count. Åke Tott had to write repeatedly to Per Brahe promising to protect Christina Brahe's rank with all his might and courage. When the wedding at last did happen in 1638 Per Brahe had forbidden his nine-year-old daughter Elsa Beata to attend as she might not be able to protect her rank. 'When my sister Christina celebrates her wedding, I on no account want my daughter Elsa Beata to be present, as I know she will be handled with disrespect in that some people want to go before her who are not entitled to it and she is young and cannot deal with it'.[9]

In the mid-seventeenth century the Brahes and De la Gardies had reached so high that several family members married into the admired German princely dynasties. Magnus Gabriel De la Gardie married Queen Christina's cousin, Maria Eufrosyne – daughter of a German prince Johan Casimir of Pfalz-Zweibrücken and a Swedish Princess. Per Brahe's own daughter, Elsa Beata, known as 'the little doll', was intended by her father as the bride of Heinrich von Thurn.[10] He was not wealthy or personally distinguished but he was a German count, son of a Bohemian refugee in Sweden. The Thurn family was crushingly aristocratic and claimed a doubtful descent from a Della Torre family. Indeed they were rumoured to be able to show their descent back to the fourth century. This was a match that would further merge the Brahes with the German princely families and elevate them above mere Swedish aristocracy. Unfortunately, on his travels Heinrich von

[8] C.M. Stenbock (ed.), *Ett 300-årigt Vasaminne. Brefväxlingen mellan Gustaf II Adolf och Ebba Brahe I* (Stockholm: Norstedt, 1915). The whole (little) volume consists of these love letters.

[9] Ellen Fries, *Teckningar ur svenska adelns familjelif i gamla tider* (Stockholm: Norstedt, 1910), 1: 114.

[10] Fries, *Teckningar*, 1: 119.

Thurn proved to be so unsatisfactory that Per Brahe eventually tired of paying his debts and helping him. He was written off and instead married a daughter of the Maregrave of Baden-Hochberg. The aim to marry into a German princely family, however, remained and Per Brahe was nothing if not persistent. In 1649 Elsa Beata Brahe married Queen Christina's cousin, Maria Eufrosyne's brother, the Count Palatine Adolf Johan. The Queen celebrated the marriage in a splendid fashion and arranged a tournament. After Elsa Beata Brahe's death in 1653 Adolf Johan married her cousin Elsa Elisabeth Brahe.

In return, the German princes grew increasingly interested in these Swedish marriages. In 1660 Per Brahe's 57-year old sister Margareta Brahe (widow of Axel Oxenstierna's son Johan) received no fewer than two proposals of marriage from German princes. The first was from the 66-year-old Landgrave Ludwig Heinrich of Nassau-Dillenburg. He was a widower with 17 children and seemed certain of success. Then he was put in the shade by the more dashing 27-year-old Landgrave Friedrich of Hesse-Homburg – called Friedrich with the silver leg. The outraged Ludwig Heinrich wrote a pamphlet entitled *Die untreue Margaretha Brahe* in order to drag her name through the mud.[11] Even so – this illustrates that the De la Gardies and the Brahes had arrived.

Stones, Castles and Towns – Creating Dynastic Facts on the Ground

Having established the ancient lineage of the Brahes and De la Gardies and having married into the right families another step was to make the families visible and to erect various forms of memorials. To do so a family seat that could be turned into a shrine was needed. If the genealogical part of the dynastic memory had been created buildings and objects could further strengthen and give more meaning to the dynastic memory. Already in the 1540s Per Brahe rebuilt parts of his castle Rydboholm. Here he erected a new tower. In the following decades the most luxurious chamber in the tower was given expensive wood panelling with pictures of Roman emperors and of Per Brahe's parents Joakim Brahe and Margareta Vasa.

In 1561 Per Brahe was elevated to one of Sweden's first three counts. When he the following year was given a county to go with the title he switched his dynastic pretensions from Rydboholm to his new county of Visingsborg. The centrepiece of the county was the island of Visingsö and in the 1560s Per Brahe began building a new castle for his family there. He looted the Cistercian monastery of Alvastra and the old royal ruin of Näs for masonry and evicted peasants from three old villages. The castle of Visingsborg was to be built in grand style.[12]

11 Ludwig Heinrich, *Die vntrewe Margaretha Brahe, Grävin zu Wisingsburg* (s.l., 1661).

12 Bo Eriksson, *I skuggan av tronen. En biografi över Per Brahe d.ä.* (Stockholm: Prisma, 2009), 285.

In 1600 the county of Visingsborg was transferred to Per Brahe's younger son Magnus as the older one, Erik Brahe, had to flee Sweden as a catholic and adherent of the deposed King Sigismund. During Magnus Brahe's lifetime Visingsborg was further improved. In the 1620s the south wing and a large banqueting hall was added. The walls of the banqueting hall were decorated by 22 portraits of members of the Brahe family and of the family of Saint Bridget.[13]

In 1633 Magnus Brahe was succeeded as count by his nephew Per Brahe the Younger (1602–1680). During his almost 50 years as count the celebration of the Brahe dynasty reached new heights. Now the county of Visingsborg had grown to the same size as the German principality of Mecklenburg-Schwerin. To Per Brahe it was always the goal to be considered the equal of minor German princes. He would also refer to himself as 'ruling count' and talk about 'his rule' and his 'subjects'.[14] Per Brahe the younger continued the rebuilding of Visingsborg and added niches in the courtyard where painted sculptures of Brahe members were placed. The Eastern side of the castle overlooking the lake Vättern was also decorated with sculptures of Brahes.

A further way of commemorating a dynasty was to name places after family members. In a similar fashion Cardinal Richelieu founded the town Richelieu but it seems more prevalent in Sweden. The Brahes and De la Gardies likewise strove to create monuments to their families by naming towns and castles after themselves. In the centre of Visingsborg county Per Brahe the younger began the building of the castle Brahehus in the 1630s. Close to Brahehus a small hunting lodge called Brahehälla was also erected. Furthermore a manor Braheberg was named after Carl Brahe in the 1630s. The indomitable Per Brahe also founded the town Brahea in 1653 in Carelia during his time as Governor of Finland. The little town never flourished, though a school was set up here. The year before Brahea was founded Per Brahe had founded another Finnish town, Brahestad, in 1652. It never became important although it managed to survive and could boast very geometrical, baroque town planning. He also created a new parish named Kristina, possibly after his first wife Kristina Stenbock. In 1652 he also founded the town Brahe-Gränna just across from Visingsborg castle.

Not content with this, Per Brahe littered his county with stones carved with his name.[15] At least 16 memorial stones were erected during his time as count. A very long inscription from 1653 details names and dates of the Brahe family since Per Brahe the elder. Other stones are more terse and just give the name and dates of a single count (usually Per Brahe the younger himself). At least one of the inscriptions is carved not on a stone but on the actual rock. These stones are quite telling in their phrasing about how many years various Brahe counts ruled ('rexit').

---

13 Erik Pettersson, *Den skoningslöse: En biografi över Karl IX.* (Stockholm: Natur & kultur, 2008), 96.

14 Fries, *Teckningar,* 1: 92.

15 Jes Wienberg, "Det hotade grevskapet – Per Brahe den yngres minnesmärken", *Fornvännen* 4 (2008), 260–78.

Figure 8.1 Per Brahe the Elder. The first prominent Brahe, Per Brahe the Elder, was happy to discover dubious evidence of his family as a branch of older dynasties going back to the royal Sverker dynasty in the twelfth century.

The De la Gardie family name was less suitable for place names but Christian names were used to fill the void. Thus in 1652 Jakob De la Gardie's widow Ebba Brahe (cousin of Per Brahe) founded a new Finnish town named Jakobstad after her late husband. A sumptuous new palace called Jakobsdal had already been built in the 1640s outside Stockholm. In the 1660s Jakob De la Gardie's son Magnus

Gabriel built a castle called Mariedal, named after his wife the Princess Palatine Maria Eufrosyne of Pfalz-Zweibrücken.

Churches could also be turned into family shrines of dynastic memory. The Brahe family had an edge over the De la Gardies in that the Visingsborg county was in Brahe hands for so long. That created a stable basis from which to build a set of family memorials. The De la Gardies did not have such a fixed base, but moved around during the first generations after Pontus. The first De la Gardie, Pontus, was buried in Reval, but his sons Jakob and Johan were buried in Veckholm where their father's barony was. Johan also presented the church with a pulpit carved with the De la Gardie crest. It is clear that Jakob De la Gardie intended Veckolm church to be a family shrine. In the 1650s his son Magnus Gabriel built a magnificent monument for his parents there and 10 of Magnus Gabriel's children are buried in Veckholm as well. He himself began to waiver and in the 1660s he chose the old church of Varnhem as his own resting place. Varnhem was much more imposing than Veckholm. It furthermore could boast royal tombs of the royal dynasties of the twelfth and thirteenth centuries. To be buried there would be more impressive and link the De la Gardies back to the old Swedish kings. Unfortunately it meant that Magnus Gabriel De la Gardie had to start from the beginning again in creating a family church. He built a grand tomb with colossal statues of himself and his father Jakob. However, Varnhem was never turned into a De la Gardie temple, as after Magnus Gabriel, the family ceased to use it.

Much more thorough was the approach of the Brahe family. Here too, though, no obvious family church existed from the start. Per Brahe the elder let his son Joakim be buried in Vadstena convent as a nod to the link to St Bridget. He himself and his wife were buried in Östra Ryd's church – the parish church of his castle Rydboholm. The next count, Erik Brahe, fled abroad and died in Danzig but the third count, Magnus Brahe, began the reconstruction of Ströja church on Visingsö. It was an old medieval church with links to the Sverker dynasty of the twelfth century – a dynasty of which the Brahes saw themselves as a cadet branch. Thus this church, close to Visingsborg castle, was a most suitable new family shrine. However, Magnus Brahe himself was buried in 1633 in Västerås cathedral.

Thus the Brahes had Östra Ryd and Ströja – the latter hereafter known as the Brahe church – at their disposal in the 1630s. Östra Ryd continued to be used by the family but the Brahe church on Visingsö was transformed into a memorial of the Brahe glory by the fourth count, Per Brahe the younger. When Per Brahe's younger brother Nils died at Lützen in 1632 this was manifested by a painting of the dead Nils Brahe which was hung at Rydboholm castle (later moved to Östra Ryd church). In Östra Ryd Nils Brahe was buried and his bloodied jacket along with his rapier were placed upon his coffin. In 1650 a tablet was put up telling that 'in this vault are buried the following Brahes of royal blood'.[16]

---

[16] S. Brandel and Tord Nordberg, "Östra Ryds kyrka", in *Sveriges kyrkor* (Stockholm: Almqvist & Wiksell, 1928), 345.

When Per Brahe's two children died in the mid-1630s he decided to bury them at Brahe church. This was the start of the church as a family mausoleum.[17] Per Brahe's sister Christina was careful that the ancestry of the young boy should be engraved on his little coffin.[18] When Per Brahe's aunt, Margareta Brahe, died in 1638 the Brahe church on Visingsö at last got going even more. She herself wanted to be buried alongside her late beheaded husband, Johan Sparre, at Kalmar. Her will was overturned as it turned out to be embarrassingly catholic in its provisions. Instead her body was transported to Visingsö and she was buried there. A statue was erected commemorating Margareta Brahe while the provisions she made in a will for a chantry priest were used on Visingsö.

In the following decades Brahe church was crammed full with bric-à-brac in order to elevate it into a dynastic church on a par with family churches of German princely and ducal families.[19] Not only did Per Brahe decorate it with family mementos but also a selection of curios that would fit into a Wunderkammer – such as a cup made out of a coconut and stone age tools. A box with Margareta Brahe's beheaded husband's skull was on display for centuries and it was said to be worn shiny by somewhat morbid sightseers. Statues of St Bridget, the Brahes' illustrious relative, were also set up at Brahe church and Östra Ryd with inscriptions that the saint was of 'Familia Brahe'.

In 1650 Per Brahe's first wife Christina Catharina Stenbock was interred at Brahe church. An imposing monument with statues of both her and Per Brahe was built. Her lineage was also painted extensively on the church wall. When Per Brahe's daughter, Elsa Beata (married to Queen Christina's cousin the Count Palatine Adolf Johan) died in 1653 she was also buried there. Of course an imposing family tree was painted and hung in the church (with a copy in Östra Ryd church). Busts that were obviously copies of some of the Brahe busts in the niches at Visingsborg were also placed in the church. We can see how both the Brahes and the De la Gardies created dynastic landmarks in the form of place names and memorials in churches. The Brahes were, however, even more persistent and remarkable in this respect.

Paper and Canvas – Disseminating the Brahe Glory

At Visingsborg Per Brahe the Younger collected documents and amassed a family archive to bolster the dynastic memory of his house. This included medieval documents from the family of St Bridget intended to further prove the Brahe descent from that family. The always dynastically minded Per Brahe the younger also initiated a number of publications devoted to the Brahe genealogy. His

[17] For the Brahe church on Visingsö see primarily Wilhelm Nisser, *Konst och hantverk i Visingsborgs grevskap på Per Brahe d.y:s tid* (Stockholm: G. Lindström, 1931).

[18] Fries, *Teckningar*, 1: 104.

[19] Nisser, *Konst och hantverk*, 67–119.

illegitimate cousin Johan Örnevinge composed a work called *Genealogia Braheae* which was published in 1647.[20] It included not only genealogical tables showing the Brahe family and its descent from St Bridget's family and the house of King Sverker. There were also lineages back to Charlemagne (actually more correct) as well as pictures of various Brahes and copies of documents including the canonisation documents of St Bridget. An engraving of her parents' tomb was also included. At the very end was a family tree that also combined a map of the county of Visingsborg. This was indeed a showcase for dynastic ambition.

Örnevinge's book was followed up by a similar publication by the historian Johannes Widekindi called *Imagines Illustrissimae Familiae Braheae* in 1673.[21] It was published by Per Brahe's own printing press on Visingsö. It contained the same information as *Genealogia Braheae* and began with the sentence 'The Brahes have always been the first noble family in the kingdom of Sweden'. One of the documents reprinted was the tampered-with genealogical notes from Vadstena convent.

In order that the eminence of the Brahes would not go unnoticed abroad Per Brahe presented Nicolaus Rittershusius in Nürnberg with 200 riksdaler. Rittershusius published genealogies covering royal, princely and noble houses and in 1658 the Brahes were included in his *Genealogiae imperatorum, regu, ducum, comitum*. In the Swedish volume *Suecia antiqua* compiled in the 1660s Per Brahe managed to get in not just the various Brahe castles but also an engraving of the tomb of the parents of St Bridget – the family founder. Other family members would sometimes write to Per Brahe asking for family information and he would then send them genealogical tables written out of documents in the chancery at Visingsborg. His sister Margareta Brahe would write from Hesse asking for information if they were descended from King Sverker and Charlemagne.

Per Brahe also employed a court painter of his own, Johan Werner, who painted numerous portraits of members of the Brahe family. Family portraits would be borrowed by Per Brahe and then be copied by Johan Werner. He also seems to have been at work painting various genealogical trees which were then put up in Brahe castles or the churches at Ryd and Visingsö. He also painted pictures from tombs so that Per Brahe to Tärna (uncle to Per Brahe the elder) was given a portrait (in the Brahe church) as well as the squire Nils Magnusson who died in 1484.

---

20 Johan Örnevinge, *Genealogia Braheae* (Stockholm, 1647).

21 Johannes Widekindi, *Imagines Illustrissimae Familiae Braheae* (Visingsö, 1673).

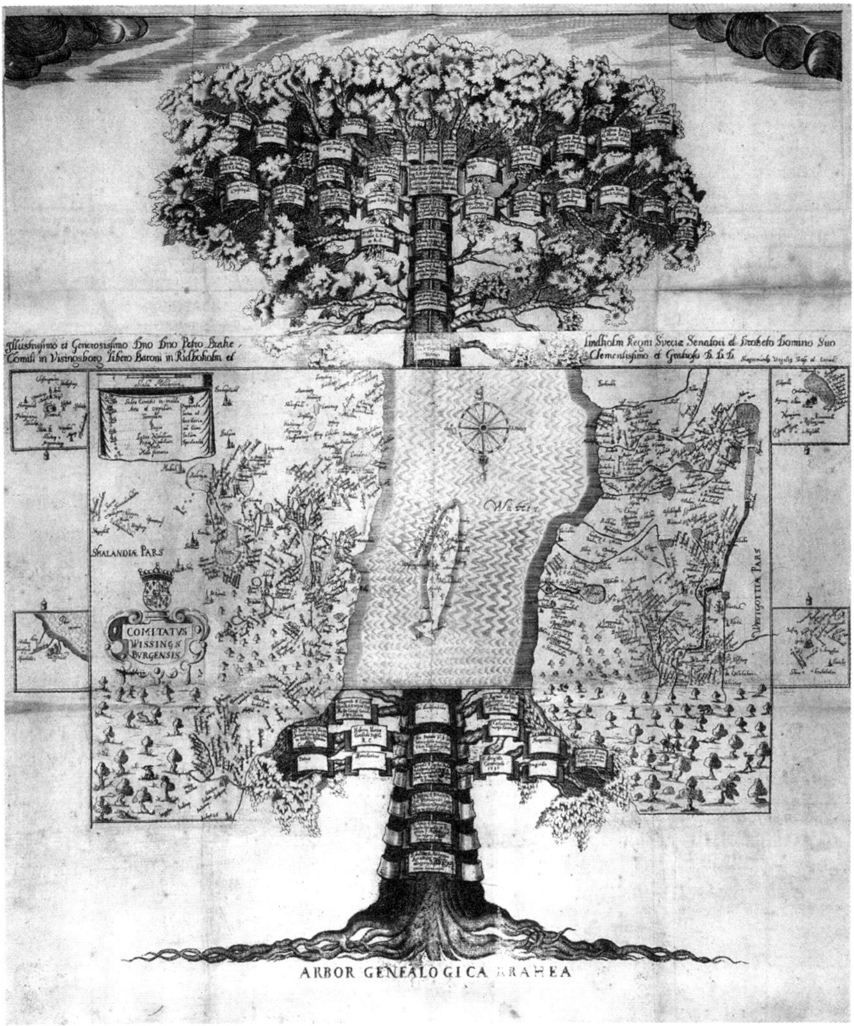

Figure 8.2 The *Genealogia Braheae* showing a combination of the Brahe family tree and a map of the county of Visingsborg.

Figure 8.3 Per Brahe the Younger would grow to be the most zealous builder of a dynastic identity in mid-seventeenth-century Sweden

Conclusion

When we look at the strategies employed by the Brahe and De la Gardie families to cement their recent aristocratic status, we can discern similarities as well as differences. They both strove to build up a dynastic memory using real ancestors as well as appropriating false ones. Both families improved their genealogical luggage. The De la Gardies did this in order to cover up their common background and the Brahes in order to further enhance their nobility and – falsely – link it to the Swedish St Bridget and the royal house of King Sverker. This was by no means unique. The period witnessed a number of noble families creating fictitious genealogies. The official genealogist Johan Peringskiöld wrote in the 1690s that 'in the ancestors of Count Lichton [I] made some up on the King's command, as knowledge otherwise could not be had without great expense from England'.[22] Peringskiöld also let his imagination run free with regard to Count Königsmarck, describing how 'several of his ancestors are made up as never existed in this world, and that to the splendour of the family'. However we should not always think of the Brahes and De la Gardies as consciously fraudulent. Of course Pontus De la Gardie knew he was born Ponce Scroperier, but his descendants probably believed in his noble status. The fabrication of noble ancestors for the Brahe family also seems to have been done by people outside the family circle. In a matter of a few years this was then accepted as a fact.

We can also see how both Brahes and De la Gardies aimed to compete not with Swedish nobility but with German princes. They wanted to distance themselves both from the lower nobility and from the ever increasing new nobility in Sweden. The obvious point of reference was German princely houses, as can be seen in the ambitious marriages contracted. The high status of the dynasties of Brahe and De la Gardie in some senses made them more a part of an international high community of princely and aristocratic families and less a part of the community of the Swedish nobility. They were thus not worried about foreigners serving at the Swedish court – unlike the lower nobility, which was outraged.

What the De la Gardies and the Brahes did dislike intensely, however, was low or newly created nobility at court or in other positions. When Queen Christina in 1647 wanted to make the brilliant diplomat Johan Adler Salvius a royal councillor the aristocratic councillors were outraged. Per Brahe said that Salvius was capable but should be given a place according to his birth. The Queen replied sharply that 'When you need good advice, you do not ask after sixteen ancestors'. Despite such reprimands Per Brahe was always a defender of aristocratic values. In 1664 he took part in a debate in the diet on rank. Brahe noted that Erik XIV had created a hierarchy within the Swedish nobility with counts and barons 'so that not everyone is like pig's feet but that some are more eminent than others'. The abolition of such an aristocratic hierarchy would leave Sweden 'worse considered by others than Turks or heathens'.

There are, however, also differences between the Brahes and De la Gardies. All said and done the De la Gardies were still more normal. Lesser nobility acted in similar ways when building a dynastic memory through decorating churches with tombs, flags and funeral crests.[23] They donated silver and clerical robes.

---

22 Bengt Hildebrand, *Handbok i släkt- och personforskning* (Stockholm: Wahlström & Widstrand, 1961), 107.

23 See for example Peter Ullgren, *Lantadel: adliga godsägare i Östergötland och Skåne vid 1600-talets slut* (Lund: Sisyfos, 2004).

The differences between the De la Gardie family and many others were, to some extent, a difference of degree.

The Brahe family was building a dynasty and a dynastic memory with a completely different zeal. Unlike the De la Gardies they began their dynastic creation earlier and with more resources. They also had the benefit of a higher degree of permanence. Whereas the De la Gardies switched between different palaces as their main abodes – such as Ekholmen, Jakobsdal, Läckö and Venngarn – the Brahe family throughout the period had Visingsborg and Rydboholm as their main seats. That also meant that the churches close to Visingsborg and Rydboholm, Brahe church and Östra Ryd, were transformed into mausoleums over the dynasty. The De la Gardies had Veckholmen but there was never any self-evident dynastic church covering several generations.

From this foundation of permanence over generations a Brahe dynasty was created in marble, paper, wood and writing. Per Brahe the Younger was instrumental in this development of a glittering dynastic memory. He ruled as count of Visingsborg for almost half a century. During that period he created a church as a family mausoleum, he founded several towns and castles named after his family, he collected and copied family portraits, he published genealogies and family documents, he decorated churches and castles with statues of Brahe family members and he managed to contract marriages with princely families.

It is no wonder that this vastly proud and ambitious man saw his family as second only to the royal family in Sweden. Around 1650 a French diplomat reported about Count Per Brahe and the possibility that Queen Christina might die without an heir: 'I don't know what Count Brahe would think about it. But I do know for sure that he thinks his own family the greatest of the realm after the royal family and has high enough ambitions to hope for anything'.[24]

The De la Gardies lacked such a person in their ranks. The contemporaries Jakob De la Gardie and Magnus Gabriel De la Gardie were certainly aware of their family's importance and eager to uphold it. They were however no match for Per Brahe in that respect. Whereas Magnus Gabriel De la Gardie's decorations in his palace of Venngarn are religious or mythical Per Brahe was robustly dynastic. Magnus Gabriel De la Gardie decorated a room at his castle Läckö to celebrate his father's military exploits but the De la Gardie family as such was not glorified for centuries back. Both families aimed to build a dynastic identity thus reflecting a general trend in early modern society. The role of individuals in creating dynastic identities was crucial. Pontus De la Gardie lay the – fraudulent – foundation of the dynastic identity of the De la Gardies. The dynastic zeal of Per Brahe the Younger brought together place names, genealogy, busts, portraits, publications and marriages. Thus the dynastic edifice of the Brahes surpassed that of the De la Gardies. Both created dynastic memories, but the Brahes were much more versatile and systematic.

---

[24] Curt Weibull, *Drottning Christina och Sverige 1646–1651: en fransk diplomat berättar (*Stockholm: Norstedt, 1970), 48.

By cultivating relations with the Vasa kings the Brahes and De la Gardies also benefitted from the growth in royal power. In that way they could secure titles, lands, offices and status in the gift of the monarch. The dazzling houses of Brahe and De la Gardie are unimaginable without strong links to and support from the royal family.

In the mid-seventeenth century the Brahes and De la Gardies had established themselves as the leading aristocratic dynasties of Sweden. Genealogies, princely marriages, paintings, castles and towns named after the families all told a story of success. This was not to last. The introduction of royal absolutism checked the princely ambitions of the great aristocratic houses. Already in 1681 counties and baronies were reabsorbed by the Crown and only the titles remained. The Brahes and De la Gardies had to pay vast amounts to the Crown for faults committed during the royal minority between 1660 and 1672. No more princely marriages would beckon and even though Brahe and De la Gardie continued to play a rôle in Swedish history their political and economical pre-eminence was now diminished. The great castle of Visingsborg fell into disrepair and ruin alongside Brahehus and Brahehälla. The families continued until the twentieth century (the De la Gardies until today) but never regained the same status, even though Magnus Brahe in the nineteenth century was a great royal favourite and power broker. When the last count Brahe died in 1930 the Archbishop of Sweden took the key to the Brahe family vault and rowed into a nearby lake and tossed it overboard. The era of the Brahes was finally over and no simple commoners would ever again disturb the rest of the ruling counts of Visingsborg in their gilded and crested coffins.

Chapter 9

The Nassau Orphans: The Disputed Legacy of William of Orange and the Construction of the Prince of Orange (1584–1675)

Liesbeth Geevers

Introduction

In 1675 Matteus Smallegange, an Orangist from Zealand, published his *Geslacht-rekening der doorluchtigste vorsten van Nassau en Oraenjen, waer in den oorspronk, aenwas en voorgank der selver, met het gene sy verricht hebben sedert den jare 682 tot het jaer 1675*: [the dynastic account of the serene princes of Nassau and Orange, in which the origins, growth and advancement of the same, with all they have achieved since the year 682 until the year 1675].[1] It is about the Nassau dynasty, which had only recently regained the stadholderate of most of the provinces of the Dutch Republic after the stadholderless era of 1650–1672. This event warranted new attention for the family's place in the history of the Dutch Republic. Accordingly, Smallegange stated in his preface that he wished to inform – or perhaps rather to remind – his fellow Dutchmen about the Nassaus, their glorious descent from the Romans and the many honours they had received over time from a list of emperors, from Julius Caesar to Charles V. His stress was on those members of the dynasty that had contributed to the defence of 'our Netherland' with their unspeakable valor, bravery and wise policy, especially William I, Maurice, Frederick Henry and – in his own time – William III.[2]

Smallegange's introductory remarks reflect his choice to focus on a select number of Nassaus. The frontispiece reinforced this message by showing a tree bearing the portraits of William the Silent, his sons Maurice and Frederick Henry, and the latter's son William II and grandson William III. In the text Smallegange narrows his focus down even further, also eliminating William II (prince of Orange and stadholder from 1647 to 1650) from his list of Nassau heroes. William the Silent's eldest son, namesake and main heir Philip William is conspicuous by his absence. He is overlooked in favour of a continuous line of Revolt heroes running

[1] Matteus Smallegange, *Geslacht-rekening der doorluchtigste vorsten van Nassau en Oraenjen, waer in den oorspronk, aenwas en voorgank der selver, met het gene sy verricht hebben sedert den jare 682 tot het jaer 1675* (Amsterdam, 1675).

[2] Smallegange, *Geslacht-rekening*, 'voorrede' (unfoliated).

from William I to William III, and, as if to underline his irrelevance, his biographical entry actually stops mid-sentence: 'he died at … '[3] After all, Philip William was no Revolt hero. In 1567, when he was a boy of 13, he had been abducted and taken to Spain as a retaliation against his father, William the Silent, who defied Habsburg authority in the Netherlands. He only returned to the Low Countries in 1596. His lengthy absence in Spain meant he had no role to play in the Dutch Revolt and could not serve as his father's political heir. Indeed, even his status as prince of Orange was debated by some. When he was about to return to the Netherlands after spending almost 30 years in Spanish captivity, his cousin William Louis did not refer to him as 'Prince of Orange' but merely as the 'lord of Buren'.[4] In a 1590 print by the Cologne engraver Conradus Goltzius Maurice had already been described as 'von gottes gnaden Printz von Auranien' while his father's escutcheon was pictured next to his portrait.[5] Smallegange was therefore in good company when he chose to make short shrift of Philip William in 1675.

It would not surprise anyone familiar with the history of the Revolt or of Dutch national identity that Philip William should be overlooked in this way. However, I will argue in this chapter that this oversight is not only the natural result of historical events, but was also part of a deliberately constructed family history that aimed to enhance the authority of his younger brother Maurice. After all, Philip William (1554–1618) was indisputably William of Orange's eldest legitimate son and heir. He was the longest serving prince of Orange of his generation, holding the title from 1584 to 1618, followed by his brothers Maurice, who became prince at 51 years of age (1618–1625) and Frederick Henry (born 1584, prince 1625–1647). Even if he was not of great political significance to the Dutch Revolt, these factors accorded him dynastic relevance and therefore a prominent place in genealogies. However, I will show how the connotation of the title 'prince of Orange' was changed in such a way, that he became as irrelevant in dynastic histories as he had been in political life – at least in the Republic. The change in connotation was first achieved by

---

3 Smallegange, *Geslacht-rekening*, 56. The Belgian historian Fernand Hermans noted in the Preface to his work *Filips Willem van Oranje* (s.l., s.n.: 1997) that he had written it to educate a Dutch audience about Philip William, since they knew almost nothing about him. He had reached this conclusion after a visit to the Nieuwe Kerk in Delft, where William the Silent is buried, where he was told by a tour guide that Philip William's place of burial was unknown. In fact, this was Diest – one of several places Philip William had chosen as a possible burial site. Hermans, *Filips Willem van* Oranje, 44–9.

4 A.Th. van Deursen, *Maurits van Nassau. De winnaar die faalde* (Amsterdam: Bakker, 2002), 151; G. Groen van Prinsterer, *Archives ou correspondance inédite de la maison d'Orange-Nassau* (2nd series, 5 vols., Leiden: S. et J. Luchtmans, 1835–1915), 1: 356. Letter dated 22 November 1595. Michel Van der Eycken, *Oranje-Nassau, Prins Filips-Willem en Diest* (Diest: Vrienden van de Sint-Sulpitiuskerk vzw, 2010), 42 even argues that the States General frequently referred to Philip William as 'lord of Buren' after his release in 1595. This statement is not corroborated by the Resolutions of the States General.

5 Kees Zandvliet (ed.), *Maurits Prins van Oranje* (Zwolle: Waanders, 2000), 186.

Maurice and the States of Holland, who were both interested in bolstering Maurice's prestige. I will argue that apart from Philip William, another 'prince of Orange' was conjured up when the States of Holland started referring to Maurice by that title.

It is perhaps not necessary to emphasise that the title 'Prince of Orange' referred to a French sovereign principality and had no connection to any office or position of power in the Netherlands, apart from the fact that its bearer counted as the highest nobleman in the Habsburg Netherlands since the Nassau family had worn it (1530). It conferred, therefore, social prestige, which was an important ingredient of high office, but did not provide access to political decision-making *per se* – neither in the Habsburg period, nor during the Dutch Republic. The title's appeal to Dutch nationalist sentiment, as opposed to that of some of its bearers, does not seem self-evident either; there was hardly any previous history between the Netherlands and Orange, although some previous generations of princes had already served Emperor Charles V. But when the States of Holland decided to start calling Maurice 'natural prince of Orange' from 1585 onwards, the title gained new meaning. By styling himself 'natural prince of Orange' Maurice acquired sovereign charisma, which, in terms of social prestige and political clout, was very real in its consequences. In return, the Dutch Republic, and especially the County of Holland, was provided with a near-monarchical military leader at no immediate cost to the Dutch ruling elites – a title with no income or inherent constitutional power. Maurice would be ruler of nowhere, yet the sovereign and ancestral charisma of the title were attached to him. The new title was only relevant to the stadholders in the Dutch Republic, referring to them in their capacity as (military) leaders of the Dutch Revolt.

Of course, the position of the Nassaus at the head of the Dutch polity always remained somewhat ambiguous and cannot be compared to the position of a hereditary monarch, but the Nassaus had a stronger, though informal, claim to hereditary power than historians usually realise. At William of Orange's funeral much effort was made to *separate* William of Orange's identities as hereditary prince of Orange and appointed stadholder in his funerary procession, as Geert H. Janssen recently showed.[6] But the equation of the hereditary French title with the non-hereditary stadholderate, or at least the military leadership of the Dutch Revolt, during Maurice's lifetime blurred the distinction between the two dignities and caused the stadholderate itself to be seen as hereditary in the Nassau line.[7] The joint effort of the States of Holland and Maurice to apply the hereditary sovereign charisma of the 'prince of Orange' to the provincial *condotierre*, was therefore the first step towards the institution of the hereditary stadholderate in the Republic. This 'more or less' hereditary status was voiced eloquently by the States of Friesland,

---

6 Geert H. Janssen, "Dynastieke transfer in de Republiek. De politieke en religieuze betekenis van de stadhouderlijke begrafenisstoet", *BMGN – Low Countries Historical Review* 122 (2007).

7 The distinction between the princes of Orange and the stadholders of the Dutch Republic is often blurred in scholarship. See for instance Herbert H. Rowen, *The Princes of Orange. The stadholders in the Dutch Republic* (Cambridge: Cambridge University Press, 1988).

Zeeland and Groningen in 1654, when the States of Holland – not so keen anymore to accept the hereditary status of the Nassaus – barred the four-year-old William III from ever holding public office in their province. The three dissenting states objected to this, referring to the 'prerogatives somewhat innate' of the young prince.[8]

This chapter will concern itself with the repercussions of adding new connotations to existing titles and the role dynastic history-writing played in this process. Such a change of meaning changed the position of its bearer. In a broader context, the development of the meaning of 'prince of Orange' shows us that titles were more than legal claims to territories, revenues and social prestige. They could be given meaning far beyond the actual power of his holder. A clear example is the title 'Duke of Burgundy', held by the Habsburgs, that constituted a link with a glorious past, rather than any serious claim to the French duchy – evoking the splendour of the 'Burgundian' court that had been Netherlandish rather than French anyway. But titles such as 'King of Jerusalem' were also clearly meaningful to the princes that claimed them – the Angevins, Habsburgs, Savoys – although none of them entertained real hopes of restoring the medieval kingdom.

To illustrate my point I will first sketch the positions of both Philip William and Maurice after the death of their father in 1584; then I will focus on their representation in contemporary or near-contemporary genealogical texts; and, to highlight the particular nature of their representation in the Republic and the contrast between the 'real' and 'new' prince of Orange, I will consider their representation in Orange at the same time – both on coins struck in their name in Orange and in an Orangeois dynastic history. Comparing their representation in two different contexts will shed light on the shifting meaning of the concept of the prince of Orange and how this affected both brothers – and, at the same time, the development of both Nassau dynastic awareness and Dutch national identity. In a broader context, my aim is to shed light on the way a title could define a dynasty, not simply by connecting it to a certain territory, but also to a set of expectations and aspirations. As I shall argue, a title could give a person prestige, revenue and territorial authority – but also a task.

The Nassaus after the Death of William the Silent: A House in Disarray

The fact that Maurice and the States General could mould the Orange legacy to their own liking was mostly due to the desperate mess William of Orange left behind at his death in 1584. His estates located in Habsburg lands had been confiscated in 1567, when he had been convicted by the Council of Trouble as a rebel against Habsburg authority; he could only dispose of his estates when these lay in territories under the rule of the rebel States-General. He had incurred huge debts in order to

[8] Serge ter Braake, *Manifest van de ware vrijheid. De Deductie van Johan de Witt uit 1654* (Arnhem: Sonsbeek Publishers, 2009), 59: ' … dat den jongen heere Prince van Oraigne ende desselfs descendenten daer door souden werden ontset vande praerogativen hen eenichtszins aangeboren'.

finance his war efforts against the king of Spain, but also his princely lifestyle, which meant the heirs could not accept the inheritance until most of the debts had been settled. The greatest creditor was William's brother John VI of Nassau.[9]

This situation made it hard to settle the estate, but it was made even more difficult by the conflicting claims of the heirs. William of Orange left behind twelve children from four different marriages. All William's marriages had been accompanied by contracts stipulating the portions for children born to the marriage and for the widow. William had three sons from three different marriages whose rights of inheritance were partly codified in the marriage contracts of their mothers, of whom only one outlived her husband to become a widow; his daughters from his third marriage were woefully under-represented and were very shabbily provided for. Still, the inheritance would be overburdened if all heirs would get what they were entitled to. The only way to allow for a definite division of the assets would be for the children to waive some of their rights, but none were prepared to do so.[10] William of Orange's involvement in the Dutch Revolt had also caused his eldest son and principal heir to be abducted to Spain, therefore he was not on the scene to negotiate with his co-heirs personally. William had envisioned a division of his estate right before his death, but this was a draft of a final testament, not a legal document itself. Therefore, the executors of the estate could only call upon the heirs not to pursue all their legal claims, but none of them paid any attention to this.

This unwillingness to compromise was a consequence of the strange positions of the two eldest sons. Philip William, the firstborn, was the principal heir, but he had been taken to Spain in 1567, when he was a boy of 13. He was the principal heir not only of the French estates (the succession to which was regulated by Salic law), but also of the Nassau holdings in Brabant, especially the barony of Breda, because Brabantine inheritance law favoured the children of the first marriage over any other children. When William had married for the second time in 1561, his prospective in-laws were well-aware of this Brabantine bias and insisted that William provide well for the children of this second marriage, including giving any son thereof (this turned out to be Maurice) the title of marquis. These requirements were hard to meet after William's death. However, the absence of Philip William meant that Maurice was in a good position to arrange a favourable inheritance for himself at his elder brother's expense. Maria, Philip William's full sister, fought Maurice every step of the way in order to preserve her brother's position.[11]

---

9 The situation of the estate and the struggles among the heirs are most clearly and in great detail explained by Pieter Scherft, *Het sterfhuis van Willem van Oranje* (Leiden: Universitaire Pers, 1966).

10 Scherft, *Sterfhuis*, 33.

11 Petra Vanhoutte, "Filips Willem van Oranje-Nassau en zijn familiale belangen en contacten in Noord en Zuid (1554–1618)", in *Het verdeelde huis: de Nederlandse adel tussen opstand en reconciliatie*, (eds) Luc Duerloo and Liesbeth De Frenne (Maastricht: Shaker, 2011).

The overburdened estate and the intransigence of the heirs meant that the estate could not be settled in the short term. This had serious repercussions. For instance, the marriage of William's eldest daughter Maria was delayed precisely because no agreement could be reached on her claims to the inheritance and thus her dowry – not only by Maurice, but also by the prospective groom's family who were not prepared to let their brother enter into a marriage that did not guarantee him anything. Also, none of the heirs could claim their part of the inheritance without a general agreement. This meant that William's younger sons were unable to take any subsidiary title, although William's last unofficial testament had intended Maurice to become the marquis of Veere and Frederick Henry the lord of Geertruidenberg.[12] For the moment, they had to remain simply counts of Nassau, a title borne by all male family members. To address the immediate needs of the estate – the servicing of the many debts – it seemed inevitable to alienate some of the property, but this would compromise some of the rights of the heirs and was therefore also deemed undesirable. Partly because of the cost of aristocratic educations, a number of William's children were taken care of by family – some by the calvinist Nassaus, others by the catholic Bourbons.[13] It took 25 years to set the affairs of William of Orange in order and decide on an acceptable division of the assets among his children. Only in 1609 were the affairs finally settled. However, William left not only a material legacy, but also a political one.

Upgrading Maurice: Count, Marquis or Prince?

After William's death, the Nassau family lacked a clear leader. Philip William, William's eldest son, would have been a natural leader of the new generation but his prolonged stay in Spain meant he had become increasingly irrelevant. Once returned, he first set himself up as a loyal subject of the archdukes before retiring to Orange. Frederick Henry, an infant when his father died, did not become an active participant in the succession squabbles until he had reached adolescence himself. The middle brother Maurice was an adolescent at William's death. As the eldest son present in the Netherlands, he played a prominent role in his father's funeral. As the nearest relative he was the evident choice to serve as primary mourner. In an engraving of the funerary procession, he is pictured right behind his father's coffin, identified as 'Sr. le conte Maurice'; referring to his title of count of Nassau, used by all Nassau relatives. The prominent seventeenth-century Dutch historian P.C. Hooft described the scene and explained Maurice's titles:

---

12 Simon Groenveld, "De Oranjes als markiezen van Veere. Hun politieke invloed in Zeeland en de stad Veere, 1581–1702", in *Borsele Bourgondië Oranje. Heren en markiezen van Veere en Vlissingen 1400–1700*, (eds) Hans Blom et al. (Hilversum: Verloren, 2009), 109.

13 Susan Broomhall and Jacqueline Van Gent, "In the Name of the Father: Conceptualizing Pater Familias in the letters of William the Silent's Children", *Renaissance Quarterly* 62 (2009), 1150.

> Then Count Maurice of Nassau, because this is how he was called at that time, according to the custom of Germany, where even the Princes' and Counts' sons who have no share in the government,[14] are called by their father's titles: and according to the custom of France, where Orange lies, the title of Prince was reserved for his eldest brother Philip William.[15]

At William's funeral Maurice served as the principal mourner,[16] but not as his father's successor as prince of Orange – indeed, even his use of the title 'count of Nassau' needed to be justified.

Despite the disputes about the inheritance and the resulting poverty of the heirs, the post-1584 Nassaus had some claim to William's political legacy; his position as leader of the Revolt and stadholder (even though his standing had been at a low ebb when he died). In recognition of this, Maurice was invited to join the Council of State set up by the States General to govern the Netherlands after William's death.[17] However, not all the provinces of the Republic saw him as an immediate heir to his father's political offices. Only the States of Holland appointed him as stadholder in his father's place, whereas count Adolf of Neuenahr was appointed to William's stadholderates of Utrecht, Gelre and Overijssel.[18]

Even though the counts of Nassau were well respected, there were very many of them. Being a count of Nassau hardly set Maurice apart and certainly did not denote any sense of dynastic or political leadership. Therefore, when the States of Holland decided to appoint Maurice to his father's offices, they also made efforts to bolster his prestige. First of all, Maurice seemed to become heir to William's hope of actually becoming Count of Holland.[19] This title and office, which were held by the sovereign States of Holland after the deposition of Philip II, would have increased Maurice's reputation tremendously without hurting his elder brother. Nor

---

14 Maurice's uncle John of Nassau actually ruled in Nassau-Dillenburg. In fact, William of Orange had tried to acquire another county in Germany earlier, because he had no say in Dillenburg. Liesbeth Geevers, "Family matters. William of Orange and the Habsburgs after the abdication of Charles V (1555)", *Renaissance Quarterly* 63 (2010), 469, n52.

15 P.C. Hooft, *Nederlandse Historiën*, in *Pieter Corneliszoon Hooft, Alle de gedrukte werken, 1611–1738*, (eds) W. Hellinga and P. Tuynman (Amsterdam: Amsterdam University Press, 1972), 906, 'voorts Graaf Maurits van Nassauw (want zoo hiette men hem op dat pas, naar de wyze van Hooghduytslandt, daar zelfs der Vorsten en Graaven zoonen, die geen deel aan de regeeringe komt, 's vaaders tytels voeren: en behield, volghends de gewoonte van Vrankryk, waarin Oranje leyt, den naam van Prins alleenlyk voor zynen oudsten broeder Philips Willem)'.

16 Janssen, "Dynastieke transfer in the Republiek", 8.

17 Rowen, *Princes of Orange*, 32.

18 Rowen, *Princes of Orange*, 34.

19 The States of Holland first offered the title to William in 1582, but the practicalities remained to be negotiated at his death. Olaf Mörke, *Wilhelm von Oranien (1533–1584). Fürst und 'Vater' der Republik* (Stuttgart: Kohlhammer, 2007), 244–5.

was it an unthinkable development, because William's elevation to this dignity had been all but finalised right before his death. However, the negotiations regarding the conditions had been tough and in the end not very favourable to William; the new count's power would have been heavily circumscribed so that William eventually actually wielded more power as a mere stadholder than as a count.

Despite William's appointment eventually falling through, the Holland pensionary Paulus Buys and Rotterdam pensionary Johan van Oldebarneveldt advocated Maurice's appointment as the new count. Maurice's installation as count was also pushed by the French faction in the Netherlands and among the heirs – most notably William's widow Louise de Coligny. In their view, Maurice should be invested as count by King Henry III of France, when the king had accepted full sovereignty of the Netherlands.[20] Both groups failed to secure the comital title for Maurice. Buys and Oldebarneveldt failed to persuade the States to grant the title, while Henry III refused to take the sovereignty of the rebellious Netherlands.[21] Maurice himself might have wanted the title of count of Holland, but also knew the States of Holland were not willing to allow him to become count, so he decided not to pursue the issue.[22] Yet, still in 1597 some of Maurice's confidants tried again to create a favourable atmosphere for Maurice's elevation to count,[23] and Maurice himself made another attempt in 1602.[24] However, all of his efforts were fruitless.

In the meantime, Maurice became marquis of Veere in 1588, although he had been using this title since 1585. Although none of the inheritance was officially settled until 1609 and Maurice could not legally take possession of the marquisate until then, he managed to convince the magistrates of the town of Veere to invest him anyway. Maurice argued that he was the rightful marquis because of his parents' marriage contract, which had stipulated that any son born of the union should become a marquis.[25] Even though Maurice would make quite a lot of use of this title,[26] it was not enough for the States of Holland, who decided to call him 'natural prince of Orange'.[27]

The decision to start using the princely title to indicate Maurice was brought on by the arrival of the Earl of Leicester in the Netherlands. Leicester had been sent

---

20 Scherft, *Sterfhuis*, 47–8; Liesbeth Geevers, "The king strikes back: the Spanish campaign to undermine the Dutch diplomatic position, 1581–1609", in *The act of Abjuration: inspired and inspirational*, (ed.) R. Kubben (Nijmegen: Wolf Legal Publishers, 2011).

21 Scherft, *Sterfhuis*, 47.

22 Scherft, *Sterfhuis*, 50.

23 Scherft, *Sterfhuis*, 214–15.

24 Scherft, *Sterfhuis*, 231–4; Rowen, *Princes of Orange*, 41–2.

25 Groenveld, "De Oranjes als markiezen", 111.

26 For instance on commemorative coins struck in 1589, 1599, 1601 and 1602. Zandvliet, *Maurits prins van Oranje*, 191–2, 219.

27 Scherft, *Sterfhuis*,p. 67. The phrase in Dutch was 'geboren prince', and in Latin 'princeps natus'. I would like to thank Jonathan Spangler for his help with translating this term to English.

to the Netherlands as a Governor-General by Elizabeth of England. The States of Holland felt they had to promote Maurice at this time to be a counterweight to the English Earl. They appointed Maurice as their stadholder, to make sure that Leicester would not appoint an Englishman; and they started to address him as 'natural prince of Orange' so that he would be an 'excellency' just like Leicester.[28] Perhaps they also wished to elevate Maurice above the other stadholders of the Republic. In any case, it is interesting to note that the title of stadholder alone apparently did not carry enough authority for the States' purpose – otherwise they would not have felt it necessary to evoke the Orange title. Using the title was a crass usurpation of course, as his brother Philip William was the only one who had the right to bear it. In reaction, Maurice's eldest sister Maria took the title 'natural princess of Orange' and had herself accepted and feted in St. Maartensdijk – part of the Buren patrimony – to secure this part of the inheritance.[29]

But Maria was not the only one to be annoyed at Maurice's new title. The Earl of Leicester considered it a slight of his own authority and demanded an explanation.[30] The historian Hooft, who was well-informed about the Dutch government, provides a clue as to how the States of Holland justified this usurpation of their English governor-general. They explained to Leicester that Maurice had a right to the princely title 'according to the German custom' and because William of Orange had granted Maurice the administration of Orange during Philip William's captivity.[31] So, according to Hooft, in 1584 German naming practices were strictly limited to the German titles of the family which made Maurice a count of Nassau, but when necessity arose, the States of Holland were justified to apply German custom to the French title of Orange – which made him a prince of Orange of sorts. This inventive shuffling of national noble customs facilitated the usurpation of the princely title by Maurice; and clearly shows the States' support of this usurpation.

Philip William and Maurice in Genealogies and Histories

How were the respective positions of the two princes of Orange reflected in the Nassau family histories? I have noted before that we do not dispose of many Nassau

28 Zandvliet, *Maurits prins van Oranje*, 18–19; Scherft, *Sterfhuis*, 67.

29 Scherft, *Sterfhuis*, 64.

30 Scherft, *Sterfhuis*, 79 argues that this conflict only erupted after Leicester had already left the Netherlands in 1587 and therefore served to sour the relationship between Holland and Elizabeth, rather than between Holland and Leicester.

31 Hooft, *Nederlandse Historiën,* 1041: 'Deezes bedryfs, als 't Leicester ter ooren quam, belghd' hy zich grootelyx, duidende t'zyner verkleeninge, dat Graave Maurits de naam van Prinse werd toegeschreeven: waarmeê men dien scheen booven hem te verheffen; … Doch, op vertoogh, dat … Prinse Maurits die tytel, naar de Duitsche wyze, toequam; te meer, dewyl zyn Heer vaader hem, by uiterste wille, de regeering van 't Prinsdoom Oranje, geduurende de gevankenis van Prinse Philips Willem, bevoolen had; liet Leicester zich needer zetten'.

genealogies in the sixteenth and early seventeenth centuries.[32] Still, genealogies are a wonderful source for dynastic identity, because it allows us to reconstruct the dynastic narrative. In constructing such a narrative, choices were made: which ancestors were deemed especially important for the family? What sort of biographical information on them was included? In short, the dynastic past could be manipulated to suit the needs of the living. Genealogies therefore tell us something about how a dynasty viewed itself or came to be viewed by its contemporaries. The same is true about the Nassaus and in the wake of William of Orange's death, genealogical texts suggest to us how his legacy was shaped and interpreted by future historians and genealogies; and how different members of the family measured up to the founder. As the following section will show, two very different dynastic narratives were developed during the seventeenth century.

In the seventeenth-century genealogies, Maurice and Philip William obviously figure rather prominently. Here, I will discuss three texts: Jan Orlers's *Geslacht-boom* of 1616 (French edition in 1615);[33] Joseph de la Pise's *Tableau d'Histoire des princes et principauté d'Orange* of 1640;[34] and Mattheus Smallegange's *Geslacht-rekening der doorluchtigste vorsten van Nassau en Oraenjen*, of 1675. Jan Orlers (Leiden, 1570–1646) was a nephew of the famous Dutch humanist Jan van Hout, who was involved with the foundation of the university of Leiden. He had been a bookseller and also served as a town councillor and burgomaster. Apart from his panegyric work on Maurice of Nassau, he wrote a description of Leiden.[35] Joseph de la Pise (1589–1648) was a notary, secretary to the stadholder in Orange and clerk of the parliament of Orange, offices his father had also held. He went to the Republic because of factional pressures. In the Republic he finished his work on the *Tableau*, based on his father's notes and papers, which was generously funded by Frederick Henry.[36] Mattheus Smallegange (Goes, 1624–1710) was a lawyer and most famous for his *New chronicle of Zealand*. He was a full member of the Reformed Church and a supporter of the prince of Orange during the stadholderless era (1650–1672). He had been exiled from Amsterdam for a year in 1666 for providing the text to a pro-William III print. He never held an official post.[37]

Both Orlers and Smallegange wrote Nassau-centred genealogies, which means they focused on the Nassau family rather than on the principality of Orange, which had been held by other dynasties. Both devote a considerable space to the

32 Liesbeth Geevers, "Being Nassau. Nassau family histories and Dutch national discourse from 1541 to 1616", *Dutch Crossing* 35 (2011).

33 Jan Orlers, *Geslacht-boom der Graven van Nassav* (Leiden, 1616)

34 Joseph de la Pise, *Tableau d'Histoire des princes et principauté d'Orange* (The Hague, 1640).

35 G.J. van Bork and P.J. Verkruijsse (eds), *De Nederlandse en Vlaamse auteurs van middeleeuwen tot heden met inbegrip van de Friese auteurs* (Weesp: De Haan, 1985), 426.

36 Marika Keblusek, *Boeken in de hofstad: Haagse boekcultuur in de Gouden Eeuw* (Hilversum: Verloren, 1997), 186–9.

37 Van Bork and Verkruijsse, *De Nederlandse en Vlaamse auteurs,* 531–2.

different Nassau branches; apart from the Nassaus of Breda/Orange, the Nassaus of Dillenburg, Beilstein, Idstein, Weilburg and mythical Guelders and Zutphen were discussed. Both devote special attention to the dynasty's star ancestor Adolf (ca. 1255–1298), who had been elected King of the Romans. The most striking characteristic of their genealogies is their emphasis on Nassau ancestors that had special merit for the Dutch Revolt. The biographical entries for most ancestors typically contain only details on birth, marriage, children etc. When the entries are more elaborate, only things that have to do with the Revolt are included. This obviously also means that the biographical entries only really become elaborate from the sixteenth century onward.

Through these little biographies, the authors can be very clear as to who matters in Nassau dynastic history – who are the 'real' or at least the 'relevant' Nassaus. They are quite explicit about this. For instance, Orlers included engravings in his work, but only for 'the most important Nassau heroes, who by their incomparable bravery, have helped to gain and guard the state of these countries', as he stated in his subtitle. The only one favoured with an engraving who falls outside this category is King Adolf. Smallegange similarly stated that 'we have mainly spoken of the glorious deeds of those who, by their unspeakable valor, bravery and wise policy … have defended, continued, confirmed, elevated and guarded the freedom of our Netherland'.[38] A nice example of how this worked can be found in Orlers's discussion of Maurice's first cousins, the sons of his uncle John VI of Nassau. Many of them had been active in the Dutch war effort, but some more than others. William Louis, John's eldest son, is famously credited with the military reforms alongside his cousin Maurice. He was granted an engraving. So was John's third son, Philip. Orlers spent over a full page discussing the exploits of both brothers. But the second son George was treated with only five lines and no engraving, despite the fact he had been active for a few years in the Dutch war, served as a regent for his elder brother in ancestral Nassau-Dillenburg and even succeeded him in the government of Nassau-Dillenburg.[39] But clearly, this did not entitle him to an engraving or even an enumeration of his deeds; Orlers only mentions the name of his wife and four sons.[40] The message is clear: William Louis and Philip matter; George does not.

---

38 Smallegange, *Geslacht-rekening*, 'voorrede', unfoliated.

39 Ernst Joachim, "Georg", in *Allgemeine Deutsche Biographie* (1878), 682. Available at: http://www.deutsche-biographie.de/pnd104279648.html?anchor=adb [accessed 19 September 2012]. A contemporary German genealogy devoted considerably more attention to George: Johannes Textor, *Nassawische Chronik* (Herborn, 1617), 168–169.

40 Orlers, *Geslacht-boom*, 44.

114 Afkomste ende Daden

van desen Doorluchtighen Nassauschen Helt al hier tot zijner eeren hebben willen verhaelen ende ghedencken. wy sullen voortgaen ende komen totte beschrijvinghe van zijne:

Kinderen van het Eerstebedde

PHILIPS *Byder Gratie Godts Prince van Orangnen, Grave van Nassau Catsenelleboge, Dietz, Vyanden, Buyren, Leerdam &c. Baron van Breda &c. Ridder van den Gulden Vliese:*

Is gheboren anno 1554.

Outsten Soone vandē Prince van Orangnen voornoemt: Is inden jaere 1554 opten 19 December des avonts gheboren. Van zijn Heer Vader tot Leuven ter scholen ghesonden wesende / omme aldaer soo wel inde Talen als ander Consten ē wetenschappen / onder wesen te werdē: so is hy uyt de selve Schoole ofte Academie

Figure 9.1 Philip (William), by the Grace of God, Prince of Orange. Engraving appearing in Jan Orlers, *Geslacht-boom der Graven van Nassaw* (Leiden, 1615), 114. Orlers gives full honours to Philip William, but would also refer to Philip William's two younger brothers as princes of Orange. Leiden University Library, Special Collections, 1158 B 11.

118 Afkomste ende Daden

MAVRITIVS AVR. PRINC. COM. NASS. etc. MARC. VERÆ etc. CONF. BEL. P. GVB

MAVRITZ, *Prince van Orangnen, Grave van Nassau, Catzenel-lebogen, Vyanden, Dietz, Meurs &c. Marquis vander Veer ende Vlissinghen, Heer van Polanen, Leck, Grave, Cuyck, St. vyt, Daesburch &c: Gouverneur ende Capiteyn Generael van Gelderlandt, Hollandt, Seelant, VVest-vrieslant, Sutphen, Vtricht ende Overyssel, &c. Admirael Generael vander See, Ridder vande Order vanden Jarretiere.*

Mauritz vā Nassau Soon van Anna van Saxen.

TWeeden Sone van Wilhelm Prince van Orangnen &c. Die hy gewonnē heeft met Anna Dochter van Keurvorst Hartoch Mauritz van Saxen, (die hy geteelt hadde met Agnesa dochter van Philips Lant-grave van Hessen) is gheboren op het Huys te Dillenburch, opten 13 November des jaers 1567.* zijn Grootva-der

* Saxoniæ Illustrata.

Figure 9.2 Although Maurice was not yet prince of Orange at the time of publication of Orlers's work, the caption underneath the engraving nevertheless identifies him as 'Prince of Orange', albeit without the addition of 'By the Grace of God'. Jan Orlers, *Geslacht-boom der Graven van Nassaw* (Leiden, 1615), 118. Leiden University Library, Special Collections, 1158 B 11.

Maurice clearly fits in the heroic category. Elsewhere I have argued that Maurice was the undisputed star of Jan Orlers's work.[41] Orlers devoted by far the most pages to him and especially to his recent membership of the English Order of the Garter. This membership elevated the entire Nassau dynasty to the ranks of royal dynasties in Europe – or rather, it confirmed that the Nassaus had ranked among them all along. Smallegange likewise described Maurice's stellar career after his father's death and gives a comprehensive list of all his victories in battle and an account of how Maurice 'secured the freedom of the state that his father had founded'.[42] Smallegange also offers lengthy entries on Frederick Henry, William II and William III.

How does Philip William fare in these genealogical works? Seventeenth-century German-minded authors, such as Jan Orlers or Mattheus Smallegange, had little to say about Philip William. He obviously does not fit the heroic profile of his Nassau relatives, but as a prince of Orange by the grace of God, he could not be entirely ignored either. His role in the family was narrowed to two aspects: the general honours bestowed on him by the kings of Spain, which reflected on the entire dynasty (the Order of the Fleece, for instance) and his role in the Dutch Revolt. This role was of course rather passive, consisting only of his abduction to Spain in 1567 when he was only 13 and his lengthy captivity until his return to the Netherlands in 1596. His biographical details (birth, titles, marriage) are also mentioned, but apart from this, he warrants little attention.[43] Both refer to him simply as Philip, omitting his father's name. Orlers, who wrote his work when Philip William was still alive, presents him as 'Philip, by the grace of God prince of Orange',[44] and refers a few pages later to Maurice as 'prince of Orange' and to their youngest brother Frederick Henry as 'natural prince of Orange'.[45] As we noticed before, Smallegange's entry on Philip William actually stops mid-sentence; in itself perhaps an indication of Philip William's lack of prestige among Nassau genealogists. It was clear to contemporary historians, and to modern ones as well, that Philip William had a limited role to play in the Dutch Revolt, that he remained a Catholic and sided with the Spanish king, so although he held an honourable position as prince of Orange, he did not really count as a Nassau.[46]

In a sense it is not surprising that Philip William should have been slightly neglected by the Nassau genealogists. But when we consult Joseph de la Pise's book on the princes of Orange, *Tableau d'Histoire des princes et principauté d'Orange*, we get quite another picture. Although this prestigious work was financed by and dedicated to Frederick Henry, it was Philip William who had ordered Joseph de la Pise to write an Orange-centred genealogy of the Nassaus. He ordered him to

41 Geevers, "Being Nassau", 16.

42 Smallegange, *Geslacht-rekening*, 57–9.

43 Orlers, *Geslacht-boom*, 114–16; Smallegange, *Geslacht-rekening*, 55–6.

44 Orlers, *Geslacht-boom*, 114.

45 Orlers, *Geslacht-boom*, 118, 137.

46 This limited perspective on Philip William is also reflected in Hermans, *Filips Willem van Oranje*.

use the documents his father Jacques had already collected to write a history of Orange in 1615.[47] This is actually the same year in which the French version of Jan Orlers's work was published (*La genealogie des illustres comtes de Nassav*, Leiden 1615), a work that presented Maurice as the top Nassau of the era.[48] Jacques de la Pise had already worked on his Orange history before 1615, so Philip William did not inspire the creation of this work, but his decision to order Joseph to finish Jacques's work in 1615 is quite coincidental. Were the Nassau brothers involved in PR warfare? In any case, De la Pise's work is in many senses nothing like Orlers's and Smallegange's genealogies. His point of departure is the principality of Orange, not the Nassau family and this different perspective leads to a very different image of Philip William and his brothers.

Whereas both Orlers and Smallegange explicitly focused on the heroic Nassaus, De la Pise stated that he wanted to give an overview of the lives and deaths of *all* princes of Orange, in order to show Frederick Henry the 'birth and origins of your sovereign state'.[49] His emphasis was on affairs of war and peace, much like Orlers and Smallegange. Although from the Chalon princes onward the relationship with the king of France and duke of Burgundy became a recurring theme, the genealogy of the princes of Orange was not connected to one overarching theme or struggle, except perhaps the fate of the principality itself. This fate had been unkind at times: 'Depuis ceste terrible & malheureuse descente des Gots en Italie, qui causa la ruine & l'abbatis de nos superbes murs anciennes, nous n'avons rencontré que malheurs, esclandres, ruines sur iceluy & toute apparence de perte inevitable'.[50]

When viewing the Nassaus from an Orangeois perspective, Philip William suddenly became a prince of relevance. Already when relating the history of Jean de Chalon (?–1418), first Prince of that House, De la Pise ruefully noted how he spent little time in Orange.[51] Jean's successors would not spend much time there either; the biographical entry on Philibert de Chalon (1502–1530) almost only describes his martial feats in the service of Charles V.[52] De la Pise devoted considerable attention to Philip William, because he was the only Nassau prince of Orange to actually reside in and rule over his principality. He was not blind to Philip William's lack of stature as compared with his father and brothers, but if William the Silent was a *pater patriae* in the Republic, his son was a 'Restaurateur de son Estat, et … Pere de son peuple'

47 Alice Colby-Hall, "Guillaume au Court Nez et les premiers historiens d'Orange", in *Studies in Honor of Hans-Erich Keller. Medieval French and Occitan literature and Romance linguistics*, (ed.) Rupert T. Pickens (Kalamazoo: Medieval Institute Publication, 1993), 157.

48 Geevers, "Being Nassau", 16.

49 De la Pise, *Tableau*, dedication, unfoliated.

50 De la Pise, *Tableau*, 205.

51 De la Pise, *Tableau*, 110.

52 De la Pise, *Tableau*, 152–99.

in Orange.[53] From the perspective of Orange, it had been indeed Philip William who had managed to end a long period during which the self-appointed governor Blacons had held power in Orange, in spite of the efforts of the 'Regent' Maurice or Philip William to oust him. In fact, for years 'governor' Blacons controlled the castle and town of Orange, while Philip William only held sway in the rest of the principality. Only in 1606, when the prince married the French king's cousin Eleanor de Bourbon and thus won Henry IV's support to regain his principality, could he return in triumph to Orange.[54] The struggle to regain control of the town and castle of Orange takes up 40 pages (554–594) of a total of 61 (553–604) of Philip William's biographical entry. Clearly, seen through Orangeois eyes, this was Philip William's crowning achievement and one for which the principality – and future princes – deserved to remember him. Also, it made Philip William an immensely politically relevant character in the history of Orange, since he had restored order after centuries of 'malheurs, esclandres, ruines … & toute apparence de perte inevitable'.

De la Pise's Orangeois take on Philip William is a reminder that Orlers's and Smallegange's interpretation of what mattered in Nassau history was not accepted by all and separates the Nassau princes of Orange from their French principality. It also serves to highlight the narrowness of their Dutch representation of Nassau dynastic history – which hardly did justice to the dynasty's international scope (also noticeable in the treatment of cousin George). They chose to associate the princes of Orange solely with the Dutch Republic and to describe only those aspects of their lives that were relevant to the Revolt – and later the maintenance of the Dutch state. Through this exclusive focus on a Dutch political context, Philip William's relevance was diminished, while Maurice and Frederick Henry became the ultimate Nassau heroes. In fact, their works constructed a definition of what it meant to be a relevant Nassau and a prince of Orange *alongside* Philip William's tenure of the sovereign dignity in Orange. When Orlers wrote his work, all three brothers were still alive. He chose to pass over the principality of Orange almost entirely and thereby to erase Philip William from the ranks of relevant Nassaus; instead he presented Maurice as the pinnacle of Nassau success because of his leadership of the Dutch Revolt, while even styling him 'prince of Orange' – a prince who was not in any way connected to his French principality. This way, he constructed the new 'Dutch' prince of Orange.

---

53 De la Pise, *Tableau*, 554. 'Et bien que sa vie ne comprene rien qui puisse aller du pair avec celles de son Pere & de ses freres des plus grands hommes de leur âages, il a eu plus faute d'occassion, que de volonté … ; rien n'a paru en luy d'indigne de la grandeur de sa maison; de coeur bon, genereux & magnanime dans tous les rencontres de la fortune. Mais sa pieté envers Dieu, sa patience en l'adversité, sa clemence a pardonner, sa liberalité à donner & à recognoistre ses serviteurs, sont les quatres vertus par lesquelles la memoire de sa vie triomphera à jamais de l'oubliance. Les soings, les peines, la despence qu'il a contribuée pour conserver dans sa famille l'Estat Soeverain de ses ancestres, en extirper la tyrannie, y establir l'ordre & par tout faire relluire la legitime authorité sans effusion de sang, luy ont justement acquis le tiltre de Restaurateur de son Estat, de Pere de son peuple'.

54 De la Pise, *Tableau*, 554–94. Van der Eycken, *Oranje-Nassau*, 44; Thera Coppens, *Buren, Egmond en Oranje* (Buren: Stichting Oud Buren, 1989), 131.

der Graven van Nassauw. 137

Des Princen Soone by zijn vierde Huysvrou geteelt zijnde is.

FR. HENRICK, *Gheboren Prince van Orangnen, Grave van Nassau, Catzenellebogen, Dietz ende Vyanden, &c. Heer van St. Geertruydenberghe, vande Hooghe ende Laghe Swaluwe, Naeldwijck, Honsholredijck, &c. Generael vande Cavallerie der vereenichde Provintien &c.*

IOngsten/eñ eenige Soone vandē Prince van Orangnen Ho. Mo. de welcke hy by zijne Vierde Huysvrouwe Loyse de Collignij, Dochter van Gasper van Collignij, geteelt ende gewonnen heeft. is binnen de Stadt Delff ghebozen opten lesten Februarij des S jaers

Frederick Henrick tot Delff gheboren anno 1584.

Figure 9.3 Orlers gave the youngest brother, Fredrick Henry, the title that the States of Holland had given to Maurice in 1585, 'natural prince of Orange' (gheboren prince van Orangnen). This title never caught on for Maurice, but appears to serve here as a courtesy title for the heir to the principality. Jan Orlers, Geslacht-boom der Graven van Nassaw (Leiden, 1615), 137. Leiden University Library, Special Collections, 1158 B 11.

The distinction between the Dutch and Orangeois princes of Orange becomes even more clear when we take a look at how they were enumerated. Mattheus Smallegange was the first of the authors under discussion who referred to William the Silent as 'William I of Orange'. It seems completely obvious to us now to refer to William of Orange in this way and apart from referring to 'prince of Orange', the title of stadholder is sometimes mentioned. But when we take a closer look at this nomenclature, it becomes apparent that it is not quite as obvious as it seems, because William I of Orange was *not* William I of Orange, and neither was he the first William to hold the stadholderate of Holland.

The enumeration of the Williams of Orange was a matter of confusion even to contemporaries. The counting of the princes of Orange is complicated by the fact that the early princes allowed all their sons to inherit the title and that some new dynasties to hold the title, started again at 'I'. Between the late eighth century and the seventeenth century, four dynasties held the title. The first is referred to as the House of Orange, followed by the Houses of Baux, Chalon and finally the Nassaus. Among these princes we find four Williams among the first house of Orange,[55] three Baux Williams (counted as I, II and III)[56] and one Chalon William (counted as VIII)[57] with any certainty. Since the Nassaus also represented a new dynasty, they might have been justified in returning to I, as the Baux Williams did. However, this does not seem to have been the case, since De la Pise counted 'our' William as William IX, while William the Silent himself had coins struck in his name bearing the inscription Guilielmus 3 or III.[58] I cannot figure out what sequence of Williams he follows here, but one thing is for certain: William the Silent was not the first prince of Orange bearing that name, instead he somehow *considered himself* to be the third. William the Silent clearly was not prince William I of Orange, but he became William I in later historiography. This was only possible after the title prince of Orange had come to mean something quite different from 'the sovereign ruler of the principality of Orange', of whom many had been called William before, but rather the symbolic leader of the Dutch Revolt. This indicates, in my opinion, that the princely title of Orange meant something quite different in the context of the Dutch Revolt than in Orange. 'The prince of Orange' was a symbolic title worn by the leader of the Dutch Revolt, constructed by Maurice, the States of Holland and publicists like Jan Orlers and Mattheus Smallegange.

---

55 De la Pise, *Tableau*, 47.

56 Wilhelm Karl von Isenburg and Frank Freytag von Loringhoven, *Europäischen Stammtafeln. Stammtafeln zur Geschichte der europäischen Staaten* (5 vols, Marburg: Stargardt,1956–1978), vol. 3, table 751–2.

57 *Europäischen Stammtafeln*, vol. 3, table 61.

58 J.R. Voûte and H.J. van der Wiel, *Les monnaies de la principauté d'Orange sous la maison de Nassau* (Bussum : Schulman, 1997), 41–2. Voûte and Van der Wiel implicitly count William as William VIII, since his grandson William II is counted as William IX.

Conclusion

In 1988 the American historian Herbert R. Rowen wrote a work titled: *The Princes of Orange. The stadholders in the Dutch Republic* (Cambridge 1988). In it, he presented sketches of the careers of those Nassaus that had also featured prominently in the works by Orlers and Smallegange. This near-equation of the two distinct dignities of prince of Orange and Stadholder in modern historiography testifies to the success of Maurice's and the States of Holland's efforts. But Maurice and the States were more concerned with the short term. They connected the count of Nassau to the Netherlands as the leader of the Dutch Revolt, providing him with the necessary prestige without giving him any real power. It was necessary to do so, because no other title fit the bill. Some alternatives had been considered. Maurice tried to upgrade his title early on by calling himself Marquis of Veere and Vlissingen, but due to the difficulties of his father's estate he had no right to take possession of these marquisates. Becoming count of Holland would certainly have given Maurice great prestige, but support for Maurice's elevation was never so broad as to make it at all possible, and the conditions were so stringent as to make it almost undesirable. The difficulty with these titles was, in a way, that they represented a political or legal reality and were therefore far more difficult to mould according to Maurice's and the States General's wishes. The use of 'prince of Orange' – more or less justified by using German noble naming practices and by the qualification 'natural' – was easier because this need not denote any actual power in Orange itself. In fact, this new prince of Orange did not exist in Orange at all.

The new meaning of the 'prince of Orange' was employed by those who wished to tie the Nassaus – all Dutch and German branches of them – closely to the Dutch Republic. This strengthened connection also helped the Nassaus to retain their dominance in the Republic. The victim was Philip William, who was relegated to polite mentions of this illustrious birth, heinous abduction, glorious acceptance of the Order of the Golden Fleece and little else. His position as a sovereign prince of Orange in the French sphere of influence – highlighted by his Bourbon marriage – was deemed irrelevant for dynastic history. In fact, Smallegange even ends his biographical sketch mid-sentence. In De la Pise's narrative, on the other hand, Philip William played a pivotal role as restorer of order in the principality – a sort of *pater patriae* in his own right.

Without the support of the state, Maurice could not have made his grab for the princely title stick. The intervention of the States-General on Maurice's side in this conflict seems to indicate that the sovereign high and mighty lords had chosen Maurice as their *condottiere*, and possibly their ruler. At the time of the usurpation of the title, no-one could have known Philip William would die childless. It is truly an intriguing question, what would have happened to 'the prince of Orange' if his marriage to Eleanor of Bourbon had borne fruit and the 'real' and 'symbolic' princes had existed next to each other for another generation. But Maurice became the legitimate prince of Orange at his brother's death in 1618 and the two versions of the prince of Orange became one: the hereditary sovereign ruler of a French principality who was the symbolic leader of the Dutch Revolt.

Conclusion

'The Line of Descent of Nobles is from the Blood of Kings': Reflections on Dynastic Identity

Hamish Scott

I

Two episodes together provide the starting point for these concluding remarks. The first concerns the duc de Saint-Simon, the celebrated chronicler of Louis XIV's fabled court at Versailles. Saint- Simon, as is well known, devoted his voluminous *Memoirs* to providing an enormously detailed account of the rivalries among the court aristocracy and the rise – and fall – of families in the entourage of the Sun King. But another aspect of the duc's life has not attracted the attention it merits: he also drew up detailed tables setting out which aristocratic lineages had in the past married a member of the French royal family. These lists survive primarily in manuscript.[1] Saint-Simon's obsessive interest in genealogy is well known, and this was a practical expression of it. He compiled these lists for one very simple reason: his conviction that such marriages added enormous and enduring lustre to the lineage in question, enhancing its prestige and boosting its status at court. Louis XIV certainly seems to have shown particular regard for these families in his treatment of them at Versailles. Between the eleventh and the sixteenth century such marriages had been concluded periodically in France.[2] After the accession of the Bourbons in 1589, however, they had all but ceased; those that did take place were mostly in unusual circumstances and attracted strong criticism at the time. The new ruling family was determined to emphasise the importance of royal blood in order to assert the dignity of the dynasty and to distance the Bourbons from even the greatest of their subjects. They therefore viewed such marriages as *mésalliances*, something which Saint-Simon clearly regretted.

---

[1] François Formel, *Alliances et Généalogie à la Cour du Grand Roi: Le souci généalogique chez Saint-Simon* (Paris: Éditions Contrepoint, 1983), 2: 1165–66, 1177–78; see also André Devyer, *Le Sang Épuré: Les préjugés de race chez les gentilshommes français de l'Ancien Régime (1560–1720)* (Brussels: Éditions de l'Université de Bruxelles, 1973), 325–52, on Saint-Simon and the 'royal blood'.

[2] Formel, *Alliances et Généalogie*, 2: 1167ff, and Arlette Jouanna, "Les Guises et le Sang de France", in *Le mécénat et l'influence des Guises*, (ed.) Yvonne Bellenger (Paris: Champion, 1997), 31, list such marriages.

The second episode is a central set piece in that great novel of aristocratic nostalgia, Marcel Proust's *À la recherche du temps perdu*.[3] In it the narrator, together with his school-friend Albert Bloch, now a rising playwright, attend an afternoon reception given by Madame de Villeparisis, a member of the aristocratic *beau-monde* of late-nineteenth-century Paris. There the two men encounter a historian, who is writing a book on the *Fronde* and is shown a celebrated portrait of the duchesse de Montmorency. The duchesse, after the execution of her husband following the great Montmorency rising in southern France in the early 1630s, had withdrawn to one of the exclusive religious houses for aristocratic women in the country's eastern regions, eventually becoming its abbess.[4] When Mme de Villeparisis is standing in front of the portrait, she notes complacently how extraordinary it is to think that the daughters of a king of France, whether Valois or Bourbon, would have been refused entry to this and similar establishments, so uncompromising were their rules governing admittance. When Bloch falls into the trap and expresses his puzzlement, she explains that this exclusion was because the ruling family lacked sufficient quarterings – that is to say, their pedigree had been compromised. This was due to their marriages into the Medici family, unions which true aristocrats – such as Mme de Villeparisis and the circles in which she moved – viewed as a *mésalliance*!

The perspective provided by these two episodes provides a very good starting point for an attempt to identify the wider themes which emerge from this volume. The point which Proust and, in a different way, Saint-Simon were making is central to all the chapters: the essential inter-connectedness of ruling and aristocratic families. Magnates inhabited the same social and political *milieu* as monarchs, to whom they were often related by ties of blood and marriage. France was unusual in the existence of the 'Princes of the Blood' (*princes du sang*) at the head of the secular aristocracy. There was no equivalent in England, with the extinction of the Tudors and the fact that James VI and I was an only son, while in Scotland a distant relationship with the Stuart monarchy did not give either the Hamiltons or the Lennoxes an exalted standing beyond their status as peers.[5] In many countries, however, the high nobility contained lineages which had begun as bastard or junior lines of a ruling dynasty. Illegitimate descent could, in certain circumstances, be circumvented and provide a route to inheritance. Theoretically, it precluded succession to titles and lands, unless removed by a subsequent act of legitimation or other legal arrangement. In practice, however, where an obvious heir or heiress was lacking, illegitimate descent would become part of the equation. In the case

3 Marcel Proust, *In Search of Lost Time: The Guermantes Way*, transl. Mark Treharne (London: Allen Lane, 2002), 195 and 185–291 *passim*; cf. William D. Godsey, Jr., *Nobles and Nation in Central Europe: Free Imperial Knights in the Age of Revolution 1750–1850* (Cambridge: Cambridge University Press, 2004), 48–9.

4 Michel Parisse and Pierre Heili (eds), *Les chapitres de dames nobles entre France et Empire* (Paris: Éditions Messene, 1998) is an informative introduction.

5 Above, Chapter 2.

of the Guise inheritance, links through bastard lines back to both the French king Henry IV (1589–1610) and to the main branch of the House of Lorraine were influential.[6]

Inter-marriage had been common in earlier times and still took place in many European countries.[7] Such links were to be found everywhere, to a greater or lesser extent. One foundation of the spectacular rise of the De la Gardie in mid-seventeenth century Sweden (above, chapter 5) was Magnus Gabriel's marriage to a cousin of Queen Christina (1632–54), whose favourite he was. This made him the brother-in-law of the next ruler, Charles X (1654–60).[8] Within a country such as Sweden, thinly populated and with an aristocracy still in the process of consolidation, the links between the ruling family and the most prominent lineages could be especially close, with the Brahe also being cousins of a sixteenth-century king, Erik XIV (1560–68), as a result of an earlier marriage between a head of the family and Gustav Vasa's sister. Indeed, the first Swedish king after the break-up of the late medieval Union of Kalmar, Gustav I Vasa (1523–60), had married as his second and third wives, prominent noblewomen.[9] Muscovy/Russia was another country where rulers intermarried with members of the social elite, though unions with leading boyar or princely families appear to have been deliberately shunned out of a fear of destabilising court politics.[10]

Where there was an established connection of this kind, it was normally incorporated into a family's coat of arms and so emphasised in the all-important visual dimension. One theme to emerge from the volume as a whole is the considerable and enduring role of heraldry in creating and highlighting identity. Marriage alliances could be celebrated, distinguished ancestry recalled and claims advertised by means of adjustments to coats of arms, which were a fluid medium. Jane Ohlmeyer's account of the remaking of Ireland's aristocracy during the tumultuous seventeenth century (Chapter 1) provides an excellent example of the importance of heraldry and, closely linked to it, genealogy within a society in which distinguished ancestry was increasingly important: whether it was genuine or, more often, problematical.[11]

---

6 Cf. above, Chapter 6; Jouanna, 'Les Guises et le sang de France'; cf. Jean-Paul Desprat, *Les bâtards d'Henri IV: L'épopée des Vendômes 1594–1727* (Paris: Perrin, 1994), a lively study of one notable group of a King's natural offspring.

7 Robert Oresko, "Bastards as Clients: The House of Savoy and its Illegitimate Children", in *Patronages et Clientélismes 1550–1700 (France, Angleterre, Espagne, Italie)*, (eds) Charles Giry-Deloison and Roger Mettam (Lille: Villeneuve d'Ascq, 1996), has some interesting reflections from a Savoyard perspective.

8 Göran Rystad, "Magnus Gabriel De la Gardie", in *Sweden's Age of Greatness 1632–1718*, (ed.) Michael Roberts (London: Macmillan, 1973), 204, 206.

9 Cf. above, Chapter 8.

10 Russell E. Martin, *A Bride for the Tsar: Bride-shows and Marriage Politics in Early Modern Russia* (DeKalb: Northern Illinois University Press, 2012).

11 See now Jane Ohlmeyer, *Making Ireland English: The Irish Aristocracy in the Seventeenth Century* (New Haven and London: Yale University Press, 2012), 73–5; cf.

Rulers and aristocrats viewed this world in similar ways, employed an identical vocabulary – that of House, lineage, and kin – and embraced the same priorities: those of conserving and, if possible, increasing their family status and building up the resources which sustained this position. Dynasticism, as Jeroen Duindam rightly notes, was an extension of the centrality of kinship to all political authority in the pre-modern world and to the importance of patriarchy and even matriarchy for this.[12] Magnates took their cue from the monarchs whom they served where succession and inheritance were concerned, often adopting primogeniture shortly after ruling dynasties had done so. Their families – exactly like those of Europe's rulers – were not compact groups of blood relatives but large and wide-ranging family complexes: as Jonathan Spangler rightly emphasises, 'A great aristocratic or princely *Maison* is an entire enterprise'.[13]

One common theme of the essays is just how wide these connections of blood and kinship – real and presumed – were in the estimation of contemporaries. Later notions of the nuclear family are of little use in understanding early modern aristocratic lineages, created and continually reinforced by marriages within a surprisingly narrow degree of kinship which could frequently exceed what was strictly permissible in canon law and were facilitated by dispensations from a complaisant Roman Catholic Church. These exemptions were often facilitated by ecclesiastical figures who were also cadets or relatives of the family in question, as younger sons followed ecclesiastical careers. The crucial importance of marriage in creating and cementing these wide family connections, and building new ones, is confirmed by many of the articles and is an established emphasis of scholarship on Europe's higher nobilities. These individual studies collectively provide further evidence for suggesting that, within the world of aristocratic and ruling lineages, 'family' could be a constructed identity, with a plasticine-like quality which made it capable of frequent refashioning. Mirella Marini's study (Chapter 5) of the various dynastic permutations supervised by Anne of Croÿ (1564–1635), duchess of Aarschot and princely countess of Arenberg during the final two decades of her life, provides an illuminating demonstration of how an aristocratic identity could be continually re-made in this way.

Within Europe's monarchies leading magnates regarded rulers as their near-equals in status. During the fourteenth and fifteenth centuries the gulf between the greatest lord and his royal master had still been relatively narrow and, though it subsequently widened as monarchy became a more exalted status during the early modern period, the sense of common values and membership of the same social and political community persisted, particularly in the perspective of a nobleman and his extended family. This was a long-established emphasis: as long ago as the

below, Section IV.

12 Above, Chapter 3. Professor Duindam has now renewed the study of dynastic power with his *Dynasties* (Cambridge: Cambridge University Press, 2015), which I was fortunate to read in typescript.

13 Above, Chapter 6.

early-eleventh century, Adalbero, the bishop of Laon, had proclaimed in a famous sentence that 'The line of descent of nobles is from the blood of kings', and this remained a widespread and enduring aristocratic assumption well into the early modern period.[14] Analysing the French monarchy in the earlier-sixteenth century, Claude de Seyssel was clear that 'Chief among the nobility are the great princes, those of the royal blood'.[15] One of the most striking illustrations of this was the plaque referred to by Fabian Persson and put up outside the burial vault in the family church of Östra Ryd, declaring it was the last resting place of 'the following Brahes of royal blood'.[16]

Historians can all-too-easily overlook this simple point, because 'monarchy' and 'nobility' have often appeared separate elements in Europe's past. Previous historiography has contributed to this, with its emphasis on how the nobility was 'tamed' by centralising absolute monarchy during the early modern centuries and so suffered an eclipse, with the traditional social elite losing out to a rising middle class.[17] Such simplicities have long been abandoned: Ronald Asch's contribution (Chapter 2) is a fine demonstration of the prism through which crown-noble relations are now viewed, with its twin emphases on the importance of co-operation and shared interests, and its revelation of the weakness and vulnerability of two new monarchs.[18] In Europe's monarchies – as in Imperial China to a significant extent – rulers depended upon co-operation with local social élites in government.[19] Yet it is all too easy to continue to view the monarchy and the higher nobility as essentially separate subjects. The essays in this volume are an important reminder that they inter-connected frequently and in significant ways, and that we should view them together, as dimensions of a larger whole.

Jeroen Duindam (Chapter 3) provides an intriguing comparative confirmation with his demonstration of the remarkable number and enduring importance of the fief-holding Imperial princes in China, particularly in the western provinces under the Ming dynasty (1368–1644), whose status derived entirely from their links with the ruling family, from which they also secured a regular income.[20] Other chapters reinforce the same point. One of the new rulers discussed by Ronald Asch came

---

14 Quoted by Raluca L. Radulescu and Edward Donald Kennedy (eds), *Broken Lines: Genealogical Literature in Medieval Britain and France* (Turnhout: Brepols, 2008), 1; cf. Formel, *Alliances et Généalogie*, 2: 1165–66, for the case of France.

15 Claude de Seyssel, *The Monarchy of France*, (eds) J.H. Hexter and Donald R. Kelley (New Haven: Yale University Press, 1981), 175.

16 Above, Chapter 8.

17 See the comments by Jeroen Duindam, above, Chapter 3.

18 The best introductions to the early modern nobility are the two overlapping syntheses by Ronald G. Asch, *Nobilities in Transition 1550–1700: Courtiers and Rebels in Britain and Europe* (London: Arnold, 2003) and *Europäischer Adel in der Frühen Neuzeit* (Vienna: Böhlau, 2008).

19 Above, Chapter 3.

20 Though in Imperial China hereditary status was less important than in Europe: above, chapter 3.

from the prominent French magnate family of Bourbon; another such lineage, its rival the House of Guise, had come close to securing the French crown at the end of the 1580s, as Jonathan Spangler notes (Chapter 6); while Liesbeth Geevers examines a transnational lineage, the House of Orange, which became rulers of the Dutch Republic (Chapter 9), and Sebastiaan Derks (Chapter 7) a Roman noble and then papal lineage which evolved into an Italian ruling dynasty, the Farnese, who were dukes of Parma and Piacenza and would eventually provide a Queen for Spain: Elisabeth Farnese, the formidable second wife of the first Bourbon ruler, Philip V (1700–46).

Looking further east, the Appanage Princes in Muscovy headed that country's protean aristocracy. These families were the descendants of the formerly independent rulers of small principalities which had become part of the Muscovite realm as it expanded through annexations and incorporations during the Later Middle Ages.[21] All were descended from a branch of the Russian or Lithuanian ruling houses, and alone enjoyed the title of prince. Everywhere, aristocrats clustered around thrones. A wish to highlight nearness to rulers of England, as well as secure status and prestige, may well have been an additional reason for the 10 Irish aristocrats buried in London's Westminister Abbey, the traditional resting place of kings, to which Jane Ohlmeyer refers; it certainly was for Magnus Gabriel De la Gardie who opted to be buried in Varnhem, alongside the remains of Sweden's twelfth- and thirteenth-century kings, even though this involved creating a new family church *ab initio*.[22] An earlier Swedish dynast – the sixteenth-century magnate Per Brahe – buried his son Joakim in the Vadstena convent church in order to highlight and reinforce the family's supposed links with the iconic St Bridget of Sweden.[23] We are used to emphasising how 'absolute' monarchs such as Louis XIV surrounded themselves with aristocrats in order to enhance their own majesty, but we need to remember that leading nobles themselves felt they secured prestige and status – as well, of course, as opportunities for income, advancement and access to patronage of all kinds – from their attendance at court and their interaction with the ruler.[24]

---

[21] The consequences are set out in the illuminating study by Nancy Shields Kollmann, *Kinship and Politics: The Making of the Muscovite Political System, 1345–1547* (Stanford: Stanford University Press, 1987).

[22] Above, Chapters 1 and 8.

[23] Above, Chapter 8.

[24] See in particular Jeroen Duindam, *Vienna and Versailles: The Courts of Europe's Dynastic Rivals 1550–1700* (Cambridge: Cambridge University Press, 2003) and the collections of essays edited by Ronald G. Asch and Adolf M. Birke, *Princes, Patronage and the Nobility: The Court at the Beginning of the Modern Age* (Oxford: Oxford University Press, 1991), and by John Adamson, *The Princely Courts of Europe 1500–1750* (London: Weidenfeld & Nicolson, 1999). A wider perspective is provided by Jeroen Duindam, Tülay Artan and Metin Kunt (eds), *Royal Courts in Dynastic States and Empires: A Global Perspective* (Leiden: Brill, 2011).

A number of prominent noble lineages actually became ruling families and established themselves upon European thrones during the early modern period. Sweden's ruling Vasa family were originally long-established members of the lesser nobility, and had been elevated to the throne in the desperate circumstances of the early 1520s, as Sweden broke free from Danish rule and established a precarious independence. Initially the crown was not even hereditary, and did not become so until 1544. During the domestic political conflicts of the second half of the sixteenth century and the first decade of the seventeenth century, there were Swedish aristocratic voices ready and willing to remind the Vasas of their modest origins. In another polity where an elective system of monarchy prevailed for much longer, that of Poland-Lithuania (which had been consolidated by the Union of Lublin in 1569), no fewer than four prominent families – Wisniowiecki, Sobieski, Leszczynski and Poniatowski – temporarily provided a king, though none was allowed to secure their family upon the throne by establishing the principle of hereditary succession. Far more enduring were the Bourbons in France (as we have seen), the Romanovs in Muscovy and the Braganças in Portugal. The Romanov family became Muscovite rulers at the end of the 'Time of Troubles' (1598–1613), while when Portugal revolted successfully in 1640 and ended the 60-year rule by Madrid, the plutocratic Bragança duke became king, successfully establishing his family on the throne.

Historians of the European nobility now agree that there was a clearly defined hierarchy within the Second Estate. It stretched up from the usually numerous and impoverished lesser nobility through more prosperous families in the middle ranks whose horizons were provincial rather than national – the *noblesse seconde* of French scholars[25] – to the great lineages, or would-be great lineages, who are the subjects of this volume: the Brahe and the Ormond, the Croÿ, the Guise and the Arenberg. But it is important to remember that the hierarchy did not stop with the magnates: it continued on upwards to reach the crown itself. France's king was seen – and, to a significant extent, saw himself, as Ronald Asch explains so clearly in the case of Henry IV[26] – as the first nobleman in the realm, able and willing to lead his armies in person on the battlefield. Many aristocrats, for their part, continued to view the king as simply *primus inter pares*, first among equals, asserting a claim to near-equality which seventeenth-century rulers were at pains to limit and even reject.[27] Sixteenth-century France contained several aristocratic lineages related to the ruling Valois family, though any claim to the throne was impossible because of the Salic Law, which precluded succession through the female line.[28] This was one reason why successive French monarchs, beginning with the first Bourbon Henry IV, particularly emphasised the sacral nature of their

---

25 For which see Laurent Bourquin, *Noblesse seconde et pouvoir en Champagne aux XVIe et XVIIe siècles* (Paris: Publications de la Sorbonne, 1994).

26 Above, Chapter 2.

27 Formel, *Alliances et Généalogie*, 2:1155–56, emphasises this for France.

28 Cf. above, Chapter 2.

kingship, intending thereby to accentuate the gulf between the ruler and even the greatest aristocrat in the realm.[29]

Behind this set of mental attitudes lay a conviction on the part of magnates that, in the past, their own predecessors had been the equals or near-equals of kings. Indeed, they had played a part in confirming rulers on the throne and even in selecting them. Whatever the truth of this – and it was idealised and exaggerated, though with some basis in past history when the gulf between rulers and their secular elites had been less than it would become by the seventeenth century – it was deeply cherished among leading families. In France it had been strengthened by the generation of intense religious and political conflict after 1562. The Valois monarchy had been at a low ebb, both in terms of prestige and of actual authority, during the later-sixteenth century Wars of Religion, at a time when magnate power had increased spectacularly, strengthening ideas of near-equality on the part of leading lineages. During the early part of the seventeenth century, noble propagandists had seriously advanced the idea that the French crown should cede more authority to aristocrats and weaken its own power. It would transform the country into a Gallic version of the *Reich* or Holy Roman Empire in which leading aristocrats enjoyed quasi-sovereign status, leaving the French king with only a position of overlordship and sharply reducing his rights. Such notions made little headway, as a stronger monarchy was created by the first Bourbon King; that they could even be advanced revealed the self-confidence and power of the leading families, after half a century of royal weakness.

The same point can be made in a rather different way. Historians of the nobility frequently emphasise how middle-ranking and especially higher nobles were accustomed to look both sideways and downwards: to the side, to scrutinise the actions of rivals and to check that they were not getting ahead in the permanent competition for status and the accompanying rewards; they also looked down, watching anxiously for the rise of a rival House which might one day threaten their own position. But the great lineages also looked upwards, modelling their lifestyles on Europe's monarchies. They created councils to advise the head of the family about dynastic strategy and to govern during any minority or the temporary absence of the head of the lineage, and administrations to supervise the collection of their revenues and the running of their estates.[30] They maintained their own courts – exactly as the Imperial princes did in China[31] – and undertook artistic and literary patronage of all kinds, creating a representational culture which, by

---

[29] Above, Chapter 2. See the suggestive studies by Paul Kléber Monod, *The Power of Kings: Monarchy and Religion in Europe, 1589–1715* (New Haven: Yale University Press, 1999), and by Ronald G. Asch, *Sacral Kingship Between Disenchantment and Re-Enchantment: The French and English Monarchies, 1587–1688* (New York: Berghahn, 2014).

[30] See, e.g., the study by Adolfo Carrasco Martínez, *El Poder de la Sangre: Los duques del Infantado 1601–1841* (Madrid: Actas, 2010), esp. part III, for a notable example.

[31] Above, Chapter 3.

the early modern period, could rival that of crowned heads.[32] The duc d'Alençon, whose early death in 1675 created the problem of the Guise succession, had an orchestra to rival that of Louis XIV together with his 'own personal composer'.[33]

Aristocrats, often accustomed to life at royal and princely courts, emulated monarchical splendour in their own extended households, which flourished particularly during the early modern centuries. One outstanding example was the court maintained by the Hungarian magnate family of Eszterházy, initially at Eisenstadt and in Vienna, and then at the fabled palace of Eszterháza – built at enormous cost on the shore of the Neusiedler See – during the reign of the celebrated Maecenas, Prince Nikolaus the Magnificent (1762–90).[34] Adorned for a generation by the noted composer Joseph Haydn as *Kapellmeister*, it rivalled the imperial court at Vienna in distinction and display, if not in size. All over Europe, leading aristocrats modelled their lifestyles and their aspirations on the rulers whom they served, to the point of adopting numerals to distinguish different members of the family with the same name and so describing themselves as 'Henri II Condé' or 'Nikolaus I Eszterházy'. Even more striking is the action of the seventeenth-century Swedish aristocrat, Per Brahe the Younger, aspiring to be a semi-sovereign ruler in his county of Visingsborg around Lake Vättern in central Sweden, which was as large as the north German Duchy of Mecklenburg-Schwerin. Brahe erected at least 16 memorial stones throughout Visingsborg, recording the length of the 'reigns' of various Brahe counts, something that is as remarkable as it is instructive.[35]

Leading nobles had always been aware of the actions of rulers, and to a significant extent copied them. One example was the way in which magnates viewed themselves in self-consciously dynastic terms: as the families studied in this volume so obviously did.[36] The sense of dynasty which is evident in all the

---

32 Two good examples are the lavishly illustrated volume edited by Marika Keblusek and Jori Zijlmans, *Princely Display: The Court of Frederik Henrik of Orange and Amalia von Solms* (The Hague and Zwolle: Waanders, 1997) and the range of cultural patronage of the sixteenth-century Guise which is made clear by the essays in Bellenger, *Le mécénat.*

33 Above, Chapter 6.

34 The articles in the 1995 exhibition catalogue *Die Fürsten Esterházy: Magnaten, Diplomaten und Mäzene*, (eds) Jakob Perschy and Harald Prickler (Eisenstadt: Amt der Burgenländischen Landesregierung, 1995) provide a helpful introduction to the family's fortunes, while its eighteenth-century ascendancy is the subject of Rebecca Gates-Coon, *The Landed Estates of the Esterházy Princes: Hungary during the Reforms of Maria Theresia and Joseph II* (Baltimore: Johns Hopkins University Press, 1994).

35 Above, Chapter 8.

36 Robert Oresko, "The Marriages of the nieces of Cardinal Mazarin: Public Policy and Private Strategy in Seventeenth-century Europe", in *Frankreich im Europäischen Staatensystem der Frühen Neuzeit*, (ed.) Rainer Babel (Sigmaringen: Thorbecke, 1995) is an illuminating examination of the Cardinal's use of dynastic marriages and a case study with wide implications; cf. ibid., 150–51, for some interesting reflections on what the author styles the 'new dynastic history' and an emphasis upon the crucial importance of female

articles first developed among ruling families and then spread downwards among the aristocrats who served them. The nobility, after all, had originated in service – mostly on the battlefield or in the council chamber – to kings and other rulers, and in the grants of land, titles and privileges which it received in return. It was perfectly natural that aristocrats should emulate the source of their own distinction. This is the first wider conclusion to emerge from the articles in this volume. Four other broad themes running through the individual essays can be identified: the importance of transnational families; the significant role of women within aristocratic lineages; the crucial importance of succession and inheritance and of arrangements to provide for these; and the numerous ways in which aristocratic identity could be represented and, more importantly, manufactured.

II

The importance of transnational families is highlighted by several articles: notably Jane Ohlmeyer's demonstration of the ways in which the Ormonds established a secure bridgehead in England while upholding their position in Ireland,[37] Violet Soen's exploration of the Croÿs poised between northern France and the Southern Netherlands, and Liesbeth Geevers's account of the way in which the House of Orange gradually withdrew from the territory in southern France which provided the very name of the dynasty and instead focused on its German lands and increasingly on the Dutch Republic, where it was intermittently Stadholder (respectively Chapters 1, 4, and 9). International marriages conferred enhanced prestige, in addition to contributing to the emergence and solidification of transnational aristocratic families, as several chapters make clear. Many aristocratic lineages acquired significant international connections, created by such marriages or by earlier service abroad, with important implications for the study of noble families. For far too long, as Violet Soen shrewdly remarks, the history of Europe's nobilities has been written almost exclusively within a national perspective, and this can easily become self-limiting.[38] Several chapters demonstrate the importance of escaping from such a restrictive framework. Living in two or more social and political worlds had obvious implications for dynastic identities, as several authors make clear. Happily, this topic is now beginning to attract the scholarly attention it merits.[39]

lines. See also Barbara Stephenson, "Maintaining the Antiquity of the House: Marguerite de Navarre, Noble Marriage and Dynastic Culture in early-sixteenth century France", *The Court Historian* 10 (2005), 15–24.

37 See also her major study: Ohlmeyer, *Making Ireland English*.

38 Above, Chapter 4.

39 Jonathan Spangler, "Those In Between: Princely Families on the Margins of the Great Powers – The Franco-German Frontier, 1477–1830", in, *Transregional and Transnational Families in Europe and Beyond: Experiences since the Middle Ages*, (eds)

Several chapters focus on what were clearly frontier zones: areas located between the powerful monarchies which increasingly dominated early modern Europe's political landscape.[40] Two such regions were of particular significance: the northern sector of the Italian Peninsula, and the extended arc of territory which stretched from the Southern Netherlands through Alsace, Lorraine, Western Switzerland and Dauphiné, into Provence, Savoy and Piedmont – the 'Middle Kingdom' first created by the division of Charlemagne's inheritance in 843 and, in its northern components, subsequently the lands of the dukes of Burgundy.

The context of Sebastiaan Derks's study (Chapter 7) is the complex political geography and territorial status of northern Italy, which remained part of *Reichsitalien*, though the precise extent and the nature of the Holy Roman Empire's authority were ambiguous and contested.[41] The Farnese were one of a number of families whose possessions lay within this zone of intense political rivalry, where Spanish and, subsequently, Austrian Habsburg interests collided with those of Valois and then Bourbon France. Its vulnerability, together with the need to pursue a balancing policy, rather than committing exclusively to one side or the other, underlay the ambiguities in political positioning skilfully detected by Derks.

The second border zone, a broad swathe of territory which bisected the emerging French monarchy to the west, and the Holy Roman Empire to the east, contained as many as 30 princely families with aspirations to independent or semi-sovereign status. It is brought into focus by three chapters: those by Mirella Marini on the Arenbergs, by Violet Soen on the Croÿs and by Jonathan Spangler on the Guises/Lorraine (Chapters 5, 4, 6). The first two, together with the Salm lineage, were the most prominent of these families, while the third was much more heavily involved within France's domestic politics in addition to its position as dukes of

Christopher H. Johnson, David Warren Sabean, Simon Teuscher and Francesca Trivellato (New York and Oxford: Berghahn, 2011), 130–54, is a helpful introduction to the situation in the borderlands between France and the Reich; I am grateful to Dr Spangler for allowing me to read this article in advance of its publication. Cf. the same author's book: *The Society of Princes: The Lorraine-Guise and the Conservation of Power and Wealth in seventeenth-century France* (Farnham: Ashgate, 2009).

40 The discussion which follows owes much to the "Introduction", in *Royal and Republican Sovereignty in Early Modern Europe: Essays in Memory of Ragnhild Hatton*, (eds) Robert Oresko, G.C. Gibbs and H.M. Scott (Cambridge: Cambridge University Press, 1997).

41 Marina Cavallera, "Les fiefs impériaux dans l'Italie nord-occidentale au XVIIIe siècle", in *Les enclaves territoriales aux Temps Modernes (XVIe-XVIIIe siècles),* (eds) Paul Delsalle and André Ferrer (Besançon: Presses Universitaires de Franche-Comté, 2000) and Blythe Alice Raviola, "The Imperial System in Early Modern Northern Italy: A Web of Dukedoms, Fiefs and Enclaves along the Po", in *The Holy Roman Empire, 1495–1806: A European Perspective*, (eds) R.J.W. Evans and Peter H. Wilson (Leiden: Brill, 2012) provide helpful discussions.

Lorraine.[42] During the fifteenth and sixteenth centuries, as ‘national’ nobilities solidified within Europe’s emerging monarchical states, families in this zone had evolved into transnational lineages and had also frequently intermarried. The Croÿs, by origin a family of modest status in the nobility of Picardy, had gravitated northwards and prospered by playing off the French King against the Burgundian ruler and, subsequently, his Austrian Habsburg and Spanish counterparts, who successively attempted to rule the Southern Netherlands from a considerable distance. The limited authority which the Austrian Habsburg Emperor, the Spanish King and the King of France were all able to exert in an area of strategic and economic importance allowed transnational lineages such as the Croÿs to prosper by playing one side off against another, thereby gaining in resources and authority.

The growing wealth and power of France’s Valois and then Bourbon monarchy, however, came to set limits to this independence. As early as the reign of Francis I (1515–47), efforts had been made to extend France’s influence into the eastern and south-eastern frontier zones by marrying the younger sons of the ruling dynasties of Lorraine, Clèves and Savoy to Valois heiresses, with the intention of drawing these polities into Paris’s political orbit. With the seventeenth-century recovery of France as a European power, this objective also came to be pursued by more direct, and often violent, means. One by-product of these initiatives had been the creation of a group of foreign princes – *princes étrangers* – at the French court: families who enjoyed dual status and who, through membership of sovereign ruling dynasties outside France, could and did claim precedence over the *ducs-et-pairs* and even the ‘*princes légitimés*’.[43] Under the Bourbon monarchy this group had grown both in size and in importance, and during a more hierarchical and status-conscious century had been a fertile source of disputes over precedence.

These clashes had revolved around the claims of such families to be considered semi-sovereign princes, and so entitled to special treatment at court due to their status as rulers of an independent territory beyond France. Such efforts naturally inspired rival claims, among a competitive and status-conscious higher nobility. During the first decade of the seventeenth century the maréchal-duc de Bouillon sought to claim this status for his possession of Sedan, which lay on the edge of the border zone along France’s north-eastern frontier.[44] Such disputes were not

42 See Jean-Marie Constant, *Les Guise* (Paris: Hachette, 1984) and, for the family’s remarkable sixteenth-century trajectory, Stuart Carroll, *Martyrs and Murderers: The Guise Family and the Making of Europe* (Oxford: Oxford University Press, 2009).

43 Robert Oresko, “Princes étrangers”, in *Dictionnaire de l’Ancien Régime*, (ed.) Lucien Bély (Paris: Presses Universitaires de France, 2003), and Guy Antonetti, “Les princes étrangers”, in *État et société en France aux XVIIe et XVIIIe siècles: Mélanges offerts à Yves Durand*, (eds) Jean-Pierre Bardet, Dominique Dinet, Jean-Pierre Poussou and Marie-Catherine Vignal (Paris: Presses de l’Université de Paris-Sorbonne, 2000) are helpful introductions, though the latter is not without shortcomings.

44 Simon Hodson, “Politics of the Frontier: Henri IV, the Maréchal-Duc de Bouillon and the sovereignty of Sedan”, *French History* 19 (2005).

confined to France. The appearance of native 'princes' in the Habsburg-governed Kingdom of Bohemia – due to the noted inflation of titles during the seventeenth century – caused similar problems in the eastern lands of the Holy Roman Empire.[45] Princely rank and the semi-sovereign status which it justified were integral to the identity of an elite group of aristocratic families scattered all across Europe, to be defended and perpetuated at all costs.

Mirella Marini's study (Chapter 5) reveals how one formidable female dynast, Anne of Croÿ, strove to perpetuate the identity and, with it, the survival of the Houses of Arenberg and Aarschot. Central to her efforts was a deliberate re-ordering of the family archives, carried out with the intention of buttressing the dynastic claims being advanced and the accompanying family realignment which she was supervising. Scholars researching the aristocracy and nobility – exactly like early modern specialists more generally – are increasingly aware that the archives they exploit are not neutral collections of documents, but were assembled and continually re-organised with distinct purposes in mind.[46] Another example of the importance of a family's archives for its identity is provided by Sebastiaan Derks, who demonstrates the importance of the consolidation of the Farnese muniments carried out by Duke Ranuccio I of Parma.[47]

The importance of sovereignty for early modern historians has usually been viewed in terms of the strengthening of monarchical authority at this time. Sovereign power has been seen as one of the essential attributes of the modern state, which was believed to have had its origins in these developments. Here there is an obvious link between the world of politics and government, and that of ideas and philosophy. During the seventeenth and eighteenth centuries, would-be absolute monarchs were quick to borrow from political theory and to support their own authority by employing the doctrine that sovereignty was complete and indivisible. This derived from the well-known writings of the sixteenth-century theorist, Jean Bodin, encapsulated in his *Six livres de la République* (1576), drawn up under the shadow of the collapse of royal authority and civil war in later-sixteenth century France. Bodin's assertion that sovereignty was complete and indivisible was seized upon by rulers, seeking a theoretical justification for efforts to increase their own authority, and employed in monarchical propaganda.

The exaggerated claims advanced on their behalf were in turn taken at face value by historians of earlier generations, particular those nineteenth- and early-twentieth century scholars searching for the origins of the homogenised 'nation-state'. They were also inspired by the writings of the German sociologist Max

---

[45] There is a valuable survey by Petr Mat'a, "Bohemia, Silesia and the Empire: Negotiating Princely Dignity on the Eastern Periphery", in *The Holy Roman Empire*, (eds) Evans and Wilson. I am grateful to Dr Mat'a for allowing me to read this article before its publication.

[46] Markus Friedrich, *Die Geburt des Archivs: Eine Wissensgeschichte* (Munich: Oldenbourg Wissenschaftsverlag, 2013) is a good introduction to the wider issues involved.

[47] Above, Chapter 7.

Weber, who credited the institutions of the state with possessing 'the monopoly of legitimate force and regularly, normally and effectively exercising domination' within a defined territorial area.[48] Such a definition assumed that sovereignty was the preserve of the ruler and, by extension, of what came to be perceived as a 'government', the existence of which derived directly from princely validation and attribution of responsibility. Though this approach was widely influential, it obscured two crucial facts. Firstly, many of what have been taken to be the attributes of the modern state – the administration of justice, the authority to tax, even the right to conduct a separate foreign policy – were at this period not the monopoly of the ruler alone, but were shared with other individuals, groups and territories within the frequently disparate lands over which the prince claimed sovereign power.[49]

In second place, the composite nature of most early modern polities has become fully apparent to historians. The debate over what came to be called 'composite monarchy' here made a major contribution. It underlined that all early modern kingdoms were collections of separate territories and provinces, each with their own distinctive constitutions, laws, political traditions and sometimes even languages. Each component part defended its own way of life and especially its fiscal, legal and (sometimes) religious privileges against central encroachment. This struggle was aided by the small size of the state apparatus and by the difficulties posed by slow and unreliable communications, highlighted by Jeroen Duindam for the very different case of China, where authority had to be exercised over a vastly greater geographical area (Chapter 3). Within every polity there were numerous smaller jurisdictional and territorial units, all anxious to retain such independence as remained. Efforts to promote greater internal cohesion could only make slow progress in the face of the enormous strength of traditional structures and established patterns of life.

---

[48] Quoted by Howard Kaminsky and James Van Horn Melton (eds), *Land and Lordship: Structures of Governance in Medieval Austria* (Philadelphia: University of Pennsylvania Press, 1992), xxiii.

[49] For its origins, see H.G. Koenigsberger, "*Dominium Regale* or *dominium politicum et regale*: monarchies and parliaments in early modern Europe" (originally an inaugural lecture delivered in 1975 and subsequently printed in the same author's *Politicians and Virtuosi: Essays in Early Modern European History* (London: Hambledon, 1986) together with the important discussion by J.H. Elliott, "A Europe of Composite Monarchies", *Past and Present* 137 (1992); see also the collection of essays edited by Mark Greengrass, *Conquest and Coalescence: The Shaping of the State in Early Modern Europe* (London: Arbold, 1991), by Petr Mat'a and Thomas Winkelbauer, *Die Habsburgermonarchie 1620 bis 1740: Leistungen und Grenzen des Absolutismusparadigmas* (Stuttgart: Steiner, 2006), and by Jon Arrieta and John H. Elliott, *Forms of Union: The British and Spanish Monarchies in the Seventeenth and Eighteenth Centuries* (Donostia: Eusko Ikaskuntza, 2009), which was published as RIEV Cuadernos 5; and Harald Gustafsson, "The Conglomerate State: A Reflection on State Formation in Early Modern Europe", *Scandinavian Journal of History* 23 (1998).

The old world of lordship thus persisted long into the early modern period, when competing jurisdictions jostled for sovereignty.[50] Powerful aristocratic dynasties were in the forefront of this struggle, sometimes acting as the agents of centralisation but more often rallying provincial resistance and in this way benefitting from the inability of dynastic monarchy to extend its authority to the extent that it wished. During the past half century, the traditional emphasis upon the emergence of a Leviathan state during the early modern period has been replaced by a recognition of the real practical limitations upon central government authority. There is now a recognition that there were a number of institutions and individuals who were attempting to establish their pre-eminence, in the process contributing to a redefinition of the idea of 'sovereignty', now seen as less a matter of legislative authority – the power to command – and more in terms of territorial, personal and practical elements rather than purely philosophical notions. Sovereignty, in other words, has ceased to be viewed through the prism provided by Bodin and, following the writings of a theorist such as the German Protestant philosopher Henning Arnisaeus (1576/79–1673), is now seen in terms of bundles of rights which might be held to a greater or lesser extent.[51] This accords with the development of ideas of sovereignty at the time. For half a century after the publication of *Six livres de la République* Bodin's theories held sway, but from the mid 1620s a view of sovereignty as something which might be divided and which accorded more with contemporary reality, was gaining ground especially within the *Reich*.

This shift in emphasis has contributed to – and been accompanied by – a recognition that many of the families discussed in this book themselves possessed a measure of sovereignty and that this was fundamental to their self-identification and self-representation. The Arenbergs, Orange and Guises-Lorraine (Chapters 5, 9 and 6) clearly were all semi-sovereign. In a similar way, early modern France contained a number of individuals, behind whom stood great family complexes, who claimed to be sovereigns in their own right. They were not the King's subjects but the juridical equals of the monarch, whom they might agree to serve.

One of the best known of these was Charles, duc de Nevers, who is most familiar for his efforts to secure the succession to the Italian duchies of Mantua and Monferrato at the end of the 1620s, which gave rise to a well-known international

[50] Otto Brunner, *Land und Herrschaft: Grundfragen der territorialen Verfassungsgeschichte Österreichs im Mittelalter* (Baden-bei-Wien: Rohrer, 1939 and subsequent editions), remains a classic study of the world of lordship; there is a notable English translation, cited in n. 48.

[51] Julian H. Franklin, "Sovereignty and the Mixed Constitution: Bodin and his Critics", in *The Cambridge History of Political Thought 1450–1700*, (eds) J.H. Burns with Mark Goldie (Cambridge: Cambridge University Press, 1991); for Arnisaeus, see ibid., 314, 320–23, 659.

crisis.[52] Nevers had a contractual view of his relationship with Louis XIII, the French King. He might and did enter French service, but he was clear that he retained his sovereign status. He always thought and acted not like a royal subject but as an independent ruler – which he was twice over, through his possession of the sovereign principalities of Bois-Belle-en-Berry, in central France, and Arches, on the north-eastern frontier. He also held and administered directly the duchies of Nevers, Rethel and (from 1621) Mayenne. The duc de Nevers's sovereignty was apparent in his ability to mint coins and to dispense justice (with no appeal to another, higher jurisdiction), and it was manifest in his resplendent court and independent military forces. This was the nub of the problem for the French crown: the existence and dual status of a number of powerful families who held ducal titles and rank, but came from sovereign princely houses and had a status which eclipsed that of most *grands*.

III

The central role which women played within these aristocratic dynasties is a further conclusion of more general importance to emerge. For far too long, female family members have been written out of the history of Europe's nobilities, in the same way that early modern and nineteenth-century genealogists and historians often omitted them, or at least many of them, from the family trees which they so laboriously constructed and the narrative histories they produced in order to create and sustain dynastic identity. Nobility was an essentially masculine status and adhered primarily in the male line, and these considerations appeared to validate the neglect of noblewomen. Where they were studied – in keeping with the approach of some early historians of gender – the emphasis was on women who substituted for men: during a husband's absence at court, on military campaign or after his death, during the minority of a child. The role they discharged was either restricted in time or essentially passive in nature.

This neglect is beginning to be remedied, as historians begin to recover the active role and central importance of the forgotten half of aristocratic lineages, and the studies in this volume advance this process.[53] They demonstrate the agency

---

[52] David Parrott, "A *prince étranger* and the French crown: Charles de Nevers, 1580–1637", in *Royal and Republican Sovereignty*, (eds) Oresko et al.; idem, "The Mantuan Succession, 1627–31: A Sovereignty Dispute in Early Modern Europe", *English Historical Review* 112 (1997); see also Ariane Boltanski, *Les ducs de Nevers et l'état royal: Genèse d'un compromis (ca. 1550- ca. 1600)* (Geneva: Droz, 2006), for the establishment of the family's power in the previous generations.

[53] By studies such as Grace E. Coolidge, *Guardianship, Gender and the Nobility in Early Modern Spain* (Farnham: Ashgate, 2011); Helen Nader (ed.), *Power and Gender in Renaissance Spain: Eight women of the Mendoza Family, 1450–1650* (Urbana: Illenois University Press, 2004); Rosine A. Lambin, *Femmes de Paix: La coexistence religieuse*

which aristocratic women possessed and exercised. An outstanding example is Jonathan Spangler's account (Chapter 6) of Mademoiselle de Guise, in the final two years of her life, so meticulously and tenaciously arranging the details of her family's succession. Another is Mirella Marini's demonstration (Chapter 5) of the key role of Anne of Croÿ in adjusting, maintaining, transmitting and so perpetuating the family identity of the Arenbergs in particular. Few lineages are as fortunate in this respect as the House of Arenberg, with a handsome and informative illustrated survey devoted to its female side, but the studies in this present volume contribute to the re-assessment which is under way and mark a further significant stage in that process.[54]

The fourth thread running through the individual chapters is the over-riding importance of succession and inheritance, which was usually a time of danger but could also be an opportunity. This is obviously central to any dynastic system, which depends upon the transmission of the human and, to a lesser extent, material resources between generations. Three articles explicitly consider this theme – those by Mirella Marini, Violet Soen and Jonathan Spangler – while others touch upon it tangentially. Its central importance is obvious: without continuity there was and, indeed, could be no dynasty, though imagined continuities could exist as well as real ones. Aristocrats – exactly like monarchs – to an extent depended upon a glorious past: one important element in a noble family's claim to high status in the present was its public contribution in former times, however idealised a version of this it cherished and presented. The renown which this conferred upon a lineage was enduring, and it was enhanced during the early modern period by the way in which noble propagandists came to embrace the notion of a noble race, which made dynastic continuity all-important.[55]

At the same time, however, the simple facts of demography and the uncertainty these created within any system dependent upon hereditary succession, however well planned, could threaten this. Dr Soen's masterly article provides a particularly instructive demonstration of the repercussions of the death of duc Guillaume de Croÿ-Chièvres (1458–1521) without a male heir (Chapter 4). This complex dispute inaugurated eight decades of conflict, culminating in prolonged litigation within the Parlement of Paris, as rival branches contested the inheritance. The outcome was the emergence of a new – French – branch of the Croÿ (supported by the King of France) in addition to the established – Burgundian and then Habsburg – line.

---

et les dames de la noblesse en France, 1520–1630 (Paris: Harmattan, 2003); Michelle L. Marrese, *A Woman's Kingdom: Noblewomen and the Control of Property in Russia, 1700–1861* (Ithaca: Cornell University Press, 2002); and Elaine Chalus, *Elite Women in English Political Life, c.1754–1790* (Oxford: Oxford University Press, 2005).

[54] Peter Neu (ed.), *Arenberger Frauen: Fürstinnen, Herzoginnen, Ratgeberinnen, Mütter* (Koblenz: Verlag der Landesarchivverwaltung Rheinland-Pfalz, 2006).

[55] Devyer, *Le sang épuré*; Arlette Jouanna, *L'idée de race en France au XVIe siècle et au début du XVIIe* (revised edition; Montpellier: Service des Publications de l'Université Paul Valéry, 1981).

Similar themes emerge from Mirella Marini's study of the Arenberg family during the sixteenth and seventeenth centuries (Chapter 5). Divisions of the family lands were often – as in the case of the Croÿs – driven by external political pressures and were a form of insurance policy. Dr Soen's article possesses a second and wider significance. It is an essential reminder of the importance of the legal context and of juridical factors, significant when present-day historians, both of the aristocracy and more generally, are prone to underestimate the importance of law. Both themes recur in Dr Spangler's revealing demonstration of Mademoiselle de Guise's preoccupation with the Guise succession and her efforts to promote dynastic continuity in the final years of her own life (Chapter 6).

Early modern aristocrats viewed the problem of succession through the prism of a demographic system which could periodically and quite unexpectedly deprive a family of the all-important male heir and sometimes of any heir at all, as in the cases of the Guise where the death of the duc d'Alençon in 1675 created the acute problems with which the last female head of the lineage struggled during the later 1680s (Chapter 6). Within a relatively stable population – as was, broadly speaking, the case in Europe until the mid-eighteenth century – the chances of any marriage producing a son who survived into adolescence have been calculated to have been no more than 60 per cent – that is to say, three out of five.[56] The likelihood of a female heir who survived, or of no children at all being born, were in each case around 20 per cent, or one in five. These figures appear to exclude deaths in warfare or from epidemic disease. Even within a society where both husbands and wives frequently remarried after they had been widowed, the permanent threat which this posed to aristocratic lineages was obvious: it is to be seen most clearly in the cases of the Croÿ (Chapter 4), Guise (Chapter 6) and the Arenberg (Chapter 5). In this latter case, Mirella Marini demonstrates the contrasting pressures arising both from the lack of a male heir and from too many children, male and female, for whom provision had to be made. Her study provides a striking reminder of the way in which family identities were fashioned and refashioned to fit the changing – and wholly unpredictable – demographic realities of an aristocratic dynasty.

In order to deal with this ever-present danger, the majority of leading families across much of Europe, in the course of the later medieval and early modern centuries, had first adopted primogeniture and then created family agreements regulating succession to the title and resources, and protecting the all-important

[56] See the comments of Michel Nassiet, "Parenté et Successions dynastiques au 14e et 15e siècles", *Annales Histoire, Sciences Sociales* 50 (1995), 621; for the original calculation, E.A. Wrigley, "Fertility Strategy for the Individual and the Group", in *Historical Studies of Changing Fertility*, (ed.) Charles Tilly (Princeton: Princeton University Press, 1978), 139ff; cf. Jack Goody, "Strategies of Heirship", *Comparative Studies in Society and History* 15 (1973) for a rather different method of calculating such probabilities which yields broadly similar results.

family patrimony at the same time.[57] Here they had been following in the footsteps of ruling dynasties: a further illustration of the diffusion downwards which took place and of the essential unity of the world of rulers and magnates. This is one of the most important categories of dynastic document for early modern aristocratic families: the family trusts which were known in England as entails and, after 1660, as strict settlements, and on the continent variously as *Fideikommisse* (German), *substitutions fidéicommissaires* or sometimes *majorats* (French), *mayorazgos* (Castilian), and *fedecommessi* (Italian). These were usually concluded upon the marriage of the eldest son, though they might also be drawn up prior to the death of the previous head of the family. Their importance within the Croÿ-Arenberg-Aarschot family complex is touched on by Mirella Marini.[58] Concentrating resources on one – usually male – heir was far from universal: Guillaume de Croÿ, for example, had initially intended to leave all his lands to one heir, but in the final days of his life divided them between two.[59] The granting of French properties to his younger nephew underlines the extent to which the succession arrangements of leading families were subject to constant revision and renegotiation, as circumstances changed and priorities evolved.

Broadly speaking – and any generalisation about what is an extremely complex subject is problematical – such agreements did three things: (1) they provided for the eldest son and his heirs to succeed to the bulk of their fathers' property, whom failing the second son and so on; (2) they placed a significant proportion of the family resources, above all the landed property, within a trust, guaranteeing to the heir in each generation a regular income but denying him or her access to the resources themselves, and in this way creating a secure material base for the family's survival through the generations; (3) they provided, sometimes in bewildering detail, for the succession if and when the direct line of the family became extinct, that is to say it failed to provide an heir. There was an analogous system of family trusts in China, as Jeroen Duindam makes clear, resembling the European entail or *Fideikommiss*.[60]

The first two of these factors – primogenitural succession and the creation of a trust – have attracted the bulk of attention from historians, and certainly the

[57] The one general study of this remains the remarkable essay by J.P. Cooper, "Patterns of inheritance by great landowners from the fifteenth to the eighteenth centuries", in *Family and Inheritance: Rural Society in Western Europe, 1200–1800*, (eds) Jack Goody, Joan Thirsk and E.P. Thompson (Cambridge: Cambridge University Press, 1976); Bartolomé Clavero, *Mayorazgo; Propiedad feudal en Castilla (1369–1836)* (Madrid: Siglo Ventiuno, 1974; 2nd ed., 1989), is in a class of its own as a national study; while the recent collection of essays edited by Anne Bellavitis, Jean-François Chauvard and Paola Lanaro, "Fidéicommis: Instruments juridiques et pratiques sociales (Italie/Europe, Bas Moyen Âge/XIXe siècle)", which was published in *Mélanges de l'École Française de Rome: Italie et Méditerranée* 124, no. 2 (2012), provides a valuable Franco-Italian perspective on the subject.

[58] Above, Chapter 5.

[59] Above, Chapter 4.

[60] Above, Chapter 3.

importance attributed to these objectives is well-merited. But providing for a similar continuity in human resources was scarcely less important, particularly in view of the real demographic uncertainties. One reason for believing that entails were dynastic arrangements tailored to a family's particular circumstances and aiming to perpetuate its power, is a very simple one: that they usually declared their aim to be exactly this. A very good example would be the English peer, the third Earl of Westmorland who, when he established such a settlement in 1668, announced that his purpose was to ensure 'that the same might continue in his name and blood and may descend with the Earldom to the heirs male of the family'.[61] The importance which families gave to securing the inheritance emerges from several chapters, which underline just how important but also how precarious aristocratic successions could be. Dynastic identity hung on a fragile demographic thread, and magnates planned as well as they could to deal with the consequences of this.

IV

The final general theme to emerge is in many ways the most important. 'Dynastic identity', as contributors repeatedly make very clear, was a constructed, manufactured commodity and not a neutral, positivistic category. In its making, present realities and requirements were more important than past history, which could be manipulated or even ignored. One of the clearest examples is provided by Liesbeth Geevers, who skilfully demonstrates (Chapter 9) the ways in which Orangist writers distorted the family's history in order to portray the House of Orange as 'a more or less hereditary ruling family'[62] and to present a record of unbroken service to the Dutch and Republican cause. Of course, history was an obvious – perhaps *the* best and most obvious – way of buttressing a family's standing in the present, by recording, creating, or improving a glorious past, as several essays underline.

Mirella Marini brings out the importance of the *Marques des Grandeurs*, an early family history finalised in 1660, for the Arenbergs (Chapter 5), while Sebastiaan Derks (Chapter 7) provides one of the most striking examples, with his account of efforts to glorify the achievements of Duke Alexander [Alessandro] Farnese, the celebrated Spanish commander and governor-general of the Low Countries (1578–92). Farnese dynastic history was woven into Paolo Rinaldi's account of Spain's struggle to defeat the Dutch rebels. Though the duke of Parma had gained renown in Madrid's service, before eventually suffering dismissal, these narratives were more ambivalent about Spain's policy than might be anticipated. One objective was certainly to recover the family's political standing by highlighting its loyalty to the Spanish Monarchy, after Alexander Farnese's fall

[61] Quoted by Sir John Habakkuk, *Marriage, Debt and the Estates System: English landownership, 1650–1950* (Oxford: Oxford University Press, 1994), 52.

[62] Above, Chapter 9.

from grace, but these efforts also took account of the Farnese position in northern Italy where Madrid's influence, based upon its control over the neighbouring Duchy of Milan, was potentially threatening. Farnese control over the dukedoms of Parma and Piacenza rested upon an earlier usurpation, and remained controversial and vulnerable. A desire to uphold family dynastic interests gave this propaganda a subtle anti-Spanish dimension.

Dr Derks's study, together with other recent studies of the Farnese, also confirms the continuing importance of artistic decoration.[63] Early modern Europe was a society and culture where visual propaganda remained a significant medium, and indeed may have been more important than the literary mode as a way of glorifying ancestors. But there were many other ways of reinforcing this. One was the practice of always baptising the eldest son with the same Christian name, which thereby became associated with the family. Another was by naming and re-naming places and settlements after the family. Between the 1630s and the 1650s the indefatigable Per Brahe the Younger created not merely the castle of Brahehus, the manor of Braheberg and the hunting lodge of Brahehälla (all within the county of Visingsborg), but the town of Brahea in Swedish Finland.[64] Aristocratic names and titles usually commemorated a location of family influence and landholding in previous centuries, and in this perspective his actions possess an obvious importance.

Genealogies, viewed in the widest sense, provided an especially significant means of manufacturing dynastic identity, and one with which historians are increasingly familiar. During the Later Middle Ages and the early modern period, these became much more numerous and also more detailed in Europe; they existed in China too.[65] Once again, magnates were following in the footsteps of the rulers they served. An excellent example is that of the arch-dynast, Per Brahe the younger, who not only sponsored two detailed family genealogies (1647, 1673: the second printed on his own press on Visingsö in Lake Vättern) but actually paid for the inclusion of his lineage in a noted German genealogical work.[66]

The inclusion of a manufactured Brahe genealogy which went back to St Bridget underlines the problems presented by such sources. Here it is important to remember the conclusions of European social anthropologists, who in the 1960s and 1970s began to study societies in Africa and Polynesia in which such records were

---

63 See also Martine Boiteux, "Le palais Farnèse: La représentation et l'identité", *Mélanges de l'École française de Rome: Italie et Méditerranée* 122 (2010), one of a series of articles in that issue devoted to the Farnese palace; Gregory Hanlon, *The Hero of Italy: Odoardo Farnese, Duke of Parma, his Soldiers, and his Subjects in the Thirty Years' War* (Oxford: Oxford University Press, 2014) is an informative study of a later Farnese duke.

64 Above, Chapter 8.

65 An informative study of developments in France, is Germain Butaud and Valérie Piétri, *Les enjeux de la généalogie XIIe-XVIIIe siècle* (Paris: Autrement, 2006); cf. above, Chapter 3.

66 Above, Chapter 8.

transmitted through a largely oral culture, rather than being written down.[67] They demonstrated how genealogies and lists of rulers essentially sought to support and justify existing social groupings and current political realities, and not to present a 'true' – and the question of authenticity will be examined shortly – version of previous events. The one group of historians who have incorporated this insight are specialists in early medieval history, obliged to work with fragmentary and imperfect sources: whether genealogies, regnal lists [lists of kings] or pedigrees of families who exercised authority.[68] It is true that early modern historians possess genealogical records which are – superficially – much better, being more detailed and seemingly more complete. But these sources are not as good, and certainly nowhere near as reliable, as we might like to think and need to be handled with considerable caution. The Italian scholar Roberto Bizzocchi who wrote a justly celebrated and quite fundamental study of this phenomenon significantly entitled his book, 'Incredible Genealogies' (*Genealogie Incredibili*).[69]

The problems which arise have recently been illuminated by Peter Mat'a in a remarkable study.[70] His subject is the way in which descent from the Orsini family was claimed by a succession of noble lineages during the Later Middle Ages and early modern period, primarily the Jouvenel des Ursins (France), the Counts of Blagaj (Croatia and Carniola, two constituent territories of the Austrian Habsburg Monarchy), the Lords of Rožmberk (Bohemia), the Counts Slavata (the successors to the social capital, though not the landed wealth of the Rožmberks when that family died out in 1611) and the Rosenbergs of Carinthia. The importance of his article lies, first of all, in its demonstration of how the quest for status drove the successive claims advanced to kinship with the celebrated Orsini family, which had provided Roman senators, cardinals in the Christian Church and even popes. The need to advance or defend a family's position was central to the adoption

[67] David P. Henige, "Oral Tradition and Chronology", *Journal of African History* 3 (1971) provides a helpful introduction.

[68] David Dumville, "Kingship, Genealogies and Regnal Lists", in *Early Medieval Kingship*, (eds) P.H. Sawyer and I.N. Wood (Leeds: University of Leeds, 1977) is a classic examination of the problems involved; while Ian Wood, "Deconstructing the Merovingian family", in *The Construction of Communities in the Early Middle Ages*, (eds) Richard Corradini, Max Diesenberger, and Helmut Reimitz (Leiden and Boston: Brill, 2003), provides an informative case study.

[69] Roberto Bizzocchi, *Genealogie incredibili* (Milan: Mulino, 1995; revised edition, 2009); Bizzocchi had earlier presented his more important conclusions in "La culture généalogique dans l'Italie du XVIe siècle", *Annales Économies, Sociétés, Civilisations* 46 (1991). There is now a French translation of the revised edition: *Généalogies fabuleuses: Inventer et faire croire dans l'Europe moderne* (Paris: Rue d'Ulm, 2010).

[70] Peter Mat'a, "The false Orsini from over the Alps: Negotiating Aristocratic Identity in Late Medieval and Early Modern Europe", *Römische Historische Mitteilungen* 55 (2013). Dr Mat'a's article originated as a paper given to the conference which was the origin of this present volume, but its length precluded its inclusion. I am grateful to him for sending me a copy.

and the pursuit of the Orsini claim, as Dr Mat'a demonstrates, in each of the interlocking cases he examines, while the identities constructed were unstable and dynamic, always likely to be amended and improved.

The modes employed were primarily the sponsoring of family histories, where he confirms the conclusions of the contributors concerning the importance of such dynastic narratives, the adoption of the Orsini name, the incorporation of its heraldic symbols of the rose and the bear into coats of arms, and the production of genealogies tracing descent in ways which indeed appear 'incredible'. Drawing on the notion of an 'imagined community' first advanced by Benedict Anderson, Dr Mat'a suggests that an aristocratic dynasty was in fact 'a constructed and reified idea which came to be perceived as the reality', a suggestion which is likely to be extremely influential.[71]

Dynastic identities were continually being constructed, defended, manipulated and even invented, as the chapters in this volume individually and collectively make clear. It would be all too easy to dismiss the undoubted distortion of past history, the improvement or invention of a genealogy, or the incorporation of another lineage's heraldic symbol into a family's coat of arms, as simple forgery. A simple 'true' or 'false' dichotomy, however, must be avoided. We need to be careful to discard twentieth-first century standards of what is authentic and can be validated historically, when considering genealogies, histories and coats of arms produced at this time, and instead see such productions through the eyes of the dynasties for whom they were intended. To view them as 'constructed' or even 'invented' would be much better than to consider them forgeries, since they blended what we would now consider fiction with fact.

Their purpose was to advance claims in the present by constructing and then drawing upon an idealised version of the dynasty's past. The Jouvenel des Ursins, Blagajs, Rožmberks, Slavatas and Rosenbergs all aspired to enhanced status, and sought to enlist real and imagined predecessors in their quest: this was an age when a lengthy and distinguished pedigree conferred status. The claim for descent from the Orsini – of which there are numerous counterparts in early modern Europe: the Hungarian House of Eszterházy, after all, claimed descent from no less a figure than Attila the Hun – should be viewed as an index of the status to which families were aspiring and believed they were entitled. Roman ancestors were particularly prized, claimed by the House of Orange and also by that of Arenberg, which improbably sought to base its claim to the title of duke not on an Imperial grant but on ducal status during the centuries of Rome's hegemony.[72] It was an important reminder of the enduring status of classical antiquity during the early modern centuries. The Guises, for their part, produced in the mid-sixteenth century a descent which extended back to Charlemagne, to the Capetians and

---

[71] Mat'a, "False Orsini", 206; cf. Benedict Anderson, *Imagined Communities: Reflections on the Origin and Spread of Nationalism* (London: Verso, 1983; 2nd ed., 1991).

[72] Above, Chapter 5.

even to the Trojans.[73] A claim of descent from the Carolingians was especially common in the early modern continental aristocracy. Other locations had their own comparable figures. The earls of Thomond in Ireland commissioned a genealogy which traced their ancestry 'to Brian boru, high king of Ireland, and Milo, the first Gaelic invader of Ireland and a descendant of the ancient Greeks'.[74] Such genealogical claims – and this is Bizzocchi's central point – were not so 'incredible' as they might seem at first sight. They were a means of legitimating social and political eminence, whether desired or already secured. Present or future grandeur demanded a glorious past, and this was then assembled for the lineage.

Two further points require to be made about genealogies and family histories, which present very similar problems. The first is that critical historical scholarship lay some way in the future, its real origins being in the later-eighteenth century.[75] Throughout the early modern period, the past was not viewed as an objective field of study, but existed primarily in order to validate the present. Montaigne went so far as to declare that a good historian should give voice to widespread beliefs, rather than create a critical dialogue between the present and the past.[76] This point is quite fundamental. Secondly, the invention of ancestors was not confined to families of recent or dubious origins. The Brahe, for example, had undoubted links to the royal family, but still traced their descent first to that fourteenth-century icon, St Bridget of Sweden, and then even further back to a twelfth-century King.[77] Long established families with no need to improve their origins, which were sufficiently distinguished, did so just as willingly: the invention of this kind of origin myth was common to almost all aristocratic Houses. These genealogies created descents, and the legends which these incorporated and came to surround them, must be taken seriously but not literally. Royal or Roman origins were particularly prized, as they furnished lineages with enormous symbolic capital which could be deployed in the permanent struggle for status and advancement.[78] The Brahes' claim that Charlemagne was one of their ancestors falls into this category.[79] By a final, delightful irony, one Italian family which created distinguished ancestors was none other than the Orsini itself![80]

In *The Leopard*, Giuseppe Tomasi di Lampedusa's striking evocation of the twilight of Sicily's aristocratic world in which he himself had grown to manhood, the ageing Prince of Salina meditates sombrely on the glue which he believed had held aristocratic lineages such as his own together over the centuries. 'The

---

73 Jouanna, "Les Guises et le sang de France", 32ff.

74 Above, Chapter 1.

75 Anthony Grafton, *What was History? The Art of History in Early Modern Europe* (Cambridge: Cambridge University Press, 2007).

76 Bizzocchi, "Culture généalogique", 796.

77 Above, Chapter 8.

78 Luc Duerloo rightly highlighted this point during the conference discussions.

79 Above, Chapter 8.

80 Bizzocchi, "Culture généalogique", 792.

significance of a noble family', Don Fabrizio concludes, 'lies entirely in its traditions, that is in its vital memories; and he was the last to have any unusual memories, anything different from those of other families'.[81] The individual elements which made up these memories and traditions, and the varied ways in which they were assembled, manipulated and transmitted down the generations, emerge in striking and persuasive detail from the studies in this volume, and are a final reminder of the central importance of dynastic identity in the history of the early modern higher nobility.

---

[81] Giuseppe Tomasi di Lampedusa, *The Leopard*, transl. A. Colquhoun (London: Vintage, 2005 ed.), 197.

Bibliography

Aalbers, Johan, H.M. Brokken, and L.J. van der Klooster. *Heren van stand: Van Wassenaer 1200–2000. Achthonderd jaar Nederlandse adelsgeschiedenis*. The Hague: Stichting Hollandse Historische Reeks, 2002.

Adams, Simon. "Spain or the Netherlands? The Dilemmas of Early Stuart Foreign Policy". In *Before the Civil War*, edited by Howard Tomlinson, 79–102. Basingstoke: Palgrave Macmillan, 1983.

———. "The Patronage of the Crown in Elizabethan Politics: the 1590s in Perspective". In *The Reign of Elizabeth I: Court and Culture in the Last Decade*, edited by John Guy, 20–45. Cambridge: Cambridge University Press, 1995.

———. "England und die Protestantischen Reichsfürsten 1599–1621". In *Dimensionen der europäischen Außenpolitik zur Zeit der Wende vom 16. zum 17. Jahrhundert*, edited by Friedrich Beiderbeck, Gregor Horstkemper, and Winfried Schulze, 61–84. Berlin: Berliner Wissenschafts-Verlag, 2003.

Adamson, John (ed.). *The Princely Courts of Europe: Ritual, Politics and Culture under the Ancien Régime 1500–1750*. Londen: Weidenfeld & Nicolson, 2000.

———. *The Noble Revolt, the Overthrow of Charles I*. London: Weidenfeld & Nicolson, 2007.

Ainsworth, John (ed). *Inchiquin Manuscripts*. Dublin: IMC, 1961.

Akkermans, Nadine, and Birgit Houben (eds). *The Politics of Female Households. Ladies-in-waiting across Early Modern Europe*. Leiden: Brill, 2013.

Anderson, Benedict R. O'G. *Imagined Communities: Reflections on the Origin and Spread of Nationalism*. London: Verso, 2006.

Anonymous. *A Brief Compendium of the Birth, Education, Heroick Exploits and Victories of the Truly Valorous and Renowned Gentleman, Thomas Earl of Ossory*. [London], 1680.

Anonymous. *An Elegy to the Memory of the Right Houorable [sic] Thomas, Earl of Ossory who depated [sic] this Life July the 30th, 1680*. London, 1680.

Antonetti, Guy. "Les princes étrangers". In *État et société en France aux XVIIe et XVIIIe siècles: Mélanges offerts à Yves Durand*, edited by Jean-Pierre Bardet, Dominique Dinet, Jean-Pierre Poussou, and Marie-Catherine Vignal, 33–62. Paris: Presses de l'Université Paris-Sorbonne, 2000.

Arenberg, Jean-Engelbert de. "De heren, graven, prins-graven en hertogen van Arenberg". In *Arenberg in de Lage Landen: een hoogadellijk huis in Vlaanderen en Nederland*, edited by Jan Roegiers et al., 13–51. Louvain: Leuven University Press, 2002.

Arrieta, Jon, and John H. Elliott. *Forms of Union: The British and Spanish Monarchies in the Seventeenth and Eighteenth Centuries*. Eusko Ikaskuntza: Editorial S.A. Sociedad de Estudios Vascos, 2009.

Asch, Ronald G. *Nobilities in Transition, 1550–1700: Courtiers and Rebels in Britain and Europe*. London: Hodder Arnold, 2003.

———. *Jakob I. (1566–1625). König von England und Schottland.* Stuttgart: Kohlhammer, 2005.

———. *Europäischer Adel in der Frühen Neuzeit*. Cologne: Böhlau, 2008.

———. *Die Stuarts. Geschichte einer Dynastie*. Munich: Beck, 2011.

———. *Sacral Kingship Between Disenchantment and Re-Enchantment: The French and English Monarchies, 1587–1688*. New York: Berghahn Books, 2014.

Asch, Ronald G., and Adolf M. Birke (eds). *Princes, Patronage, and the Nobility: the Court at the Beginning of the Modern Age c. 1450–1650*. Oxford: Oxford University Press, 1991.

Assmann, Aleida. "Re-framing Memory. Between Individual and Collective Forms of Constructing the Past". In *Performing the Past: Memory, History, and Identity in Modern Europe*, edited by Karin Tilmans, Frank van Vree, and Jay M. Winter, 35–50. Amsterdam: Amsterdam University Press, 2010.

Assman, Jan. *Das kulturelle Gedächtnis: Schrift, Erinnerung und politische Identität in frühen Hochkulturen*. Munich: Beck, 2000.

Aubert de La Chesnaye-Desbois, François-Alexandre, and J. Badier (eds). *Dictionnaire de la noblesse*, 10 volumes. Paris: Schlesinger frères, 1863–77.

Babaie, Sussan, Kathrin Babayan, Ina Baghdiantz-McCabe, and Massumeh Farhad. *Slaves of the Shah. New Elites of Safavid Iran*. London and New York: I.B. Tauris, 2004.

Backer, Anne Mieke. "Tuinkunst tijdens de Nederlandse Opstand. De prinses van Chimay, Marie de Brimeu en de 'humanisering' van de bloem 1550–1605". *Cascade. Bulletin voor Tuinhistorie* 15, no. 2 (2006): 14–39.

Baelde, Michel. *De collaterale raden onder Karel V en Filips II (1531–1578). Bijdrage tot de geschiedenis van de centrale instellingen in de zestiende eeuw*. Brussels: Koninklijke Vlaamse Academie voor Wetenschappen, Letteren en Schone Kunsten, 1965.

Balabanlilar, Lisa. *Imperial Identity in the Mughal Empire: Memory and Dynastic Politics in Early Modern South and Central Asia*. London: I.B. Tauris, 2012.

Baratier, Edouard. *Histoire de la Provence*. Toulouse: Privat, 1969.

Barilli, A. "Nuovi documenti su Alessandro Farnese", *Archivio storico per le province parmensi*, ser. III, 3 (1938), 91–2.

Barnard, Toby. "Land and the Limits of Loyalty: The Second Earl of Cork and First Earl of Burlington (1612–98)". In *Lord Burlington. Architecture, Art and Life*, edited by Toby Barnard and Jane Clark, 195–6. London: Hambledon Press, 1995.

———. *A New Anatomy of Ireland: Protestants in Ireland, 1649–1770*. New Haven: Yale University Press, 2003.

Barone, Nicola. *Notizie riguardanti l'archivio farnesiano di Napoli*. Naples: D'Auria, 1898.

Bastress-Dukehart, Erica. "Family, Property and Feeling in Early Modern German Noble Culture: The Zimmerns of Swabia". *Sixteenth Century Journal* 32 (2001): 1–19.

Bayart, Jean-François. *L'illusion identitaire*. Paris: Fayard, 1996.

———. *Les Princes de Condé: Rebelles, courtisans et mécènes dans la France du Grand Siècle*. Paris: Champ Vallon, 1999.

Béguin, Katia. "Louis XIV et l'aristocratie: coup de majesté ou retour à la tradition". *Histoire, économie et société* 19, no. 4 (2000): 497–512.

Behn, Aphra. *A Pindarick Poem on The Happy Coronation Of His Most Sacred Majesty James II And His Illustrious Consort Queen Mary*. London, 1685.

Beik, William. *Absolutism and Society in Seventeenth-Century France. State Power and Provincial Aristocracy in Languedoc*. Cambridge: Cambridge University Press, 1985.

Bellany, Alastair. "'The Enigma of the World'. Memorializing and Remembering George Villiers, First Duke of Buckingham in the Aftermath of Assassination, c. 1628–1642". In *Zwischen Schande und Ehre. Erinnerungsbrüche und die Kontinuität des Hauses. Legitimationsmuster und Traditionsverständnis des frühneuzeitlichen Adels in Umbruch und Krise*, edited by Martin Wrede and Horst Carl, 27–52. Mainz: Zabern, 2007.

Bellonci, Maria. *Segreti dei Gonzaga*, revised edition. Milan: Mondadori, 1981.

Bellù, Adele. "Margherita Farnese, sposa mancata di Vincenzo Gonzaga". *Archivi per la storia* 1 (1988): 381–420.

Bely, Lucien (ed.). *Dictionnaire de l'Ancien Régime*. Paris: Presses universitaires de France, 1996.

———. *La Société des princes, XVIe-XVIIIe siècle*. Paris: Fayard, 1999.

Bergin, Joseph. *Crown, Church and Episcopate under Louis XIV*. Yale: Yale University Press, 2004.

Bertini, Giuseppe. "Alessandro Farnese fra Italia, Spagna e Paesi Bassi". In *Uomini di governo italiani al servizio della Monarchia spagnola (secoli XVI e XVII)*, edited by Carlos José Hernando Sanchez and Gianvittorio Signorotto, 71–95. Rome: Bulzoni, 2011.

Biondi, Albano. "L'immagine dei primi Farnese (1545–1622) nella storiografia e nella pubblicistica coeva". In *Le corti farnesiane di Parma e Piacenza, 1545–1622*, vol. 1: *Potere e società nello stato farnesiano*, edited by Marzio Achille Romani and Amedeo Quondam, 189–229. Rome, Bulzoni 1978.

Bizzocchi, Roberto. "La culture généalogique dans l'Italie du XVIe siècle". *Annales. Économies, Sociétés, Civilisations* 46 (1991): 789–805.

———. *Genealogie incredibili: Scritti di storia nell'Europa moderna*. Bologna: Il Mulino, 1995, revised edition, 2009.

———. *Généalogies fabuleuses: Inventer et faire croire dans l'Europe moderne*. Paris: Editions Rue d'Ulm, 2010.

Blanquie, Christophe. "Dans la main du Grand maître. Les offices de la maison du roi, 1643–1720". *Histoire & Mesure* 13, no. 3–4 (1998): 243–88.

Bodart, Didier. "Cérémonies et monuments romains à la mémoire d'Alexandre Farnèse duc de Parme et de Plaisance". *Bulletin de l'Institut historique belge de Rome* 37 (1966): 121–36.

Bodenhorn, Barbara, and Gabriele vom Bruck. "'Entangled in Histories': An Introduction to the Anthropology of Names and Naming". In *The Anthropology of Names and Naming*, edited by Barbara Bodenhorn and Gabriele vom Bruck, 1–30. Cambridge: Cambridge University Press, 2006.

Boiteux, Martine. "Le palais Farnèse: La représentation et l'identité". *Mélanges de l'École française de Rome: Italie et Méditerranée* 122 (2010): 311–38.

Bol, Peter. "The 'Localist Turn' and 'Local Identity' in Later Imperial China". *Late Imperial China* 24, no. 2 (2003): 1–50.

Boltanski, Ariane. *Les Ducs des Nevers et l'État royal. Genèse d'un compromis (ca. 1550-ca. 1600)*. Geneva: Droz, 2006.

Bork, Gerrit Jan van, and Peter Jozias Verkruijsse (eds). *De Nederlandse en Vlaamse auteurs van middeleeuwen tot heden met inbegrip van de Friese auteurs*. Weesp: De Haan, 1985.

Born, Robert. *Les Croÿ, une grande lignée hennuyère d'hommes de guerre, de diplomates, de conseillers secrets, dans les coulisses du pouvoir, sous les ducs de Bourgogne et la Maison d'Autriche (1390–1612)*. Brussels: Editeurs d'art associés, 1981.

Bouchard, Constance Brittain. *'Those of my blood'. Constructing Noble Families in Medieval Francia*. Pennsylvania: University of Pennsylvania Press, 2001.

Bourquin, Laurent. *Noblesse seconde et pouvoir en Champagne aux XVIe et XVIIe siècles*. Paris: Publications de la Sorbonne, 1994.

Bouvet, Joachim. *Histoire de l'empereur de la Chine*. Paris, 1697.

Braake, Serge ter. *Manifest van de ware vrijheid. De Deductie van Johan de Witt uit 1654*. Arnhem: Sonsbeek Publishers, 2009.

Brandel, Sven, and Tord Nordberg. *Östra Ryds kyrka. Sveriges kyrkor*. Stockholm: Almqvist & Wiksell, 1928.

Brook, Timothy. *The Troubled Empire. China in the Yuan and Ming Dynasties*. Cambridge, MA: Harvard University Press, 2010.

Broomhall, Susan, and Jacqueline Van Gent. "Corresponding Affections: Emotional Exchange Among Siblings in the Nassau Family". *Journal of Family History* 34 (2009): 143–65.

Broomhall, Susan, and Jacqueline Van Gent. "In the Name of the Father: Conceptualizing Pater Familias in the letters of William the Silent's Children". *Renaissance Quarterly* 62 (2009): 1130–66.

Broomhall, Susan, and Colette H. Winn. *Les femmes et l'histoire familiale (xvie-xviie siècle)*. Paris: Champion, 2008.

Brown, B. Bradford, Reed W. Larson, and T. S. Saraswathi (eds). *The World's Youth: Adolescence in Eight Regions of the Globe*. Cambridge: Cambridge University Press, 2002.

Brown, Keith M. "The Scottish Aristocracy, Anglicization and the Court, 1603–38". *The Historical Journal* 36 (1993): 543–76.

Brown, Michael. "Aristocratic Politics and the Crisis of Scottish kingship, 1286–1296". *The Scottish Historical Review* 90 (2011): 1–26.

Brown, Peter. *Power and Persuasion in Late Antiquity, Towards a Christian Empire*. Wisconsin: University of Wisconsin Press, 1992.

Brunelli, Giampiero. "'Sopra tutto fu inclinatissimo alla religione'. La *Vita dell'illustrissimo signor Camillo Orsino* di Giuseppe Orologi". In *Nunc alia tempora, alii mores. Storici e storia in età postridentina. Atti del convegno internazionale, Torino, 24–27 settembre 2003*, edited by Massimo Firpo, 429–52. Florence: L.S. Olschki, 2005.

Brunnner, Otto. *Land und Herrschaft: Grundfragen der territorialen Verfassungsgeschichte Österreichs im Mittelalter*. Baden-bei-Wien: Rohrer, 1939.

Burke, Peter. *Cultural Hybridity*. Cambridge: Cambridge University Press, 2010.

Butaud, Germain and Valérie Piétri. *Les enjeux de la généalogie XIIe-XVIIIe siècle: pouvoir et identité*. Paris: Autrement, 2006.

Butler, Lee. *Emperor and Aristocracy in Japan, 1467–1680: Resilience and Renewal*. Cambridge, MA: Harvard University Press, 2002.

Buylaert, Frederik. "Edelen in de Vlaamse stedelijke samenleving: een kwantitatieve benadering van de elite van het laatmiddeleeuwse en vroegmoderne Brugge". *Tijdschrift voor sociale en economische geschiedenis* 4 (2007): 29–56.

———. *Eeuwen van ambitie. De adel in laatmiddeleeuws Vlaanderen*. Brussels: Koninklijke Vlaamse Academie van België der Wetenschappen, 2010.

———. "La noblesse et l'unification des Pays-Bas. Naissance d'une noblesse bourguignonne à la fin du Moyen Âge?" *Revue historique* 653 (2010): 3–25.

Buylaert, Frederik, and Jan Dumolyn. "L'importance sociale, politique et culturelle de la haute noblesse dans les Pays-Bas Bourguignons et Habsbourgeois (1475–1525): un état de la question". In *Entre la ville, la noblesse et l'état: Philippe de Clèves (1456–1528), homme politique et bibliophile*, edited by Jelle Haemers, Céline Van Hoorebeeck and Hanno Wijsman, 279–94. Turnhout: Brepols, 2008.

Caball, Marc. "Bardic Poetry and the Analysis of Gaelic mentalities". *History Ireland* 2 (1994): 46–50.

Cabourdin, Guy. *Encyclopédie illustrée de la Lorraine: Les temps modernes. Vol 1: De la Renaissance à la guerre de Trente ans*. Nancy: Éd. Serpenoise u.a., 1991.

Cadoppi, Alberto. *Gabriele Bombasi, letterato reggiano (1531–1602): una vita fra l'Ariosto, il Correggio, i Farnese e i Carracci*. Modena: Nuova Futurgraf, 2010.

Calendar of the Manuscripts of the Marquess of Ormonde, preserved at Kilkenny Castle. Old and New Series, 11 vols. London 1895–1920.

Callaey, Fredegand (religious name Fredegand van Antwerpen). *La vie religieuse et familiale en Belgique au XVIIe siècle: étude sur le Père Charles d'Arenberg, frère-mineur capucin (1593–1669)*. Paris: Librairie Saint François, 1919.

Canny, Nicholas. *The Upstart Earl. A Study of the Social and Mental World of Richard Boyle First Earl of Cork, 1566–1643*. Cambridge: Cambridge University Press, 1982.

———. *Making Ireland British, 1580–1650*. Oxford: Oxford University Press, 2001.

Canosa, Romano. *I segreti dei Farnese*. Rome: Sapere, 2001.

Cappelli, Adriano. "Alessandro Farnese ed i Parmigiani alla Battaglia di Lepanto". *Aurea Parma* 2, fasc. 1–2 (1913): 4–9.

Caputo, Vincenzo. *La 'bella maniera di scrivere vita': biografie di uomini d'arme e di stato nel secondo Cinquecento*. Naples: Edizioni scientifiche italiane, 2009.

Carl, Horst, and Martin Wrede (eds). *Zwischen Schande und Ehre. Erinnerungsbrüche und die Kontinuität des Hauses. Legitimationsmuster und Traditionsverständnis des frühneuzeitlichen Adels in Umbruch und Krise*. Mainz: Zabern, 2007.

Carrasco Martínez, Adolfo. *El Poder de la Sangre: Los duques del Infantado 1601–1841*. San Sebastian de los Reyes: Actas Editorial, 2010.

Carroll, Stuart. *Martyrs and Murderers. The Guise Family and the Making of Europe*. Oxford: Oxford University Press, 2009.

Carte, Thomas. *The Life of James Duke of Ormond*, 6 volumes. Oxford: Oxford University Press, 1851.

Cassol, Allessandro. *Vita e scrittura. Autobiografie di soldati spagnoli del Siglo de Oro*. Milan: LED, 2000.

Cauchie, Alfred, and Léon van der Essen. *Inventaire des archives farnésiennes de Naples au point de vue de l'histoire des Pays-Bas catholiques*. Brussels: Kiessling, 1911.

Cavallera, Marina. "Les fiefs impériaux dans l'Italie nord-occidentale au XVIIIe siècle". In *Les enclaves territoriales aux Temps Modernes (XVIe-XVIIIe siècles)*, edited by Paul Delsalle and André Ferrer, 185–208. Besançon: Presses Universitaires de Franche-Comté, 2000.

Chalus, Elaine. *Elite Women in English Political Life, c.1754–1790*. Oxford: Clarendon, 2005.

Chan, Hok-Lam. "Ming Taizu's Problem with His Sons: Prince Qin's Criminality and Early-Ming Politics". *Asia Major* 20, no. 1 (2007): 45–103.

Châtelet, Albert. "Antoine de Croÿ et Hugo van der Goes". In *Der Fall des Günstlings. Hofparteien in Europa vom 13. Bis zum 17. Jahrhundert*, edited by Jan Hirschbiegel and Werner Paravicini, 481–7. Stuttgart: Thorbecke, 2004.

Chen, Jack W. *The Poetics of Sovereignty: On Emperor Taizong of the Tang Dynasty*. Cambridge, MA: Harvard University Press, 2010.

"Chronique: L. van der Essen (Louvain), Une source inconnue pour l'histoire du gouvernement d'Alexandre Farnèse aux Pays-Bas espagnols", *Revue belge de philologie et d'histoire* 9 (1930): 685.

Chung, Priscilla Ching. *Palace Women in the Northern Sung 960–1126*. Leiden: Brill, 1981.

Clarendon, Edward Hyde, earl of. *The History of the Rebellion and Civil Wars in England*. Edited by William Dunn Macray. 6 volumes. Oxford: Oxford University Press, 1888.

Clarke, Aidan. "The Policies of the 'Old English' in Parliament, 1640–1". In *Historical Studies V*, edited by J. L. McCracken, 85–102. London: Books for Libraries Press, 1965.

———. "Colonial Identity in Early Seventeenth Century Ireland". In *Historical Studies XI. Nationality and the Pursuit of National Independence*, edited by T.W. Moody, 57–71. Belfast: Appletree Press, 1978.

Clavero, Bartolomé. *Mayorazgo: Propriedad feudal en Castilla 1369–1836*. Madrid: Siglo Veintiuno, 1974; 2nd ed., Madrid: Siglo XXI de España, 1989.

Clunas, Craig. *Screen of Kings: Royal Art and Power in Ming China*. London: Reaktion, 2013.

Cockerham, Paul. "'To mak a Tombe for the Earell of Ormon and to set it up in Iarland': Renaissance Ideals in Irish Funeral Monuments". In *Ireland in the Renaissance, c.1540–1660*, edited by Thomas Herron and Michael Potterton, 195–230. Dublin: Four Courts Press, 2007.

Cocula, Anne Marie. "Les trois dimensions de la conspiration de Biron". In *Les lettres au temps de Henri IV = L'Avènement d'Henri IV, quatrième centenaire*, edited by Association pour la Commémoration de l'Avènement d'Henri IV au Trône de France, vol. 4, 341–58. Pau: Association Henry IV, 1989–1991.

Cogswell, Thomas. *The Blessed Revolution: English Politics and the Coming of War, 1621–1624*. Cambridge: Cambridge University Press, 1989.

———. "The People's Love: The Duke of Buckingham and Popularity". In *Politics Religion and Popularity in Early Stuart Britain*, edited by Thomas Cogswell, Richard Cust, and Peter Lake, 211–34. Cambridge: Cambridge University Press, 2002.

Colby-Hall, Alice. "Guillaume au Court Nez et les premiers historiens d'Orange". In *Studies in Honor of Hans-Erich Keller. Medieval French and Occitan Literature and Romance Linguistics*, edited by Rupert T. Pickens, 151–64. Kalamazoo: Medieval Institute Publication, 1993.

Cole, Mary Hill. *The Portable Queen. Elizabeth I and the Politics of Ceremony*. Amherst: University of Massachusetts Press, 1999.

Coloma, Carlos. *Las guerras de los Estados Bajos, desde el año de 1588 hasta el de 1599*. Madrid: Ediciones Atlas, 1948.

Commentario del coronel Francisco Verdugo de la guerra de Frisa en XIIII años que fue governador y capitan general de aquel estado y exercito por el rey D. Phelippe II, nuestro senor, edited by Henri Lonchay. Brussels: Kiessling, 1899.

Constant, Jean-Marie. *Les Guise*. Paris: Hachette, 1984.

———. *La vie quotidienne de la noblesse française aux XVIe et XVIIe siècles*. Paris: Hachette, 1985.

———. *La folle liberté des baroques (1600–1661)*. Paris: Perrin, 2007.

Coolidge, Grace E. *Guardianship, Gender and the Nobility in Early Modern Spain*. Farnham: Ashgate, 2011.

Cools, Hans. "Noblemen on the Borderline: The Nobility of Picardy, Artois and Walloon Flanders and the Habsburg-Valois Conflict, 1477–1529". In *Secretum Scriptorum. Liber alumnorum Walter Prevenier*, edited by Wim Blockmans, Marc Boone, and Thérèse de Hemptinne, 371–82. Leuven and Apeldoorn: Garant, 1999.

———. *Mannen met Macht. Edellieden en de Moderne Staat in de Bourgondisch-Habsburgse landen (1475–1530)*. Zutphen: Walburg, 2001.

Cooper, J.P. "Patterns of inheritance by great landowners from the fifteenth to the eighteenth centuries". In *Family and Inheritance: Rural Society in Western Europe, 1200–1800*, edited by Jack Goody, Joan Thirsk and E.P. Thompson, 192–327. Cambridge: Cambridge University Press, 1976.

Coppens, Thera. *Buren, Egmond en Oranje*. Buren: Stichting Oud Buren, 1989.

Coreth, Anna. *Pietas austriaca: Ursprung und Entwicklung barocker Frömmigkeit in Österreich*. Munich: Oldenbourg, 1959.

Cornette, Joel (ed.). *Mémoires, suivis de Manière de montrer les jardins de Versailles*. Paris: Tallandier, 2007.

———. *Henri IV à Saint-Denis. De l'abjuration à la profanation*. Paris: Belin, 2010.

Costa Gomes, Rita. *The Making of a Court Society: Kings and Nobles in Late Medieval Portugal*. Cambridge: Cambridge University Press, 2003.

Courcelles, Jean-Baptiste de. *Histoire généalogique et héraldique des pairs de France ... et maisons princières de l'Europe*. Paris, 1822–1833.

Crawford, Katherine. "The Politics of Promiscuity: Masculinity and Heroic Representation at the Court of Henry IV". *French Historical Studies* 26 (2003): 225–62.

Cressy, David. "Binding the Nation. The Bonds of Association, 1584 and 1696". In *Tudor Rule and Revolution*, edited by Delloyd J.Guth and John W. McKenna, 217–34. Cambridge: Cambridge University Press, 1982.

Crouch, David. *The Birth of Nobility. Constructing Aristocracy in England and France 900–1300*. Harlow: Pearson/Longman, 2005.

Crouzet, Denis. *Charles de Bourbon, Connétable de France*. Paris: Fayard, 2003.

Cuddy, Neil. "Anglo-Scottish Union and the Court of James I, 1603–1625". *Transactions of the Royal Historical Society*, Fifth Series 39 (1989): 107–24.

Cunningham, Bernadette. "Irish Language Sources for Early Modern Ireland". *History Ireland* 4 (1996): 41–8.

———. "Colonized Catholics: Perceptions of Honour and History in Michael Kearney's Reading of *Foras feasa ar Éirinn*". In *Taking Sides. Colonial and Confessional Mentalités in Early Modern Ireland*, edited by Vincent P. Carey and Ute Lotz-Heumann, 150–64. Dublin: Four Courts Press, 2003.

Cunningham, Bernadette, and Raymond Gillespie. "Brian Maguire of Knockninny and his manuscripts". *Clogher Record* 13 (1988): 38–49.

Dai, Yingcong. "Broken Passage to the Summit: Nayancheng's Botched Mission in the White Lotus War". In *Agents and Interactions. The Dynastic Center and the Provinces,* edited by Jeroen Duindam and Sabine Dabringhaus, 49–73. Leiden and Boston: Brill, 2014.

Damen, Mario. "Heren met banieren. De baanrotsen van Brabant in de vijftiende eeuw". In *Bourgondië voorbij. De Nederlanden 1250–1650*, edited by Mario Damen and Louis Sicking, 139–58. Hilversum: Verloren, 2010.

Damen, Mario. "Rivalité nobiliaire et succession princière: La lutte pour le pouvoir à la cour de Bavière et à la cour de Bourgogne". *Revue du Nord* 91 (2009): 361–83.

Dangeau, Philippe de Courcillon, marquis de. *Journal*. Edited by E. Soulié et al. Paris: Firmin Didot frères, 1854–60.

Dansaert, Georges and Thierry de Limburg-Stirum, *Guillaume de Croÿ-Chièvres*. Kortrijk: J. Vermaut, 1942.

Daussy, Hugues. *Les Huguenots et le roi. Le combat politique de Philippe Duplessis-Mornay (1572–1600)*. Geneva: Droz, 2002.

Davis, Rees. "The Medieval State: The Tyranny of a Concept?" *Journal of Historical Sociology* 16 (2003): 280–97.

Daybelle, James (ed.). *Women and Politics in Early Modern England, 1450–1700*. Aldershot: Ashgate, 2004.

De Clercq, Wim, Jan Dumolyn, and Jelle Haemers. "Material Culture and Elite Identity in Late Medieval Flanders". *Journal of Interdisciplinary History* 38 (2007): 1–31.

De Fraine, Piet. "Gouvernés et gouvernants au pays et duché d'Aerschot". In: *500 jaar parlementair leven in België: assemblées d'états, 1464–1964*, 183–94. Louvain: Nauwelaerts, 1966.

———. "1612–1640: le Duché d'Aerschot passe de la Maison de Croy à la Maison d'Arenberg". *Le Folklore Brabançon* 173 (1967): 67–89.

De Groof, Bart. "Alexander Farnese and the Origins of Modern Belgium". In *La dimensione europea dei Farnese*, edited by Bart de Groof and Eugenio Galdieri, 195–219. Rome and Brussels: Institut historique belge de Rome, 1993.

———. "Una questione di priorità: spagnoli, italiani e fiamminghi alla morte di Alessandro Farnese". In *I Farnese. Corti, guerra e nobiltà in antico regime. Atti del convegno di studi, Piacenza, 24–26 nov. 1994*, edited by Antonella Billotto, Piero Del Negro and Cesaro Mozzarelli, 167–87. Roma: Bulzoni, 1997.

Delaborde, Jules. "Antoine de Croy, Prince de Porcien". *Bulletin de la société de l'histoire du protestantisme français* 18 (1896): 7–10.

de la Cuadra Blanco, Juan Rafael. "La idea original de los enterramientos reales en El Escorial". *Boletín de la Real Academia de Bellas Artes de San Fernando* 85 (1997): 375–413.

De la Gardiska archivet eller handlingar ur Grefl. Dela Gardiska Bibliotheket på Löberöd. Edited by Peter Wieselgren. Lund: Hörberg, 1836.

Delannoy, Yves. *La cession de la seigneurie d'Enghien par Henri IV à Charles d'Arenberg en 1607*. Gemeentekrediet historische uitgaven. Reeks in-8° 76. Brussel: Gemeentekrediet, 1988.

Delorme, Pierre. *Les Grimaldi. 700 ans d'une dynastie*. Poitiers: Aubin Imprimeur, 1998.

Demel, Walter. "Die Spezifika des europäischen Adels. Erste Überlegungen zu einem globalhistorischen Thema". *Zeitenblicke* 4, 3 (2005).

Dempsey, Charles. "Annibale Carrache au Palais Farnese", in *Le Palais Farnèse*. Rome: Ecole française de Rome, 1981.

Denunzio, Antonio Ernesto. "Strategie diplomatiche e vicende dinastiche: le pretese dei Farnese nella successione al trono di Portogallo (1578–1580)". In *Maria di Portogallo, sposa di Alessandro Farnese, principessa di Parma e Piacenza dal 1565 al 1577*, edited by Giuseppe Bertini, 224–58. Parma: Ducati, 2001.

Derks, Sebastiaan. "Le ricompense della guerra: giustificazione e rappresentazione di Alessandro Farnese nel Liber relationum di Paolo Rinaldi". In Giuseppe Bertini (ed.), *Militari italiani dell'esercito di Alessandro Farnese nelle Fiandre. Atti della giornata di studio, Fontevivo, 24 settembre 2011*, edited by Giuseppe Bertini, 205–30. Fidenza: Mattioli, 2013.

Schepper, Hugo de. "De katholieke Nederlanden van 1589 tot 1609". In *Algemene Geschiedenis der Nederlanden*, edited by D.P. Blok et al., 15 vols, vol. 6, 279–97. Haarlem: Fibula-Van Dishoeck, 1977–1983.

———. "Le gouverneur général Peter Ernst von Mansfeld et les agents espagnols Fuentes e Ibarra aux Pays Bas en 1593". In *España y los Países bajos, siglos XVI-XVII. Agentes e identidades en movimiento*, edited by René Vermeir, Maurits Ebben, and Raimond Fagel, 89–112. Madrid: Silex, 2011.

Descimon, Robert. "Les noblesses à l'époque moderne: chercher de nouvelles voies pour interpréter les phénomènes nobiliaires dans la France moderne: la noblesse, 'essence' ou rapport social?" *Revue d'Histoire Moderne et Contemporaine* 46 (1999): 5–21.

———. "*Nobles de lignage* et *Noblesse de service*. Sociogenèses comparées de l'épée et de la robe (XVe-XVIIIe siècle)". In *Épreuves de noblesse. Les expériences nobiliaires de la haute robe parisienne (XVIe-XVIIIe siècle)*, edited by Robert Descimon and Élie Haddad, 277–302. Paris: Les Belles lettres, 2010.

Desprat, Jean-Paul. *Les bâtards d'Henri IV: L'épopée des Vendômes 1594–1727*. Paris: Perin, 1994.

Deursen, Arie Theodorus van. *Maurits van Nassau. De winnaar die faalde*. Amsterdam: Bakker, 2002.

De Vries, Joyce. *Caterina Sforza and the Art of Appearance: Gender, Art and Culture in Early Modern Italy*. Farnham: Ashgate, 2010.

De Waele, Michel. "Clemence royale et fidelités françaises à la fin des Guerres de Religion". *Historical Reflections* 24 (1998): 232–52.

———. "Henri IV, politicien monarchomaque? Les contrats de fidelité entre le roi et les Français". In *Le traité de Vervins*, edited by Jean-François Labourdette, Jean-Pierre Poussou, and Marie-Catherine Vignal, 120–31. Paris: Presses de l'Université de Paris-Sorbonne, 2000.

Dewald, Jonathan. *The European Nobility 1400–1800*. Cambridge: Cambridge University Press, 1996.

De Win, Paul. "Antoine de Croy, seigneur de Crouy, comte de Porcien". In *Les chevaliers de l'Ordre de la Toison d'or au XVe siècles. Notice bio-bibliographiques*, edited by Ralph De Smedt, 34–6. Frankfurt am Main: Peter Lang, 2000.

Devyer, André. *Le Sang Épuré: Les préjugés de race chez les gentilshommes français de l'Ancien Régime (1560–1720)*. Brussels: Editions de l'Université de Bruxelles, 1973.

Dickerman, Edmund H., and Anita M. Walker. "Thc Choice of Hercules: Henry IV as Hero". *Historical Journal* 39 (1996): 315–37.

Dickerman, Edmund H., and Anita M. Walker. "The Politics of Honour. Henri IV and the Duke of Bouillon, 1602–1606". *French History* 14 (2000): 383–407.

Di Cosmo, Nicola. "Qing Colonial Administration in Inner Asia". *International History Review* 20, no. 2 (1998): 287–309.

——— (ed.). *Military Culture in Imperial China*. Cambridge, MA: Harvard University Press, 2009.

Dierickx, Michel. "Les Carte Farnesiane de Naples par rapport à l'Histoire des anciens Pays-Bas, après l'incendie du 30 septembre 1943". *Bulletin de la Commission royale d'histoire* 112 (1947): 111–26.

Doran, Susan. "James VI and the English Succession". In *James VI and I: Authority, Ideas and Government, 1566–1625*, edited by Ralph Houlbrooke, 25–42. Aldershot: Ashgate, 2006.

Drei, Giovanni. *I Farnese: grandezza e decadenza di una dinastia italiana*. Rome: La Libreria dello Stato, 1954.

Duerloo, Luc. "*Pietas Albertina*. Dynastieke vroomheid en herbouw van het vorstelijk gezag". *BMGN – Low Countries Historical Review* 112 (1997): 1–18.

———. "Arenberg in de Habsburgse Nederlanden". In *Arenberg in de Lage Landen: een hoogadellijk huis in Vlaanderen en Nederland*, edited by Jan Roegiers et al., 58–80. Louvain: Leuven University Press, 2002.

———. "Het blazoen ontsmet. Adellijke heraldiek als toe-eigening van eer en deugd, 1550–1750". *BMGN – Low Countries Historical Review* 123 (2008): 633–54.

———. *Dynasty and Piety: Archduke Albert (1598 – 16 21) and Habsburg Political Culture in an Age of Religious Wars*. Aldershot: Ashgate, 2012.

Duerloo, Luc, and Liesbeth De Frenne (eds). *Het verdeelde huis: De Nederlandse adel tussen opstand en reconciliatie*. Maastricht: Shaker, 2011.

Du Halde, Jean Baptiste. *Description géographique, historique, chronologique, politique, et physique de l'empire de la Chine et de la Tartarie chinoise*. The Hague: 1736–1737.

Duhamelle, Christophe. "The Making of Stability: Kinship, Church, and Power among the Rhenish Imperial Knighthood, Seventeenth and Eighteenth Centuries". In *Kinship in Europe. Approaches to Long-Term Development*

(1300–1900), edited by David Warren Sabean, Simon Teuscher, and Jon Mathieu, 125–44. New York and Oxford: Berghahn Books, 2007.

Duindam, Jeroen. *Myths of Power. Norbert Elias and the Early Modern European Court*. Amsterdam: Amsterdam University Press, 1995.

———. *Vienna and Versailles. The Courts of Europe's Dynastic Rivals*. Cambridge: Cambridge University Press, 2003.

———. "Versailles, Vienna, and Beyond: Changing Views of Household and Government in Early Modern Europe". In *Royal Courts in Dynastic States and Empires: A Global Perspective*, edited by Jeroen Duindam, Metin Kunt and Tulay Artan, 401–31. Leiden, Boston: Brill, 2001.

———. *Dynasties. A Global History of Power 1300–1800*. Cambridge: Cambridge University Press, 2015.

Duindam, Jeroen, Tülay Artan and Metin Kunt (eds). *Royal Courts in Dynastic States and Empires: A Global Perspective*. Leiden: Brill, 2011.

Dumont, Henri (ed.). *Corps universel diplomatique du droit des gens*. 4 vols. Amsterdam, 1739.

Duncan, Sarah. *Mary I: Gender, Power, and Ceremony in the Reign of England's First Queen*. New York: Palgrave Macmillan, 2012.

Dumville, David. "Kingship, Genealogies and Regnal Lists". In *Early Medieval Kingship*, edited by Peter H. Sawyer and Ian N. Wood, 72–104. Leeds: University of Leeds, 1977.

Eastman, Lloyd E. *Family, Fields, and Ancestors. Constancy and Change in China's Social and Economic History*. Oxford and New York: Oxford University Press, 1988.

Ebrey, Patricia B. "Shifts in Marriage Finance from the Sixth to the Thirteenth Century". In *Marriage and Inequality in Chinese Society*, edited by Rubie S. Watson and Patricia Buckley Ebrey, 97–132. Berkeley: University of California Press, 1991.

——— (ed.). *Chinese Civilization: A Sourcebook*. New York: Free Press, 1993.

———. "Succession to High Office: The Chinese Case". In *Culture, Technology and History: Implications of the Anthropological Work of Jack Goody*, edited by David R. Olson and Michael Cole, 49–71. Lawrence: Psychology Press, 2006.

Edwards, David. *The Ormond Lordship in County Kilkenny, 1515–1642. The Rise and Fall of Butler Feudal Power*. Dublin: Four Courts Press, 2003.

Edwards, Kathryn. *Families and Frontiers. Recreating Communities and Boundaries in the Early Modern Burgundies*. Leiden: Brill, 2002.

Eisenberg, Andrew. "Weberian Patrimonialism and Imperial Chinese History". *Theory and Society* 27, no. 1 (1998): 83–102.

Eglauer, Martina. "Family and Household in Late-Imperial China". In *Agriculture, Population and Economic Development in China and Europe*, edited by Rolf Peter Sieferle and Helga Breuninger, 276–310. Stuttgart: Breuninger-Stiftung, 2003.

Elias, Norbert. *Die höfische Gesellschaft*. Darmstadt and Neuwied: Luchterhand, 1969.

———. *The Court Society*. New York: Pantheon, 1983.

Elliott, J.H. "A Europe of Composite Monarchies". *Past and Present* 137 (1992): 48–71.

Elliott, Mark C., *The Manchu Way: The Eight Banners and Ethnic Identity in Manchu China*. Stanford: Stanford University Press, 2001.

Elman, Benjamin A. "Political, Social, and Cultural Reproduction via Civil Service Examinations in Late Imperial China". *The Journal of Asian Studies* 50, no.1 (1991): 7–28.

———. "The Social Roles of Literati in Early to Mid-Ch'ing', in *The Cambridge History of China*, vol. 9, *The Ch'ing Empire to 1800*, vol 1. 360–427. Cambridge: Cambridge University Press, 2002.

Eriksson, Bo. *I skuggan av tronen. En biografi över Per Brahe d.ä.* Stockholm: Prisma, 2009.

Esherick, Joseph. *Ancestral Leaves: A Family Journey Through Chinese History.* London, Berkeley, Los Angeles: University of California Press, 2011.

Esherick, Joseph W. and Mary Backus Rankin, "Concluding remarks", *Chinese Local Elites and Patterns of Dominance*, edited by Joseph W. Esherick and Mary Backus Rankin. Berkeley: University of California Press, 1990.

Esteban Estríngana, Alicia. *Guerra y finanzas en los Países Bajos católicos: De Farnesio a Spínola, 1592–1630.* Madrid: Laberinto, 2002.

Evans, R.J.W. *The Making of the Habsburg Monarchy 1550–1700. An Interpretation.* Oxford: Clarendon Press, 1979.

Expilly, Jean-Joseph. *Dictionnaire géographique, historique et politique des Gaules et de la France.* 6 vols. Amsterdam, 1764.

Fantoni, M. (ed.). *Il 'perfetto capitano'. Immagini e realtà (secoli XV-XVII): atti dei seminari di studi Georgetown University a Villa 'Le Balze', Istituto di Studi Rinascimentale di Ferrara 1995–1997.* Rome: Bulzoni, 2001.

Farmer, Edward. *Zhu Yuanzhang and Early Ming Legislation: The Reordering of Chinese Society Following the End of Mongol Rule.* Leiden: Brill, 1995.

Fea, P. *Alessandro Farnese, duca di Parma, narrazione storica e militare, scritta colla scorta di documenti inediti.* Rome, 1886.

———. *Il duca Alessandro Farnese e le carte dell'Archivio napoletano.* Parma: 1914.

Fernández Abaladejo, Pablo (ed.). *Los Borbones: Dinastía y memoria de nación en la España del Siglo XVIII.* Madrid: Marcial Pons/Casa de Velázquez, 2001.

Fletcher, Joseph. "Turco-Mongolian Monarchic Tradition in the Ottoman Empire". *Harvard Ukrainian Studies* 3–4 (1979–1980): 236–51.

Fletcher, Reginald J. (ed.). *The Pension Book of Gray's Inn 1569–1669.* London, 1901.

Filangieri, Riccardo. *L'Archivio di Stato di Napoli durante la seconda guerra mondiale*, edited by Stefano Palmieri. Naples: Arte Tipografica, 1996.

Finucci, V. *The Prince's Body: Vincenzo Gonzaga and Renaissance Medicine.* Cambridge, MA: Harvard University Press, 2015.

Formel, François. *Alliances et Généalogie à la Cour du Grand Roi: Le souci généalogique chez Saint-Simon.* 4 vols. Paris: Éditions Contrepoint, 1983.

Francisco Verdugo: Verslag over mijn jaren als legerleider en gouverneur namens Filips II in Stad en Lande van Groningen, Drenthe, Friesland, Overijssel en Lingen (1581–1595), edited by J. van den Broek. Assen: Koninklijke Van Gorcum, 2009.

Franklin, Julian H. “Sovereignty and the Mixed Constitution: Bodin and his critics”. In *The Cambridge History of Political Thought 1450–1700*, edited by J.H. Burns and Mark Goldie, 298–328. Cambridge: Cambridge University Press, 1991.

French, Nicholas. *The Unkinde Desertor of Loyall Men and True Frinds* [Paris], 1676.

Friedeburg, Robert von. “In Defense of Patria: Resisting Magistrates and the Duties of Patriots in the Empire from the 1530s to the 1640s”. *Sixteenth Century Journal* 32 (2001): 357–82.

Friedrich, Markus. *Die Geburt des Archivs: Eine Wissensgeschichte.* Munich: Oldenbourg Wissenschaftsverlag, 2013.

Fries, Ellen. *Teckningar ur svenska adelns familjelif i gamla tider.* Stockholm: Norstedt, 1910.

Fuchs, Lawrence H. *The American Kaleidoscope: Race, Ethnicity, and the Civic Culture.* Middletown: Wesleyan University Press, 1990.

Gaber, Stephane. *Et Charles V arrêta la marche des Turcs ... Un lorrain sauveur de l'occident chrétien.* Nancy: Presses universitaires de Nancy, 1986.

Gachard, Louis Prosper. “Les archives farnésiennes à Naples”. *Compte rendu des séances de la Commission royale d'histoire* 9 (1869).

Galloway, Bruce. *The Union of England and Scotland, 1603–1608.* Edinburgh: John Donald, 1986.

García García, Bernardo J. “Ranuccio I Farnesio y la gloria del principe”. In *I Farnese. Corti, guerra e nobiltà in antico regime. Atti del convegno di studi, Piacenza, 24–26 nov. 1994*, edited by Antonella Billotto, Piero Del Negro and Cesaro Mozzarelli. Roma: Bulzoni, 1997.

——— “Mansfeld contre Farnèse. Dessins satiriques de Charles de Mansfeld contre le gouvernement du duc de Parma, Alexandre Farnèse”. In *Un prince de la renaissance. Pierre Ernest de Mansfeld (1517–1604). II. Essais et catalogue*, edited by J.-L. Mousset and K. De Jonge, 129–34. Luxemburg: Musée national d'histoire et d'art, 2007.

Gates-Coon, Rebecca. *The Landed Estates of the Esterházy Princes: Hungary during the Reforms of Maria Theresia and Joseph II.* Baltimore: Johns Hopkins University Press, 1994.

Geevers, Liesbeth. ‘Family Matters. William of Orange and the Habsburgs after the Abdication of Charles V (1555)”. *Renaissance Quarterly* 63 (2010): 459–90.

———. “Being Nassau. Nassau Family Histories and Dutch National Discourse from 1541 to 1616”. *Dutch Crossing* 35 (2011): 4–19.

———. "The King strikes Back: the Spanish Campaign to Undermine the Dutch Diplomatic Position, 1581–1609". In *The Act of Abjuration: Inspired and Inspirational*, edited by R. Kubben, 81–95. Nijmegen: Wolf Legal Publishers, 2011.

Giesey, Ralph E. "The Juristic Basis of the Dynastic Right to the French Throne". *Transactions of the American Philosophical Society*, New Series, 51, no. 5 (1961): 3–47.

Gilbert, John Thomas (ed.). *A Contemporary History of Affairs in Ireland, from AD 1641 to 1653*. 3 vols. Dublin: Irish Archaeological Society, 1879.

——— (ed.). *History of the Irish Confederation and the War in Ireland, 1641–1649*. 7 vols. Dublin, 1882–91.

Gillespie, Raymond. "The Making of the Montgomery Manuscripts". *Familia* 2, no.2 (1980): 23–9.

———. *Colonial Ulster. The Settlement of East Ulster 1600–1641*. Cork: Cork University Press, 1985.

———. "The Image of Death, 1500–1700". *Archaeology Ireland* 6 (1992): 8–10.

Godsey, William D. *Nobles and Nation in Central Europe: Free Imperial Knights in the Age of Revolution, 1750 – 1850*. Cambridge: Cambridge University Press, 2004.

González de León, Fernando. *The Road to Rocroi. Class, Culture and Command in the Spanish Army of Flanders, 1567–1659*. Leiden and Boston: Brill, 2009.

Goodare, Julian. *State and Society in Early Modern Scotland*. Oxford: Oxford University Press, 1999.

———. *The Government of Scotland 1560–1625*. Oxford: Oxford University Press, 2004.

Goodare, Julian, and Michael Lynch (eds). *The Reign of James VI*. East Linton: Tuckwell Press, 2000.

Goody, Jack (ed.). *Succession to High Office*. Cambridge: Cambridge University Press, 1966.

———. "Strategies of Heirship". *Comparative Studies in Society and History* 15 (1973): 3–20.

———. *Production and Reproduction: A Comparative Study of the Domestic Domain*. Cambridge: Cambridge University Press, 1976.

———. *The Development of the Family and Marriage in Europe*. Cambridge: Cambridge University Press, 1983.

Goody, Jack, Joan Thirsk, and E.P. Thompson (eds). *Family and Inheritance: Rural Society in Western Europe, 1200–1800*. Cambridge: Cambridge University Press, 1976.

Goody, Jack, and S.J. Tambiah, *Bridewealth and Dowry*. Cambridge: Cambridge University Press, 1973.

Gosellini, G. *Vita del prencipe don Ferrando Gonzaga*. Milan, 1574.

Gossart, Ernest. *La Révolution des Pays-Bas au XVIe siècle dans l'ancien théâtre espagnol*. Brussels: Hayez, 1910.

Grafton, Anthony. *What was History? The Art of History in Early Modern Europe.* Cambridge: Cambridge University Press, 2007.
Greengrass, Mark. *Conquest and Coalescence: The Shaping of the State in Early Modern Europe.* London: Arnold, 1991.
Greengrass, Mark. *France in the Age of Henri IV.* 2nd edn. London: Longman, 1995.
Grell, Chantal, Werner Paravicini and Jürgen Voss (eds). *Les princes et l'histoire du XIV*[e] *au XVIII*[e] *siècle.* Bonn: Bouvier, 1998.
Groen van Prinsterer, Guillaume. *Archives ou correspondance inédite de la maison d'Orange-Nassau.* 2nd series, 5 vols. Leiden, 1835–1915.
Groenveld, Simon. "'Natie' en 'patria' bij zestiende-eeuwse Nederlanders". In *Vaderland: een geschiedenis van de vijftiende eeuw tot 1940*, edited by N.C.F. van Sas, 55–81. Amsterdam: Amsterdam University Press, 1999.
———. "De Oranjes als markiezen van Veere. Hun politieke invloed in Zeeland en de stad Veere, 1581–1702". In *Borsele Bourgondië Oranje. Heren en markiezen van Veere en Vlissingen 1400–1700*, edited by Hans Blom et al., 105–52. Hilversum: Verloren, 2009.
Grosart, Alexander B. (ed.). *The Lismore Papers.* *First [and the second] series ... Edited with Introd. and Notes by Alexander B. Grosart from the Original MSS. belonging to the Duke of Devonshire preserved in Lismore Castle.* 10 vols. London, 1886–88.
Guisso, Richard. *Wu Tse-t'ien and the Politics of Legitimation in T'ang China.* Bellingham: Western, 1978.
Gustafsson, Harald. "The Conglomerate State: A Reflection on State Formation in Early Modern Europe". *Scandinavian Journal of History* 23 (1998): 189–213.
Haan, Bertand. *Une paix pour l'éternité. La négociation du traité du Cateau-Cambrésis.* Madrid: Casa de Velázquez, 2010.
Habakkuk, Sir John. *Marriage, Debt and the Estates System: English Landownership, 1650–1950* (Oxford: Oxford University Press, 1994.
Haddad, Élie. *Fondation et ruïne d'une "maison". Histoire sociale des comtes de Belin (1582–1706).* Limoges: Pulim, 2009.
———. "La 'maison' noble: pistes de recherches concernant les contraintes de la transmission dans la noblesse française des XVIe et XVIe siècles". In *Mobilité et transmission dans les sociétés de l'Europe moderne,* edited by Anna Bellavitis, Laurence Croq, and Monica Martinat, 203–18. Rennes: Presses Universitaires de Rennes, 2009.
Haemers, Jelle, Wim De Clercq, and Jan Dumolyn, "Sumptuary Legislation, Material Culture and the Semiotics of 'Vivre Noblement' in the County of Flanders (14th – 16th centuries)". *Social History* 36 (2011): 393–417.
Hamilton, Gary G. "Patriarchalism in Imperial China and Western Europe: A Revision of Weber's Sociology of Domination". *Theory and Society* 13, no. 3 (1984): 393–425.
Hammer, Paul E.J. *The Polarisation of Elizabethan Politics. The Political Career of Robert Devereux, 2nd Earl of Essex.* Cambridge: Cambridge University Press, 1999.

Hanley, Sarah. "The Family, the State, and the Law in Seventeenth- and Eighteenth-Century France: The Political Ideology of Male Right versus an Early Theory of Natural Rights". *The Journal of Modern History* 78, no. 2 (2006): 289–332.

Hanlon, Gregory. *The Hero of Italy: Odoardo Farnese, Duke of Parma, his Soldiers, and his Subjects in the Thirty Years' War.* Oxford: Oxford University Press, 2014.

Harari, Yuval Noah. *Renaissance Military Memoirs: War, History, and Identity, 1450–1600.* Woodbridge: Boydell, 2004.

Harding, Robert R. *Anatomy of a Power Elite. The Provincial Governors of Early Modern France.* New Haven, London: Yale University Press, 1978.

Harris, Amy Louise. "Tombs of the New English in Late Sixteenth and Early Seventeenth-Century County Dublin". *Church Monuments* 11 (1996): 25–41.

Harsany, Zoltan. *La Cour de Léopold, duc de Lorraine et de Bar.* Nancy: Idoux, 1939.

Heinrich, Ludwig. *Die vntrewe Margaretha Brahe, Grävin zu Wisingsburg.* s.l., 1661.

Hemptinne, Thérèse de, and Jan Dumolyn. "Historisch adelsonderzoek over de late middeleeuwen en de vroegmoderne periode in België en Nederland: een momentopname". *Bijdragen en Mededelingen betreffende de Geschiedenis der Nederlanden* 103 (2008): 481–489.

Henige, David P. "Oral Tradition and Chronology". *Journal of African History* 3 (1971): 371–89.

Hermans, Fernand. *Filips Willem van Oranje.* s.l., s.n.: 1997.

Herrup, Cynthia. "'To Pluck Bright Honour from the Pale-Faced Moon': Gender and Honour in the Castlehaven Story". *Transactions of the Royal Historical Society*, sixth series, 6 (1996): 137–60.

Hildebrand, Bengt. *Handbok i släkt- och personforskning.* Stockholm: Wahlström & Widstrand, 1961.

Hill, George (ed.). *The Montgomery Manuscripts (1603–1706). Compiled from the Family Papers by William Montgomery of Rosemount* ... Belfast, 1869.

Hirschbiegel, Jan, and Werner Paravicini (eds). *Das Frauenzimmer: Die Frau bei Hofe in Spätmittelalter und früher Neuzeit.* Stuttgart: Thorbecke, 2000.

Hjärne, Harald. "Ur brefvexlingen emellan konung Johan III och tsar Ivan Vasilievitj". *Historiskt bibliotek* 7, no. 8 (1880): 531–4.

Hodson, Simon. "Politics of the Frontier: Henri IV, the Maréchal-Duc De Bouillon and the Sovereignty of Sedan". *French History* 19, no. 4 (2005): 413–39.

Hoffmans, Landelin. *Les portraits des d'Arenberg dans les tableaux religieux des XVIIe et XVIIIe siècles à Enghien.* Enghien: Imprimerie Delwarde, 1941.

Hohkamp, Michaela. "Do Sisters have Brothers? The Search for the *'rechte Schwester'*: Brothers and Sisters in Aristocratic Society at the Turn of the Sixteenth Century". In *Sibling Relations and the Transformation of European Kinship, 1300–1900*, edited by Christopher H. Johson and David Warren Sabean, 65–84. New York: Berghahn Books, 2011.

Holmgren, Jennifer, "Imperial Marriage in the Native Chinese and Non-Han State, Han to Ming", in *Marriage and Inequality in Chinese Society*, edited by Rubie S. Watson and Patricia Buckley Ebrey. Berkeley: University of California Press, 1991.

Hooft, Pieter Cornelisz. *Nederlandse Historiën*, in *Pieter Corneliszoon Hooft, Alle de gedrukte werken, 1611–1738*, edited by W. Hellinga and P. Tuynman. Amsterdam: Amsterdam University Press, 1972.

Hooker, Edward N., and H.T. Swedenberg, Jr. (eds). *The Works of John Dryden*. 20 vols. Berkeley and Los Angeles: University of California Press, 1953–2000.

Horowski, Leonhard. *Die Belagerung des Thrones. Machtstrukturen und Karrieremechanismen am Hof von Frankreich 1661–1789*. Ostfildern: Thorbecke, 2012.

Hortal Muñoz, J. Eloy. "La visión de un ministro 'castellanista' sobra la situación de los Países Bajos al final del siglo XVI: los advertimientos de Esteban de Ibarra". *Bulletin de la Commission royale d'histoire* 174 (2008): 89–166.

Houben, Birgit. *Wisselende gedaanten. Het hof en de hofhouding van de landvoogden Isabella Clara Eugenia (1621–1633) en de kardinaal-infant don Fernando van Oostenrijk (1634–1641) te Brussel*. Unpublished doctoral dissertation Ghent University. Ghent 2009.

Hsieh, Bao Hua. "From Charwoman to Empress Dowager: Serving-Women in the Ming Palace". *Ming Studies* 42 (2000): 26–80.

Hübner, Joseph Alexander von. *Sixte-Quint: d'après des correspondances diplomatiques inédites tirées des archives d'État du Vatican, de Simancas, Venise, Paris, Vienne et Florence*. Paris: A. Franck 1870.

Hucker, Charles O. "Introduction: Governmental Organization Era by Era". In *Dictionary of Official Titles in Imperial China*, 2–96. Stanford: Stanford University Press, 1985.

Humblot, Emile, and Roger Luzu. *Les seigneurs de Joinville*. Saint-Dizier: Impr. A. Brulliard, 1964.

Ianziti, Gary. "I 'Commentarii': appunti per la storia di un genere storiografico quattrocentesco". *Archivio storico italiano* 50 (1992): 1029–63.

Ibn Khaldun. *The Muqaddima. An Introduction to History*. Edited by Franz Rosenthal. Princeton, Oxford: Princeton University Press, 1967.

Ingrao, Charles, and Andrew L. Thomas. "Piety and Patronage: The Empresses-Consort of the High Baroque". *German History* 20 (2002): 20–43.

Irwin, Robert. "Toynbee and Ibn Khaldun". *Middle Eastern Studies* 33, no.3 (1997): 461–79.

Isenburg, Wilhelm Karl von, and Frank Freytag von Loringhoven. *Europäischen Stammtafeln. Stammtafeln zur Geschichte der europäischen Staaten*. 5 vols, Marburg: Stargardt, 1956–1978.

Janssen, Geert H. "Dynastieke transfer in de Republiek. De politieke en religieuze betekenis van de stadhouderlijke begrafenisstoet". *BMGN – Low Countries Historical Review* 122 (2007): 208–32.

Janssens, Paul. *De evolutie van de Belgische adel sinds de late Middeleeuwen.* Brussels: Gemeentekrediet, 1998.

———. “De la noblesse médiévale à la noblesse moderne. La création dans les anciens Pays-Bas d’une noblesse dynastique (XVe-début XVIIe siècle)”. *BMGN – Low Countries Historical Review* 123 (2008): 490–516.

Johnson, Christopher H., and David Warren Sabean. “Introduction. From Siblingship to Siblinghood: Kinship and the Shaping of European Society (1300–1900)”. In *Sibling Relations and the Transformation of European Kinship, 1300–1900*, edited by Christopher H. Johnson and David Warren Sabean, 1–28. New York: Berghahn, 2011.

Jope, Edward Martyn. “Scottish Influences in the North of Ireland: Castles with Scottish Features, 1580–1640”. *Ulster Journal of Archaeology* third series 14 (1951): 31–47.

Jouanna, Arlette. *L’idée de race en France au XVIe siècle et au début du XVIIe.* Revised edition; 2 vols. Montpellier: Service des Publications de l’Université Paul Valéry, 1981.

———. *Le devoir de révolte. La noblesse française et la gestation de l’État moderne, 1559–1661.* Paris: Fayard 1989.

———. “Les Guise et le sang de France”. In *Le mécenat et l’influence des Guises*, edited by Yvonne Bellenger, 23–38. Paris: Champion, 1997.

Kagan, Richard L. *Clio and the Crown: The Politics of History in Medieval and Early Modern Spain.* Baltimore: Johns Hopkins University Press, 2009.

Kamen, Henry. *The Escorial. Art and Power in the Renaissance.* New Haven and London: Yale University Press, 2010.

Kaminsky, Howard, and James Van Horn Melton (eds). *Land and Lordship: Structures of Governance in Medieval Austria.* Philadelphia: University of Pennsylvania Press, 1992.

Kane, Brendan. “Making the Irish European: Gaelic Honor Politics and its Continental Contexts”. *Renaissance Quarterly* 61 (2008): 1139–1166.

———. “From Irish Eineach to British Honor? Noble Honor and High Politics in Early Modern Ireland, 1500–1650”. *History Compass* 7 (2009): 414–30.

———. *The Politics and Culture of Honour in Britain and Ireland, 1541–1641.* Cambridge: Cambridge University Press, 2010.

———. “Scandal, Wentworth’s deputyship and the breakdown of Stuart honour politics”. In *Reshaping Ireland 1550–1700. Colonization and its consequences*, edited by Brian MacCuarta, 147–62. Dublin: Four Courts Press, 2011.

Kaske, Elisabeth. “Fund-Raising Wars: Office Selling and Interprovincial Finance in Nineteenth-Century China”. *Harvard Journal of Asiatic Studies* 71/1 (2011): 69–141.

Kaufmann, Thomas DaCosta. *Towards a Geography of Art.* Chicago: University of Chicago Press, 2004.

Keblusek, Marika. *Boeken in de hofstad: Haagse boekcultuur in de Gouden Eeuw.* Hilversum: Verloren, 1997.

Keblusek, Marika, and Jori Zijlmans. *Princely Display: The Court of Frederik Hendrik of Orange and Amalia von Solms*. The Hague and Zwolle: Waanders, 1997.

Keller, Katrin. "Frauen in der höfischen Gesellschaft des 17. Jahrhunderts: Amtsinhabe und Netzwerke am Wiener Hof". *Zeitblicke* 4 (2005).

Kelly, James. *That Damn'd Thing Called Honour: Duelling in Ireland, 1570–1860*. Cork: Cork University Press, 1995.

Kerlouégan, Jérôme. "Printing for Prestige? Publishing and Publications by Ming Princes". *East Asian Publishing and Society* 1 (2011): 39–73.

Klaniczay, Gábor. *Holy Rulers and Blessed Princesses. Dynastic Cults in Medieval Central Europe*. Cambridge: Cambridge University Press, 2007.

Klein, Lawrence E. "Sociability, Politeness and Aristocratic Self-formation in the Life and Career of the Second Earl of Shelburne". *The Historical Journal* 55 (2012): 653–77.

Knecht, Robert J. *The French Civil Wars, 1562–1598*. Harlow: Longman, 2000.

Koenigsberger, Helmut Georg. "*Dominium Regale* or *dominium politicum et regale*: Monarchies and Parliaments in Early Modern Europe". In *Politicians and Virtuosi: Essays in Early Modern European History*, edited by Helmut Georg Koenigsberg, 1–26. London: Hambledon Press, 1986.

Kohnle, Armin (ed.). *Das Vermächtnis Kaiser Karls V. Die Politische Testamente*. Darmstadt: Wissenschaftliche Buchgesellschaft, 2005.

Koller, Alexander. "Reichsitalien als Thema in den Beziehungen zwischen Kaiser und Papst: Der Fall Borgo Val di Taro". In *Das Reich und Italien in der Frühen Neuzeit* (Contributi dell'Istituto storico italo-germanico in Trento 17), edited by M. Schnettger and M. Verga, 323–45. Bologna: Mulino, 2006.

Labatut, Jean-Pierre. *Les noblesses européennes de la fin du XVe siècle à la fin du XVIIIe siècle*. Paris: Presses universitaires de France, 1978.

Lambin, Rosine A. *Femmes de Paix: La coexistence religieuse et les dames de la noblesse en France, 1520–1630*. Paris: Harmatta, 2003.

Langlois, Charles-Victor. *Les hôtels de Clisson, de Guise & de Rohan-Soubise au Marais*. Paris: J. Schemit, 1922.

La Rochefoucauld, Edmée de. *Flashes*. Paris: B. Grasset, 1982.

Lawrence, Richard. *The interest of Ireland in its trade and wealth stated in two parts: first part observes and discovers the causes of Irelands not more increasing in trade and wealth from the first conquest till now: second part proposeth expedients to remedy all its mercanture maladies ... by which it is kept poor and low; both mix'd with some observations on the politicks of government relating to the incouragement of trade and increase of wealth: with some reflections on principles of religion as it relates to the premises*. Dublin, 1682.

Lee, Maurice. *Government by Pen: Scotland under James VI and I*. Urbana: University of Illinois Press, 1981.

———. "The Gowrie Conspiracy Revisited". In *The Inevitable Union and Other Essays on Early Modern Scotland*, edited by Maurice Lee, 99–115. East Linton: Tuckwell Press, 2003.

Leerssen, Joep. *Mere Irish and Fíor-Ghael. Studies in the Idea of Irish Nationality, its Development and Literary Expression Prior to the Nineteenth Century.* Cork: Cork University Press, 1996.

Leferme-Falguières, Frédérique. "La noblesse de cour aux XVIIe et XVIIIe siècles. De la définition à l'autoreprésentation d'une élite". *Hypothèses* 4 (2000): 87–98.

Lefèvre, J. "Le Tribunal de la Visite (1594–1602)". *Archives, bibliothèques et musées de Belgique* 9 (1932): 65–85.

Lépine, Jean-Baptiste. *Histoire de Château-Portien (Ardennes).* Vouziers, 1858.

Leuschner, Eckhard. "Francesco Villamena's 'Apotheosis of Alessandro Farnese' and Engraved Reproductions of Contemporary Sculpture around 1600". *Simiolus* 27 (1999): 145–67.

Lewis, Mark. *China's Cosmopolitan Empire. The Tang Dynasty.* Cambridge, MA: Harvard University Press, 2009.

———. *The Early Chinese Empires: Qin and Han.* Cambridge, MA: Harvard University Press, 2010.

Liedgren, Jan. "Föreställningar om den heliga Birgittas släkt: traditioner och konstruktioner". *Personhistorisk Tidskrift* 79 (1983): 1–16.

Lipp, Charles. "Being Noble in the Borderlands: The Family de Mahuet of Lorraine, 1599–1737". *Proceedings of the Western Society for French History* 29 (2001): 72–9.

Lindley, David. *The Trials of Frances Howard: Fact and Fiction at the Court of James I.* London: Routledge, 1993.

Little, Patrick. "The Earl of Cork and the Fall of the Earl of Strafford". *Historical Journal* 39 (1996): 619–35.

Livingstone, Amy. "Kith and Kin: Kinship and Family Structure of the Nobility of Eleventh- and Twelfth-Century Blois-Chartres". *French Historical Studies* 20 (1997): 419–58.

Livingstone, Amy. *Out of Love for my Kin: Aristocratic Family Life in the Lands of the Loire, 1000–1200.* Ithaca: Cornell University Press, 2010.

Loades, David. "The English State and the Death of Mary, Queen of Scots". In *Murder and Monarchy: Regicide in European History, 1300–1800*, edited by Robert von Friedeburg, 159–75. Basingstoke: Macmillan, 2004.

Loeber, Rolf. "Sculptured Memorials to the Dead in Early Seventeenth-Century Ireland". *Proceedings of the Royal Irish Academy* 81, Section C (1981): 267–93.

Louis XIV, *Mémoires de Louis XIV pour l'instruction du Dauphin*, edited by Charles Dreyss. Paris: Didier, 1860.

Lowe, John (ed.). *Letter-Book of the Earl of Clanricarde 1643–1647.* Dublin: IMC, 1983.

Lowry, T.K. (ed.). *Hamilton Manuscripts: containing some account of territories of Upper Clandeboye, Great Ardes, Dufferin in the county of Down, by Sir William Hamilton, afterward Viscount Clandeboye.* Belfast, 1867.

Mac Craith, Mícheál. "The Gaelic Reaction to the Reformation". In *Conquest and Union. Fashioning a British State, 1485–1725*, edited by Steven Ellis and Sarah Barber, 139–61. Harlow, Longman, 1995.

MacHardy, Karin. "Cultural Capital, Family Strategies and Noble Identity in Early Modern Habsburg Austria 1579–1620". *Past & Present* 163 (1999): 36–75.

———. *War, Religion and Court Patronage in Habsburg Austria: The Social and Cultural Dimensions of Political Interaction, 1521–1622.* Basingstoke: Palgrave, 2003.

Malettke, Klaus. *Die Bourbonen.* Vol. 1, *Von Heinrich IV. bis zu Ludwig XIV, 1589–1715.* Stuttgart: Kohlhammer, 2008.

Manning, Roger B. *An Apprenticeship in Arms: the Origins of the British Army; 1585 – 1702.* Oxford: Oxford University Press, 2006.

Manning, Roger B. *Swordsmen: the Martial Ethos in the Three Kingdoms.* Oxford: Oxford University Press, 2003.

Marini, Mirella. "Female Authority in the *Pietas Nobilita*: Habsburg Allegiance during the Dutch Revolt". *Dutch Crossing: Journal of Low Countries studies* 34, no. 1 (2010): 5–24.

———. "Interlocking dynasties: netwerking en huwelijkspolitiek van de familie Arenberg tijdens de Opstand". In: *Het verdeelde huis: de Nederlandse adel tussen opstand en reconciliatie*, edited by Liesbeth De Frenne and Luc Duerloo, 55–78. Maastricht: Shaker Publishing, 2011.

———. "Pendanten in leven en dood: Vroomheid, identiteit en autoriteit in de testamentaire beschikkingen van Anna van Croy, hertogin van Aarschot en prinses-gravin van Arenberg (1564–1635)". In *Graven spreken. Perspectieven op grafcultuur in de middeleeuwse en vroegmoderne Nederlanden*, edited by Peter Bitter, Vera Bonenkampova and Koen Goudriaan, 153–70. Hilversum: Verloren, 2013.

———. "Dynastic Relations on an International Stage. Margaret de la Marck (1527–1599) and Arenberg Family Strategy during the Dutch Revolt". In *Women, Diplomacy and International Politics since 1500*, edited by Glenda Sluga and Carolyn James, 46-67. London: Routledge, 2015.

Marrese, Michelle Lamarche. *A Woman's Kingdom: Noblewomen and the Control of Property in Russia, 1700–1861.* Ithaca: Cornell University Press, 2002.

———. "'The Poetics of Everyday Behaviour' Revisited: Lotman, Gender and the Evolution of Russian Noble Identity". *Kritika: Explorations in Russian and Eurasian History* 4 (2010): 701–39.

Marshall, Peter, and Geoffrey Scott. *Catholic Gentry in English Society. The Throckmortons of Coughton from Reformation to Emancipation.* Farnham: Ashgate, 2009.

Martin, Georges. *Histoire et généalogie de la Maison de Croÿ.* Lyon: s.n. 2001: s.n.,1981[1].

———. *Histoire et généalogie des Maisons de Ligne et d'Arenberg.* 2 vols. Lyon: G. Martin, 2003.

Martin, Russell E. *A Bride for the Tsar: Bride-shows and Marriage Politics in Early Modern Russia.* DeKalb: Northern Illinois University Press, 2012.

Maurice, Jean Baptiste. *Le Blason des Armoiries de tous les Chevaliers de l'Ordre de la Toison d'Or depuis la première institution iusques à present. Avec leurs noms, surnoms, titres et cartiers. Ensemble leurs Eloges déscrites en bref.* The Hague, 1667.

Mat'a, Petr. "Bohemia, Silesia and the Empire: Negotiating Princely Dignity on the Eastern Periphery". In *The Holy Roman Empire, 1495–1806: A European Perspective*, edited by R.J.W. Evans and Peter H. Wilson, 143–65. Leiden: Brill, 2012.

———. "The false Orsini from over the Alps: Negotiating Aristocratic Identity in Late Medieval and Early Modern Europe". *Römische Historische Mitteilungen* 55 (2013): 155–213.

Mat'a, Petr, and Thomas Winkelbauer. *Die Habsburgermonarchie 1620 bis 1740: Leistungen und Grenzen des Absolutismusparadigmas*. Stuttgart: Steiner, 2006.

Mayes, Charles R. "The Sale of Peerages in Early Stuart England". *The Journal of Modern History* 29 (1957): 21–37.

McCluskey, Philip. *Absolute Monarchy on the Frontiers: Louis XIV's Military Occupations of Lorraine and Savoy.* Manchester: Manchester University Press, 2013.

McDonnell, Hector. "A Fragment of an Irish Manuscript History of the MacDonalds of Antrim". *Ulster Journal of Archaeology* 64 (2005): 140–53.

McDonnell, Hector, and Jane Ohlmeyer (eds). "New Light on the Marquis of Antrim and the 'Wars of the Three Kingdoms'", *Analecta Hibernica* 41 (2009).

McKenny, Kevin. 'The Restoration Land Settlement in Ireland: a Statistical Interpretation". In *Restoration Ireland. Always Settling and Never Settled*, edited by Coleman Dennehy, 35–52. Aldershot: Ashgate, 2008.

Mears, Natalie. "Courts, Courtiers, and Culture in Tudor England". *The Historical Journal* 46 (2003): 703–22.

Méndez Silva, Rodrigo. *Nacimiento y bautismo del Serenissimo Infante de España, D. Fernando Tomas de Austria.* Madrid, 1659.

Mettam, Roger C. *Power and Faction in Louis XIV's France.* Oxford, New York: Blackwell, 1988.

Monod, Paul Kléber. *The Power of Kings: Monarchy and Religion in Europe, 1589–1715.* New Haven: Yale University Press, 1999.

Monter, William. *A Bewitched Duchy: Lorraine and its Dukes, 1477–1736.* Geneva: Libr. Droz, 2007.

Montpensier, Anne Marie Louise de Bourbon, Mlle de. *Mémoires de Mlle de Montpensier, petite-fille de Henri IV*, edited by A. Chéruel. 4 vols. Paris: Charpentier, 1858.

Mörke, Olaf. *Wilhelm von Oranien (1533–1584). Fürst und "Vater" der Republik.* Stuttgart: Kohlhammer, 2007.

Morrice, Thomas (ed.). *A Collection of the State Letters of ... Roger Boyle, First Earl of Orrery ...* London, 1742.
Mote, F.W. "Becoming an Emperor". *Proceedings of the Denver Museum of Natural History* 3, no. 15 (1998): 11–25.
Motta, U. *Antonio Querenghi (1546–1633). Un letterato padovano nella Roma del tardo Rinascimento.* Milan: Vita e Pensiero, 1997.
Munns, Jessica, Penny Richards, and Jonathan Spangler (eds). *Aspiration, Representation and Memory: The Guise in Europe, 1506–1688.* Farnham: Ashgate, 2015.
Nader, Helen (ed.). *Power and Gender in Renaissance Spain: Eight women of the Mendoza Family, 1450–1650.* Urbana: University of Illinois Press, 2004.
Naquin, Susan, and Evelyn Rawski. *Chinese Society in the Eighteenth Century.* New Haven: Yale University Press, 1987.
Nassiet, Michel. "Parenté et Successions dynastiques au 14e et 15e siècles". *Annales Histoire, Sciences Sociales* 50 (1995): 621–44.
———. *Parenté, noblesse et états dynastiques XVe-XVIe siècles.* Paris: Ecole des hautes études en sciences sociales, 2000.
Nelson, Eric. "Royal Authority and the Pursuit of a Lasting Religious Settlement". In *Politics and Religion in Early Bourbon France*, edited by Alison Forestal and Eric Nelson, 107–31. Basingstoke: Palgrave Macmillan 2009.
Nenner, Howard. *The Right to be King: The Succession to the Crown of England, 1603–1714.* Basingstoke: Macmillan, 1995.
Neu, Peter. *Die Arenberger und das Arenberger Land.* 6 vols. Koblenz: Verlag der Landesarchivverwaltung Rheinland-Pfalz, 1989–2001.
——— (ed.). *Arenberger Frauen: Fürstinnen, Herzoginnen, Ratgeberinnen, Mütter.* Koblenz: Verlag der Landesarchivverwaltung Rheinland-Pfalz, 2006.
Neumann, F. *Geschichtsschreibung als Kunst. Famiano Strada S.I. (1572–1649) und die ars historica in Italien.* Berlin-Boston: De Gruyter, 2013.
Nierop, Henk van. *The Nobility of Holland: From Knights to Regents 1500–1650.* Cambridge: Cambridge University Press, 1993.
Nierop, Henk van. *Van ridders tot regenten. De Hollandse adel in de zestiende en de eerste helft van de zeventiende eeuw.* Amsterdam: De Bataafsche Leeuw, 1984.
Nijsten, Gerard. *In the Shadow of Burgundy: the Court of Guelders in the Late Middle Ages.* Cambridge: Cambridge University Press, 2004.
Nisser, Wilhelm. *Konst och hantverk i Visingsborgs grevskap på Per Brahe d.y:s tid.* Stockholm: G. Lindström, 1931.
Nori, G. "Pomponio Torelli: una ignorata missione diplomatica in Spagna (1598–1599)". *Archivio storico per le province parmensi* ser. IV, 29 (1977): 279–310.
———. "Una biografia parallela di Alessandro Farnese: Pomponio Torelli e Cesare Campana". *Aurea Parma* 62, fasc. I (1978): 33–41.
Numers, Lorenz von. *De hemliga rummen.* Stockholm: Norstedt, 1980.
Ó Buachalla, Breandan. "James Our True King. The Ideology of Irish Royalism in the Seventeenth Century". In *Political Thought in Ireland since the*

Seventeenth Century, edited by D. George Boyce, Robert Eccleshall and Vincent Geoghegan, 7–35. London: Routledge,1993.

O'Connor, Thomas (ed.). *The Irish in Europe, 1580–1815*. Dublin: Four Courts Press, 2001.

Ohlmeyer, Jane. "The Baronial Context of the Civil War in Ireland". In *The English Civil War. Conflicts and Contexts, 1640–49*, edited by John Adamson, 106–24. Basingstoke: Palgrave Macmillan, 2009.

———. "New Light on the Marquis of Antrim and the 'Wars of the Three Kingdoms'". *Analecta Hibernica* 41 (2009): 67–82.

———. *Making Ireland English. The Irish Aristocracy in the Seventeenth Century.* New Haven: Yale University Press, 2012.

———."Scottish peers in seventeenth-century Ireland" in *Scots in early Stuart Ireland*, edited by David Edwards, 62-94. Manchester: Manchester University Press, 2015.

Ohlmeyer, Jane, and Steven Zwicker. "Patronage and Restoration Politics: John Dryden and the House of Ormond". *Historical Journal* 49 (2006): 677–706.

Oresko, Robert. "The Marriages of the Nieces of Cardinal Mazarin: Public Policy and Private Strategy in Seventeenth-century Europe". In *Frankreich im europäischen Staatensystem der Frühen Neuzeit*, edited by Rainer Babel, 109–51. Sigmaringen: Torbecke, 1995.

———. "Bastards as Clients: The House of Savoy and its Illegitimate Children". In *Patronages et Clientélismes 1550–1700 (France, Angleterre, Espagne, Italie)*, edited by Charles Giry-Deloison and Roger Mettam, 39–67. Lille: Villeneuve d'Ascq, 1996.

———. "Maria Giovanna Battista of Savoy-Nemours (1644–1724): Daughter, Consort and Regent of Savoy". In *Queenship in Europe, 1660–1815: The Role of the Consort*, edited by C. Campbell-Orr, 16–55. Cambridge: Cambridge University Press, 2004.

Oresko, Robert, G.C. Gibbs and H.M. Scott (eds). *Royal and Republican Sovereignty in Early Modern Europe: Essays in Memory of Ragnhild Hatton.* Cambridge: Cambridge University Press, 1997.

Orlers, Jan. *Geslacht-boom der Graven van Nassav.* Leiden, 1616.

Örnevinge, Johan. *Genealogia Braheae*. Stockholm, 1647.

Palmer, William. "That 'Insolent Liberty': Honor, Rites of Power, and Persuasion in Sixteenth-Century Ireland". *Renaissance Quarterly* 46 (1993): 308–27.

Paravicini, Werner. "Moers, Croy, Burgund. Eine Studie über den Niedergang des Hauses Moers in den zweiten Hälfte des 15. Jahrhunderts". *Annalen des Historischen Vereins für den Niederrhein* 179 (1978): 7–113.

Parisse, Michel, and Pierre Heili (eds). *Les chapitres de dames nobles entre France et Empire.* Paris: Editions Messene, 1998.

Park, Nancy E. "Corruption in Eighteenth-Century China". *The Journal of Asian Studies* 56, no. 4 (1997): 967–1005.

Parkes, Peter. "Fostering Fealty: A Comparative Analysis of Tributary Allegiances of Adoptive Kinship". *Comparative Studies in Society and History* 45, no. 4 (2003): 741–82.

Parrott, David. "A *prince étranger* and the French crown: Charles de Nevers, 1580–1637", in *Royal and Republican Sovereignty in Early Modern Europe: Essays in Memory of Ragnhild Hatton*, edited by Robert Oresko et al. Cambridge: Cambridge University Press, 1997.

———. "The Mantuan Succession, 1627–31: A Sovereignty Dispute in Early Modern Europe". *English Historical Review* 112 (1997): 20–65.

———. *Richelieu's Army: War, Government and Society in France, 1624–1642.* Cambridge: Cambridge University Press, 2001.

Pečar, Andreas. *Die Ökonomie der Ehre: der höfische Adel am Kaiserhof Karls VI. (1711–1740).* Darmstadt: Wissenschaftliche Buchgesellschaft, 2003.

Peirce, Leslie. *The Imperial Harem. Women and Sovereignty in the Ottoman Empire.* New York, Oxford: Oxford University Press, 1993.

Perceval-Maxwell, M. *The Scottish Migration to Ulster in the Reign of James I.* London: Routledge, 1973.

———. "Sir Robert Southwell and the Duke of Ormond's Reflections on the 1640s". In: *Kingdoms in Crisis. Ireland in the 1640s*, edited by Micheál O Siochru, 229–43. Dublin: Four Courts, 2001.

Perdue, Peter C. *China Marches West: the Qing Conquest of Central Eurasia.* Cambridge, MA: Harvard University Press, 2005.

Pérez Bustamante, Ciriaco. *El cronista Antonio de Herrera y la historia de Alejandro Farnese.* Madrid: Olózaga, 1933.

Perschy, Jakob, and Harald Prickler (eds). *Die Fürsten Esterházy: Magnaten, Diplomaten und Mäzene.* Eisenstadt: Amt der Burgenlañdischen Landesregierung, 1995.

Petiot, Alain. *Au service des Habsbourg. Officiers, ingénieurs, savants et artistes lorrains en Autriche.* Paris: Messene, 2000.

Pettersson, Erik. *Den skoningslöse: En biografi över Karl IX.* Stockholm: Natur & kultur, 2008.

Pise, Joseph de la. *Tableau d'Histoire des princes et principauté d'Orange.* The Hague, 1640.

Piot, Charles. "Melun (Pierre de)". *Biographie Nationale* XIV, 332–335. Brussels, 1897.

Pitts, Vincent J. *Henry IV of France: His Reign and Age.* Baltimore: Johns Hopkins University Press, 2009.

Polybius. *The Histories.* Edited by F.W. Walbank, Chr. Habicht and W.R. Paton. Cambridge, MA: Harvard University Press, 2011.

Potter, David. "A Treason Trial in Sixteenth-Century France: The Fall of Marshal du Biez, 1549–1551". *English Historical Review* 105 (1990): 595–623.

———. *War and Government in the French Provinces, Picardy 1470–1560.* Cambridge: Cambridge University Press, 1993.

Poull, Georges. *La maison ducale de Lorraine.* Nancy: Presses Universitaires de Nancy 1991.

Poutrin, Isabelle, and Marie-Karine Schaub. "Introduction – Pour une histoire des princesses européennes à l'époque moderne". In: *Femmes & pouvoir politique. Les princesses d'Europe XVe-XVIIIe siècle*, edited by I. Poutrin and M.-K. Schaub, 7–57. Rosny-sous-Bois: Bréal, 2007.

Prendergast, John P., and Charles William Russell (eds). *Calendar of State papers, relating to Ireland, of the reign of James I.* 5 vols. London: Longman & Co, 1872–1880.

Primi Visconti, Giovanni-Battista, conte di San Maiolo. *Mémoires sur la Cour de Louis XIV, 1673–1681*, edited by J.-F. Solnon. Paris: Perrin, 1988.

Proust, Marcel. *In Search of Lost Time: The Guermantes Way*. Translated by Mark Treharne. London: Allen Lane, 2002.

Puddu, Raffaele. *Il soldato gentiluomo: autoritratto d'una società guerriera, la Spagna del Cinquecento.* Bologna: Il Mulino, 1982.

Puppel, Pauline. "Der 'Traum' einer jeden Schwiegermutter. Gräfin Elisabeth Charlotte von Nassau-Dillenburg-Schaumburg und Prinz Lebrecht von Anhalt-Bernburg". *Zeitblicke* 8 (2009).

Radulescu, Raluca L., and Edward Donald Kennedy (eds). *Broken Lines: Genealogical Literature in Medieval Britain and France.* Turnhout: Brepols, 2008.

Raeymaekers, Dries. *One Foot in the Palace: The Habsburg Court of Brussels and the Politics of Access in the Reign of Albert and Isabella, 1598–1621.* Louvain: Leuven University Press, 2013.

Ramacciotti, G. "Le vicende storiche dell'Archivio Farnesiano a Napoli e la sua reale consistenza". *Archivio storico per le province parmensi*, ser. IV, 2 (1949–1950) and 4 (1951).

Rankin, Deana. *Between Spenser and Swift. English Writing in Seventeenth-Century Ireland.* Cambridge: Cambridge University Press, 2005.

Ranum, Patricia. "Mademoiselle de Guise, ou les défis de la quenouille". *XVII*[e] *siècle* 144 (1984): 221–31.

———. *Portraits Around Marc-Antoine Charpentier.* Baltimore: Dux Femina Facti, 2004.

Rapple, Roy. *Martial Power and Elizabethan Political Culture. Military Men in England and Ireland, 1558–1594.* Cambridge: Cambridge University Press, 2009.

Raviola, Blythe Alice. "The Imperial System in Early Modern Northern Italy: A Web of Dukedoms, Fiefs and Enclaves along the Po". In *The Holy Roman Empire, 1495–1806: A European Perspective*, edited by R.J.W. Evans and Peter H. Wilson, 217–36. Leiden: Brill, 2012.

Rawski, Evelyn S. *The Last Emperors: A Social History of Qing Imperial Institutions.* Berkeley: University of California Press, 1998.

Redworth, Glyn. *The Prince and the Infanta: the Cultural Politics of the Spanish Match.* New Haven: Yale University Press, 2003.

Reiffenberg, baron de. *Une existence de grand seigneur au seizième siècle: Mémoires autographes du Duc Charles de Croy*. Brussel: Muquardt, 1845.

Riordan, Michelle. *The Gaelic Mind and the Collapse of the Gaelic World.* Cork: Cork University Press, 1990.

———. "'Political' Poems in the Mid-Seventeenth-Century Crisis". In *Ireland from Independence to Occupation*, edited by Jane Ohlmeyer, 112–27. Cambridge: Cambridge University Press, 1995.

Rizzo, Mario. "Gli Austrias e l'Italia centrosettentrionale nella prima età moderna. Una rapsodia geopolitica". In *Feudi di Lunigiana tra Impero, Spagna e Stati italiani (XV-XVIII secolo)*, edited by E. Fasano Guarini and F. Bonatti, 82–100. La Spezia: Accademia lunigianese di scienze Giovanni Capellini, 2008.

Robaulx de Soumoy, A.L.P. de (ed.). *Mémoires de Frédéric Perrenot, sieur de Champagney, 1573–1590.* Bruxelles: Société de l'histoire de Belgique, 1860.

Robertson, Claire. "Osservazioni sul mecenatismo del Cardinale Odoardo Farnese". In *I Farnese. Arte e collezionismo. Studi*, edited by L. Fornari Schianchi, 70–9. Milan: Electa, 1995.

———. *The Invention of Annibale Carracci.* Milan: Silvana 2008.

Robinson, David. "Princely Courts of the Ming Dynasty". *Ming Studies* 65 (2012): 1–12.

———. "Princes in the Polity: The Anhua Prince's Uprising of 1510". *Ming Studies* 65 (2012): 13–56.

———. *Martial Spectacles at the Ming Court of China, 1368–1568.* Cambridge, MA: Harvard University Press, 2013.

Robinson, Philip. *The Plantation of Ulster. British Settlement in an Irish Landscape, 1600–1670.* Dublin: Gill and Macmillan, 1984.

Roche, Daniel. "Aperçus sur la fortune et les revenus des princes de Condé à l'aube du XVIIIe siècle". *Revue d'histoire moderne et contemporaine* XIV (1967): 217–43.

Rodríguez Pérez, Yolanda. *The Dutch Revolt through Spanish Eyes. Self and Other in Historical and Literary Texts of Golden Age Spain (c. 1548–1673).* Bern: Peter Lang, 2008.

Rodríguez Salgado, Maria José. "Philip II and the Post-Armada Crisis: Foreign Policy and Rebellion, 1588–1594". In *IX Jornadas de Historia Maritima. Despues de la Gran Armada: la historia desconocida (1588–16.)*, 51–89. Madrid: Instituto de Historia y Cultura Naval, 1993.

———. "Ferrante Gonzaga: the Champion of Innocence". In *Ferrante Gonzaga. Il Mediterraneo, l'Impero (1507–1557). Atti del convegno di studi, Guastalla, 5–6 ottobre 2007*, edited by G. Signorotto, 139–96. Rome: Bulzoni, 2009.

———. "Almost a Royal Eagle. Alexander Farnese and the Spanish Monarchy". In *Alexander Farnese and the Low Countries*, edited by Krista De Jonge, Sebastiaan Derks and Hans Cools. Turnhout: Brepols, forthcoming.

Roegiers, Jan, Mark Derez, Marc Nelissen, Jean-Pierre Tytgat and Anne Verbrugge (eds). *Arenberg in de Lage Landen. Een hoogadellijk huis in Vlaanderen & Nederland.* Louvain: Universitaire Pers, 2002.

Roeykens, Auguste. "Une grande dame de nos provinces au XVIe siècle: Marguerite de la Marck, Princesse-Comtesse d'Arenberg". *Annales du Cercle Archéologique d'Enghien* 15 (1967–1969): 297–424.

Romani, Marzio Achille. "Finanza pubblica e potere politico: il caso dei Farnese (1545–1593)". In *Le corti farnesiane di Parma e Piacenza (1545–1622)*, edited by M.A. Romani, 3–85. Rome: Bulzoni, 1978.

Rowe, William T. "Social Stability and Social Change". In *Cambridge History of China.* Vol. 9, *The Ch'ing Empire to 1800*, edited by Willard J. Peterson, vol. 1, 476–562. Cambridge: Cambridge University Press, 2003.

Rowen, Herbert H. *The Princes of Orange. The Stadholders in the Dutch Republic.* Cambridge: Cambridge University Press, 1988.

Rowlands, Guy. "Louis XIV, Aristocratic Power and the Elite Units of the French Army". *French History* 13 (1999): 303–331.

———. *The Dynastic State and the Army under Louis XIV.* Cambridge: Cambridge University Press, 2002.

Rust, George. *A Sermon Preached at New-town the 29 of Octob. 1663. At the Funeral of the Right Honourable Hugh Earl of Mount-Alexander, Lord Viscount Mountgomery of Ards, Late Master of the Ordnance, and one of His Majesties Most Honourable Privy Council in Ireland.* Dublin, 1664.

Rystad, Göran. "Magnus Gabriel De la Gardie". In *Sweden's Age of Greatness 1632–1718*, edited by Michael Roberts, 203–36. London: Macmillan, 1973.

Sabatier, Gérard, and Margarita Torrione (eds). *Louis XIV espagnol? Madrid et Versailles, images et modèles.* Versailles: Centre de Recherche du château de Versailles, 2009.

Sabbadini, Roberto. *La grazia e l'onore. Principe, nobiltà e ordine sociale nei ducati farnesiani.* Rome: Bulzoni, 2001.

———. "L'uso della memoria. I Farnese e le immagini di Alessandro, duca e capitano". In *Il 'perfetto capitano'. Immagini e realtà (secoli XV-XVII): atti dei seminari di studi Georgetown University a Villa 'Le Balze', Istituto di Studi Rinascimentale di Ferrara 1995–1997*, edited by M. Fantoni, 155–82. Rome: Bulzoni, 2001.

Sabean, David Warren. "Kinship and Class Dynamics in Nineteenth-Century Europe". In *Kinship in Europe. Approaches to Long-Term Development (1300–1900)*, edited by David Warren Sabean, Simon Teuscher, and Jon Mathieu, 301–13 New York: Berghahn Books, 2007.

Sabean, David Warren, and Simon Teuscher. "Kinship in Europe. A New Approach to Long Term Development". In *Kinship in Europe. Approaches to Long-Term Development (1300–1900)*, edited by David Warren Sabean, Simon Teuscher and Jon Mathieu, 1–32. New York: Berghahn Books, 2007.

Sahlins, Peter. *Unnaturally French: Foreign Citizens in the Old Regime and After.* Ithaca: Cornell University Press, 2004.

Sainte-Marie, Père Anselme de. *Histoire Généalogique et Chronologique de la Maison Royale de France, des Pairs, des Grands Officiers de la Couronne & de la Maison du Roy, des anciens Barons du Royaume, avec les qualitez, l'origine, le progrès et les armes de toutes leurs familles.* 9 vols. Paris: La Compagnie des libraires, 1726–33.

Saint-Simon, Louis de Rouvroy, duc de. *Mémoires*, edited by A. de Boislisle. Paris: Hachette, 1879–1928.

———. *Mémoires*, edited by Y. Coirault. 8 vols. Paris: Gallimard, 1983.

Samson, Alexander (ed.). *The Spanish Match: Prince Charles's Journey to Madrid, 1623.* Aldershot: Ashgate, 2006.

Samuelson, Jan. *Aristokrat eller förädlad bonde?* Lund: Lund University Press, 1993.

Sánchez, Magdelena S. *The Empress, the Queen, and the Nun: Women and Power at the Court of Philip III of Spain.* Baltimore: Johns Hopkins University Press, 1998.

Sandberg, Brian. *Warrior Pursuits: Noble Culture and Civil Conflict in Early Modern France.* Baltimore: Johns Hopkins University Press, 2010.

Schattkowsky, Martina (ed.) *Witwenschaft in der Frühen Neuzeit: Fürstliche und adlige Witwen zwischen Fremd- und Selbstbestimmung.* Leipzig: Leipziger Universitätsverlag, 2003.

Scherft, Pieter. *Het sterfhuis van Willem van Oranje.* Leiden: Universitaire Pers, 1966.

Schilling, Heinz. "Die Konfessionalisierung von Kirche, Staat und Gesellschaft – Profil, Leistung, Defizite und Perspektiven eines Geschichtswissenschaftlichen Paradigmas". In *Die katholische Konfessionalisierung*, edited by W. Reinhard and H. Schilling, 1–49. Gütersloh: Mohn, 1995.

Scohier, Jean. *La généalogie et descente de la très illustre maison de Croÿ.* Douai, 1596; anastatic reprint Brussels, 1996.

Scott, Hamish S. (ed.). *The European Nobilities in the Seventeenth and Eighteenth Centuries. Northern, Central and Eastern Europe.* London: Longman 1995; second revised edition Basingstoke: Palgrave Macmillan, 2007.

———. *Forming Aristocracy: the Reconfiguration of Europe's Nobilities, c. 1300–1750.* Oxford: Oxford University Press, forthcoming.

Semedo, Álvaro de. *The History of That Great and Renowned Monarchy of China.* London, 1655.

Seyssel, Claude de. *The Monarchy of France*, edited by J.H. Hexter and Donald R. Kelley. New Haven: Yale University Press, 1981.

Sharpe, Kevin M. *Selling the Tudor Monarchy: Authority and Image in Sixteenth-Century England.* New Haven: Yale University Press, 2009.

———. *Image Wars: Promoting Kings and Commonwealths in England, 1603–1660.* New Haven: Yale University Press, 2010.

———. *Rebranding Rule: the Restoration and Revolution Monarchy, 1660–1714.* New Haven: Yale University Press, 2013.

Shields Kollmann, Nancy. *Kinship and Politics: The Making of the Muscovite Political System, 1345–1547.* Stanford: Stanford University Press, 1987.

Signorotto, Gianvittorio. "Identità e interessi nell'Italia dei potentate". In *Le sentiment national dans l'Europe méridionale aux XVIe et XVIIe siècles*

(France, Espagne, Italie), edited by A. Tallon, 33–50. Madrid: Casa de Velázquez, 2007.

Skinner, William. "Introduction: Urban Development in Imperial China". In *The City in Late Imperial China*, edited by William Skinner, 3–32. Stanford: Stanford University Press, 1977.

Slos, Karel. *Karel van Croy en de recuperatie van de Zuid-Nederlandse adel onder de aartshertogen.* Unpublished Master's Thesis History. Louvain: Katholieke Universiteit Leuven, 1997.

Smallegange, Mattheus. *Geslacht-rekening der doorluchtigste vorsten van Nassau en Oraenjen, waer in den oorspronk, aenwas en voorgank der selver, met het gene sy verricht hebben sedert den jare 682 tot het jaer 1675.* Amsterdam, 1675.

Smith, Paul J., and Richard von Glahn. *The Song-Yuan-Ming Transition in Chinese History.* Cambridge, MA: Harvard University Press, 2003.

Smuts, Malcolm. "The Making of Rex Pacificus. James VI and I in an Age of Religious War". In *Royal Subjects. Essays on the Writings of James VI and I*, edited by Daniel Fischlin and Mark Fortier, 371–88. Detroit: Wayne State University Press, 2002.

Snow, Vernon F. *Essex the Rebel: The Life of Robert Devereux, the Third Earl of Essex, 1591–1648.* Lincoln: University of Nebraska Press, 1970.

Soen, Violet. "Philip II's Quest. The Appointment of Governors-General during the Dutch Revolt". *The Low Countries Historical Review* 126 (2011): 3–29.

——— "La Causa Croÿ et les limites du mythe bourguignon: la frontière, le lignage et la mémoire (1465-1475)" in *Mémoires conflictuelles et mythes concurrents dans les pays bourguignons (ca. 1380-1580),* (eds) Jean-Marie Cauchies and Petit Peporte, 81-97, Neuchâtel: Publications du Centre d'études bourguignonnes, 2012.

——— "Nobility", in *Oxford Bibliographies in Renaissance and Reformation,* (ed) Margaret King, New York: Oxford University Press, online since January 2015, DOI: 10.1093/OBO/9780195399301-028

——— and Hans Cools, "L'aristocratie transrégionale et les frontières: les processus d'identification politique dans les maison de Luxembourg-Saint-Pol et de Croÿ (1470-1530)" *L'identité au pluriel. Jeux et enjeux des appartenances autour des anciens Pays-Bas, XIVe-XVIIIe siècles. Identity and Identities. Belonging at Stake in the Low Countries 14th-18th Centuries,* (eds.) Violet Soen, Yves Junot and Florian Mariage, 209-28, Villeneuve d'Ascq: Revue du Nord, Hors série, collection Histoire 30, 2014.

Sommerville, Johann P. "James I and the Divine Right of Kings: English Politics and Continental Theory". In *The Mental World of the Jacobean Court*, edited by Linda Levy Peck, 55–70. Cambridge: Cambridge University Press, 1991.

Soulié, Eudore, and Edouard de Barthélemy (eds). *Journal de Jean Héroard sur l'enfance et la jeunesse de Louis XIII (1601–1628).* Paris, 1868.

Sourches, Louis-François du Bouchet, marquis de. *Mémoires sur le règne de Louis XIV*, edited by G.-J. de Cosnac and A. Bertrand. 13 vols. Paris: Hachette, 1882.

Spade, Joan Z., and Catherine G. Valentine (eds). *The kaleidoscope of Gender: Prisms, Patterns, and Possibilities.* Los Angeles: Sage, 2011.

Spagnoletti, A. “Quale patriottismo per i soldati napoletani al servizio della Monarchia Cattolica?” In *Guerra y sociedad en la monarquía hispánica: política, estrategia y cultura en la Europa moderna (1500–1700)*, edited by E. García Hernán and D. Maffi. Madrid: Laberinto, 2006.

———. “Onore e spirito nazionale nei soldati italiani al servizio della monarchia spagnola”. In *Militari e società civile nell'Europa dell'età moderna (secoli XVI-XVIII)*, edited by C. Donati and B.R. Kroener. Bologna: Mulino, 2007.

———. “Le dinastie italiane e la guerra delle Fiandra”, *Società e storia*, n. 125 (2009).

Spagnoli, Paul. “The Revolution Begins: Lambesc's Charge, 12 July 1789”. *French Historical Studies* 17 (1991): 466–97.

Spangler, Jonathan. “Benefit or Burden? Elite Widows in Seventeenth-Century France”. *Proceedings of the Annual Meeting of the Western Society for French History* 31 (2003): 65–83.

———. *The Society of Princes: The Lorraine-Guise and the Conservation of Power and Wealth in Seventeenth-Century France.* Farnham: Ashgate, 2009.

———. “Those in Between: Princely Families on the Margins of the Great Powers – The Franco-German Frontier, 1477–1830”. In *Transregional and Transnational Families in Europe and Beyond: Experiences since the Middle Ages*, edited by Christopher H. Johnson, David Warren Sabean, Simon Teuscher, and Francesca Trivellato, 131–54. New York/Oxford: Berghahn Books, 2011.

———. “Material Culture at the Guise ‘Court’: A Tapestry, a Bed and a Devotional Dollhouse as Expressions of Dynastic Pride and Piety in Seventeenth-Century Paris”. *Seventeenth-Century French Studies* 34, no. 2 (2012): 158–75.

Spangler, Jonathan, Jessica Munns and Penny Richards (eds). *Aspiration, Representation and Memory: The Guise in Europe, 1506–1688.* Farnham: Ashgate, 2015.

Spanheim, Ezéchiel, baron. *Relation de la Cour de France en 1690*, edited by E. Bourgeois. Paris: Mercure de France, 1973.

Spence, Jonathan. *Emperor of China. Self-portrait of Kang-Hsi.* New York: Knopf, 1974.

Steensel, Arie van. “Kinship, Property and Identity: Noble Family Strategies in Late-Medieval Zeeland”. *Journal of Family History* 37 (2012): 247–69.

Stenbock, Carl Magnus (ed.). *Ett 300-årigt Vasaminne. Brefväxlingen mellan Gustaf II Adolf och Ebba Brahe I.* Stockholm: Norstedt, 1915.

Stensland, Monica. *Habsburg Communication in the Dutch Revolt.* Amsterdam: Amsterdam University Press, 2012.

Stephenson, Barbara. “Maintaining the Antiquity of the House: Marguerite de Navarre, Noble Marriage and Dynastic Culture in Early Sixteenth-Century France”. *The Court Historian* 10 (2005): 15–24.

Stevenson, John Home. "The Law of the Throne – Tanistry and the Introduction of the Law of Primogeniture". *Scottish Historical Review* 25 (1927/8): 1–12.

Stewart, Alan. *The Cradle King: A Life of James VI and I.* London: Chatto & Windus, 2003.

Stone, Lawrence. *The Crisis of the Aristocracy, 1558–1641.* Oxford: Clarendon Press, 1965.

Strada, Famiano. *Della guerra di Fiandra, deca prima.* Rome, 1638.

Struve, Lynn A. (ed.). *The Qing Formation in World-Historical Time.* Cambridge, MA: Harvard University Press, 2004.

Sturges, Robert S. "The Guise and the Two Jerusalems: An Early Modern Family's Medievalism". In *Aspiration, Representation and Memory: The Guise in Europe, 1506–1688*, edited by Jessica Munns, Penny Richards and Jonathan Spangler Farnham: Ashgate, 2015.

Subrahmanyam, Sanjay. "Sixteenth Century Millenarianism from the Tagus to the Ganges". *From the Tagus to the Ganges: Explorations in Connected History*, vol. 2, 102–137. Oxford: Oxford University Press, 2007.

Swann, Julian. *Provincial Power and Absolute Monarchy: The Estates General of Burgundy, 1661–1790.* Cambridge: Cambridge University Press, 2003.

Swope, Kenneth M. "A Few Good Men: the Li Family and China's Northern Frontier in the Late Ming". *Ming Studies* 49 (2005): 34–81.

Szonyi, Michael. *Practicing Kinship. Lineage and Descent in Late Imperial China.* Stanford: Stanford University Press, 2002.

Tait, Clodagh. "Colonising Memory: Manipulations of Death, Burial and Commemoration in the Career of Richard Boyle, First Earl of Cork (1566–1643)". *Proceedings of the Royal Irish Academy* 101 Section C (2001): 107–34.

Tait, Clodagh. *Death, Burial and Commemoration in Ireland, 1550–1650.* London: Palgrave Macmillan, 2002.

Terrasa-Lozano, Antonio. "Legal Enemies, Beloved Brothers. High nobility, Family Conflict and the Aristocrats' two Bodies in Early-Modern Castile". *European Review of History* 17, no. 5 (2010): 719–34.

Textor, Johannes, *Nassawische Chronik*. Herborn: Christoff Raab, 1617.

The Great Ming code. Da Ming Lü, edited by Jiang Yonglin. Seattle, London: University of Washington Press, 2005.

Thielemans, Marie-Rose. "Les Croy, conseillers des ducs de Bourgogne. Documents extraits de leurs archives familiales, 1357–1487". *Bulletin de la Commission Royale d'Histoire* 124 (1959): 1–141.

Thiesse, Anne-Marie. *La création des identités nationales: Europe XVIIIe-XXe siècle.* Paris: Éditions du Seuil, 2001.

Thomas, Andrew L. *A House Divided: Wittelsbach Confessional Court Cultures in the Holy Roman Empire, c. 1550–1650.* Leiden: Brill, 2010.

Thomas, Werner, and Luc Duerloo (eds). *Albert & Isabella 1598–1621: Essays.* Turnhout: Brepols, 1998.

Tocci, Giovanni. *Le terre traverse. Poteri e territori nei ducati di Parma e Piacenza tra Sei e Settecento.* Bologna: Mulino, 1985.

Togan, Isenbike. "Court Historiography in Early Tang China: Assigning a Place to History and Historians at the Palace". In *Royal Courts in Dynastic States and Empires: a Global Perspective*, edited by Jeroen Duindam, Metin Kunt and Tulay Artan, 171–98. Leiden, Boston: Brill, 2011.

Tomas, Natalie R. *The Medici Women: Gender and Power in Renaissance Florence.* Aldershot: Ashgate, 2003.

Tomasi di Lampedusa, Giuseppe. *The Leopard*, translated by A. Colquhoun. London: Vintage, 2005.

Trompf, G.W. *The Idea of Historical Recurrence in Western Thought, From Antiquity to the Reformation.* Berkeley, Los Angeles, London: University of California Press, 1979.

Twitchett, Denis. "The T'ang Imperial Family". *Asia Major* 7, no. 2 (1994): 1–60.

———. "How to be an Emperor: T'ang T'ai-tsung's Vision of His Role". *Asia Major* 3rd ser. 9 (1996): 1–102.

———. "Chen gui and Other Works Attributed to Empress Wu Zetian". *Asia Major* 16, no. 1 (2003): 33–109.

Typotius, Jacob. *Relatio historica de regno Sveciae.* Frankfurt,1605.

Tytgat, Jean-Pierre. "Van rentmeesters en intendanten: het beheer van de Arenberggoederen". In *Arenberg in de Lage Landen: een hoogadellijk huis in Vlaanderen en Nederland*, edited by J. Roegiers et al., 132–44. Louvain: Leuven University Press, 2002.

Ullgren, Peter. *Lantadel: adliga godsägare i Östergötland och Skåne vid 1600-talets slut.* Lund: Sisyfos, 2004.

Van den Gheyn, Joseph-Marie. *Catalogue des manuscrits de la Bibliothèque royale de Belgique.* Brussels: Lamertin, 1901.

Van der Essen, Léon. "Le testament politique d'Alexandre Farnèse. Dernières instructions du gouverneur général à son fils, Ranuccio Farnèse, au sujet des affaires des Pays-Bas (novembre 1592)". *Bulletin de la Commission royale d'histoire* 86 (1922): 171–215.

———. *Alexandre Farnèse, prince de Parme, gouverneur général des Pays-Bas (1545–1592).* 5 vols. Brussels: Librairie nationale d'art et d'historie, 1933–1937.

———. "Une critique de l'administration d'Alexandre Farnèse aux Pays-Bas par Don Juan de Idiáquez, secrétaire d'Etat de Philippe II (1592)". *Bulletin de la Commission royale d'histoire* 100 (1936): 167–80.

———. *De auteur en de beteekenis van de Liber relationum eorum quae gesta fuere in Belgio et alibi per serenissimum D. Ducem Alexander Farnesium.* Antwerp, Utrecht: Standaard, 1943.

———. *Kritische inleiding tot de studie van het Spaanse leger en van zijn oorlogvoering in de Nederlanden gedurende de XVIe eeuw.* Brussels: Paleis der Academiën, 1949.

———. "Alexandre Farnèse 1545–1592: les principaux aspects de sa personnalité". *Revue générale belge* 68 (1951): 220–43.

———. "Correspondance de Cosimo Masi, secrétaire d'Alexandre Farnèse, concernant le gouvernement de Mansfeld, de Fuentes et de l'Archiduc Ernest aux Pays-Bas, 1593–1594". *Bulletin de l'Institut historique belge de Rome* 27 (1952): 358–60.

Van der Eycken, Michel. *Oranje-Nassau, Prins Filips-Willem en Diest.* Diest: Vrienden van de Sint-Sulpitiuskerk, 2010.

Vanhoutte, Petra. "Filips Willem van Oranje-Nassau en zijn familiale belangen en contacten in Noord en Zuid (1554–1618)". In *Het verdeelde huis: de Nederlandse adel tussen opstand en reconciliatie*, edited by Luc Duerloo and Liesbeth De Frenne, 11–22. Maastricht: Shaker Publishing, 2011.

Van Laer, An-Katrien. *Ceste servirat pour vous baiser humblement les mains: de mentaliteit van de hoge adel gezien door de familiecorrespondentie van Karel van Arenberg en Anne van Croy (1600–1635).* Unpublished Master's Thesis in History. Louvain: Katholieke Universiteit Leuven, 1988.

Vázquez, Alonso. *Los Sucesos de Flandes y Francia del Tiempo de Alejandro Farnesio.* 3 vols. Madrid: Miguel Ginesta, 1879–1880.

Vermeir, René. "Le duc d'Arschot et les conséquences de la conspiration des nobles (1632–1640)". In *Beleid en bestuur in de oude Nederlanden: liber amicorum Prof. dr. M. Baelde*, edited by H. Soly and R. Vermeir, 477–89. Ghent: Gent RUG, 1993.

Vermeulen, Roger. "Vorselaar, Retie en Lichtaart". In *Arenberg in de Lage Landen: een hoogadellijk huis in Vlaanderen en Nederland*, edited by J. Roegiers et al., 153–6. Louvain: Leuven University Press, 2002.

Verstegen, Ian (ed.). *Patronage and Dynasty: The Rise of the della Rovere in Renaissance Italy.* Kirksville: Truman State University Press, 2007.

Verstraten, Freya. "Naming Practices among the Irish Secular Nobility in the High Middle Ages". *Journal of Medieval History* 32 (2006): 43–53.

Villermont, Marie de. *Grands Seigneurs d'autrefois: Le duc Charles de Croy et d'Arschot et ses femmes Marie de Brimeu et Dorothée de Croy.* Brussels: Dewit, 1923.

Visceglia, M.A. *Roma papale e Spagna. Diplomatici, nobili e religiosi tra due corti.* Rome: Bulzoni, 2010.

Vocelka, Karl. *Die Familien Habsburg und Habsburg-Lothringen. Politik – Kultur – Mentalität.* Vienna: Böhlau, 2010.

Vocelka, Karl, and Lynne Heller. *Die Lebenswelt der Habsburger: Kultur- und Mentalitätsgeschichte einer Familie.* Graz: Styria, 1997.

Vocelka, Karl, and Lynne Heller. *Die private Welt der Habsburger. Leben und Alltag einer Familie.* Graz: Styria, 1998.

Volpi, Caterina. "Odoardo al bivio. L'invenzione del Camerino Farnese tra encomio e filosofia". *Bollettino d'arte* 83 (1998): 87–93.

———. "Odoardo e il Camerino Farnese. 'Virtù' politica o 'Virtù' privata". In *Studi di Storia dell'Arte in onore di Denis Mahon*, edited by M.G. Bemardini, S. Danesi Squarzina and C. Strinati, 81–94. Milan: Electa, 2000.

Voûte, J.R., and Hendrik J. van der Wiel. *Les monnaies de la principauté d'Orange sous la maison de Nassau.* Bussum: Schulman, 1997.

Wakeman jr., Frederic. *The Fall of Imperial China.* New York: Free Press, 1977.

Wakeman jr., Frederic. *The Great Enterprise. The Manchu Reconstruction of Imperial Order in Seventeenth-Century China.* Berkeley, Los Angeles, London: University of California Press, 1986.

Wandruzka, Adam. "Ein Freskenzyklus der 'Pietas Austriaca' in Florenz". *Mitteilungen des Österreichischen Staatsarchivs* 15 (1962): 495–99.

Wang, Liping, and Julia Adams. "Interlocking Patrimonialisms and State Formation in Qing China and Early Modern Europe". *Annals of the American Academy of Political and Social Science* 636 (2011): 164–81.

Wang, Richard G. *The Ming Prince and Daoism: Institutional Patronage of an Elite.* Oxford: Oxford University Press, 2012.

Wang, Shuo. "Qing Imperial Women: Empresses, Concubines, and Aisin Gioro Daughters". In *Servants of the Dynasty. Palace Women in World History*, edited by Anne Walthall, 137–58. Berkeley, Los Angeles: University of California Press, 2008.

Watson, James L., and Patricia B. Ebrey (eds). *Kinship Organization in Late Imperial China 1000–1940.* Berkeley, Los Angeles, London: University of California Press, 1986.

Watson, Rubie S. "Corporate Property and Local Leadership in the Pearl River Delta, 1898–1941". In *Chinese Local Elites and Patterns of Dominance,* edited by Joseph W. Esherick and Mary Backus Rankin, 239–60. Berkeley: University of California Press, 1990.

Watson, Rubie S. and Patricia Buckley Ebrey (eds). *Marriage and Inequality in Chinese Society.* Berkeley: University of California Press, 1991.

Weber, Wolfgang E.J. "Dynastiesicherung and Staatsbildung. Die Entfaltung des frühmodernen Fürstenstaates". In *Der Fürst. Ideen und Wirklichkeiten in der europäischen Geschichte*, edited by Wolfgang E.J. Weber, 91–136. Cologne : Böhlau, 1998.

Weiand, Kerstin. "De 'Roi de Guerre' à 'Warrior King'. Réflexions sur un transfert politique et culturel considéré comme enjeu mémoriel". In *Les funérailles princières en Europe, XVIe – XVIIIe siècle*. Vol. 3, *Mémoire monarchique et la construction de l'Europe. Les stratégies funérailles des dynasties princières, 16e et 17e siècle,* edited by Juliusz Chrosciscki, Mark Hengerer and Gérard Sabatier. Paris: Presses Universitaires de Rennes, forthcoming.

Weibull, Curt. *Drottning Christina och Sverige 1646–1651: en fransk diplomat berättar.* Stockholm: Norstedt, 1970.

Weiss, Charles (ed.). *Papiers d'État du Cardinal de Granvelle d'après les manuscrits de la bibliothèque de Besançon.* 9 vols. Paris: Imprimerie Royale/ Imprimerie Nationale, 1841–52.

Wendt, Alexander. *Social Theory of International Politics.* Cambridge: Cambridge University Press, 2009.

Wheatcroft, Andrew. *The Habsburgs. Embodying Empire.* London: Viking, 1996.

Widekindi, Johannes. *Imagines Illustrissimae Familiae Braheae.* Visingsö, 1673.

Wienberg, Jes. "Det hotade grevskapet – Per Brahe den yngres minnesmärken". *Fornvännen* 4 (2008): 260–78.

Wieselgren, Peter (ed). *De la Gardiska archivet eller handlingar ur Grefl. Dela Gardiska Bibliotheket på Löberöd* (Lund: Hörberg, 1836

Witte, A. "The Farnese Salone as Failed Memorial to Alessandro Farnese", in *Alexander Farnese and the Low Countries*, edited by Krista de Jonge, Sebastian Derks and Hans Cools. Turnhout: Brepols, forthcoming.

Woeckel, Gerhard P. *Pietas bavarica: Wallfahrt, Prozession und Ex-voto-Gabe im Hause Wittelsbach in Ettal, Wessobrunn, Altötting und der Landeshauptstadt München von der Gegenreformation bis zur Säkularisation und der 'Renovatio Ecclesiae'.* Weissenhorn: A.H. Konrad, 1992.

Wolffson, Michael, and Thomas Brechenmacher. "Nomen est Omen: The Selection of First Names as an Indicator for Public Opinion in the Past". *International Journal of Public Opinion Research* 13 (2001): 116–39.

Wood, Ian. "Deconstructing the Merovingian family". In *The Construction of Communities in the Early Middle Ages*, edited by Richard Corradini, Max Diesenberger, and Helmut Reimitz, 149–71. Leiden and Boston: Brill, 2003.

Wormald, Jenny. "James VI and I – Two Kings or One". *History* 68 (1983): 187–209.

———. "Gunpowder, Treason and Scots". *Journal of British Studies* 24 (1985): 141–68.

Wrede, Martin. "Zwischen Mythen, Genealogen und der Krone. Rivalisierende Familiengedächtnisse im französischen Hochadel des 17. Jahrhunderts: die Häuser Bouillon, Noailles und Bourbon". *Zeitschrift für Historische Forschung* 32 (2005): 17–43.

———. *Ohne Furcht und Tadel. Für König und Vaterland. Frühneuzeitlicher Hochadel zwischen Familienehre, Ritterideal und Fürstendienst.* Ostfildern: Jan Thorbecke Verlag, 2012.

Wrigley, E.A. "Fertility Strategy for the Individual and the Group". In *Historical Studies of Changing Fertility*, edited by Charles Tilly, 135–54. Princeton: Princeton University Press, 1978.

Yardeni, Myriam. *La Conscience Nationale en France pendant les guerres de Religion (1559–1598).* Louvain: Éditions Nauwelaerts, 1971.

Yun Casalilla, Bartolomé. "Localism, Global History and Transnational History. A Reflection from the Historian of Early Modern Europe". *Historisk Tidskrift* 127 (2007): 659–78.

———. "Introducción. Entre el imperio colonial y la monarquía compuesta. Élites y territorios en la Monarquía Hispánica (ss. XVI y XVII)". In *Las redes del Imperio. Élites sociales en la articulación de la Monarquía Hispánica, 1492–1714*, edited by Bartolomé Yun Casalilla, 11–35. Madrid: Marcial Pons, 2009.

Zandvliet, Kees (ed.). *Maurits Prins van Oranje.* Zwolle: Waanders, 2000.

Zapperi, Roberto. "Le Cardinal Odoardo et les Fastes Farnese". *Revue de l'art* 11 (1987).

———. "Odoardo Farnese principe e cardinale". In *Les Carrache et les décors profanes*, edited by École française de Rome, 335–58. Rome: École française de Rome, 1988.

———. *Eros e Controriforma. Prehistoria della galleria Farnese.* Turin: Bollati Boringhieri, 1994.

———. "Per la storia della Galleria Farnese. Nuovi ricerche e precisazioni documentarie". *Bollettino d'arte* 84 (1999): 87–102.

——— "Annibale Carracci e Odoardo Farnese". *Bollettino d'Arte* 95 (2010).

Zimmerman, T.C. Price. *Paolo Giovio: The Historian and the Crisis of Sixteenth-Century Italy.* Princeton: Princeton University Press, 1995.

Zmora, Hillay. *Monarchy, Aristocracy, and the State in Europe.* London: Routledge, 2001.

———. "The Princely State and the Noble Family: Conflict and Co-operation in the Margraviates Ansbach-Kulmbach in the Early Sixteenth Century". *The Historical Journal* 49 (2006): 1–21.

Zuber, Henri. "La noblesse protestante (1584–1598). Histoire politique des rapports entre Henri IV et les grands réformés". In *Avènement d'Henri IV. Quatrième Centenaire.* Vol. 3, *Henri IV. Le roi et la reconstruction du royaume*, edited by Association Henry IV, 73–93. Pau: Association Henry IV 1989, 1990.

Zurndorfer, Harriet. "From Local History to Cultural History Reflections on Some Recent Publications". *T'oung Pao*, Second Series, 83, no. 4–5 (1997): 386–424.

———. "What is the Meaning of 'War' in an Age of Cultural Efflorescence? Another Look at the Role of War in Song Dynasty China (960–1279)". In *War in Words: Transformations of War from Antiquity to Clausewitz*, edited by Marco Formisano and Hartmut Böhme, 89–110. Berlin, New York: De Gruyter, 2011.

———. "Meta-narratives of Song Dynasty Regional Society: An Historiographical Analysis of Western-language Scholarship since 1950". In *Chugoku suka no chiiki-zo: Hikaku-shi kara mita sensei kokka to chiiki*, edited by Ihara Hiroshi, 55–86. Tokyo: Iwata-shoin, 2013.

Index